TRUTH OR DARE

TRUTH OR DARE

Encounters with Power, Authority, and Mystery

STARHAWK

1817

Harper & Row, Publishers, San Francisco

Cambridge, Hagerstown, New York, Philadelphia, Washington
London, Mexico City, São Paulo, Singapore, Sydney

Grateful acknowledgment is made for use of the following: Passages and poetry from *Treasures of Darkness,* by Thorkild Jacobsen. Copyright © 1976 by Yale University Press. Used by permission. The Twelve Steps reprinted with permission of Alcoholics Anonymous World Services, Inc. Interpretations are solely the author's, not those of Alcoholics Anonymous. Excerpt from the *She Who* poems is taken from *The Work of a Common Woman* by Judy Grahn (Crossing Press, 1984). Copyright Judy Grahn, 1984. Used by permission. Lyrics from the song "Fierce Love" by Charlie Murphy. Copyright © Out Front Music, P.O. Box 12188, Seattle, WA 98102. Used by permission. Sections from *The Ancient Near East, Vol. 1: An Anthology of Texts and Pictures* edited by James B. Pritchard. Copyright © 1958 by Princeton University Press. Reprinted by permission. Sections from *The Epic of Gilgamesh* translated by N. K. Sandars (Penguin Classics, 1960, 1964), copyright © N. K. Sanders 1960, 1964. Used by permission. Passages and poetry from *Inanna, Queen of Heaven and Earth: Her Stories and Hymns from Sumer* by Diane Wolkstein and Samuel Noah Kramer (Harper & Row, Publishers, Inc.). Copyright © Diane Wolkstein and Samuel Noah Kramer, 1983. Used by permission. Biblical quotations are taken from the Holy Bible: King James Version. Nashville, TN: Thomas Nelson, 1977. Cover drawing by Robert Thawley.

FIRST EDITION

Designed by Donald Hatch

Library of Congress Cataloging-in-Publication Data

Starhawk.
  Truth or dare.

  Bibliography: p.
  Includes index.
  1. Witchcraft. 2. Ritual. I. Title.
BF1566.S773 1987 299'.93 87–45197
ISBN 0–06–250812–1

---

87 88 89 90 91 HC 10 9 8 7 6 5 4 3 2 1

Contents

Acknowledgments

This book arises from a matrix of community. I want to acknowledge and thank the members of many groups: the Reclaiming Collective, whose present and some former members seem to include Arachne, Bone Blossom, Cybelle, Diane, Iris May, Kay Kat, Leslie, Raven, Rick Dragonstongue, Robin K., and Robin G., Roddy, Rose May Dance, Roy, Vibra, and Amy, who also assisted me in the preparation of this manuscript and has tried her best to get me organized, a thankless task. My magic is sustained by my covens, the Wind Hags: Arachne, Carol, Pandora, and Rose; and Matrix: David, Deborah, Iris, Kelly, Roddy, and Rose. The Black Cats, my household, have fed me, entertained me, and put up with me through this process, thanks to Bill (the Cat), Brook, Iris, Jamie, Karen, Marian, Phebe, and Rose, and of course the Black Cat dogs, who kept me company through all those long nights at the word processor. I also thank the women of the WomanEarth Feminist Peace Institute, including Gen Vaughn, Gwyn Kirk, Luisah Teish, Margie Mayman-Park, Rachel Bagby, Rachel Sierra, and especially Ynestre King, who inspired us to begin the project and sustained it through the tough times. Deb Slager nurtured us all. The women of Greenham Common are exploring the frontiers of ideas of nonhierarchy and provide a continuing example of fierce love. All the people who organized and took part in the actions described here—the Abalone Alliance, the Livermore Action Group, Witness for Peace, and Vandenberg Action Coalition—and all who take action to resist the structures of domination deserve acknowledgment.

My students at Antioch West provided a forum for the development of these ideas, and insisted on a future that includes chocolate. Ani Mander of Antioch's Women's Studies Program is always a source of support. Matthew Fox of the Institute for Culture and Creation Spirituality inspired me to explore new cosmologies. Brian Swimme gave me a scientific/poetic understanding of creation, and Buck Ghosthorse shared with me Native American creation myths. My colleagues and students in the Creation Spirituality program have given me appreciation for the life-affirming streams in Christianity. And the women and men who have taken part in rituals and workshops with me have opened themselves and enriched my understanding.

I thank Ruby Rohrlich and Merlin Stone for their critical readings of chapter 2 and helpful comments, and Robert Thawley for his cover drawing. Discussions with Bill Moyer helped form ideas in chapters 10 and 12. Susan Davidson, Terry Gips, and Sago taught me much about sustainability and permaculture. Charlie Murphy and Jami Sieber let me draw on their music.

Rose reassured me in the middle of the night that I was not channeling Thomas Paine or the young Marx; Isis chided me for not having fun, and I'm waiting for her to provide it; Paula accompanied me to Nicaragua and helped me to integrate the meaning of our experiences there; Jonathan attempted to distract me; and Teish has kept me sane in many weird situations and I hope I've done the same for her. Bethany and Yarrow allowed me to draw on their experiences of coming of age. Amy, Corian, Delaney, Guthrie, Juliana, Morgan, Morgan Renee, Maurice, Nathan, Shannon, Rael, Sidra, Vanessa, and Zachary inspired my ideas about children.

Finally, my editor, Marie Cantlon, deserves praise and thanks. Her contributions to this book are unseen but basic to its flow and form. She has a catalytic effect on my own creativity, and I feel grateful to have worked with her once again.

This book is dedicated to all prisoners, and to the unborn.

Starhawk
Ides of Leafy Moon, 1987
San Francisco

How to Read This Book

This is a book of theory and practice. You can read it straight through and find them mixed together. You can also use it as a resource book or workbook; to aid you I have prepared a List of Processes, Exercises, Rituals, and Meditations for Individuals and Groups.

Each chapter is introduced by a story or litany. The stories can be read separately, or all together in sequence. You can also read them aloud, and some of them can be used as guided visualizations.

Several of the stories are a retelling of the myth of the Descent of Inanna. In the orginial, she passes through seven gates to the underworld. In my retelling, there are only five—because that is the number of gates I needed. When the myths come alive for us, they change.

I draw on many stories and experiences of myself, clients, and friends. To protect the innocent, the guilty, and the privacy of everyone involved, I have changed names and identifying details of each story unless I had permission from the person involved to use a real name. I have kept the essence of each story intact. If you think you know who I'm talking about, you don't.

The material in this book is essentially from a collective storehouse that I have drawn upon. Many of the rituals evolved in the Reclaiming Collective, in classes, or in workshops. None of them are my creation alone.

Now this material is yours to use as is, change, or to inspire you to create your own.

LIST OF PROCESSES, EXERCISES, RITUALS , AND MEDITATIONS FOR INDIVIDUALS AND GROUPS

A Story of Beginnings

Out of the point, the swelling
Out of the swelling, the egg
Out of the egg, the fire
Out of the fire, the stars
Out of the rain of stars
   the congealing, molten world

The fire remains, see it burn in the center of the circle
Watch the flames, filled with points of light that
   spark and dance
Watch the fire, as in and out of your lungs flows breath
   the most ancient river
The air you breathe passed through the lungs of dinosaurs
   and chittering, big-eyed lemurs, ancestors
Feel yourself rocking
   cradled in the night sky womb arching around you
   alive with a billion billion dancing points of light
Breathe
Watch the flame
Listen to the voice of the story, the first story
   whispered in the secret heart of your encoded
   memories
Hear the story woman

She says
   The labor is hard, the night is long
   We are midwives, and men who tend the birth
    and bond with the child
   We are birthing, and being born
   We are trying to perform an act of magic—
   To pull a living child out of a near-corpse
    of the mother we are simultaneously poisoning,
    who is also ourselves

She is alive in you as you in her
Warm your human hands at the watchfire
See the stains on the cloak
Feel the wounds too deep for healing

There are times, sisters and brothers
   when we are afraid that we will die
   and take the whole great humming dance of life
   with us
Something must change, we know that

But are we strong enough?
And will we be given time?

This is the story we like to tell ouselves
   in the night
   when the fire seems nothing but dying embers winking
   out
   and the labor is too hard and goes on too long
   when we can't believe that we can make it
We like to tell ourselves
   that we remember the First Mother

She is alive in you as you in her
A power keener than the weapon's edge, a healing deeper
   than the wound
Feel her in your belly, at the bottom of breath
Her power is life; it is stronger

She is a being who is spinning, fire covered with a
   sweet crust shell
Feel her pulse, remember in your nerves winks
   the spark of the first fire
You are alive in her as she in you
You are her
Your misty breath great clouds of gasses set in motion
   by your spinning dance
   swirl and cool and rain
   for thousands and thousands of years
   while you build up, tear down, and rearrange
   the ridges and valleys of your skin
   carve and smooth your wrinkles
And the water
   softens every sharp edge into soil
   fills the basins of your oceans
In your veins flows ocean water
Remember the lightning, sparks striking into being
   something new
Life, teeming, greedy life
That grows, cell by swelling cell, divides, devours, unites
   and changes, filling your ocean belly, flinging a green
   cloak over the land, learning to swim, crawl, run,
   stalk, fly, caress, and stand erect, made of
   earth air water fire
   and what goes beyond these and unites these
   the mystery

She is alive in us: we are alive in her as in each other
   as all that is alive is alive in us
   and all is alive

When we are afraid, when it hurts too much
We like to tell ourselves
   stories of power
   how we lost it
   how we can reclaim it
We tell ourselves
   the cries we hear may be those of labor
   the pain we feel may yet be that of birth

Truth or Dare

Because the woman runs screaming into the gym, because she dives into the center of our meeting, because we are in jail, because six guards are after her, because spontaneously we surround her and protect her, we encounter mystery. The terrain of the mysteries is the edge where power encounters power, for mystery is the arising of powers that are uncharted and untamed, that will not follow the logic of naked force, and so act in unexpected ways. Mystery is surprise.

Six hundred women are crowded into the gym at Camp Parks. All of us have been arrested for blockading the Livermore Weapons Lab, one of the two facilities in the United States where nuclear weapons are designed and developed. We are irritable and uncomfortable. The day is hot; voices ricochet off the walls and bounce on the wood floor. The scanty food runs short at every meal. No one has slept well and we have no doors to close out the crowd, the constant meetings, the decisions to be made; no way to withdraw or be alone.

We are not complaining. In the fervor of the action, we are willing to face horrors much worse than the discomfort of this makeshift lockup in an old World War II Japanese relocation camp. Nevertheless, we feel secure in our knowledge that we probably won't have to. We expect our courage to be tested only a little. Although many women, at booking, gave their names as Karen Silkwood, we are not at risk of being run off the road for our stand. Although we sing songs about Victor Jara and Hannah Senesh, we are not facing massacre or torture, nor do we face, as did the Japanese who preceded us here, long years of custody and loss of our homes, our businesses, our community. Stories of martyrs inspire us but also make us feel slightly guilty, for we know that we are not great heras, or saints. We are a small legion of a more common breed of ordinary, irritable people, able sometimes to be somewhat brave.

On our second day in custody, we are massed in the center of the floor, having an endless meeting that has become an extended argument. We are arguing about solidarity, about militancy, about violence and nonviolence, about sexuality and spirituality and how polite we should or should not be to the guards. We have learned from our lawyers that the gym we are held in has been the site of experiments with radioactive substances for twenty years. We are arguing about who knew this fact ahead of time and why they didn't tell us and what we should do about it. Outside is nothing but dust, smog, and barbed wire. Inside are six hundred women rapidly getting sick of each other and feeling that the line they have put their bodies on is getting rather frayed.

And then the woman runs in. She bursts through the open doorway that leads to the concrete exercise yard outside. Six guards are after her. "Grab her! Grab her!" they yell. The woman dives into our cluster, and we instinctively surround her, gripping her arms and legs and shielding her with our bodies. The guards grab her legs and pull; we resist, holding on. The guards and the women are shouting and in a moment, I know, the nightsticks will descend on kidneys and heads, but in that suspended interval before the violence starts we hold our ground.

And then someone begins to chant.

The chant is wordless, a low hum that swells and grows with open vowels as if we had become the collective voice of some ancient beast that growls and sings, the voice of something that knows nothing of guns, walls, nightsticks, mace, or barbed-wire fencing, yet gives protection, a voice outside surveillance or calculation but not outside knowledge, a voice that is recognized by our bodies if not our minds and is known also to the guards whose human bodies, like ours, have been animal for a million years before control was invented.

The guards back away.

"Sit down," a woman whispers. We become a tableau, sitting and clasping the woman as if we are healing her with our voices and our magic. The confrontation has become a laying on of hands.

The guards stand, tall, isolated pillars. They look bewildered. Something they are unprepared for, unprepared even to name, has arisen in our moment of common action. They do not know what to do.

And so, after a moment, they withdraw. The chant dies away. It is over. For a moment, mystery has bested authority.

The moment passes. We take a deep breath, return to our arguments and irritation. The encounter does not transform us into saints, or even make us all get along much better. The implications of the incident are too much for us to take in fully: we wall it off, returning to our usual games and strategies.

Yet what has taken place is an act that could teach us something deep about power. In that moment in the jail, the power of domination and control met something outside its comprehension, a power rooted in another source. To know that power, to create the situations that bring it forth, is magic.

MAGIC AND ITS USES

Magic is a word that can be defined in many ways. A saying attributed to Dion Fortune is: "Magic is the art of changing consciousness at will." I sometimes call it the art of evoking power-from-within. Today, I will name it this: the art of liberation, the act that releases the mysteries, that ruptures the fabric of our beliefs and lets us look into the heart of deep space where dwell the immeasurable, life-generating powers.

Those powers live in us also, as we live in them. The mysteries are what is wild in us, what cannot be quantified or contained. But the mysteries are also what is most common to us all: blood, breath, heartbeat, the sprouting of seed, the waxing and waning of the moon, the turning of the earth around the sun, birth, growth, death, and renewal.

To practice magic is to tap that power, to burrow down through the systems of control like roots that crack concrete to find the living soil below.

We are never apart from the power of the mysteries. Every breath we take encompasses the circle of birth, death, and rebirth. The forces that push the blood cells through our veins are the same forces that spun the universe out of the primal ball of fire. We do not know what those forces are. We can invoke them, but we cannot control them, nor can we disconnect from them. They are our life, and when we die, decay, and decompose, we remain still within their cycle.

Yet somehow we human beings, made of the same materials as the stars, the eucalyptus, the jaguar, and the rose, we who inherit four billion years of survival have managed to create a culture in which the power of the mysteries has been denied and power itself has been redefined as power-over, as domination and control. Wielding that false and limited power, we create misery for each other and devastation for the other life forms that share this earth.

In a warped way, such an achievement is almost grimly inspiring. We are like a friend I had in the sixties who, while wheelchair-bound, paraplegic, and needing constant care, managed to deal drugs successfully until he killed himself with an overdose of heroin. We have overcome every handicap and surmounted every obstacle to self-destruction.

We are not particularly happy in this condition. We do not enjoy being the targets of nuclear warheads or developing cancer from our polluted environment. We do not enjoy starving, or wasting our lives in meaningless work, nor are we eager to be raped, abused, tortured, or bossed around. Whether the bosses enjoy their role is not the issue. The question is, How are the rest of us controlled? Or, even more to the point, How do we break control and set ourselves free?

This book is a text of magic, a liberation psychology. It holds tools, not answers, for the mysteries do not offer answers, but questions that in time, may change us.

Those who practice magic can be called many things: magicians, shamans, mystics. I myself am a Witch. *Witch* comes from the Anglo-Saxon root *wic,* meaning to bend or shape—to shape reality, to make magic. Witches bend energy and shape consciousness. We were—and are—shamans, healers, explorers of powers that do not fit the usual systems of control. Those powers are rightly perceived as dangerous to the established order, and so we have been taught to view them as evil or delusionary. We imagine Witches flying around on brooms or brewing up noxious potions.

Actually, Witchcraft is a mystery religion, based on ritual, on consciously structured collective experiences that allow us to encounter the immeasurable. It is the old, pre-Christian, tribal religion of Europe. Like other earth-based, tribal traditions, Witchcraft sees the earth as sacred.

To Witches, the cosmos is the living body of the Goddess, in whose being we all partake, who encompasses us and is immanent within us. We call her Goddess not to narrowly define her gender, but as a continual reminder that what we value is life brought into the world. The great forces of the spirit are manifest in nature and culture. The Goddess is fertile earth and ripened fruit, and she is also the storehouse, where the earth's fruits are collected, guarded, and given out. She is the virgin grove of redwoods and also the carved shape that speaks through art of the wood's power. She is wildfire and hearthfire, the star's core, the forge, and the poetic fire of inspiration. She has infinite names and guises, many of them male: the Gods, her consorts, sons, companions. For what we call Goddess moves always through paradox, and so takes us into the heart of the mysteries, the great powers that can never be limited or defined.

However they name their Gods, tribal cultures across the world have always shared a common understanding: that the sacred is found here, where we are, immanent in the world. In Europe, long after Christianity had become the official faith, the more ancient understanding persisted in folk customs and beliefs, in ways of healing, and in the practices of the Witches, the dedicated few who preserved remnants of the Old Religion.

In the sixteenth and seventeenth centuries, the Catholic and Protestant churches began systematic Witch persecutions. Witches were accused by both Catholic and Protestant churches of worshiping the devil, but in reality our tradition has nothing to do with Satanism, a peculiarly Christian heresy.[1] Accused Witches were subjected to horrifying tortures and execution. The persecutions fractured peasant class solidarity, and marked off the domain of healing and midwifery as the preserve of upper-class, university-educated male "experts." The old organic worldview, the vision that saw sacred presence in all of life, was made illegitimate in Western culture. What remained of the value system of immanence was discredited. The living world became viewed as a machine, something made of non-living, atomized parts that could ultimately be completely known and controlled. That worldview in turn justified increased social control, isolation, and domination.[2]

Maligned and persecuted for four hundred years, the Craft went underground, became a closed and secret society that is only now reemerging.

I call myself a Witch even though I am fully aware that the word often produces fear.[3] Until we confront the fears and stereotypes evoked by the word, we cannot contact the powers that are also embedded there.

The word *Witch* throws us back into a world who is a being, a world in which everything is alive and speaking, if only we learn its language. The word brings us back to the outlawed awareness of the immanence of the sacred, and so it reeks of a holy stubbornness, an unwillingness to believe that the living milk of nurture we drink daily from the flowing world can be reduced to formula administered from a machine.

To be a Witch is to make a commitment to the Goddess, to the protection, preservation, nurturing, and fostering of the great powers of life as they emerge in every being. In these discussions of power, that, then, is my bias: I am on the side of the power that emerges from within, that is inherent in us as the power to grow is inherent in seed. As a shaper, as one who practices magic, my work is to find that power, to call it forth, to coax it out of hiding, tend it, and free it of constrictions. In a society based on power-over, that work inevitably must result in conflict with the forces of domination, for we cannot bear our own true fruit when we are under another's control.

To practice magic is to bear the responsibility for having a vision, for we work magic by envisioning what we want to create, clearing the obstacles in our way, and then directing energy through that vision. Magic works through the concrete; our ideals, our visions, are meaningless until they are in some way enacted. So, if our work is to evoke power-from-within, we must clearly envision the conditions that would allow that power to come forth, we must identify what blocks it, and create the conditions that foster empowerment. Given a world based on power-over, we must remake the world.

THE THREE TYPES OF POWER

The conflicts brewing today are only superficially questions of who will take power. Underneath is a deeper struggle: to change the nature of the power in which our society is rooted. The root question is, How do we define the world? For it is an old magical secret that the way we define reality shapes reality. Name a thing and you invoke it. If we call the world nonliving, we will surely kill her. But when we name the world alive, we begin to bring her back to life.

Reality, of course, shapes and defines us. Only when we know how we have been shaped by the structures of power in which we live can we become shapers. A psychology of liberation can become our *athame,* our Witch's knife, the tool of magic that corresponds with the East, the element air: mind, clarity, vision. It is the knowledge and insight we need to carve out our own freedom.

Witches have a saying: "Where there's fear, there's power." It also works backward: "Where there's power, there's fear." We are afraid to look at power because one of the deepest prohibitions is that against seeing how power operates. Psychoanalyst Alice Miller, in her analysis of what she calls "poisonous pedagogy," shows "the overriding importance of our early conditioning to be obedient and dependent and to suppress our feelings."[4] "The more or less conscious goal of adults in rearing infants is to make sure they will never find out later in life that they were trained not to become aware of how they were manipulated."[5] We are afraid of the pain of seeing how deeply we have been shaped by systems of control.

Those systems and that power are built of the earth's charred bones and cemented with her stripped flesh. In this chapter, I will explore three types of power: power-over, power-from-within, and power-with. Power-over is linked to domination and control; power-from-within is linked to the mysteries that awaken our deepest abilities and potential. Power-with is social power, the influence we wield among equals.

Power-over comes from the consciousness I have termed estrangement: the view of the world as made up of atomized, nonliving parts, mechanically interacting, valued not for what they inherently are but only in relation to some outside standard. It is the consciousness modeled on the God who stands outside the world, outside nature, who must be appeased, placated, feared, and above all, obeyed. For, as we will see in chapter 2, power-over is ultimately born of war and the structures, social and intrapsychic, necessary to sustain mass, organized warfare. Having reshaped culture in a martial image, the institutions and ideologies of power-over perpetuate war so that it becomes a chronic human condition.

We live embedded in systems of power-over and are indoctrinated into them, often from birth. In its clearest form, power-over is the power of the prison guard, of the gun, power that is ultimately backed by force. Power-over enables one individual or group to make the decisions that affect others, and to enforce control.

Violence and control can take many forms. Power-over shapes every institution of our society. This power is wielded in the workplace, in the schools, in the courts, in the doctor's office. It may rule with weapons that are physical or by controlling the resources we need to live: money, food, medical care; or by controlling more subtle resources: information, approval, love. We are so accustomed to power-over, so steeped in its language and its implicit threats, that we often become aware of its functioning only when we see its extreme manifestations. For we have been shaped in its institutions, so that the insides of our minds resemble the battlefield and the jail.

In the Livermore action described in the opening of this chapter, we were relying on a different principle of power, one that I call power-from-within, or empowerment. The root of the word *power* means to be able. We were acting as if we were able to protect our friend. Our strength came not from weapons, but from our willingness to act.

Power-from-within is akin to the sense of mastery we develop as young children with each new unfolding ability: the exhilaration of standing erect, of walking, of speaking the magic words that convey our needs and thoughts.

But power-from-within is also akin to something deeper. It arises from our sense of connection, our bonding with other human beings, and with the environment.

Although power-over rules the systems we live in, power-from-within sustains our lives. We can feel that power in acts of creation and connection, in planting, building, writing, cleaning, healing, soothing, playing, singing, making love. We can feel it in acting together with others to oppose control.

A third aspect of power was also present in the jail at Camp Parks. We could call it power-with, or influence: the power of a strong individual in a group of equals, the power not to command, but to suggest and be listened to, to begin something and see it happen. The source of power-with is the willingness of others to listen to our ideas. We could call that willingness respect, not for a role, but for each unique person. We joined in the chanting begun by one woman in the jail because we respected her inspiration. Her idea felt right to us. She had no authority to command, but acted as a channel to focus and direct the will of the group.

In the dominant culture, power-with has become confused with power-over. When we attempt to create new structures that do not depend upon hierarchy for cohesion, we need to recognize power-with, so that we can work with it, share and spread, and also beware of it. For like the Witch's knife, the *athame,* power-with is double-bladed. It can be the seedbed of empowerment, but it can also spawn oppression. No group can function without such power, but within a group influence can too easily become authority.

AUTHORITY AND OBEDIENCE

The *Oxford English Dictionary* defines *authority* first as "the power to enforce obedience: moral or legal supremacy: the right to command, or give an ultimate decision." Authority is also "power to influence the conduct and actions of others . . . title to be believed . . . one whose opinion is entitled to be accepted—an expert in any question."

The influence, the respect commanded by an authority is different from the respect we give to an equal. The influence of authorities comes from their roles or positions in a hierarchy. They have a *title,* a named role, which *entitles* them to influence others. Ultimately, their entitlement derives from their power to enforce obedience.

Authority does not depend on the personal qualities of the individual. The guards in the jail expected us to respect their commands not because of who they were as individuals or because of the worth of their ideas, but because they were in a position to control us. Respect for authority is fear of power-over.

The woman in our group who suggested we sit down and chant had no position of authority. She was not designated as our leader. We did not fear her. Yet she exercised leadership in a positive sense; she put forth a plan of action, and we followed because we believed the plan good.

Power-with is more subtle, more fluid and fragile than authority. It is dependent on personal responsibility, on our own creativity and daring, and on the willingness of others to respond.

Through our willingness to respond, we can also throw away our own power, letting the "experts," tell us what to think and do, forgetting that true respect implies the possibility of challenge.

In a culture based on domination, authority and power-with are often confused, and the boundaries can be fuzzy. A teacher, for example, may impart valuable skills and knowledge in ways that empower us. We may rightfully respect such a person. Another teacher, however, may treat us in ways that establish her or his superiority and make us feel inferior. When we are required to act respectfully toward such a teacher's authority, we show deference to the role, not the person. We ignore our actual experience of her or his teaching, and by speech and gesture confirm our acceptance of our lesser status, adopting corresponding roles of our own: the good student, the teacher's pet, the rebel, and so on. Once in those roles, we are no longer thinking freely or acting freely, but reacting in set ways that reinforce the patterns of domination.

Our conditioning to obey authority is the foundation of the culture of domination. It is embedded in us so deeply that we are rarely aware of it. My own vision has been sharpened by the experience of doing direct action—of deliberately deciding to break an unjust law, to challenge authority on its home ground. In the jail, when every moment we face the decision of whether to resist or to comply, the strength of our conditioning to obey becomes clear. The guards say, "Give me your name and address," "Get on the bus," "Bend over and spread your cheeks," and we do. Only when someone refuses, resists, does another possibility reveal itself. Until then, we do not realize that we could say no.

Nazi Germany, My Lai, and many other examples have shown us how the conditioning to obey can override moral compunctions and human compassion. Another example comes from psychological experimentation.

In the 1960s, psychologist Stanley Milgram conducted a series of experiments in which he asked subjects to administer electric shocks to volunteers in what was presented as a learning experiment. The learners, who were actually actors, were to be given shocks when they failed at a memorization task, and the shocks were to gradually increase in intensity past a level clearly marked Danger. The shocks were simulated, but those who administered them believed they were real. The actors screamed and pleaded with the subjects to stop the shocks. The experimenters encouraged subjects to continue, and a frighteningly high percentage did so, over half continuing to the highest level of shock available.

Milgram commented, "Subjects have learned from childhood that it is a fundamental breach of moral conduct to hurt another person against his will. Yet twenty-six (out of forty) subjects abandon this tenet in following the instructions of an authority who has no special powers to enforce his commands. Subjects often expressed deep disapproval of shocking a man in the face of his objections, and others denounced it as stupid and senseless. Yet the majority complied with the experimental commands."[6]

Because of our experience in a society based on domination, we often expect to find a system of power-over operating in any new situation. We feel uneasy when we don't know who is in charge, and look to others to take responsibility.

In the same jail setting I described at the beginning of this chapter, I was waiting in a long lunch line one afternoon when I heard a woman behind me grumble to her friend, "Boy, would I ever have a thing or two to tell this organization if I could ever figure out who it is!" I turned to her. "But you are the organization—we all are!" I said.

Her friend poked her and stage-whispered, "She's one of the leaders."

The woman blushed. "I shouldn't have said anything."

"But I'm not a leader," I protested. "We have no leaders. And anyway—we really want to know what you think."

She proceeded to tell me a long list of things "the organizers" were doing wrong. I suggested she take responsibility for making some changes.

"I'm not in charge," she said.

Systems of domination destroy power-with, for it can only truly exist among those who are equal and who recognize that they are equal. The woman in the lunch line could not recognize that she had a right equal to anyone's to shape decisions and influence the action. She would not accept the responsibility that went with that right. And so she lost her power, and the group was deprived of her perspectives.

Power-with is always revocable. The group may consider our ideas, but it does not automatically adopt them or obey them. And if we misuse our influence, we may lose it.

For women, power-with is especially elusive. We are not taught to expect that our ideas, our contributions, will be valued equally with men's. Women defer to men in discussions, and are more hesitant to speak out in mixed groups of women and men. When researcher Matina Horner presented college students with the task of finishing a story that began,

"At the end of first term finals, Anne finds herself at the top of her medical school class," she found that students predicted tragedies and disasters for Anne, while a group given the identical sentence about a male predicted great achievements and good fortune. Concluded Horner, "For most women, the anticipation of success in competitive achievement activity, especially against men, produces anticipation of certain negative consequences, for example, threat of social rejection and loss of femininity."[7] We fear the achievements that might gain us respect and admiration, for loneliness is the price we expect to pay for esteem.

Perhaps we also fear power-with because we do not recognize it as different from power-over. Women have been victims of power-over, and we hesitate to step into the role of dominators. We are aware of the hostility directed toward women who wield power. For while we rarely reach the higher echelons of power-over, women most often fill the ranks of those who directly administer the decrees or impose the sanctions of the authorities. We rarely are the politicians who cut benefits to the hungry, but we are often the social workers who are forced to refuse the claims. We staff the front desks and answer the phones, and we receive the rage and frustration that really belongs elsewhere. And so the image in our minds of women in power becomes that of the Big Nurse, the hated, petty tyrant, someone we shrink from becoming, not someone we aspire to be.

In tribal and traditional societies, power-with, influence, increased with age and experience. "Old age was equated with wisdom and learning in most Native American societies, and aged persons were treated with deference and respect. In many tribes, women gained more power as they became older."[8] The elder, the clan mother, the chief, the person whose wisdom and judgment were acknowledged by the group, was listened to. Her or his opinions were sought on important matters, and were followed not because they were backed by law or force but because the experience of the group over time proved their consistent wisdom. Conrad Arensberg describes the informal gathering of old men in an Irish village of the thirties:

"O'Donoghue is the 'judge' in this gathering. . . . He is regarded as a wise man. All must defer to his opinions. Usually he contents himself with a word of affirmation, or now and again, a slow, measured judgment upon a current topic. He initiates nothing. . . .

"Silent as this shrewd old man is, his is the central position in the group. Comments and questions are phrased through him. . . . And, when agreement is finally reached, it is his quiet 'so it is' that settles the point for good."[9]

Power-with retains its strength only through restraint. It affirms, shapes, and guides a collective decision—but it cannot enforce its will on the group or push it in a direction contrary to community desires. The elders, the wise ones, retain our respect when we see them as working for the good of the whole. Should O'Donoghue attempt to influence the group for his own personal benefit at the community's expense, the good will upon which his influence rests would rapidly disappear. Were he in a role of authority or a position to wield control, the community might obey his directives, but they would not trust his judgment. The limits of influence are inherent in its nature.

ROOTS OF THE THREE TYPES OF POWER

Power-over, power-from-within, and power-with are each rooted in a mode of consciousness and a worldview that can be identified. Each speaks in its own language and is supported by its own mythologies. Each depends upon distinct motivations.

The consciousness that underlies power-over sees the world as an object, made up of many separate, isolated parts that have no intrinsic life, awareness, or value. Consciousness is fragmented, disconnected. In *The Spiral Dance* I compared it to seeing by flashlight with a narrow beam that illumines one separate object at a time, but cannot reveal the fabric of space in which they interconnect. Relationships between objects are described by rules. We believe that we can, in the end, find rules to describe all things and their relationships, to predict what they will do, and allow us to control them.

The language of power-over is the language of law, of rules, of abstract, generalized formulations enforced on the concrete realities of particular circumstances.

In the worldview of power-over, human beings have no inherent worth; value must be earned or granted. The formulation of Fall/Redemption-oriented Christianity is that we are born in original sin and we can be saved only by grace.[10] In the secular world, the worth we acquire is constantly rated against that of others, in school, in the workplace, by potential mates and lovers. We internalize a primal insecurity about our own right to be, which drives us to compete for the tokens of pseudo-value.

Mechanistic science provides us with the technology of power-over. Technology gives us power entirely split from any questions of meaning or purpose. The nuclear bomb is perhaps the ultimate symbol of power-over and the ultimate irony, as nuclear physics has "proven" that the mechanistic model of the universe is overly simplistic.

Power-over motivates through fear. Its systems instill fear and then offer the hope of relief in return for compliance and obedience. We fear the force and violence of the system should we disobey, and we fear the loss of value, sustenance, comforts, and tokens of esteem.

In the jail story, our victory came when we ceased to act from fear. Systems of domination are not prepared to cope with fearlessness, because acts of courage and resistance break the expected patterns.

Power-from-within stems from a different consciousness—one that sees the world itself as a living being, made up of dynamic aspects, a world where one thing shape-shifts into another, where there are no solid separations and no simple causes and effects. In such a world, all things have inherent value, because all things are beings, aware in ways we can only imagine, interrelated in patterns too complex to ever be more than partially described. We do not have to earn value. Immanent value cannot be rated or compared. No one, nothing, can have more of it than another. Nor can we lose it. For we are, ourselves, the living body of the sacred. This is what Witches mean when we say, "Thou are Goddess," and also what mavericks and heretics have always read into the biblical account of the creation of the world in the image of God.

Immanent value does not mean that everyone is innately good, or that nothing should ever be destroyed. What is valued is the whole pattern, which always includes death as well as birth. I pull snails off the iris leaves and crush them—they are out of pattern here. They have no natural predators and devour the diversity of the garden. A hundred years ago they escaped from a Frenchman who brought them to California so he could continue to eat escargot. Now they ravage plants all up and down the West Coast. Yet I do not expect to completely kill them off. We will, at best, strike a balance, a new pattern. Nor will I put out poison, which disrupts larger patterns still. I will be predator, not poisoner.

The language of power-from-within is poetry, metaphor, symbol, ritual, myth, the language of magic, of "thinking in things," where the concrete becomes resonant with mysteries that go beyond its seeming solid form. Its language is action, which speaks in the body and to all the senses in ways that can never be completely conveyed in words.

The technology of power-from-within is magic, the art of changing consciousness, of shifting shapes and dimensions, of bending reality. Its science is a psychology far older than Freud, Jung, or Skinner. And its motivations are erotic in the broadest sense of the deep drives in us to experience and share pleasure, to connect, to create, to see our impact on others and on the world.

Power-with also embodies a particular consciousness, language, and set of motivations. It bridges the value systems of power-from-within and power-over. Power-with sees the world as a pattern of relationships, but its interest is in how that pattern can be shaped, molded, shifted. It values beings, forces, and people according to how they affect others and according to a history based on experience. It can recognize inherent worth, but can also rate and compare, valuing some more highly than others.

The language of power-with is gossip. Gossip has a bad reputation as being either malicious or trivial. But in any real community, people become interested in each others' relationships within the group, love affairs, quarrels, problems. The talking we do about each other provides us with invaluable information; it makes us aware of whom we can trust and whom we distrust, of whom to treat carefully and whom to confront, of what we can realistically expect a group to do together.

Gossip maintains the social order in a close-knit society more effectively than law. Margery Wolf describes how she observed women's informal groups working in rural Taiwan: "A young woman whose mother-in-law was treating her with a harshness that exceeded village standards for such behavior told her woes to a work group, and if the older members of the group felt the complaint was justified, the mother-in-law would be allowed to overhear them criticizing her, would know that she was being gossiped about, and would usually alter her behavior toward her daughter-in-law. Every woman valued her standing within the women's circles because at some time in her life she might also need their support. . . . In the Taiwanese village I knew best, some women were very skilled at forming and directing village opinion toward matters as apparently disparate as domestic conflicts and temple organization. The women who had the most influence on village affairs were those who worked through the women's community."[11]

The art of wielding power-with, of gaining influence and using it creatively to empower, is probably intuitive to great and charismatic leaders. We can, however, observe and study it, both to improve our ability to use influence constructively and to identify the qualities we expect of those who assume leadership.

SEEING POWER AS IMMANENT

Power is exerted in the material world. Power-over has a clear material base, as it is grounded in the ability to punish by imposing physical or economic sanctions. Constructed from the demands of war, domination in turn builds in us a continuing psychological readiness to accept and administer control, a willingness to obey.

Power-from-within and power-with are grounded in another source, akin not to violence but to spirit. Because power-over works by creating false divisions, we have been trained to see spirit as something severed from the material world and from the world of real political and economic struggle. The split between spirit and matter, which locates God and the sacred outside the world of form and earth and flesh, allows exploitation and destruction of human beings and the earth's resources. The model of God in patriarchal religion furnishes the model that lends authority to all hierarchies.

In my earlier book, *Dreaming the Dark: Magic, Sex and Politics,* I spoke of another model of spirit, as a presence immanent in the world, in nature, in the body, in the human community and all its creations. "Spirit" can be another way of saying "immanent value." When matter is sacred, there is no split, no severing of value from the here and now. Immanent spirit is the ground of the European Goddess tradition, as it is the ground of Native American, African, and other tribal traditions and of shamanistic practices everywhere.

In Latin America, liberation theology, the response of radical Catholics to conditions of poverty and oppression, inspires revolution. In the peace movement church-based groups form the backbone of resistance to militarism. A neo-Pagan movement allied to a radical vision is also growing rapidly.

Still, the linking of politics and spirit among politically minded people is often greeted with embarrassment or fear. Marx's famous quote, "Religion is the opiate of the people," still holds sway. No one can deny that patriarchal religions often have served to drug people into submission, but the assumption that all spirituality inevitably functions oppressively in every culture and context misses the perspective held by most of the world's peoples.

I was made aware of that gap one afternoon when I visited the *assiento* of my friend Luisah Teish. Teish was being initiated into the Afro-Cuban religion of Lucumi as a priestess of Oshun, the Yoruban goddess of love. During the several days of the *assiento,* the new initiate receives friends while seated on the throne of the Goddess. The whole community comes to visit and bring gifts and offerings of sacred foods.

I walked into a room full of food, color, noise, and laughter. Teish was sitting in state, draped in golden cloth in the back bedroom. The front room was crowded with women in flowing white dresses, their heads bound in colorful cloths. Men wore whites or the colors of the *orishas,* the Yoruba goddesses and gods: the gold of Oshun, the red of Chango, the blue of Yemaya. Some of the participants were black, others Hispanic. I was the only white person in the room.

I set my food down in the kitchen, and began talking to Teish's *padrino,* the priest who had officiated at the ceremony. Teish had told him that I was a Witch, and soon a number of us were discussing the similarities and differences between our traditions. Teish's friends seemed amused that I called myself a Witch. They knew the term only as an insult, a way of discounting their rich religious tradition.

After a while, one of the older women called me over and gestured toward the chair next to her. She spoke with a soft Spanish accent, and patted my hand in a motherly way.

"Tell me," she asked, "Do you have trouble being accepted by white people?"

I looked at her, somewhat stunned. I'd certainly had my share of trouble in life but it had never occured to me to look at it in that way. As I thought it over, I realized that she was quite right. The shift of perspectives was both dizzying and exhilarating. The spiritual/political split is a problem of white people. The dominant culture can afford to cast power purely in terms of power-over, for it has at its disposal the backing of that power: the guns, the prisons, the laws, the economic wealth.

The resistance to questions of spirit among radicals is itself born of the white culture's delusion that power-over can be countered only by power-over, that spirit, mystery, bonding, community, and love are weak forces at best, and at worst, distractions from serious struggle.

But the dispossessed, to survive, to have power at all, must seek another source. They know the power of the common bonds of culture, of song, of ritual, of drum and dance, of healing to sustain hope and strength to resist oppression. The authorities know also. The slave owners outlawed the drum, the dances, and the African languages. The landowners of Europe in the sixteenth and seventeenth centuries persecuted the ancient peasant celebrations and traditions and labeled their healers Witches. The United States government removed Native American children from their families to place them in boarding schools where they were indoctrinated into Western culture and religion.

The women's question had jolted me into an awareness I might have intuited from my own Jewish history. Power-from-within, the bonding power of the spirit, sustained Jewish communal life through two thousand years of landlessness and persecution. Knowing my own people's history, I knew that the dispossessed can arise again and again out of that cohesive spirit to become a political force, and although those risings may bring tragedy as well as liberation, they represent forces that must be reckoned with.[12]

Culture describes reality, and different cultures develop different descriptions of what reality encompasses. Modern Western culture is perhaps unique in pushing spirit outside the boundaries of what we call real.

Spirituality was a powerful force in the black civil rights movement, not just because many of its leaders came from the Church, but in the way it was experienced in the lives of ordinary people. Alice Walker wrote: "I sometimes think that it was literally the prayers of people like my mother and father. . . that kept Dr. King alive until five years ago. For years we went to bed praying for his life."[13] In the movement for justice for Native Americans and indigenous peoples, religion plays a central role.

Myth is enacted in the world according to its theology or thealogy, to use Naomi Goldenberg's term for a feminist knowing of the sacred.[14] The mythology of Christ has certainly been used as much as any ideology in history to support oppression and the status quo. On the other hand, although its imagery for women is always problematic, Christianity also can inspire struggles for liberation. In December of 1984, I spent two weeks in Nicaragua with a Jewish delegation of Witness for Peace, a group that brings North Americans into the war zones to see firsthand the effects of our country's policies. As I heard individuals tell of how they became involved in the Revolution, I began to realize that liberation theology has developed an understanding of Jesus as immanent, alive in the world, especially in the poor. A verse from the "Missa Campesino," the Peasant's Mass, goes: "Jesus is a truck driver fixing the wheel on a truck . . . Jesus is a man in the park buying a snow cone and complaining that he didn't get enough ice." An old man in a border cooperative told us, "The revolution reminds us of when Christ walked on the earth."

"There are two churches here," one woman told us. "The church of the poor and the church of the capitalists." The Christ they invoke in the church of the poor is a Christ who, like the other fallen heroes and martyrs, is still *presente,* who walks among us and within us. The church of the poor is the church of the Delegates of the Word, lay preachers, *campesinos* themselves, who teach and encourage the people to read the Gospels and to interpret the stories for themselves. In the slow and dusty villages of the border, the life of Jesus seems contemporary. He too lived in sunbaked shacks like these, with the animals wandering in and out, with the people trudging off to the fields behind the oxen. And what the people read in the Gospels becomes the concrete practice of revolution: to serve the poor, to work for justice, to share what people have.

Spirituality promotes passivity when the domain of spirit is defined as outside the world. When this world is the terrain of spirit, we ourselves become actors in the story, and this world becomes the realm in which the sacred must be honored and freedom created.

If we are to be allies in struggle with people of different backgrounds, we need to respect different worldviews. The debate about the linking of the spiritual and the political too often takes place in terms that discount or make invisible the experience of the nondominant world. Such cultural imperialism is itself a form of racism. It is hard for us to acknowledge that powers and dimensions of reality with which we are unfamiliar may be more than quaint hangovers from a prescientific age, that they represent people's real experience and that we might have something to learn from them. Or, if we do bring ourselves to admit that the dominant description of reality is too narrow, we may run slavishly after other spiritual traditions, eager to acquire experiences of nonordinary consciousness as if they were Gucci bags or Cuisinarts, commodities we can use to bolster our status. We become spiritual colonialists, mining the Third World for its resources of symbols and shamans, giving nothing back, in a way that cheapens both the traditions we seek to understand and our own spiritual quests.

To find the point of balance, where we can learn from and share other peoples' cultural riches, we must be grounded in the experience of our own mysteries. That grounding is a difficult process, for the remnants of the mysteries in the West have been described to us for the last four hundred years as evil and frightening. The Witches, our Western shamans and healers, have been portrayed as either demonic or ludicrous. We fear identification with that tradition, and expect the mysteries to be strange, occult, and bizarre. Yet the mysteries are made up of the stuff of everyday life. They center on the most common of human experiences: birth, death, love, nurture, challenge, passion, time. We make mystery ourselves out of our everyday lives, and so we must discover the mysteries that will take us to the heart of our world.

The terrain of the mysteries is the ordinary. To seek out mystery, we don't have to go anywhere. We must simply change our perception, our description, our consciousness of where we are.

DEVELOPING A PSYCHOLOGY OF LIBERATION

The skills, the descriptions, the tools of magic are road maps. I offer the principles of magic not as a belief system to be proved or disproved, but as an alternative descriptive system that can help us develop a psychology of liberation. An alternative is necessary because, in Audre Lorde's words, "the master's tools will never dismantle the master's house."[15] The way we describe the world determines how we will value and experience the world. The descriptive systems of psychology, of science, of patriarchal religion are not objective. Embedded in them are values. If we describe the world as being separate from God, we have devalued the world. If we say that only quantifiable experiences are true, we have not eliminated what cannot be measured, but we have devalued it. We are unlikely to encounter it in our texts or the works of the authorities, however often we may encounter it in our lives.

Language is political. A liberation psychology cannot be written in the standard jargon of the psychologists, because such language is designed to exclude those who do not have the approved training and credentials. For example: "In the less-structured personality, therefore, the technical problem is not to make the unconscious conscious, but to make the ego capable of coping with the drives by means of neutralizing libido and aggression, thereby making them available for the building of higher levels of object relations."[16] This statement could be roughly translated into advice for beginning therapists: "When you're dealing with someone who is really unstrung, don't delve into their dreams and fantasies, help them gain some self-control, at which point they might have hope of making friends or even attracting a lover." More than its content, the language and form of the statement embody attitudes about power, knowledge, and value. The statement reserves power for someone steeped in the training necessary to translate it. It assumes that knowledge can be conveyed separately from feeling, that the process of healing is directed and understood by the healer, not the patient. Furthermore, it presents itself as a statement of fact. Its abstracted language seems scientific but is not, in reality, either objective or verifiable. The statement actually is an unpoetic metaphor. It implies that the human psyche is constructed like a machine, fueled by twin drives of sex and aggression. If all the parts are not firmly bolted together, the fuel will spill out, possibly igniting explosions, and the engine will go nowhere.

An overt metaphor is a map, a description we may find useful or not, may accept or reject. A covert metaphor is an attempt to restructure our reality by leading us to accept the map as the territory without questioning where we are going or whose interests are being served.

A liberation psychology, like liberation theology, maintains an "option for the poor." It allies itself with the dispossessed, with those resisting oppression, not with the forces of control. It must be useful to those who may not have formal education, or state-issued licenses. Therefore, it must be understandable. It is not anti-intellectual, but it realizes that intellect divorced from feeling is itself part of our pain. Its insights are conveyed in a language that is concrete, a language of poetry, not jargon; of metaphors that clearly are metaphors; a language that refers back to the material world, that is sensual, that speaks of things that we can see and touch and feel. It is a vocabulary not of the elite but of the common, and its concepts can thus be tested by experience.

A psychology that can lead us to encounter the mysteries must be rooted in an earth-based spirituality that knows the sacred as immanent. What is sacred—whether we name it Goddess, God, spirit, or something else—is not outside the world, but manifests in nature, in human beings in the community and culture we create. Every being is sacred—meaning that each has inherent value that cannot be ranked in a hierarchy or compared to the value of another being. Worth does not have to be earned, acquired, or proven; it is inherent in our existence.

Earth-based spirituality values diversity, imposes no dogma, no single name for the sacred, no one path to the center. But at this moment in history, the mythology and imagery of the Goddess carry special liberating power. They free us from the domination of the all-male God who has so strongly legitimized male rule, and by extension, all systems of domination. The Goddess represents the sacredness of life made manifest. All of the symbols and practices associated with her reaffirm her presence in this world, in nature and culture, in life and death. She does not symbolize female rule over men—but freedom from rule. She herself has male aspects who are earth Gods, alive in nature, in the wildness and cycles of transformation. The mystery, the paradox, is that the Goddess is not "she" or "he"—or she is both—but we call her "she" because to name is not to limit or describe but to invoke. We call her in and a power comes who is different from what comes when we say "he" or "it." Something happens, something arises that challenges the ways in which our minds have been shaped in images of male control. The hum of bees drowns the sound of helicopters.

A liberation psychology, based on the acknowledgment of the inherent worth of each person, views each person's truth and emotions with respect, sees resistances as evidence of strength, and knows that each process of change proceeds at its own pace.

When we see spirit as immanent, we recognize that everything is interconnected. All the beings of the world are in constant communication on many levels and dimensions. There is no such thing as a single cause or effect, but instead a complex intertwined feedback system of changes that shape other changes. The destruction of the Amazon rain forest changes our weather. The murder of a health-care worker in Nicaragua by the Contras affects our health. And so our health, physical and emotional, cannot be considered out of context. To change ourselves, we must change the world; to change the world we must be willing to change, ourselves.

When the sacred is immanent, the body is sacred. Woman-body, man-body, child-body, animal-body, and earth-body are sacred. They have an inherent integrity and inherent worth. All of our bodily processes, especially the deep, pleasure-giving force of our sexuality, are sacred processes. A psychology of liberation is not one of repression, nor does earth-based spirituality call us to asceticism. The times may demand courage and self-sacrifice, but we have no spiritual need for martyrdom. The celebration of life is our value.

With the AIDS epidemic threatening so many lives, it is more important than ever to assert the sacred value of the erotic. Caution about transmitting AIDS may restrict some aspects of erotic expression, but AIDS does not change the sacred nature of our sexuality any more than it invalidates the medical use of blood transfusions.

Society's response to AIDS reflects our fear and hatred of sexuality. The disease is used as an excuse to tell us, once again, that sex is dirty, nasty, and wrong—especially when not done in the approved manner. Out of fear of AIDS, people can be manipulated to accept schemes for concentration camps, identity cards, and other forms of social control. Punishment is our central social metaphor: we are eager to see AIDS as some form of divine or cosmic punishment, to blame its victims instead of assuming the responsibilities of caring. In a culture that valued the erotic, a disease that attacked our free expression of love would be a top research priority. Instead, we see funds diverted or denied. In a culture that valued the inherent worth of every being, no disease would lead us to shun the sick or deny them treatment, care, or dignity.

By shoving our noses in the face of death, one of the great mysteries, AIDS can be a powerful teacher. The largescale breakdown of immune systems warns us that our environment is dangerously overloaded with toxins. The disease challenges us to speak publicly and graphically about sexual practices, ending hypocritical censorship. Most of all, AIDS challenges us to mobilize the erotic force of love to create communities of healing and care.

Earth-based spiritual traditions are rooted in community. They are not religions of individual salvation, but of communal celebration and collective change. Community includes not just the human but the interdependent plant, animal, and elemental communities of the natural world, and is both a model of and limit to what we can become. A psychology of liberation is one whose primary focus is the communities we come from and create. Our collective history is as important as our individual history. A liberation psychology is more concerned with how structures of power shape and bind us than with the particular events of our individual childhoods. Those events are important, but to focus on them outside of the context of the whole is misleading. Individual therapy may be helpful, and sometimes necessary, but a liberation psychology is more concerned with ways of creating communal healing and collective change. For it is our responsibility to bring into being a culture that will nourish, heal, and sustain us in freedom.

The model we use is not one of health or sickness, but one of personal power. We each strive to increase our power-from-within, and this growth in power is beneficial as long as we remain centered and in balance. Many roads lead to power-from-within: among Witches, some of the traditional ways have been through knowledge of nature, through healing practices, through ritual, through trance, through the erotic, through the provision of food, through divination. Among Native Americans, magic, war, healing, peacemaking, and the vision quest can be roads to power. Pathways to power may be extraordinary or very ordinary. Sister José Habday, a Native American teacher and Franciscan sister, speaks of being called to power by the road of giving gifts to those who don't deserve them.[17]

The Yoruba term for personal power is *ache*. Luisah Teish writes, "Replenishing the 'ache' is a prime reason for the existence of individual and group rituals and the use of charms.

"There is a regulated kinship among human, animal, mineral and vegetable life. Africans do not slaughter animals wholesale, . . . nor do they devastate the fields that serve them. It is recognized that they have been graced with the personal power to hunt, farm and eat; but it is also recognized that they must give back that which is given to them."[18]

Personal power, *ache*, power-from-within, depends on a moving, living balance of the energies that sustain interconnected life. To misuse it is to lose it. Energy, like water, has power to shape only when it is in motion. Dammed, it stagnates and evaporates.

In Witchcraft, the model of balance is the magic circle that we cast by calling four directions and four elements, which each correspond to qualities within a human being. Correspondences vary among different groups, but in the tradition I learned, East corresponds to air and the mind, South to fire and energy, West to water, emotion, and sexuality, North to earth and the body. We need to be in touch with all aspects of ourselves. Each informs, but none controls, the others. When we develop personal power, we learn to move freely around the wheel, and in and out of the center—to evoke the aspect of ourselves that we need, to become whole.

THE PRINCIPLES OF MAGIC

Magic, as I have said, can be called the art of evoking power-from-within. Art implies skill and knowledge that empowers us to create. The skills of magic are the techniques of moving and shaping energy, of work, celebration, and ritual, of making the proper offerings and giving the right gifts. The knowledge magic teaches is that reality is deeper, more complex, more intricate, than it appears. We can swim, but not measure, its depths.

What we call magic is a body of knowledge compiled from many sources, and a tool that has been used to build many systems, some of them as hierarchical as any construction of mechanistic science. A liberation psychology understands the principles of magic and uses its tools to challenge hierarchies that keep us unfree and create structures that embody values of immanent spirit, interconnection, community, empowerment, and balance.

Magic teaches that living beings are beings of energy and spirit as well as matter, that energy—what the Chinese call *chi*—flows in certain patterns throughout the human body, and can be raised, stored, shaped, and sent. The movements of energy affect the physical world, and vice versa. This is the theory that underlies acupuncture and other naturopathic systems of healing, as well as the casting of spells and magical workings.

Energy can be formed; "structures," stable patterns, can be created by focused visualization. Energy structures influence physical reality. Physical beings are energy structures. Events in the physical world shape energy into patterns that in turn shape events that themselves move energy. The material world and the nonmaterial world are a mutually influencing system, a continuous feedback loop.

Of course, our power to shape reality has limits. Reality also has the power to shape us, and its power is usually stronger than ours. We do not say, as do some fashionable New Age philosophies, that we create our own reality. Such an idea can only conceivably make sense for white, upper-middle-class Americans, and then only some of the time. It is clearly senseless and becomes a form of victim blaming when applied, for example, to a Nicaraguan peasant child murdered by the Contras. We come into a reality that is already a given; within those sets of circumstances, we can make choices that will shape our future, but reality is a collective event and can be changed only by collective action. The peasants of Nicaragua did collectively shape their reality. Many individual changes in consciousness eventually sparked the actions that led to revolution. For action, ultimately, shapes reality. A change in consciousness changes our actions, or it is no true change. Only through action can magic be realized. And when we have acted, our actions shape a new reality that in turn shapes us, as the revolution in Nicaragua, in turn, changed individuals' ideas of who they were and what they could be.

Energy is directed by visualization, by imagining what it is we want to do. What we envision determines how we act. Our vision is distorted if we discount any aspect of reality. We cannot ignore the political, the spiritual, the social, the physical, the emotional, or any dimension of our lives. Again, the goal is balance, the image that of the magic circle where all forces come together equally.

Energy is erotic. Erotic energy is a manifestation of the sacred. Our mysteries draw on the erotic; respect our drives and know that they have their own rhythms and cycles, their own regulatory principle. Control of sexuality by others is a primary way in which our sense of worth is undermined, and is a cornerstone of the structures of domination.

The tangible, visible world is only one aspect of reality. There are other dimensions that are equally real although less solid. Many cultures acknowledge other realms of existence, and there are many different systems for naming them. Ron Evans, a Native American shaman, identifies eight worlds—the Inner World, the Outer World, the Mist World, the Pollen World, the Dawn World, the Dusk World, the Dream World, the Dark World—each of which has a precise use and is entered by a different type of drumming.[19] The Western theosophists spoke of different planes of existence. Witches, also, speak of different worlds, and read myths and symbols as maps to other dimensions. Tir-Na-Nog, the Land of Youth in Irish mythology, is not a metaphor nor archetype—it is a real place that can be visited, but its reality is not a physical one and the visits do not take place in the physical body.

Beings also exist in those other realms. The Goddesses, Gods, the ancestors, the Beloved Dead are more than symbols; they are powers, consciousnesses, intelligences, perhaps of a different order than our own, but nonetheless real. When we name them, call them, we open a doorway and power enters, for we are naming the great patterns that move and shape life.

"The African observed the voluptuous river, with its sweet water and beautiful stones and surmised *intuitively* that it was female. They named the river *Oshun,* Goddess of Love. They further noticed that a certain woman carried the flow of the river in her stride. . . so they called her the daughter of Oshun. They know that the river came before the woman, and that the woman's stride is affected by the flow of the river."[20]

The gods themselves may be shaped by how we perceive them. Our images of the gods in turn influence our acts. When our Goddess is voluptuous, flowing, erotic, so will be our dances, the rhythms of our drums and chants, our bodies. When the Inquisition became obsessed with the devil, it performed acts of evil, torturing and murdering suspected Witches. To say the Goddess is reawakening may be an act of magical creation.

Just as individuals have an identity, a form, and a corresponding energy form, so do groups. The idea of a "group mind" or a "group soul" is, again, not just a metaphor but a reality in subtler dimensions than the physical.

To expand our vision of reality does not diminish the immanent value of the material world. The ancestors are revered, but not more so than the living. The Goddess, the Gods, the great powers, are the material world, are us. If they extend beyond us they do so like the sun's corona flaring beyond its core. No power is entirely separate from our own power, no being is entirely separate from our own being.

THE DARE

Any psychology, to be useful, must look at two basic questions: How did we get into this mess? and How do we get out of it? A psychology of liberation, rooted in the magical description of the world, sees that the process of getting into our mess is long, complex, and historic; that we are in pain because we live in psychic and social structures that destroy us.

Our way out will involve both resistance and renewal: saying no to what is, so that we can reshape and recreate the world. Our challenge is communal, but to face it we must be empowered as individuals and create structures of support and celebration that can teach us freedom. Creation is the ultimate resistance, the ultimate refusal to accept things as they are. For it is in creation that we encounter mystery: the depth of things that cannot be wholly known or controlled, the movement of forces that speak through us and connect us at our core.

To value the mysteries we must describe the world in ways that make possible encounter with mystery. When we view the world through the lens of that description, the old systems and structures may themselves be revealed as distortions.

The core of the mysteries is the understanding that truth is always deeper and richer than any description of it. To change lenses and face a fuller spectrum of that truth can be frightening, shattering. It requires daring.

And so I have named this book after the game of Truth or Dare, a favored pastime in groups suffering enforced boredom or confinement. I have played it waiting in traffic jams and in holding cells after being arrested. The rules are simple. One person is "it." Anyone else in the group can ask that person a question, preferably intimate, sometimes embarrassing. "What would you like to do sexually that you can't ask for?" "What is your most exciting fantasy?" "Who in this room do you find most attractive?"

When you are "it," you are required to tell the truth—or else you must face the dare. No one knows what the dare is, but everyone knows it will be worse than the question.

So the game becomes an endlessly fascinating stripping process, a collective demand to speak the unspeakable, reveal what we have always been warned not to reveal. Secrets become common knowledge. Love affairs are sparked.

In the process, we learn something important about our own secrets: that they too, like the great mysteries, are common. What shames us, what we most fear to tell, does not set us apart from others; it binds us together if only we can take the risk to speak it.

"Let everything private be made public" was a Situationist slogan of the sixties.

The slogan and the core of these encounters with common mysteries is this:

Truth is the dare.

A Story of Change

The fire remains
See it burn in the center of the circle
   where it has burned for a thousand thousand years
A living flame in a dying landscape
   a beacon surrounded by fences, walls, concrete, and barbed wire
Watch the flame
Hold out your human hands
Feel the fragile warmth
Breathe deep

This is the story we like to tell ourselves
   as the bars of the cage rise around us
We tell ourselves
   that there once was a time when we were free . . .

Remember
   the green plains of Africa
   lion and gazelle
   the trackless forest
   coco and fruit
The First Mother stands erect
   cries out in a human voice
   gives birth
   to a child with human hands
   again and again
And her children grow, change, wander
We fill the plains, we fill the forest
We follow the herds and the wild grass seeds
   into every land
   mountain and glacier, desert and fertile valley,
   jungle and seacoast, riverbank and tundra
And we change

We change the way we get our food, our songs, our shelters,
   the rhythm of our drums, our dances, our magic
   the way we wear our hair
   the color of our skin
And always we remember

She lives in us as we
   in her as in each other

And we fill the earth with color, and dancing, and shaping
And we change

We tame the herds, breed goats to woolly sheep,
  wild aurochs to milk cows
Poke seeds into the earth, tend them,
Harvest, winnow, and store them
Changing the grasses to bread wheat, rice, millet, corn, barley,
Shaping wet clay to fired pot—the vessel
Weaving the basket, the cloth
Forming the bricks, building the walls, thatching the roofs
  of our shelters
Singing litanies of praise, painting and carving images
  to remind us

All that is alive is alive in us
  and all is alive

The First Mother is a wise mother
She knows that to be a mother is to let go
She leaves us free to change
  to become something
  different from herself
Free even to forget
  who we are

And so we changed
And perhaps in a valley between two rivers
  or a plateau high above a jungle
  or in many places, many times
We discovered a power
  that could turn in the hand to a cutting edge
  and be wielded over
  what lives
  that we have forgotten
  lives in us

Remember
  for this memory also is ours:
The intoxication of rule
  to command, and be obeyed
  to threaten, and be feared
  to be exalted over others
Feel the rush in your veins
You are like the gods
They give life but you wield
  death
It is stronger

And the circle was broken

And the people splintered

To rule or be ruled
To stand above or below
   men over women, light skin over dark, rich over poor,
   the few over the many
   human gain over the living balance of the earth
And the rulers forged weapons,
   waged endless wars, twisted the old songs and stories,
   wrote new hymns that exalted battle,
   sacrificed to gods of conquest
   and feared
   the memory of the living dance of the Mother
   that lives in the heart
   like a watchfire
   giving courage
   to resist
   giving strength
   to create
The rulers tried to destroy her
   pierced her skin with weapons,
   salted her living fields,
   drenched clean rivers with blood and poison,
   weighted her down with stones and walls and fences,
   murdered children,
   cursed her name and called it evil,
   carved her body into pieces and sold them
And what was done to the earth was done
   on the living bodies of women and men
And we who are alive in her as she in us
   were fettered, beaten, raped, tortured,
   burned, poisoned, and
   dismembered . . .
And almost destroyed.

Breathe deep
Feel the pain
   where it lives deep in us
   for we live, still,
   in the raw wounds
   and pain is salt in us, burning
Flush it out
Let the pain become a sound
   a living river on the breath

Raise your voice
Cry out. Scream. Wail.
Keen and mourn
for the dismembering of the world

2

The Dismembering of the World

We like to tell ourselves that there once was a time when we were free, that power-over is a human invention, not an imperative of nature. In our dreams, in our deepest minds, sleeps a memory that stirs in the presence of certain ancient things. From the earliest times, the mother-times, no texts have come down to us, no writing, no records of laws or lineages or events, only objects that wake in us some intuitive sense of what was. When we hold in our hands a reproduction of a heavy-hipped Paleolithic Venus, when we see the solid thighs and bountiful breasts of the Anatolian mother enthroned between lions, we feel a sense of power in our own bodies, in curve and swelling. When we contemplate the beaked bird-pots of Old Europe, painted with breasts and wings, we sense some deep connection between nurturing and flight.

Scholars, including some feminists, argue about whether such times existed. We cannot prove to them that the mother-times were real, for the academy accepts only written evidence. Their definition of what can be considered fact claims to be objective, but it is inevitably skewed. For texts do not preserve the mysteries, nor can they fully record the reality of oral cultures. And texts are written by people with biases and interests to preserve. It was not in the interests of the rulers to preserve records of a time of freedom, or of woman's power. Yet traces survive.

Carol Christ writes, "In the case of the New Testament, Schüssler Fiorenza argues that any scrap of evidence about women's liberation or women's religious leadership within the Jesus movement must be given weight, because it was not in the interests of the increasingly androcentric church to preserve such information. The same can be said of the historical (written) records concerning the Goddesses. . . . The gaps and silences in the androcentric tradition deny women a potentially empowering knowledge of history. When Goddesses are dismissed without careful consideration of all the evidence from prehistory, scholars perpetuate an inexcusable ignorance about the prehistoric Goddesses and the power of women in prehistory, an ignorance which serves to bolster patriarchy."[1]

The story of the rise of power-over is the story of the literal dismemberment of the world, the tearing apart of the fabric of living interrelationships that once governed human life. It is a tragic story that names our condition as one of loss, that gives us a vehicle through which we can feel our pain, grieve, rage, heal, and fight.

Without the story, we don't know what's wrong with us. Western culture is rooted in myths of progress. We like to think we are challenging the system when often we are simply putting forth new ways of framing the same false picture. The myth of the New Age would tell us that progress has given us understanding of the human potential that will illumine us, and wean us comfortably away from destruction without requiring us to give up anything. Simplified Freudian theory would tell us that the sublimation of our instinctual drives is the necessary sacrifice that allows us to build higher civilization. Some Jungians believe that patriarchy was a painful but necessary advance over matriarchy because it allowed the differentiation of the individual.[2] A certain feminist position would tell us that women have always been oppressed, but now through cultural advancement, technological development, and the women's liberation movement, we can gain control over our capacity for production and reproduction and free ourselves. "The story of civilization," writes Gerda Lerner, "is the story of men and women struggling up from necessity, from their helpless dependence on nature, to freedom and their partial mastery over nature."[3] Her statement identifies progress and freedom with removal from nature. It embodies the same patriarchal attitudes that treat the natural world as an object to be exploited and assumes that we can somehow remove ourselves from what we are.

The arguments among feminists about women's power in early times are not actually about evidence but about progress and values. For the story of the rise of power-over resembles a myth of regress. It tells us that things are not always getting better and better, that in fact they were better in some ways in the past and have been getting worse.

To be a woman, to be a person of color, to be a tribal person in the dismembered world, to be among the dispossessed and disempowered, is to suffer continual loss. We suffer loss precisely because we have something to lose: a heritage, the rich gifts of a culture, a way of being. The myth of progress denies that loss, makes us unable to name our grief.

Frozen sorrow paralyzes. To unlock our energies, to empower ourselves again, we must mourn and rage. And so the first healing task of a psychology of liberation is to teach us our history.

In looking at the past, we can look for the evidence of things—the artifacts that still speak the language of magic. We can read texts for their hints of power and mystery as well as their concrete content.

Clearly, we cannot look at all of history everywhere. The history of Western culture has too often been assumed to be the history of *all* culture. I do not want to perpetuate that assumption. Nevertheless, our first question is: how did we get into this mess? and the mess is integrally bound up with Western culture. We must therefore examine its roots, which are to be found in Mesopotamia. We will explore, especially, the transition to patriarchy, to an organization of society around the principles of domination and the rule of men over women, and over other men.

THE MOTHER TIMES

A Story of the Birth Chamber

You enter the shrine from above, through the roof hole, the smoke of the hearthfire curling around you as you descend the ladder made of lashed saplings. Smoke purifies. The roof hole is an opening as the vagina is a passageway. Emerge and return.

The shrine is a square room of whitewashed mud-brick walls. On a raised platform heaped high with skins and woven blankets, the old women sit, playing their round, flat drums and chanting. Behind them, on the wall, a paint and plaster image of the Goddess raises her arms and legs and gives birth to three sculptured bulls' heads.

In the corner stands the birth stool, its high back carved into sacred horns. On the stool squats a sweating woman, breathing hard in heavy labor. Women support her back and grasp her sides. You join them, sponging her face with cool water as the chief midwife rubs her vulva with warm oil.

The old women chant:

> Great Woman
> Mother of birds
> Your shrine is sticky with beeswax and
>   feathers
> Your shrine is loud with bird cries and
>   throbs
>   with the beat of wings
> You are the vessel
>   beaked and breasted
> You contain us
>   as earth contains us
>   as sky contains stars
>   our ancestors   our yet unborn
> We pour through you
>   life after life
>   the vessel dips into the river
>   water pours out on thirsty earth
>   earth drinks of us
>   as corn sucks rain from your breast
>   as rain feeds the river
> Great Sky Woman
>   your shrine is deep in the cradling earth
>   your shrine is the spirit's resting place
>   beginning place
> We are your vessel

You are milk on the wing
We contain you
    as the body contains breath
    as the breast contains milk
You pour through us
    life after life
        as breath pours through us
        the ancestors   the yet unborn   return
        our bodies are their vessels
        earth drinks of us
        as rain feeds the river
    The spirit rises on the wing

The room hums with power; you hear bees; you taste honey. The woman cries out, her contractions ripple through you like the beat of wings that carry you up as you match breath with breath as you have been trained to do. The bird comes for you and you ride her out into the free sky where the stars are smeared like breast milk in a vessel of dark brew. They are the souls of the dead; they are the unborn. They are a vast field of grain and here is your grandmother walking toward you holding three different stalks of wheat from three fields.

"Plant these together," she says. Then she is gone.

The bird plucks a star like a glowing fruit with her beak. The wings beat with your breath.

"She's crowning!" the women cry. "Bear down. Push!"

You cry out together with one voice. The child slides free.

"A girl!" the women cry in delight. They give her to her mother, who holds her close as the old women chant a song of praise:

        A great gift, a precious gift
        Has come to us . . .

You catch the birth blood in a bowl to pour over the fields. The child's skin is covered with the waxy vernix that protected her in the womb. The old women rub it into her body and smear some on their faces. "It will make you beautiful," they say. The shrine is filled with song and laughter.

Tomorrow you will walk the fields. You will find seeds of three different kinds of grain and plant them together. When you have planted and harvested and planted again, season after season, your daughters and daughters' daughters following after, you will have something new: a heavy-headed kernel, easy to thresh, a gift to the people from the ancestors. You have brought the knowledge through, for you are a priestess of the women's mysteries, shaman of the birth chamber, ancestor-speaker, the bird's rider, a woman of knowledge.

The beginnings of Mesopotamian history are to be found in what went before. Human beings began as scavengers, and over millennia learned to gather and hunt. Gathering and hunting cultures are generally egalitarian, and women seem to have been held in high regard.[4] The earliest works of art are the voluptuous Venuses of France and central Europe that show veneration and respect for the power embodied in women.

The great divide in human history came with the development of agriculture. In the Middle East and Anatolia (now Turkey), the cultivation of crops and the breeding of animals are over ten thousand years old.[5] Women, who gathered seeds and herbs and intimately knew the habits of plants, may have been the first to deliberately plant and tend seeds. Women and children may have cared for or tamed wounded or orphaned animals, and so may have begun the process of domestication.[6]

The first farmers had no body of accumulated knowledge to draw upon. Their grains were wild grasses with small kernels, hard to thresh and harvest. Their flocks and herds had no genetic heritage of tractability and had not yet been bred to produce milk, wool, meat. The first agriculture was probably a supplement to gathering and hunting. Only after millennia would agriculture become the mainstay of a culture.[7]

By the seventh millennium B.C.E.,[8] villages and even small cities had been established. One of the finest examples is the Anatolian city of Çatal Hüyük, excavated by archaeologist James Mellaart in the 1960s. Çatal Hüyük, the imagined setting for my story of the birth chamber, flourished from 6500 to 5650 B.C.E. Its dwellers farmed, bred stock, hunted wild cattle, deer, boar, and leopards, and controlled the important trade in obsidian from nearby active volcanoes. Reports Mellaart: "The standard of agriculture is amazing: emmer, einkorn [both are varieties of wheat], bread wheat, naked barley, pea, vetch and bitter vetch, were widely grown. Vegetable oil was obtained from crucifers and from almonds, acorn and pistachio . . . and it may certainly be assumed that beer was also known."[9]

Çatal Hüyük looked somewhat like a Pueblo Indian village. Flat-topped adobe houses, crowded closely together, were entered by ladders from their roofs. Many small shrines served the city; there was no centralized temple. In plan, the shrines were like the houses, square, windowless structures of mud brick, but their walls were lavishly decorated with paintings and relief sculptures of birth.

According to Mellaart, "The supreme deity was the Great Goddess."[10] The Goddess appears in twin aspects, of birth and death, fertility and age. She may appear with a daughter or a young son, or a bearded god associated with the bull. Many reliefs show her giving birth to a bull's head. Others show her as the vulture, as death. "The whole aim of the religion [was] to ensure the continuity of life, in every aspect: wildlife for the hunter, domesticated life for the civilized communities, and finally the life of Neolithic man [sic] himself."[11]

Statues of the Goddess show ties to even earlier Paleolithic art, and to Goddess figures found throughout the Middle East and Old Europe.[12] Çatal Hüyük was part of a civilization in which women were leaders, priestesses, revered and respected members of society. Murals show that women participated in hunting, and women were buried with hoes and adzes, the tools of the farmers. Children were buried with their mothers, indicating that society was matrilineal.[13] We could call it matriarchal, but the term might mislead us if we read it as the reverse image of patriarchy. For women had power at a time when power-over had not yet been institutionalized.

The images, the objects, we find in Çatal Hüyük do not reflect structures of domination. Little differentiation is present in grave goods to indicate class divisions. Although the town was several times destroyed by fire, it was never destroyed by war. We find no images of war, of kings or conquests. "It was apparent from the absence of blood pits and animal bones that there was no sacrificing of animals in the shrines."[14] Nor was human sacrifice practiced. "In this society," states Ruby Rohrlich, "the focus was on the conservation of life."[15]

MESOPOTAMIA AND THE TIMES OF TRANSITION

The earliest settlements in Mesopotamia were similar to Çatal Hüyük.[16] In the fifth millennium B.C.E., the vast valley of Mesopotamia, hot, dry, and potentially fertile, lay cradled in the arms of two great rivers, Idiglat and Burunum—the Tigris and the Euphrates. Mud-brick villages of simple houses and small shrines dotted the plain. Their inhabitants made decorated pottery and statues of the Goddess with round hips and belly and carefully emphasized eyes. They practiced agriculture and stockbreeding. They buried their dead with offerings and belongings that show no great differences in wealth or class.[17]

The people of the valley thrived. By the last quarter of the fifth millennium, the 'Ubaid culture, forerunner of the Sumerian civilization, had been established.[18] Population grew and new settlements were founded. Irrigation developed more land for agriculture and encouraged larger-scale organization. Trade was extensive. Some of the villages began to grow into small cities.

The scale of collective life changed. Cities may have grown up for defensive reasons. "The impulse to urbanization seems to have occurred when the Neolithic villages and towns drew together into larger territorial and political units in defense against periodic raids by nomadic pastoralists."[19] Or they may have grown because increases in population and agricultural efficiency made them possible, or because people found them convenient and desirable.

As the cities grew, the small shrines of the early period were replaced by the first great central temples. "Nothing . . . more clearly demonstrates the change in culture than the monumental temples which were now built in the cities. . . . They dominated the cities from the top of ancient mounds. At Eridu they were set on mud-brick platforms, the origin of the temple tower or Ziggurat."[20]

Throughout the fourth millennium, as the 'Ubaid cultures gave way to the cultures we call Sumerian, the power of the temples increased. They became business centers surrounded by workshops and warehouses.

The traditional system of land tenure was based on clans and kinship groups that held land in common. The clans may have undertaken the first irrigation projects as a communal effort to improve their land. Over time, however, the scale of the projects tended to encourage large-scale organization, often directed by the temple priesthood. Mesopotamia's dry climate, arid but fertile land, and erratically flooding rivers made agriculture difficult and unpredictable for small farmers with limited resources, but rewarded massive irrigation and storage projects.

Irrigation made some land enormously more productive, and therefore more valuable than other land. Some groups and individuals became rich; others were gradually made poor. "By engendering inequalities in access to productive land, irrigation contributed to the formation of a stratified society. And by furnishing a reason for border disputes between neighboring communities, it surely promoted a warlike atmosphere that drew people together in offensive and defensive concentrations."[21]

The clans were strongholds of the old egalitarian, matrifocal order. As control of the land passed into the hands of the temple priesthood, so did the surplus wealth of agricultural production, and with it, power. "By Protoliterate times [around 3500 B.C.E.], . . . the farmers had lost their autonomy as they were forced to cultivate the private lands of the elite."[22]

At first, women retained power in the new priestly hierarchy. The word *en,* which denotes both religious and political leadership, first appears in this period "when female deities outnumbered male deities as temple patrons and the 'ens' were mainly women. . . . Women priests were not only administrators and officials in the temples, they were also very active in the arts, especially in music and literature . . . they also organized large choirs and orchestras, in which trained, gifted women of all classes performed."[23] Writing, education, science, and account keeping were the domains of a Goddess, Nidaba, and women were scribes and scholars, poets and composers of religious texts. Writing first appears in the form of pictographs used to keep accounts in the Temple of Inanna, Queen of Heaven, in Uruk, and was most likely invented by women.[24] The patroness of medicine was the Goddess Gula, and throughout the third millennium most doctors were probably women.[25]

"In the early Sumerian myths, the female deities are the creators of all life."[26] Nammu, the ocean, was revered as the primal ancestress, mother of heaven and earth. Ninhursaga—or Ninmah, Nintur, Aruru, Belit-ili, or Mama, to list just a few of her names—was one of the original triad of most powerful deities, representing the productivity of the earth. Her name means Lady of the Foothills or Lady of the Stony Ground.[27] Inanna, the most revered of Sumerian deities, was originally the goddess of the date palm and the communal storehouse. She symbolized "the authority of women as producers and distributors of staple food and clothing."[28]

"Her emblem—that is to say, her preanthropomorphic form—confirms this, for it is . . . a gatepost with rolled up mat to serve as a door, a distinguishing mark of the storehouse."[29]

"From the third through the first millennium, the wide spectrum of activities attributed to goddesses was matched by the wide-ranging powers of gods, and both shared sovereignty over fertility, life and death, war, justice, wisdom, social order, and the arts of civilization . . . . Gender as a category . . . was not seen as a necessary or natural correlative of power or powerlessness."[30]

It is likely that many women opposed the growing centralization of power. Others, who may have benefited by the change, probably supported it. These women could not foresee that centralized power would ultimately lead to changes that would wrest power from all women and most men.

As power in Sumer became more centralized, secular political power developed. In the Protoliterate period, political authority was invested in an assembly, which was at first broadly democratic and included women as well as men.[31] Later, "convoked only to meet sporadic external threat, the assembly's task was merely to select a short-term war leader."[32]

By about 2600 B.C.E., the time of the reign of Gilgamesh in Uruk, the assembly excluded women, marking "the basic step in the breakdown of the democratic kinship group, which paved the way for the next step, the 'divine' appointment, instead of the election, of the king."[33]

Warfare gradually became more and more common. Wars may have been fought first to repel nomadic invaders. The geography of Sumer, with its many prosperous, independent city-states, may have offered attractive targets for nomad chiefs or ambitious leaders. Some scholars believe that concepts of kingship and male rule were imposed by patriarchial conquerors. Others believe that intracity conflicts arose from within Sumerian society and spawned chronic war. However war began, it developed a self-perpetuating quality. To understand Sumerian society and our own, we must understand how chronic war restructured culture and human personality in the image of domination.

Andrew Bard Schmookler, in *The Parable of the Tribes,* suggests that societies develop to maximize power. "The parable of the tribes begins: 'Imagine a group of tribes living within reach of one another. . . . What are the possible outcomes for those tribes threatened by a potent and ambitious neighbor?' We discover that the possibilities are quite limited." Each tribe may try to withdraw, may submit to destruction, may survive conquest but find its culture transformed, or may imitate the invaders and itself become warlike and belligerent. "They all amount fundamentally to the same thing: the inescapable permeation of the entire system by the ways of power. It is, therefore, a parable about the theft of free human choice."[34]

The story of the transition to patriarchy is the history of the maximization of power. It came about through choices made by both men and women to preserve what they saw as their best interests. Although we can see, with hindsight, what each change led to, or imagine other choices, they could not. Perhaps the clans said, "We will accept a war leader temporarily to pull us through this crisis," never intending the change to become permanent. But crisis followed crisis, and as warfare between city-states became endemic, "successful war leaders were retained even in times of peace. Herein lies the apparent origin of kingship."[35] Kings found their power extended by war, and so had incentive to wage war. So the cycle continued.

The Sumerian dynasties were succeeded by the Akkadians and Babylonians. Each change in political power represented a new stage in the transition to a hierarchical, patriarchal, militarist society. Feminist scholars, among them Ruby Rohrlich, Merlin Stone, and Gerda Lerner, have traced the erosion of women's power through changes in laws, religious practices, records of customs and transactions, and myths.[36] I have chosen to focus on the myths because they reveal to us most clearly how the outer changes reshaped the landscape of the psyche.

Although all written records of myths and ceremonies date from the transitional period, they record clear traces of the earlier order. But myths and religious images change as political structures change. They may change organically, as new powers arise and old ones wane, or they may be changed deliberately, to consolidate the power of a new political order, to discourage beliefs that might foster resistance, to close the doors to one kind of power and open the gates to another.

We can hear in the Mesopotamian myths echoes of the changes in the structures of power upon which the society was based. We will examine three mythic cycles: the Sacred Marriage cycle of the late fourth and third millennium B.C.E.; the Epic of Gilgamesh from the mid-second millennium B.C.E.; and the *Enûma elish,* the Babylonian creation myth from the late second millennium B.C.E.[37] Together, they tell the story of the rise of power-over.

As an exercise in imagining what might have been, I will introduce each section with a story of my own.

THE SACRED MARRIAGE

A Temple Story

You wake early and throw open the shutters of your east-facing window to welcome the first rays of dawn. It is the day, the great day. The walls of the temple are cool, of plastered brick, and as you breathe deep you can smell the city below, the dampness of the canal, the freshness of the palm grove, the ripe odor of animal and human dung. You begin to hear the sounds of the city awakening. In the distance, a farmer swears at a donkey. From the terrace above you, a hymn to Inanna drifts through the air.

It is to you they are singing. You are Inanna's daughter, her vessel. The door opens and the women come to greet you. You go with them to bathe in the courtyard pool. They pour warm water over your body and rub you with oil and sweet scents, praising the beauty of your body and teasing each other as you all groom.

"Look at those lovely breasts—like ripe pomegranates!"

"Do you think the God will pluck them?"

"He might try to suck their juice!"

"We better taste them, to make sure they're sweet!"

"Oh, but what a lovely vulva! See how the little hairs stand up around it like stalks of barley in a field."

"Who will plow it, do you think?"

"The God, of course—if he has a plow equal to the task!"

You splash water at them, and they laugh. But their teasing and stroking has a purpose. Every word, every touch calls the Goddess into you.

The day is spent in preparation. You are bathed and dressed in your finest clothing, white linen, the ropes of beads of precious stone, the rare gold of your dangling earrings shaped in stars and crescents. You bring offerings to all the Goddesses and Gods, descending at last to a small shrine in the temple's deepest chamber, where you pour out milk and grain for the earth Goddess.

The women say, in the temple, that once all power belonged to the Mother. That in her wisdom she allowed women, and then men, to bring that power to the earth. Once grain and fruit grew only where the Mother's power bade them grow; now human hands plant seeds and open the date bud to the pollen. And so the Mother gave to the people the rite of the Sacred Marriage as a reminder lest they come to think their power greater than hers. On the festival, the women who rule and manage let go their responsibilities to dance for the Goddess, to become her daughter, to let her currents flood them and carry them away, spilling out fertile waters on the earth.

For you do not spend every day in teasing and play. Were this any other day, you might be closeted with the scribes reviewing temple accounts or greeting trade delegations from distant cities. You draft letters and hold audiences with people seeking judgments in disputes. You are in charge of preparations for all the rituals. Sometimes it all seems too much. You barely have time for making hymns and songs. Sometimes you long for the simpler days when you were a minor priestess of a small clan shrine. The statue of the Mother gazes at you with implacable eyes. Here you must speak truth, even to yourself. You like being who you are: chief priestess of the Eanna, Inanna's Temple of Uruk. You like being the important one, the one at center. And so it is fitting for you to have to put yourself aside and let Inanna enter. For the mysteries remind us of the limits of our power.

You are the Shepherd of the People. All day you, too, have been bathed, oiled, prepared. You have fasted; tonight you will taste the marriage feast. You have checked that each animal in the long train of cattle, goats, and sheep is perfect, without flaw or blemish, brushed and bedecked in a newly braided collar. You think about the baskets of dates, the grain, the vegetables. It is a rich offering, a fitting reflection of your power to feed the people. You feel proud, and just a little nervous. It is said sometimes in the temple that the reason men were admitted to the sacred rite is to keep them humble and remind them of where their power ends.

Breathe. See the full moon rise above the temple terrace. Hear the drums and voices of the procession: he comes, bringing rich offerings, cattle and grain, milk and fruit to fill the storehouse. You will be filled. He ascends the stairs, he comes up. Moonlight glints on bare arms. The women dance, arms upraised to the moon, hips curving, as the drums beat and the chants rise in the night air.

You ascend. The drums call you. Your shoulders shake; your feet pound out the rhythm. The women sing the courting songs and the calling songs. On the high wind a voice sings out:

"She has called for it! She has called for it!"

"She has called for the bed!" The people answer with one throat.

"She has called for the bed of heart's delight!"

"She has called for the bed!"

The drums beat faster. A sweetness rises in you. You are Inanna's priestess: she fills you. You are Dumuzi's priest; in you he swells. You find each other: you can't remember who you are, only that you are a living vessel of honey, only that touch is fire, is sweet cool water, only that you can pour yourself out like rich creamy milk, a foam that pours over the people, over the herds and groves and fields and soaks into the living loam.

And so life is renewed.

"The ancient Mesopotamian, it would seem, saw numinous power as a revelation of indwelling spirit, as power at the center of something that caused it to be and to flourish."[38] "The earliest form of Mesopotamian religion was worship of powers of fertility and yield, of the powers in nature ensuring human survival."[39]

The rite of the sacred marriage of Inanna, Goddess of the storehouse, patroness of civilization, and her consort Dumuzi were central to the religion of Sumer for centuries. The texts record practices—they are liturgies, as well as stories. They tell us not just what people believed, but what they did: that they called the Goddess and God to take possession of priestess and priest and so enacted the renewal of the world through the life-sustaining power of the erotic.

The rites were celebrated in ways that reflected the unique ecology and economy of each place through Dumuzi's changing attributes. Among the date growers, Dumuzi was named Amaushumgalana, meaning the One Great Source of the Date Clusters. He was "the personified power in the one enormous bud which the date palm sprouts each year, and from which issue the new leaves, flowers, and fruits." He represented what was to be stored in the storehouse; and Inanna herself was originally named Ninanna(k), Lady of the Date Clusters.[40] Elsewhere, among the herders, Dumuzi was the Wild Bull, "a Sumerian metaphor for 'shepherd'—originally, probably for 'cowherd.' "[41] The erotic metaphors of the Sacred Marriage texts here center around milk and cream. Inanna asks Dumuzi "to make the milk yellow—that is, creamy and fat—for her. She asks for cow's milk, goat's milk, and even for camel's milk." She praises her vulva and compares it to "a field ready for the fertilizing seed plough—an image, incidentally, which still does not take us outside the herder's world since the plough oxen were provided by the cowherders."[42]

These early myths celebrate the presence of immanent power in the natural and human world, in the seasonal rhythms of renewal and withering, in food, and in sexuality. The erotic power of woman is venerated, seen as a force that generates good for all the community, and as a power that woman herself takes pride in. In the herder wedding text, "Inanna's pride appears focused . . . on her own bodily charms, so much so indeed that she wants them celebrated in a song. She calls upon the girl singer and girl elegist who accompany her and orders them to weave her praise of her charms into a song for all to sing. . . .

> "The young lady was praising her parts
> and the elegist was weaving it into a song,
> Inanna was praising them,
> had her parts extolled in song.
>
> '(My crescent-shaped) "Barge of Heaven,"
> so (well) belayed,
> full of loveliness, like the new moon,
> my untilled plot,
>   left so fallow in the desert,
> my duck field so studded with ducks,
> my hillock land, so (well) watered,
> my parts, piled up with levees,
>   (well) watered.' "[43]

(The translator rushes to assure us that the phrase "well-watered" refers to Innana having just bathed.)

Inanna is so enamoured of her own body that she wants it celebrated in poetry. The image of a young woman frankly praising her own vulva is hard for us to comprehend in a world in which women are conditioned to hate their bodies. The song represents a fundamentally different understanding of what it is to be a woman. For although Inanna is eager to join with Dumuzi in sexual union, to have "the ploughman . . . the man of my heart" plough those well-watered hillock fields and lowlands, she does not derive her sense of worth from Dumuzi or look to him to give her value. It is she herself who celebrates her own being, who finds herself beautiful in her own eyes, and who lives in a world in which there is no conceivable reason why she should hesitate to express and rejoice in that beauty.

Women sing the praises of a woman's body. Although the context of the Sacred Marriage seems a heterosexual one, the texts again and again show us women's erotic celebration of each other. Inanna's girlfriends praise her sexual parts as if they have intimate knowledge of them. In a society in which the erotic was seen as sacred, sexual identity may have been much more fluid than it is today. The texts that have been preserved sing of heterosexual sex; we don't know what chants were sung that were not preserved. But Inanna represents the woman who is neither heterosexual nor lesbian, but simply sexual—and proud of it!

With all the celebration of fertility implicit in these texts, Inanna never gets pregnant. Her sexuality is celebrated for its power to give pleasure and renew all the life of the earth, not for reproduction.[44]

Male sexuality is also identified as a fructifying force, a force that awakens new life:

> "At its mighty rising, at its mighty rising,
> did the shoots and the buds rise up.
> The king's loins! At its mighty rising
> did the vines rise up, did the grains rise up,
> did the desert fill (with verdure)
> like a pleasurable garden."[45]

Here is no suggestion of male erotic power as linked with the power of conquest, no force or violence, no rulership. The penis, in its mysterious swelling, rising, and withering, is linked magically with the swelling of buds and the rising of new shoots of grain, the swelling of the date clusters and the cow's udders. Male sexual power is life-sustaining, is food itself:

> "He has sprouted, he has burgeoned,
> He is lettuce planted by the water,
> He is the one my womb loves best. . . .

> "His hand is honey, his foot is honey,
> He sweetens me always. . . .

> "Make your milk sweet and thick, my bridegroom.
> My shepherd, I will drink your fresh milk. . . .

Let the milk of the goat flow in my sheepfold.
Fill my holy churn with honey cheese."[46]

Inanna is depicted as both sexually agressive and eager for satisfaction, and there is no hint of disparagement nor any suggestion that she is expected to be the passive partner. On the contrary, it is Inanna who chooses her bridegroom:

"I had in view having the nation multiply,
chose Dumuzi for (personal) god of the country . . ."[47]

It is she who calls for the bed, and its royalty reflects her status:

"She has called for the bed for sweetening the loins,
She has called for the bed!
She has called for the royal bed!
She has called for the bed!
She has called for the queenly bed!
She has called for the bed!"[48]

It is she who decrees Dumuzi's fate:

"Inanna, the First Daughter of the Moon,
Decreed the fate of Dumuzi:
'In battle I am your leader,
In combat I am your armor-bearer,
In the assembly I am your advocate,
On the campaign I am your inspira-
tion.' "[49]

The sexual passion of their union is not divorced from emotion:

"Not only is it sweet to sleep hand in hand with him,
sweetest of sweet is too the loveliness
of joining heart to heart with him."[50]

The early myths celebrate burgeoning life, but they also center on mourning and death. The sacred marriage with the young Dumuzi is balanced by the rite of grieving for the dying God. The penis swells, rises, spills its seed, and then shrivels, as the grain sprouts green in the spring and then withers under the scorching sun, as the young animal grows older and yields its life to the slaughterer's knife. Dumuzi dies, and Inanna mourns him, often accompanied by his sister and his mother.

An immanent spirituality cannot deny death. Death is part of life. When we embrace life, we must also embrace the sorrow at its ending, just as to deeply feel erotic pleasure is to feel the sadness that it cannot last forever.

Collective myths of loss and rituals of mourning create strong communal bonds. They provide a framework for grieving personal losses in a context that links them with the larger forces of death and regeneration. So the mourning for Dumuzi served as a purging for the community.

Various texts depict Dumuzi's death in many different ways. In some, he is attacked by robbers; in others, by evil beings from the underworld. In one text, called "Dumuzi's Dream," he has premonition of evil and suffers from disturbing dreams. The focus, however, is on the mourning. "[He] asks all of nature to lament him—the high desert and the swamps, the crayfish and the frogs in the rivers—and he hopes that his mother Dutter will cry out in her grief, 'He was [worth] any five! He was worth any ten!' "[51] In most of the texts, Inanna is depicted as stricken with grief, yet helpless to save Dumuzi from a fate stronger than her:

"The most bitter cry [of commiseration]—because of her husband,
[the cry] to Inanna, because of her husband . . .
Inanna weeps bitter tears for her young husband."[52]

The mourning rituals for Dumuzi have been taken by some scholars as evidence of the literal killing of the king at periodic intervals. The actual Dumuzi texts, however, show Inanna as lamenting Dumuzi but not as a cause of his death, except for the one version known as "The Descent of Inanna." "The Descent of Inanna," however, is not a record of liturgy used in ritual, as are many of the others; rather, it is "an entirely literary composition,"[53] and its meaning is complex. It records Inanna's descent to the underworld, a journey that can be read as a shamanic initiation. My own retelling of this myth can be found in the stories linking the later chapters of this book.

When Inanna descends to the underworld, she dies, but is returned to life when her faithful woman helper seeks aid from the gods. But she must provide the underworld with a substitute to pay for her own life. She is unwilling to sacrifice her faithful attendant Ninshubur, but she flies into a rage when she sees Dumuzi enjoying himself on her throne. She sends the demons after him, and although he runs for help to his sister and mother, they eventually find him. His sister, in turn, offers herself as a sacrifice, and she and Dumuzi alternate terms in the underworld. They may represent the grain and the vine; their alternate terms below may reflect that both wine and beer are fermented in the dark storehouse, but in different seasons.[54]

The tale may also be one of warning, aimed at kings who usurp too much power. Or it may be an early attempt to identify women's power as being dangerous and destructive to men. It clearly reflects a time of transition, when issues of power and gender had become concerns in Sumer.

There is no archeological evidence for human sacrifice in the mother-times. No human sacrifices are found, for example, in Çatal Hüyük, or elsewhere in Old Europe.[55] In Sumer, human sacrifice is found only in one limited period, in the Royal Tombs of Ur, which date from the mid-third millennium B.C.E., when the transition to patriarchy was already underway. "The burial of the kings was accompanied by human sacrifice on a lavish scale, the bottom of the grave pit being crowded with the bodies of men and women who seemed to have been brought down here and butchered where they stood."[56] The dead retainers seem to have been themselves of high rank, and may have considered themselves honored to follow their ruler into death. But they were followers sacrificed *to* the king. Nowhere do we find any evidence that the king was sacrificed to assure blessings to his followers.

Sacrifice is thus found at the beginning of the era in which kingship, hierarchy, war, and class stratification were being consolidated. In the Royal Tombs, queens as well as kings were honored by a retinue of sacrifices. "Ruling queens shared in the status, power, wealth, and ascription of divinity with kings. . . . But the overwhelming preponderance of female skeletons over male among the buried retainers also speaks to their greater vulnerability and dependency as servants."[57] The appearance of sacrifice marks the erosion of women's power and the shift from the celebration of the Goddess of life, to glorification of the divinity of rulers. Human sacrifice must have been a dramatic and terrible way of impressing the people with the concept of the king's absolute power, making resistance to the new order seem futile and helping to establish the authority of rule.[58]

In contrast, the celebratory myths of The Sacred Marriage show us a time in which the world was still a living being, infused with erotic, fructifying power. Women are shown as powerful and autonomous, full members of a society that had not yet identified power with only one gender. Although images of war and rule appear, they are not the central themes of the myths, which derive their inspiration from the common material of mystery: sex and food, life and death.

As society developed to maximize power-over, however, the myths changed. We can see the transition in the Epic of Gilgamesh.

THE EPIC OF GILGAMESH

The Priestess's Story

The woman is bleeding. Red stains on the stone of the temple court—not the first, not the last. You run practiced hands over her limbs, feel her pulse, soothe the reddened energy that darts and shoots around her body like the corona of a bruised sun. You massage her belly, call for the proper brews and poultices.

"Will she live?" the women ask.

"She will live," you say, and they sigh, but you are angry, for this has become an everyday occurence. You can hardly walk out on the city streets without women throwing themselves at your feet, clasping your knees, and begging you to take them as servants. Men return from the wars, and treat their own women as they did the women of their enemies. Hard times.

"What is your name?" you ask the woman.

"I am Ninti, daughter of the First Clan of Kish," she says. "I was a priestess in the temple before the city was sacked."

Your priestesses do not cease dressing the woman's wounds or stroking her bruised limbs. You imagine, nevertheless, that they draw away. For this woman is their mirror. Tomorrow, or a year from tomorrow, any one of you could be lying in your own blood on strange stones.

It is no wonder that many of the women support the king. The city walls he built gave the people a sense of safety.

Only you question what the people are becoming behind those walls. Not many others do. The people grumble, but in the end they are afraid to oppose the king. No one can deny he is a brilliant general—and politician. You remember when he was a young battle leader, chosen to lead the fight against the northern invaders. How he distinguished himself! Then there was the threat of war with Kish, who in former days were your allies, and then crisis after crisis, each demanding a strong leader, more of the people turning to soldiers, more wealth poured into war. And the priests supporting him, with their made-up myths and their hero gods, until it seemed natural to everyone that the king reigned in power, permanently.

In the city, they whisper that you are bitter, frustrated because the king refuses you the sacred marriage rite. Hah! You know you aren't missing much there. For all the man's physical strength, he is not a man who can face the Goddess. What heats his blood is death, not the letting go and the rising in the whitewater streams of life. A disease is spreading among the men, and some of the women, too. No wonder the fields no longer produce as they did in your grandmother's, or even your mother's, time. You have read the old temple records, you know that where you get one basket of grain today, four grew in former times. But the king takes the farmers to be soldiers and the dikes are destroyed in the battles that waste the land.

The king sent you a letter filled with insults when he suspended the sacred marriage rite. You could have flung a few of your own. Why, the man was a wastrel, a plough made of wax that melted at the first touch, a dog that couldn't raise its own head, a . . . but that line of thinking was stale and unproductive. For now you are faced with a more immediate problem. The woman. Should you heal her only to send her back to a master, for more of the same treatment? But you cannot keep her here: your power in the city, the delicate balance that preserves your women's rights to such power as you have, can be tipped and lost by an accusation that you steal and harbor runaway slaves.

The arrogance of that man! Sometimes you wonder why the demons of the underworld don't rise up and carry him away.

But if they did, would you lie where the woman lies now? And would some priestess at some other temple in some far city be deciding your fate? That is the hard and distasteful truth of it. Would you yourself destroy the king even if you could, even seeing, clearly as you do, the twisting of the people into something mean and bloody?

Bad times, and getting worse. But the end will not come today, and here before you is a living need.

"Find her a bedchamber," you instruct your women. You touch her hand.

"Rest, sister," you say. "You are safe here."

"For now," you add silently.

The change in mentality with the coming of kingship can be clearly seen in the Gilgamesh stories. With Gilgamesh, we move out of the realm of myth, the stories that link us to the great rounds of birth, death, and renewal; and into epic, the tales that recount the deeds of the hero, the war leader, the great man. Yet the Gilgamesh stories are ancient enough that they preserve traces of the older order, and of the dissatisfactions and disruptions brought by the new dominion.

Gilgamesh was a historical king of Sumer in approximately 2600 B.C.E. He first appears as an epic hero in fragments of stories about him that date from 2100 B.C.E., from the Third Dynasty of Ur. The complete epic, however, dates from a later period, about 1600 B.C.E.—a time when the full transition to patriarchy had been made.[59] The epic belongs to the Old Babylonian era, the culture that superceded the Sumerian but incorporated much of their culture and traditions. Although the epic itself is Babylonian, some of its sources are rooted in earlier Sumerian tales.[60]

The Gilgamesh epic shows us a period in which kingship had become institutionalized. The war leader was now the permanent holder of political power. "New leaders emerged who were preoccupied with, and committed to, both defensive and offensive warfare against neighboring city-states."[61] Kings made war for glory and for profit—and war consolidated the power of kings.

Gilgamesh is king of Uruk, the strongest warrior in the land. Yet his people complain: "His arrogance has no bounds by day or night. No son is left with his father, for Gilgamesh takes them all, even the children; yet the king should be a shepherd to his people. His lust leaves no virgin to her lover, neither the warrior's daughter nor the wife of the noble; yet this is the shepherd of the city, wise, comely and resolute."[62]

Although Gilgamesh is king, the people have clearly not forgotten an earlier, more egalitarian order. They chafe under his domination.[63]

In the Gilgamesh epic the view of the erotic has changed. No longer is sexuality the source of fertility, joy, and abundance. Now the erotic is linked in the same breath with war and conquest. Sex has become a prerogative of the ruler.

The gods, to contain Gilgamesh, decide to create his equal as friend, rival, and counterforce. They create the wild man Enkidu, who lives in the forest with the beasts. A trapper wishes to tame him, but does not know how. The trapper's father advises: "Ask [Gilgamesh] to give you a harlot, a wanton from the temple of love; return with her, and let her woman's power overpower this man. When next he comes down to drink at the wells she will be there, stripped naked; and when he sees her beckoning he will embrace her, and the wild beasts will reject him."[64]

This is a different world from the one in which Inanna and her friends blissfully sang of their sacred sexual parts. Now, women belong to men. Where the erotic once linked the human and natural worlds, now sex is seen to separate the wild man from nature. Where Inanna chose her bridegroom, now the king disposes of a woman's body. The woman involved has no choice in how her body is used. She is an object, a trap.

Whereas Dumuzi derived his status and power from Inanna, and their sexual union was seen as bringing great good to all the land, here sexual union with a woman is seen to rob a man of his power. Sexual intercourse is still termed "the woman's art,"[65] but after six days and seven nights of it, the game flees from Enkidu. He cannot even follow: "His body was bound as though with a cord, his knees gave way when he started to run, his swiftness was gone. . . . Enkidu was grown weak."[66]

True, six days and seven nights of hot sex might leave any strong man winded, but the sense of this passage is closer to the superstition that loss of semen drains a man's strength. Male power is endangered by women. And, of course, forced sex with a woman who has no choice and a man who most likely has no technique will hardly open the sluices of the world-renewing waters of life.

When Enkidu is brought to the city, he hears the people complain against Gilgamesh. "He does strange things in Uruk, the city of great streets. At the roll of the drum work begins for the men, and work for the women. Gilgamesh the king is about to celebrate marriage with the Queen of Love, and he still demands to be first with the bride, the king to be first and the husband to follow."[67]

Again, the people complain even as they comply with the king's demands. The *droit de seigneur* is one of the traditions by which kings and lords impress upon their subjects the absoluteness of their power-over. Woman is now property of man—but all property belongs first to the king. Sexuality has become debased to a means of proving ownership, and this change reflects the shift in values to those that serve the needs of war.

Enkidu attacks Gilgamesh at the very threshold of the temple where Gilgamesh is about to celebrate the Sacred Marriage with Ishtar, the Babylonian Inanna, the Queen of Love. They fight, equally matched, destroying the threshold and doorpost in their battle. In the manner of brawling boys, the strength of each inspires respect in the other. They embrace and become friends. And perhaps more than just good friends: the coming of

Enkidu has been prophesied to Gilgamesh. "This is the strong comrade, the one who brings help to his friend in his need. . . . You will love him like a woman, and he will never forsake you."[68]

After their comradeship is established, the Sacred Marriage is forgotten. The epic perhaps records the portentous abandonment of the ancient custom. Gilgamesh does not offer his body to the Goddess, nor will he submit to the power of the erotic. The destruction of the doorway may symbolically represent the destruction of the Goddess: Inanna's emblem was the threshold and doorway of the storehouse. So male comradeship here supercedes the old rites of love and fertility.

The love between Gilgamesh and Enkidu may replace sexual love for women, and may itself be sexual, but it is different from the Dumuzi tales with their open delight in sensuality and their celebration of the world-renewing power inherent in the male body. The matter-of-fact tone of the above passage implies that homosexuality was commonplace and accepted. But now its character is also changed, subsumed to the demands of war as men's love for each other is twisted to reinforce the new values of patriarchy. Denial of feeling replaces erotic celebration.

Gilgamesh and Enkidu love like comrades in war. They undertake heroic adventures together, killing the demon Humbaba of the faraway forest. Much of the poem can, in fact, be read as a paean to male comradeship, to the strength of the male bond in battle. The new order is a heroic order in which men expect each other to be brave and chide each other when they falter: "Then Enkidu called out to Gilgamesh, 'Do not go down into the forest; when I opened the gate my hand lost its strength.' Gilgamesh answered him, 'Dear friend, do not speak like a coward. Have we got the better of so many dangers and travelled so far, to turn back at last? You, who are tried in wars and battles, hold close to me now and you will feel no fear of death; keep beside me and your weakness will pass, the trembling will leave your hand. Would my friend rather stay behind? No, we will go down together into the heart of the forest. Let your courage be roused by the battle to come; forget death and follow me, a man resolute in action, but who is not foolhardy. When two go together each will protect himself and shield his companion, and if they fall they leave an enduring name.' "[69]

Here is the ideology of warfare. To understand the militarization of Sumerian society (and our own) we must understand that war creates its own psychology. War was defined as a male preserve, and manhood was defined by the qualities that made a successful soldier. Although myths seem to indicate that at first women participated in war, even led attacks as generals, they were "gradually ousted from military activities and decision making and thereby excluded from important public roles."[70]

The question of why war became a male activity is not simple to answer. Many women are as strong as most men. Women are more hampered by pregnancy and childbirth, but castes of female warriors who chose not to bear children could have developed and legends of Amazon tribes indicate that in some areas, they did. But in Sumer, as in most places, war became a male preserve.

The new bronze technology spurred the development of more deadly and efficient weapons. Armed with metal spears and swords, armies were now capable of conquest on a scale never known before. As war became an organized instrument of state, it made unprecedented demands on those who took part in it. It required the reshaping of the human psyche in a mold of obedience to authority. War became male, and men ruled, not because males were innately better at war or inherently more brutal, but because societies that adopted patriarchy, the social system based on the principle of hierarchical rule, proved most effective at maximizing power.

War changed its character when it transformed from tribal raid to instrument of policy. The hit-and-run tactics of tribal wars and raids may have been "an exciting and dangerous game," but they were "not about power in any recognizable sense of the word, and . . . most certainly . . . not about slaughter." Typically, "very few people got killed: there were no leaders, no strategy, and no tactics."[71] "Civilized" war, in contrast, requires a level of organization, obedience, and discipline that runs deeply counter to instinct.

In tribal wars, a moment's courage was accompanied by action, and the individual can choose what level of risk to take. "Civilized" warfare, from Sumerian times on, has been characterized by the need for masses of soldiers to act together as parts of a whole, to face danger and relinquish the right to make an individual decision about whether to stand or run. In all ancient warfare, from Gilgamesh to the disciplined Roman legions, battles turned and fell on whether or not formations held together.

"It is the formations themselves that count . . . those carefully aligned and articulated ranks of thousands of well-drilled troops."[72] Armies that fight with sword or spear can only fight toward their front. If gaps open in the formation, if they are attacked from rear or side, disaster will result. Another danger is crowding: if the men get pushed together so closely that they cannot swing their arms or hurl their weapons, they will be slaughtered. "A great deal of the endless drill goes into training the soldiers to maintain that vital three-foot interval at all costs."[73]

When armies joined in battle, the spearmen were massed together in large groups. The men in the front ranks would fight, and as they fell they would be replaced from behind. The turning point would come when one side or the other attempted to break their opponents' line with a massive shove forward. Battles were won or lost not by individual heroes, but by the mass formation, for if it held, the army remained strong, and if it broke, the "formation would crumble, men would turn to flee, and the massacre would begin."[74] Mass obedience, not individual courage, won battles.

The organization of the armies reinforced class differences. The earliest armies of the Sumerian cities were composed of nobles and citizen levees, who had obligations to do military service.[75] From the beginning, they composed two very different classes. The nobility provided the army with its mobile striking force of chariots. These armored carts, at first four-wheeled and cumbersome, later two-wheeled and lightweight, were drawn by onagers (asses) in early Sumer, later by swifter horses.[76] The ordinary foot soldiers came from the poorer classes of society. They carried spears and shields, but wore little or no armor.

The common foot soldiers were anonymous and unsung, important only as part of a mass. They composed the formations that actually won or lost wars, but it was the deeds of the nobility that were glorified and celebrated. The role of the common soldier was to remain in that solid, unbreakable line, to advance when ordered or to hold firm against the onrush of the enemy. Any individual action on his part could cause disruption in the lines, wavering, even panic. Obedience to authority was the prime quality necessary for the common soldier.

As warfare became chronic, Sumerian society was restructured in the image of war. Myth, epic, religion, and customs changed to perpetuate a new ideology of control.

Unquestioning obedience is not a trait that is easy to instill. Strong motivations were needed. Soldiers fought for pay and for plunder, but obedience that would hold a man still in line while chariots thundered down the field and arrows rained on him could not be inspired by the hope of booty alone. It had to be etched in the psyche, too deep to be questioned, and reinforced by training, religion, and ideology.

Comradeship is one strong motivation. Gilgamesh, who after all was an experienced and successful war leader, understood that the presence of a comrade is strengthening. Comradeship becomes a powerful incentive to fight, as a World War II veteran expressed: "I was not a brave young man (but after I was wounded) I went back because I learned that my regiment was going to . . . land behind the Japanese lines, and I felt that if I were there I might save men who had saved my life many times, and the thought of not being there was just intolerable. I missed them, I yearned for them—it was, as I say, a variety of love, and I was joyful to be reunited with them."[77]

"Numberless soldiers have died . . . because they realized that by fleeing their post and rescuing themselves, they would expose their companions to greater danger. Such loyalty to the group is the essence of fighting morale."[78]

Let us listen to Gilgamesh again: "Would my friend rather stay behind? No, we will go down together into the heart of the forest."

In contrast, the earlier Inanna/Dumuzi texts stress the superiority of women's help and the blood ties central to a matrifocal society. When the demons of the underworld attack Dumuzi, he turns to his sister and his mother for help. His sister protects him, though the demons torture her.

She shows courage, which is expected of her even by the demons because of the strength of the familial bond. His friend, however, betrays him:

"My sister saved my life,
My friend caused my death!"[79]

Comradeship, friendship, loyalty, mutual aid, and self-sacrifice are beautiful qualities. But the comradeship of war is purchased at a price. The value gained by being one of the company of warriors is a substitute for the lost value of the self. In the passage from the Gilgamesh epic we can already hear the underlying price of the male bond of war. "Do not speak like a coward," Gilgamesh says. Ignore your feelings, for cowards do not make good comrades.

Good soldiers are those who would rather die than be thought cowards. Clearly, the personality of such a soldier cannot be structured around a conviction of his immanent worth. Such obedience can come only from a fundamental insecurity about one's own value, an uneasiness so deep that obedience and even death seem a small price to pay for an assurance of one's value.

Patriarchy creates that insecurity, making manhood and womanhood into qualities that have to be achieved. Now it becomes somehow possible to be an "unreal man," a characterization that has nothing to do with one's sexual equipment, but with failure to live up to certain standards that combine willingness to obey with willingness to brutalize. An "unreal man" is an unworthy man—unworthy to live and, in fact, under conditions of battle, more likely to die or to cause the death of his companions should he fail in courage and run.

A "real woman," then, becomes defined as one who is also willing to obey, to train her children in obedience, to offer her children up to war. She, too, must be made insecure.

The ideology of warfare is founded on contempt for women. The gulf between women and men that establishes men's superior status is used to keep men striving to be unlike women, and hence, good soldiers. *Woman*, in fact, becomes a dirty word, an insult to be hurled at one who fails to act like a "real man." "When one does not sufficiently act like a man in military training, the drill instructor may bark, 'What's the matter, girl?' Or a foul description of a part of a woman will be used. It is as if the next thing worse to The Enemy is a woman."[80] The denigration of women is an inherent part of basic military training today: "Marine Corps slang for any woman who isn't the wife, mother, or daughter of anyone present is 'Suzie.' It is short for 'Suzie Rottencrotch.' "[81]

At the same time as women are denigrated, they become the prizes of war. The real situation of women in a militaristic male-dominant culture becomes one of continual insecurity.

For women to become the sexual rewards of men, they must be removed from positions of power. When women are present as comrades, leaders, and fighters, men are less likely to perceive them as objects available to be used.

Although we like to think of rape as an aberration of war, as something only the enemy does, rape has been an omnipresent aspect of warfare in all times. In the ancient world, rape was the normal, expected reward of a victorious army, and some of the fruits of battle were the captured women who could be brought home to serve as slaves and concubines.

Homer's *Iliad,* from a later era, gives us a clear picture of the psychology of warfare for plunder. It opens with the famous quarrel between Agamemnon and Achilles over their "prizes"—the women they have captured in battle. Achilles rails at Agamemnon: "You shameless schemer," he cried, "always aiming at a profitable deal! How can you expect any of the men to give you loyal service when you send them on a raid or into battle? . . . Now comes this threat from you of all people to rob me of my prize, my hard-earned prize, which was a tribute from the ranks."[82]

A commander's hold over his men was dependent on his fairness in distributing the booty of war. The possession of "prize" women also marked the status of nobles. Agamemnon's reply to Achilles demonstrates how women's bodies had become the proving ground for men's rivalry: "I am going to pay a visit to your hut and take away the beautiful Briseis, your prize, Achilles, to let you know that I am more powerful than you, and to teach others not to bandy words with me and openly defy their King."[83]

Warfare in Sumer institutionalized slavery, which made all women vulnerable, for any woman could be captured in war, and women could also be sold as slaves by their husbands or fathers to pay debts. Men might also be sold into slavery as punishment for crimes or debts, but slavery for women was sexual slavery: concubinage or forced prostitution to enrich her owner. The institutions such as the temple priesthood in which women still held power might have resisted the extension of warfare, but the threat of rape and slavery made all women dependent on the armed might of the state for protection.

Mass rape may have been adopted as a deliberate tactic to devalue women and undermine the older, matristic values. Men who could use enemy women as objects began to see women of their own people as objects. Rape as a weapon of war contaminated every act of love, for it introduced power-over into the realm of the erotic. And so the erotic became transformed from the source of life-renewing energy to the reward for violence and brutality. Sex and violence became linked. Inanna, and her later Babylonian incarnation Ishtar, became Goddesses of love and war.

Changed values are reflected in myth and law. In early Sumer, "rape was considered a heinous crime, punishable by exile even for the king. When Enlil rapes the goddess Ninlil . . . despite the fact (that he) heads the pantheon, he is seized and arrested as a sex criminal and banished from his own city of Nippur to the nether world."[84] Yet is is possible that even in the transcription of the myth, the new ideology justifying rape and capture was creeping in, for Ninlil is reported to have followed Enlil to the underworld and there bore three more children to him, a chain of events described by Sumerologist Kramer as "a passionate love affair."[85]

The roles established by war were institutionalized by new laws and forms of marriage in the patriarchal family, which became a primary arena for the teaching of hierarchical power relations. The patriarchal family created in its children a fundamental insecurity about their own worth. A child had literally no independent right to live. "The father had the power of life and death over his children. He had the power to commit infanticide by exposure or abandonment. He could give his daughters in marriage . . . or he could consecrate them to a life of virginity in the temple service. . . . A man could pledge his wife, his concubines and their children as pawns for his debt; if he failed to pay back the debt, these pledges would be turned into debt slaves."[86]

The presence of slaves and concubines, women who had even fewer rights than wives, and the hierarchy of status among them, must have been a constant reaffirmation of the superiority of male power.

Male control over women and children ingrained the patterns of domination into children too young to challenge or resist, who then accepted the patterns of power-over as unquestionable givens in life. Within the family, children's basic sense of identity and orientation to their own sexuality were formed in the model of domination.

With patriarchy came also inheritance through the father, making control of women's sexuality necessary. The new ideology saw women's power and sexuality as inherently dangerous and destructive. To institute control over sexuality, patriarchy had to destroy the old order that affirmed the cyclical round of life and death, the erotic, the primal pleasure of touch. Society necessarily came to identify the erotic with all that undermined its good.

When Gilgamesh returns victorious from the battle with the forest demons, Ishtar chooses him as consort and offers all the gifts of abundance and power that are hers to bestow: "Come to me, Gilgamesh, and be my bridegroom; grant me seed of your body, let me be your bride and you shall be my husband. I will harness for you a chariot of lapis lazuli and of gold . . . and you shall have mighty demons of the storm for draft-mules. When you enter our house in the fragrance of cedar-wood, threshold and throne will kiss your feet. Kings, rulers and princes will bow down before you; they shall bring you tribute from the mountains and the plain. Your ewes shall drop twins and your goats triplets . . . and your chariot horses shall be famous far-off for their swiftness."[87]

Gilgamesh responds arrogantly. His words recall the ancient connection of Inanna/Ishtar with the date palm and the sacred marriage rite, but now these are identified with rot and poison. After a string of insults, he says: "And did you not love Ishullanu, the gardener of your father's palm-grove? He brought you baskets filled with dates without end; every day he loaded your table. Then you turned your eyes on him and said, 'Dearest Ishullanu, come here to me, let us enjoy your manhood, come forward and take me, I am yours.' Ishullanu answered, 'What are you asking from me? My mother has baked and I have eaten; why should I come to such as you for food that is tainted and rotten?' "[88]

In the era of the Gilgamesh story, power had become power-over. Even the gifts of the Goddess had changed: Recall Ishtar's words, "Kings, rulers and princes will bow down before you. . . ." Male domination of women set the pattern for all domination. Continual warfare increased class differences. Kings and nobles got the largest share of plunder, and so the wealth of the upper classes was increased by warfare, while working conditions for the free poor were undermined by slave labor.

The world of Gilgamesh had changed radically from the earlier world of the sacred marriage texts. In those texts, which date from a time when the transition to patriarchy was in its early stages, the gifts of the Goddess do include rulership:

> "Grant him a royal throne, firm in its foundations;
> grant him a scepter righting wrongs in the land,
>   all shepherds' crooks. . . ."[89]

But primarily they are gifts of fertility for crops, game, and foodstuffs, gifts that literally spring up under his feet:

> "May there be vines under him,
>   may there be barley under him,
> may there be carp-floods in the river under him . . .
> may fishes and birds sound off in the marshes under
>   him. . . ."[90]

And the whole tone of the passage is peaceful:

> "May there be long life in the palace under him. . . .
> O milady, Queen of heaven and earth. . . .
> May he live long in your embrace!"[91]

The long life, the good life, the abundant life, the peaceful life, are here still valued beyond the short life of fame, heroism, and battle. Dumuzi's power is power-from-within, the erotic power inherent in his magically rising penis, the power in the earth and the plants that makes them grow, the power in animals that makes them breed. Dumuzi is king and consort by virtue of being a good provider and hard worker:

> "He is the man of my heart. . . .
> Working the hoe, heaping up piles of grain,
> bringing the grain into the barn,

the farmer whose grain is of hundreds of piles
the shepherd whose sheep are laden with wool. . . ."[92]

But he is no warrior. He is never praised for his strength in arms or prowess in battle. Male sexuality is not identified with violence, but with food. War and weapons are barely mentioned in the early texts; where they are, Inanna proclaims: "In battle, I am your leader. . . ."[93]

By the time of Gilgamesh, war had become society's central concern, transforming every aspect of culture. The erotic also had become diminished for men. The male body had become a weapon, no longer a source of nourishment, comfort, and delight.

Myth and religion had changed to reflect the new ideology of hierarchy. The great female powers of creation had lost prominence or changed aspects. Nammu, the creatrix, had become merely the consort of the sky God An.[94] Inanna/Ishtar, whose appeal was so great that she remained central in the Mesopotamian pantheon even when patriarchy was well established, had become the goddess of love and war. "War deities become female after women were no longer involved in military activities."[95]

Perhaps the Goddess's patronage was required to legitimize war to the common people. Perhaps, as Rohrlich suggests, "the feminization of war deities may also be an example of making the victim the criminal, attributing to women the causes of intercity discord long after they have had no voice in military decision making."[96] In any case, the dual role of Inanna/Ishtar as Goddess of erotic activities and war, reflects the yoking together of sex and violence that occurred as Sumer became militarized. "In protohistorical Sumer there were no goddesses of love. The early female deities were patrons of the various aspects of agriculture, as well as of the arts and crafts."[97]

In the era of Gilgamesh, women retained some power as priestesses in the temples, although their roles and activities became more restricted as society became more patriarchal. The high-ranking Sal-Me priestesses continued to practice matrilineal descent long after patrilineality had been established in secular Sumer.[98] The so-called temple prostitutes were in reality women who reserved for themselves the ancient prerogative to choose their own lovers and bear children who would inherit their property. *Kadishtu,* or *qadishtu,* a word often translated by male scholars as "harlot," literally means "holy woman." "Women who made love in the temples were known in their own language as 'sacred women,' 'the undefiled' . . . the use of the word 'prostitute' as a translation for *qadishtu* not only negates the sanctity of that which was held sacred, but suggests . . . an ethnocentric subjectivity on the part of the writer."[99]

Prostitution did exist outside the temples. Law codes refer to "the harlot from the public square."[100] But prostitution, far from being the oldest profession, "emerged after the professions of priest, scribe, merchant, and warrior had become predominantly male, when women had been made legally and economically dependent on men."[101]

Prostitution, of course, is the handmaiden of war. Access to the bodies of women is assured to soldiers not only through rape and capture, but by designating a certain class of women as available for purchase. "The two acts—raping an unwilling woman and buying the body and services of a more or less co-operating woman—go hand in hand with a soldier's concept of his rights and pleasures."[102]

War also transformed the concept of wealth. Ishtar's offer to Gilgamesh reflects a new order in which wealth is measured in gold, precious stones, metals, and chariots, the new technology of war. The new economy is removed from the land and its fruits, which are no longer the prime measures of abundance. Ishtar's powers of fertility here are named only in conjunction with herd animals. Gone are the plant and tree imagery of the earlier tales.

The change in imagery may also reflect ecological change in the Mesopotamian landscape. As the ownership of the land changed from clans to absent nobles who owned large estates, care for the land declined. When nobles needed money to support their wars they may have instituted land use practices designed to bring quick profits rather than safeguard the land's long-term viabilty. For the land, too, the ideology of the short, heroic life replaced the values of longevity and abundance.

"Mesopotamia is an artifact: before that soil . . . could support the cities of Lagash and Niniveh, Ur and Babylon . . . it had to be made. And what is made, if it be thereafter neglected, decays."[103]

The soil of Mesopotamia was made by extensive irrigation. Yet the very processes of centralization, urbanization, and extensive irrigation that are linked with the rise of cities may have, by this era, depleted the fertility of the soil. Over time, irrigated fields become salt-laden and infertile. Certainly, the power centers in Mesopotamia moved gradually northward—from Sumer to Akkad, from Akkad to Babylonia, later still farther north to Assyria. Exhaustion of the soil in the older centers of civilization may have been the underlying cause of the shift in political power. "The rise of great military powers meant the waste of soil fertility in war, that waste meant gradual impoverishment of the whole region, especially in man-power: that impoverishment entailed neglect of the irrigation works, and such neglect the ruin of the soil itself."[104]

The decline in the soil's productivity may have contributed to the decline of the older religious traditions that celebrated the Goddess as storehouse of the land's fertility. When Gilgamesh spurns Ishtar's invitation to the Sacred Marriage, his retorts reflect a sense of disappointment and betrayal: "Your lovers have found you like a brazier which smolders in the cold, a backdoor which keeps out neither squall of wind nor storm, a castle which crushes the garrison. . . ."[105]

Women, and also men, must certainly have resisted the changes. Long and hard battles may have been fought. The *Enûma elish,* the Babylonian creation myth we will examine next, may reflect one such power struggle. The transition took thousands of years and was perhaps never entirely completed. To this very day, some of us are not yet reconciled to the rule of patriarchy and hierarchy.

The Gilgamesh epic shows us a society in transition, in which differing values and models of power clash. Although the story records the rise of male power, in the end even Gilgamesh must face the limits of power. After a long quest in search of eternal life, he finds the plant that grants immortality. As he bathes, it is stolen from him by a serpent, who thus acquires the ability to shed its skin and be renewed.[106] Gilgamesh must die. The snake, however, has always been the symbol of the Goddess. Reading the story through a Witch's eyes, we can find hope in its outcome. In the end, all kings must die, but the great energies of life have the power to renew themselves and rise again.

THE *ENÛMA ELISH*

A Battle Story

They are coming. Over the farmland kicked and trodden to dust, over the broken dikes and the drained canals, they are coming. From the north, in close formations, they are coming. In horsedrawn chariots, sun glinting on bronze spears, they are coming. Armed and shielded, fierce and invincible, they are coming.

You stand on a small rise in the ground. You can see them, a line of dust under the shimmering heat waves that rise from the baked ground. You adjust your leather corselet, grip your bronze spear. Your consort stands at your side; you remember twining together in the passion of serpents, shedding your skin to be renewed. Now he, too, is armed for war. He says your name, "Tiamat."

Behind you stretches the army of the south, great in number, shielded in leather, armed with bronze, ready to march in close formation over the wasted land, ready to fight to the end. You look before you: across the plain they are coming. You look behind you, at the formations you lead; you have become the mirror image of your enemies.

So much, so much, is already lost.

They outnumber you. They will defeat you. They will carve their world out of the corpse of these dead lands. You will die.

What will be remembered is this battle, your fierceness, your serpent's teeth.

What will be forgotten are the tender, iridescent moments of emerging in a new skin.

What will be remembered is your mask, your war cry.

What will be forgotten is your living face, your own true voice.

As war reshaped culture, it reshaped the self in the image of war. As unthinking obedience on the battlefield became the prime determinant of winning or losing, surviving or going down in defeat, the group mind became obsessed with images of obedience.

> "Thou art the most honored of the great gods,
> Thy decree is unrivalled, thy word is Anu. . . .
> Thy utterance shall be true,
> Thy command shall be unimpeachable.
> No one among the gods shall transgress thy bounds."[107]

Thus do the Gods of Mesopotamia declare their obedience to Marduk, whom they have made king, in the *Enûma elish,* the Babylonian creation myth probably dating from the early second millennium B.C.E. (although none of the extant texts dates from earlier than the first millennium).[108] The myth reflects the triumph of the patriarchal order over the old mother-right, describing the battle of Marduk, champion of the gods, with Tiamat, original progenitrix, primal sea.

Tiamat is the original mother, the matrix of creation, and her imagery reflects that of the Great Goddess. The myth, written of course by the victors, identifies the new order of Marduk with movement and activity, "contrast(ing) sharply with the older (Gods) who stand for rest and inactivity."[109] In fact, the battle is joined presumably because the old, primal powers find their sleep disturbed by the play and dancing of the gods, and determine to destroy their own noisy offspring. Tiamat is at first reluctant to destroy her children. When her consort, Apsu, suggests killing the young Gods:

> "Tiamat, when she heard this
> became upset, cried out against her husband. . . .
> 'How could we destroy
> what we (ourselves) have brought into being?
> Though their ways be noisome,
> let us bear it in good part!' "[110]

When, after Apsu is killed, Tiamat is finally pressed to fight, she gives birth to an army of serpent dragon monsters.

> "Mother Hubur—molding everything—
> added irresistible weapons, bore monster serpents. . . .
> Fierce dragons she clothed in terror,
> crowned them with glories
> and made them like gods . . ."[111]

The serpent from the time of prehistory has been associated with the Great Goddess. "The Snake and Bird Goddess, whose imagery was linked with that of life-giving waters, was a predominate image in the pantheon of Old Europe . . . inherited from the Magdalenian culture of the Upper

Paleolithic. . . . She is the feminine principle. . . . The upper and lower waters which she controlled were represented by labyrinthine meanders and snake spirals . . . she was a mistress of life-generating cosmic forces."[112]

Just as in the Gilgamesh myth the erotic power of the Goddess was seen as poisonous and dangerous, the ancient snake, earth-dragon, serpent of the regenerating waters, now becomes the poison-dripping monster. The symbols of life-renewing female power are twisted to make female power seem dangerous and destructive.

Tiamat, the enemy, has been demonized, turned into something bearing no resemblance to our common being. War demands the creation of an "other" who is different, inhuman. "Most soldiers are able to kill and be killed more easily in warfare if they possess an image of the enemy sufficiently evil to inspire hatred and repugnance."[113] Slavery, war's camp follower, is dependent on "the possibility of designating the group to be dominated as entirely different from the group exerting dominance."[114] Marduk's authority, the legitimacy of his role as protector and conqueror, demand as their counterpoint the enemy/other—demonic, poisonous, female. Conquest is justified by dehumanizing and denigrating the conquered. Racism is born of the same forces that spawned patriarchy.

Tiamat is also accused of exercising the ancient prerogative of women to choose their own consorts and lovers.

> "Thou hast appointed Kingu as consort,
> Conferring upon him the rank of Anu,
> not rightfully his."[115]

Where Inanna was expected to choose her mate, where Dumuzi's rank and status stemmed from her, now Tiamat is castigated for exercising choice. Female will and autonomy have become a crime.

Do we hear the echoes of an ancient power struggle? Does Tiamat represent a historical woman, a priestess-queen, who refused the mate to whom she was given under the new patriarchal order and chose her own consort in the old way? And were there men, perhaps her own sons and clan brothers, who also opposed the new order and refused to give their allegiance to the patriarchy?

Jacobsen suggests the myth may reflect an actual struggle for supremacy between the rising Babylonian civilization of the north and the "Sealand," the southern cities of old Sumer.[116] Clearly the myth reflects a battle against a Goddess culture.

The result of Marduk's victory is the establishment of permanent kingship. Marduk is first elected as war leader of the Gods. He carries a spear "named for his mandate 'Security and Obedience.' "[117] Security, protection, life itself are linked with obedience to authority in the new order of the war-state.

Marduk triumphs over Tiamat, and creates the world out of her dismembered body:

> "He split her like a shellfish into two parts:
> Half of her he set up and ceiled it as sky,
> Pulled down the bar and posted guards.
> He bade them to allow not her waters to escape."[118]

The world has been dismembered. The living body of the Goddess has been torn apart: the patriarchal world, the world of hierarchy, racism, and domination, the world in which we still live today, exists literally within the pulsating remains of her corpse.

Like a fun house mirror, the new myth preserves a distorted reflection of the old order of immanent spirit. And in Tiamat's very fierceness and rage, we retain an image of the power of woman:

> "Towards the raging Tiamat he set his face. . . .
> As he looks on, his course becomes upset,
> His will is distracted, and his doings are confused. . . .
> Tiamat emitted [a cry] without turning her neck,
> Framing savage defiance in her lips. . . ."[119]

The Gods swear allegiance to Marduk as permanent monarch. They employ a new formula in swearing their allegiance: "Benefits and Obedience."[120]

The king commands. It is the power of his word to order reality that is the essence of his authority. Obedience to that word is the primary condition of the relationship between king and subject. Under patriarchy, we internalize the image of the King, which becomes an entity within, a psychic structure that assures our obedience to authority.

In the *Enûma elish,* we can already see Marduk functioning in the five roles that provide the underlying architecture of kingship: Conqueror, Orderer of the Universe, Judge, Master of Servants, and Censor.

> "O Marduk, thou art indeed our avenger
> We have granted thee kingship over the universe entire.
> When in Assembly thou sittest, thy word shall be supreme.
> Thy weapons shall not fail, they shall smash thy foes!
> O Lord, spare the life of him who trusts thee,
> But pour out the life of the God who seeks evil."[121]

He is praised as avenger and judge: he has ordered the cosmos out of Tiamat's corpse, and now out of the blood of her consort, Kingu, he creates humanity to be the servant of the gods.

> "I will create Lullu, 'man' be his name. . . .
> Let him be burdened with the toil of the gods,
>   that they may freely breathe."[122]

Marduk is less obviously the censor, the one who controls speech. Yet the actual law codes of Mesopotamia saw wrong speech (especially for women) as a serious crime. The earliest code, that of Urukagina dating to 2415 B.C.E., states: "If a woman said to a man '. . . ' [unfortunately the text is unintelligible at this crucial point], her teeth were crushed with burnt bricks."[123]

The command, the word of the king, has a numinous, magical power.

> "He spoke, and at his word
>   the constellation was destroyed.
> He spoke again,
>   and the constellation was
>   [re]constructed.
> The Gods, his fathers,
>   seeing (the power of) his word,
>   rejoiced, paid homage: 'Marduk is
>   king.' "[124]

The king's word has to be powerful if he is to command armies, for soldiers must above all obey the word of their commanders. For the king's word to be so powerful, all other speech must be subordinate. If a commander says "Advance!" a soldier cannot begin an argument, discussion, or shout "Retreat!" So the king's power to order reality through his word becomes also the power to control the speech of others.

When Marduk carved the world out of the dismembered corpse of Tiamat, a new psychic reality was created. As society was reshaped by systems of power-over, the individual self was reshaped to fit those systems. The institutionalization of war and patriarchy required the construction of a new human personality conditioned to obedience. As obedience to authority became a primary social value, authority became internalized. The King lives within us, and possesses us.

War and patriarchy have remained institutionalized since the times of Sumer in Western civilization, and so has the self that reflects the structure of war. Inside our minds, we live in a dismembered world, on a battlefield peopled by Conqueror and Enemy, Master and Slave, Judge, and Censor imposing their own order. Outside, the living earth has become one vast potential battlefield.

PATRIARCHAL RELIGION AND THE CONSTRUCT OF THE KING

The entity of the King-within has been fed by imagery, mythology, and religious doctrine since it first appeared. God-language is important, for the imagery of religion shapes the self by defining what value is. How we see God literally shapes and limits who we can become. The work of Marduk was continued by those who dismembered the ancient Goddess religions and molded patriarchal culture and values.

As we have seen, the transition to patriarchy took place long before the biblical era, and male rule was established centuries before the first books of the Bible were codified and written down in the late first millennium B.C.E.

The Hebrews certainly did not invent patriarchy, and blaming male domination on the Jews is another form of anti-Semitism. Nevertheless, the Bible is directly rooted in the mythology of Mesopotamia, and while containing much that can be liberating, it also perpetuates the images of God and kingship that evolved in the militaristic, hierarchical, male-ruled society of the Near East. Both the Jewish and Christian Bibles have been prime sources of myths, stories, and imagery that transmit those values in Western culture. Images of God as King—Orderer of the Universe, Conqueror, Judge, Master of Servants, and Censor—abound in both Testaments.

God is the Conqueror, who defends his people and avenges wrongs: "Arise O Lord; save me, O my God: for thou hast smitten all mine enemies upon the cheek bone: thou hast broken the teeth of the ungodly" (Ps. 2:7); "And out of his mouth goeth a sharp sword, that with it he should smite the nations: and he shall rule them with a rod of iron: and he treadeth the winepress of the fierceness and wrath of Almighty God. / And he hath on his vesture and on his thigh a name written, KING OF KINGS AND LORD OF LORDS" (Rev. 19:15–16).

He orders the universe, creating by his command, and distributes his creation. God is the Master, we are his servants. God is the Censor, regulating speech, thought, and belief: "The Lord shall cut off all flattering lips, and the tongue that speaketh proud things: / Who have said, With our tongue will we prevail; our lips are our own: who is lord over us?" (Ps. 12:3–4); "He that believeth not shall be damned" (Mark 16:16).

And of course, he is the Judge, who gives laws, rewards obedience, and punishes transgressions and rebellions: "And he shall judge the world in righteousness, he shall minister judgment to the people in uprightness" (Ps. 9:8); "And I saw a great white throne, and him that sat on it, from whose face the earth and the heaven fled away: and there was found no place for them. / And I saw the dead, small and great, stand before God: and the books were opened: and another book was opened, which is the book of life: and the dead were judged out of those things which were written in the books, according to their works. / And whosoever was not found written in the book of life was cast into the lake of fire" (Rev. 20:11–15).

The imagery of king is welded to that of father: "Our father which art in heaven, Hallowed by thy name. Thy kingdom come. Thy will be done, as in heaven, so in earth" (Luke 11). He offers benefits in return for obedience—the benefits expected of a father. He provides for us, protects us, cares for us.

Just as the king is seen as father, so the father is seen as king. The patriarchal family itself is modeled on authority. Fathers no longer have the rights of life and death over their wives and children, but they inherit a four-thousand-year-old tradition of domination. Like the king, the father in a traditional patriarchal family is expected to defend his dependents. His work, his needs, his career, order the family's universe, establish their status and determine what level of privilege they can claim. His wife is expected to serve his needs, provide for his comfort and sexual satisfaction, rear his children, and subordinate her own impulses and desires. He is the family disciplinarian, the one no one talks back to, the authority everyone must respect.

This model of the family is changing for many people, and even in families that follow the old model, authority may be mitigated by love. Patriarchs have feelings, too. But whether we internalize a loving or a stern authority, the model of authority itself teaches us that our worth is not a given but must be earned and subordinated to the value of someone else whose status is higher than ours.

Because the essential quality of the king/authority is its attack on our inherent worth, we internalize it as the self-hater, the inner voice that judges and attacks. Doris Lessing describes it in *The Four-Gated City:* "It was as if she had an enemy who hated her in her head, who said she was wicked and bad and disobedient and cruel to her father. . . . She tried to behave well because of this cruel tormentor in her head. She kept quiet."[125]

We are open to possession by self-hate because the ground of self-love has been undermined in us: our inherent worth is denied by our culture. Unsure of our own value, insecure about our own truth, we accept the reality defined for us by the rules and structures of the authorities.

The self-hater's five faces are those of the internalized King: the Conqueror, treating the self and those around us as enemies to be feared, demonized, and destroyed; the Orderer, imposing a rigid control on the self and the environment; the Master of Servants, demanding that we deny our own needs and desires to serve others' ends; the Censor, keeping us isolated in silence; and the Judge, offering to restore value to us in return for obedience, and threatening us with further loss of value, if we resist.

The roles of the king are determined by the demands of war for obedience, for a rigid order in the face of the chaos of battle, for control. The systems of control that serve authority are systems of punishment. To serve war, society itself becomes the big jail.

The system that developed to maximize power-over is as dependent on all the varieties of oppression as my Toyota's engine is on pistons, carburator, spark plugs, and starter. Male domination, racism, economic exploitation, war, centralized control, heterosexism, religious persecution, human dominance over nature and animals, all drive the machine that is taking us somewhere nobody wants to go.

To change direction, or better, to dismantle the machine altogether, we must recognize that the system does not just act upon us—it shapes us and acts within us. Patriarchy has created us in its image.

Once we see that image, however, it no longer possesses us unaware. We can reshape it, create something new. Once we understand how we react to systems of control, we can choose to actively resist domination. We can develop the tools of vision and the structures of support that will enable us to heal the wounds of the world and bring her back to life. We can become agents of the earth-soul, raging, passionate, and fearless in our labor, bringing to birth what perhaps has never been: a world in which no one is ruled or ruler, where no promise of heaven offers us false compensation for our present pain, but where we tend together the earth's living, fruitful flesh to grant each other the long life, abundant and peaceful, shared as equals and lived in freedom.

A Story of Masks

What has been done to the earth
   has been done to you
      as to us all
Every murder, every rape, every act of torture
   leaves its scar on the landscape of the self
   and the outer bars
      cast shadows in our mind

Feel them
   they are your wounds
   they are all you might have been
      and will not be
Cry for it   mourn   rage
There are toxins in your blood
Your dismembered parts
   lie scattered around you
You prowl your own borders
   looking for escape
The wall is invisible
   like glass, but stronger
   you can't get over it
   you can't get under it
   you can't get around it

So you put on the mask
   that hides you
   and try to slip through
How do you walk in this mask?
How does your body feel?
The mask covers you
It hides the barrier
And suddenly you can't remember
   where you were going or why
   and none of it seems very important
   so you stop and sit
And there you can remain
   forever
Or you can take the mask off

And put on the tricky mask
   the deceiving mask
   and try to slip through
How do you walk in this mask?

How does your body feel?
And the barrier disappears
  and you walk through
  and the path is clear and green and pleasant
  and you know it's the right way
  although from time to time
    you suspect
  that you really haven't gone anywhere
  that you are back where you started from
And there you can remain
  forever
Or you can take the mask off

And you put on the mask
  that pleases
  and try to slip through
How do you walk in this mask?
How does your body feel?
And everyone at the barrier is charming
  they make polite conversation
  they serve tea
  they sympathize with your difficulties
  with how hard it is to break through
  and you wouldn't want to offend them
  so you stay where you are
And there you can remain
  forever
Or you can take the mask off

And you put on the ugly mask
  and try to smash through
How do you walk in this mask?
How does your body feel?
You don't care who you offend, or what you
break
  the pleasant people scatter
  the teacups shatter
  and you bash into the barrier
  again and again
  your flesh becomes pulp
  your own bones break
And there you can remain
  forever
Or you can take the mask off

Unmasked

Turn your naked face
  to the fire
  that remains
An ember in the center
  juice of the earth's living heart
The fire survives
  as you survive
  and all may yet survive in you
Beside the fire
She is still sitting
  the story woman
Her whisper makes
  a dry sound
  like the sliding of snakes
  coupling and uncoupling
  at the cell's core
Like the memory of
  being alive
  with all life living in you

She says
    There is another way
    You knew it once
    Remember

Memory sleeps coiled
  like a snake in a basket
  of grain
  deep in the storehouse
Breathe deep
Let your breath take you down

    Find the way there
    And you will find the way out

3

Fierce Love:
Resisting the Weapons the Culture Has
Devised against the Self

There is no mystery waiting
for the asking
No one can bring in the harvest alone
The hour is late and it demands hard questions
It's gonna take a fierce love
To get us home before the sun goes down
CHARLIE MURPHY, FROM THE SONG "FIERCE LOVE"

In the morning, after getting out of jail, I awaken with a voice in my dream saying: "They can let you out of jail, because now they've put the jail inside your mind."

The jail is inside my mind: it appears in my dreams nightly. I am, inside my mind, in jail, surrounded by the concrete walls, the barbed wire, steel grids on the windows. In jail something is always blocking your view. Over the fence we can see only a slice of the distant mountains. In the dining hall, blue glass screens the faces of the women who serve the food: the hands scooping mashed potatoes onto our tin plates seem disembodied, cut off. Those who serve, those who are served, cannot look each other in the face.

There is an image in my mind in jail: a vise. A pair of tongs. A clamp— a clampdown, like in the Clash song:

You start wearing blue and brown
You're working for the clampdown
Now you got someone to boss around
And it makes you feel big now . . .

One arm of the clamp is made of threats. What they can do to you. There is always someplace worse they can put you. The barracks where we are held are not awful. They are large enough and clean enough and we have each other to talk to. The lockup cells are worse: tiny, with barely room to turn around, and the windows are painted over. When you are in lockup they can threaten you with the rubber room. It is bare and padded, with only a hole in the floor to piss in, and they take away your clothes and leave you there, alone.

The other arm of the clamp is made of promises. What they will give you if you obey. Privileges. A chance to buy shampoo at the commissary. Letters. Visits. Your good time and your work time. They will let you out.

Between the two arms of the clamp we are controlled. No matter how hard we try not to reach for the carrot or flinch from the stick, our fear and our hunger betray us. We who are in jail here are women willing to risk more than many; even so, there is a point beyond which we will not go. So we come out of jail hating ourselves a little bit—for we have been forced to see too clearly how we are controlled.

Outside of jail, something is always blocking our view. The promises are plastered across every magazine and billboard: they shriek at us over the radio and dance on the TV screen. The jail itself, the mental hospital, the prison, the gun, stand as the threats, the worst place they can send us if we scream too loud. But it is not that we go around in fear, it is that we don't fear, we think this is just the way things are, the only way they can be, and the pervasive uneasiness, the dull rage, is some flaw in us.

When we discover that within us is also a part that holds the gun, we think we are uniquely evil—as if our minds could be anything but mirrors of the culture in which we are raised. As if we could be anything but victims—at best, survivors—of the weapons our culture has devised against the self.

RESPONSES TO SYSTEMS OF PUNISHMENT

We have seen how the needs of war reshape society into systems of control. Just as Marduk encaged the corpse of Tiamat:

> ". . . Pulled down the bar and posted guards.
> He bade them to allow not her waters to escape,"

the living flow of life force that yet remains in us must trickle through the bars of the big jail. We can, nevertheless, still drink from that water. We can be more than victims or survivors. We can resist systems of control, renewing the world with other powers.

Systems of punishment bring the war home. We enact its battles within the self, becoming our own conquerors and judges. We reproduce war's hierarchies in relationships and social structures.

War demands obedience to authority, and in systems of domination obedience is deeply ingrained in us. If we are not to obey passively and automatically, we must decline the offered security of obedience and listen, instead, to our own true passions and desires. We must begin to understand how systems of punishment function and how we react to them, so that we can replace our conditioned responses with conscious choices.

Both reward and punishment are dependent on a worldview that has destroyed immanent value, the sense of the sacred present in each of us. For when the sacred is present, all things have inherent value. But when value has to be earned, proven, it becomes a scarce commodity. The self-hater's coin of trade is the granting and withholding of value.

Punishment can be inflicted overtly in a variety of ways: through the infliction of physical pain and damage; through the withholding of resources necessary for survival or desired for pleasure; through restriction of action and movement; through humiliation; and, more subtly, through the eroding of a person's value as experienced by the self and viewed by others.

In *Discipline and Punish,* Foucault describes five distinct ways in which systems of punishment function:[1]

1. "The art of punishment . . . refers individual actions to a whole that is at once a field of comparison, a space of differentiation and the principle of a rule to be followed." Judgment itself is part of the operation of punishment. When we are valued for how closely we approximate an imposed standard, we are not valued for who we are. So, for example, the operation of an ideal of feminine beauty sets up a field upon which all women can be rated and compared. A student told me she once polled her male friends on what a woman should weigh. They all answered "110 pounds." She then asked them what a man should weigh. "That depends," they all said, "on his height, his body type, his musculature. . . ." Our value becomes dependent on how closely we conform to the rule; our unique beauty is rendered invisible, worthless. A woman's own body becomes her enemy, her betrayer, by its insistence on shaping itself according to its own organic imperatives.

2. Punishment "differentiates individuals from one another, in terms of the following overall rule: that the rule be made to function as a minimal threshold, as an average to be respected or as an optimum towards which one must move." When our organic individuality has been devalued, we are given back a false individuation. We can tell who we are not because we hear the song of our bodies or love the largeness or smoothness or hairiness of our flesh, but because we know our measurements and how they compare to the standardized charts.

3. Punishment "measures in quantitative terms and hierarchizes in terms of value the abilities, the level, the 'nature' of individuals." It is not just that we pass or fail; we are given "grades," A's or B's, a 96 on the final or a 75. So we strive for gradations of improvement: we

work to achieve a B+ even when we know we cannot aspire to an A. The hierarchy gives us many shades and subdivisions of value, finer grades of comparison, the illusion of more individuation that becomes a more refined means of control.

4. Punishment "introduces, through this 'value-giving' measure, the constraint of a conformity that must be achieved." We attempt to live in the illusory world where all women weigh 110, where all children learn at the same rate, and where differences are seen as deviations.

5. Lastly, punishment "traces the limit that will define difference in relation to all other differences, the external frontier of the abnormal." Every hierarchy has a cutoff point, a mark beyond which one is no longer part of the whole, where you are no longer acceptable in the school system, on the job, where your failure to conform to the rule may relegate you to the worst place: the mental hospital, the back ward, skid row. That fear, of finally being forced out from the circle of value, makes us all work harder to keep a safe cushion between ourselves and the pit of worthlessness.

Going to jail is a succinct way to learn about punishment. In jail, there are no clouds of daily details and none of the substances we use to soothe ourselves. The bare strategies of power-over are revealed, clean as gnawed bones. So are the patterns in which we respond to systems of punishment. For human beings are creatures of context. Although we imagine that our choices are free, our responses are greatly determined by the situations in which we find ourselves.

A system of punishment is a system of roles that shapes who we are and how we act. In a classic experiment, psychologists Haney, Banks, and Zimbardo set up a mock prison in the basement of a building at Stanford University. They staffed their jail and filled it with randomly chosen "guards" and "prisoners," selected from volunteers carefully screened for "normality." Guards and prisoners adapted so quickly and thoroughly to their roles that the experiment had to be stopped after six days because the brutality of the guards and the demoralization of the prisoners had progressed so far that the experimenters feared permanent damage might result.[2]

When we are conditioned to obey authority, we try to behave as authority expects, looking to others for confirmation and reinforcement, denying our own perceptions. Solomon Asch conducted an experiment in which volunteers were asked to compare the length of lines on cards. The subject was unaware that the rest of the group were deliberately giving false answers. A significant percentage literally denied the evidence of their own senses in order to agree with the majority.[3]

In war, too, "the most potent quieters of conscience are evidently the presence of others who are doing the same things and the consciousness of acting under the orders of people 'higher up' who will answer for one's deeds."[4]

Authority relieves us of the responsibility of independent action. Instead, we react in set and patterned ways. Systems of punishment generate four basic responses. We can comply, rebel, withdraw, or manipulate. All confirm the power of the system because they respond to rather than challenge the reality the system has created.

Another sort of response is possible. I call it resistance, or empowered action—action that does not accept the terms of the system, action that creates a new reality.

"Creating your own reality" is a New Age watchword, but many of those who espouse it really mean "take the best of what the system has to offer for yourself"—an option open only to a few of the more privileged among us. But to actually change the terms of reality itself, to generate new systems based on different values, is a far more demanding, dangerous, and revolutionary task.

Punishment systems define what is real by defining what is valued. In essence, punishment is based on the destruction of value. The jail is an analogy that reveals the workings of all the systems that destroy our sense of worth.

From Haney and Zimbardo, and the laboratory of my own jail experiences, I have identified ten principal ways in which the prison undermines value. My experiences in jail for short periods with other political activists are a world apart from the experience of those who are imprisoned alone, unsupported, or for long terms. The structures identified here then become even more extreme, destructive, and all-encompassing. But the same structures are to varying degrees inherent in all punishment systems. For the prison we could substitute the school, the job, the corporation, the hospital, the mental hospital, the government office, the welfare system, the military, the cult, the church. We do not generally think of all these institutions as systems of punishment, but all of them are involved in the rule-giving, rating, and comparing that deny immanent value.[5]

1. Individual worth is defined by the person's status in the system. The prisoner, the mental patient, is placed outside the bounds of the normal. In the corporation or the graduate school, the inmates are considered to have a superior rather than inferior status. Yet that status exists only as long as the person meets the demands of the system. The threat of being cast out is always present, and to be cast out of a system that defines one as valuable is itself a punishment to be feared.
2. The individual must be watched. Prisoners are kept under constant surveillance. Students are tested, workers supervised. We learn,

also, to observe ourselves, to impose the standards of the Judge on our own emotions, bodies, and spirits.

3. Jails are ugly. They provide minimum sensory variation. Boredom is punishment. Corporate offices are bland; windows become identified with privilege because they represent access to stimulation outside the system's control.

4. Prisoners, outsiders, are shorn of identity and individuality. Anonymity is enforced, often symbolized by uniformity of dress and appearance, even actual uniforms—whether of the prisoner's khaki or the executive's dress-for-success variety.

5. Punishment systems limit choices. In jail, the coffee comes with sugar already added. At work, the hours and conditions are imposed. Little or no room is made for negotiations and individual variations.

6. Punishment institutions are controlled by rules, and rules define reality. In the workplace, the rule that workers must be there between the hours of 9:00 A.M. to 5:00 P.M. creates a reality of massive traffic jams and downtown areas that go dead in the evening. In jail, the rule against touching makes expressions of affection, comfort, and sexuality illegal. The emotional reality becomes inevitably grim and harsh.

7. Emotional expression is required to be suppressed, for feelings are not amenable to control. Prisoners are not allowed to get angry; managers are not supposed to cry. The erotic, too, must be suppressed.

8. Time itself becomes distorted, becomes an instrument of punishment. Prisoners count the days; workers and students watch the clock.

9. Punishment systems are ultimately based on force and the potential of violence and/or deprivation of resources and opportunities.

10. In the most vicious systems, force and power are applied unpredictably and inconsistently, which further undermines the individual's sense of control. In the Nazi concentration camps, perhaps the most extreme system of punishment ever devised, "the SS could kill anyone they happened to run into. Criminal *kapos* would walk about in groups of two and three, making bets among themselves on who could kill a prisoner with a single blow."[6] When punishment is predictable, when it is bound somewhat by its own rules, the individual can maintain some sense of power and control. But when death comes at random, the last shreds of personal power are undermined.

Punishment systems and their agents—the Conqueror, the Orderer, the Master of Servants, the Censor, the Judge—attack our inherent value. The roles that we play in response confirm our lack of value.

Resistance, in contrast, asserts the value of the self, arising from values outside the realm of punishment. Unless we at times inhabit a realm of freedom, we may never get a chance to learn empowered action.

We can create systems and relationships that liberate and empower, where we can learn free action, in which we can be seen rather than watched. Such structures, whether they are organizations, love affairs, or architecture, can generate beauty and pleasure, can provide a richness of the senses and a celebration of individuality and diversity. They can provide choice whenever possible, and affirm emotional and erotic expression. Instead of force, cooperation and interdependence can bind us together; instead of rules to define reality, we can let reality itself reveal its inherent demands. Time can become a blessing, not a burden.

This vision may sound utopian, yet the models we might take are common: a forest ecosystem in which each tree, each plant, each insect and animal performs a vital function that sustains the whole by acting in accord with its own nature; an organic garden in which the demands of work are determined not by clock time but by wind and weather and the cycles of the earth's turning. We might even imagine walking the streets of a free city: see them lined with gardens and fruit trees that offer sustenance to travelers; see children playing on wide walkways and in small parks knowing they are safe, imagine big houses and small where people live in a hundred diverse ways—in families, in couples, in big collective groupings, in splendid solitude; feel the excitement as night falls and the lights go on and people come out to dance in the streets, fearing no one. See their faces of different shapes and colors, their eyes alive with pride in their own history and culture. Imagine walking through those varied streets, going to a workplace where the work you do has value because it contributes sustenance or pleasure or knowledge to the community and because you share equally with others in its rewards and responsibilities. You can bring a sick child here, or your dog; you can grow fresh vegetables outside and cook them up for lunch; and you can cry if you want to, or laugh, or flirt, or paint your walls with exuberant murals, for you and your co-workers all know that the way you treat and value each other is as important as anything you produce.

Reshaping the world in the image of freedom requires action that is freely chosen. To make those choices, we must recognize the patterns of unfree action we adopt in response to punishment. We must recognize the jail inside our own minds.

COMPLIANCE

We are in jail at the Lompoc Federal Prison. The women are held in a recreation hall, now covered wall-to-wall with mattresses. It seems a haven of peace and safety to me after the past few days, hiking in pouring rain through the backcountry to reach the missile silos of Vandenberg Air Force

Base. We have spent a horrible night locked up in a cold, damp classroom, and a long, tense day resisting being booked, in solidarity with some of our fellow blockaders who were isolated. We refused to move, going limp as the military police dragged us away. We are bruised, sore: I am covered with the itching rash of poison oak and coughing from bronchitis.

But now it is morning. We have time to relax, to talk about life, sex, relationships, and finally to hold a meeting and begin to organize. This is the first time most of us have encountered the federal legal system. Because I have done some of the trainings for the action, I am briefed on the legal information and I share it with the group.

After the meeting, we resume our major occupation for the day—hanging out. There is nothing else to do, nowhere to go. A guard comes up and calls out a couple of numbers. I recognize my own. We have not yet given our names to the authorities, so our numbers are our only identities.

Without thinking, I respond. "Don't answer," my friend Jeri whispers, but too late.

"Get your things," the guard says. "You're going to the doctor."

"I don't want to go to the doctor," I say. "I don't need to."

"You said you've got poison oak. The doctor's got to look at you."

"I don't need a doctor for poison oak. I'm fine."

"It's not up to you to decide. We're in charge here—not you. Now get going."

A second woman has been called along with me. We confer. "I don't want to go," she says. "Don't go," my friends say. I know that if the guards were to try to take me away, the women would surround me and resist. But I put on my shoes. I comply.

"Let's get it over with," I say. The two of us are escorted into a car, driven by an older man in a gray suit who is accompanied by a woman. They drive us around the prison grounds—and then we realize suddenly that we are on the open road, headed in some unknown direction. "Where's the doctor?" my friend asks. "What doctor?" replies the man.

"I thought we were being taken to see a doctor."

"You're not going to any doctor. You're being turned over to the federal marshals."

Paranoid visions flash through our minds—solitary cells, rubber hoses. But the marshals simply throw us out of jail, released without charges or explanations.

On the street again, waiting outside the K-Mart for our supporters to pick us up, we are furious. We want to be in jail, with the group, with our friends, part of the action and the solidarity that we feel we have inadvertently betrayed.

Mostly, I am furious at myself. "How could you be so stupid?" I say to myself over and over again. "You know that's the oldest trick in the book—the medical call. Stupid, stupid, stupid!"

Only much later, after the fever of the action has subsided, am I able to put the question to myself not in an orgy of self-hate but a spirit of inquiry: "How, indeed, could I be so stupid?" How is it I could act without thinking clearly, could obey so automatically against my own wishes and interests? For in looking back, in trying to remember my thoughts and feelings at the moment I made the decision to go, all I find is a curious blankness, as if my critical self, my emotions, had somehow switched off. I could only recognize that blankness after it was over, when I had come back to myself. At the time I was not aware of being unconscious.

Obedience is so deeply ingrained, compliance comes so naturally, that it sneaks up on us even when we intend the opposite. It's not that we don't think about what we're doing, its that we are in a state in which we cannot think. We run on automatic.

Such automatic obedience is required of soldiers in war. One of the subjects of the Milgram experiments, in a later interview, expressed his rationale for continuing to administer shocks to the "learner" even when he believed the other person might be unconscious or dead: "I figured: well, this is an experiment, and Yale knows what's going on, and if they think it's all right, well, it's all right with me. They know more than I do. . . . This is all based on a man's principle in life, and how he was brought up and what goals he sets in life. . . . I know that when I was in the service. . . . If the lieutenant says, 'We're going to go on the firing range, you're going to crawl on your gut,' you're going to crawl on your gut. And if you come across a snake, which I've seen a lot of fellows come across, copperheads, and guys were told not to get up, and they got up. And they got killed."[7]

Compliance begins with belief. The authority, the institution, constructs reality for us, by limiting our sources of information and giving us the information it wants us to believe. "I have to teach you about sex—all daddies do this," says the father. We believe because we have no way to know what not to believe. In the jail, we cannot tell what is real.

Awareness is the beginning of all resistance. We can only resist domination by becoming and remaining conscious: conscious of the self, conscious of the way reality is constructed around us, conscious of each seemingly insignificant choice we make, conscious that we are, in fact, making choices. Resistance becomes a discipline of awareness, akin to any spiritual discipline that demands we remain present to our experience. When we resist domination, we must practice magic—the art of changing consciousness at will.

The jail constructs reality also, as we have seen, through rules. "Rules are the backbone of all institutionalized approaches to managing people."[8] The rules tell us how to behave, what to do and what not to do, and how we will be punished if we disobey. When we are brought into jail, we are immediately handed a list of rules.

"Rules can come to define reality for those who follow them. Since the *definition* of the situation frequently *is* the situation, violations and not rules are defined as the problem. . . ."⁹ In the Stanford experiment, "when the guards . . . threatened to suspend visiting privileges unless a prisoner who was fasting ate his dinner, the other prisoners turned violently against *him* . . . not against the guards for their arbitrary rule. They had accepted the guards' definition of the situation and regarded the prisoner's defiance as blameworthy, rather than as a heroic, symbolic act to instill the courage they so desperately needed."¹⁰

Compliance destroys the unity of resistance. When we accept the authority's reality, when we blame the rule-breakers, blame the victims, we cannot see our own victimization or act against it. Resistance demands clarity. We cannot mistake the rule for the reality; we must continuously search behind the rules for the assumptions they represent and the power relations they enforce.

The jail wants us to comply, and it will exert all its power to see that we do. And we do comply, part of the time, for no one has the energy to rebel or resist completely.

March 1982, I write in my journal: "Intimidation: In jail, they pull one of the women out of our group, lock her up in someplace worse

so that we see their power
so that we become fearful
they pick the woman who makes us most uncomfortable, who is most loud and angry, least respectable, who least fits in
so that we do not really want to extend ourselves, to risk ourselves, for her
so that we can justify not risking ourselves, telling ourselves that there is nothing we can do (even though all of us are here in jail because we will not accept that there is nothing we can do)
so that we don't try to do anything, telling ourselves
we don't have enough information to act
that it is not yet the right time to act
that if we try to act we will make the situation worse:
that it is better to let someone else (our lawyers, the experts) act for us
that she may have done something to deserve it
that she created her own situation

"These are the voices that silence us, that keep us powerless inside the jail, and they are the same voices that silence us, that keep us powerless, on the outside. We can recognize the excuses when we hear them, but when we are scared enough we don't hear them anymore, we simply do not act. And if at one time we can overcome them enough to speak and act, then another time they will overcome us, for if we are not afraid of one thing there will always be something worse they can do that we will be afraid of. There is always a rubber room—and when we are in the rubber room already, there is something beyond that."

So we obey, because it is to dangerous not to, or simply too hard to fight every battle, because our chronic vigilance has left us exhausted, or because we cannot tolerate the isolation we suffer if we don't comply. For us, as for the soldier, disobedience "means to set oneself against others and with one stroke lose their comforting presence. It means to cut oneself free of doing what one's superiors approve, free of being an integral part of the military organism with the expansion of the ego that such belonging brings. Suddenly the soldier feels himself abandoned and cast off from all security."[11]

To obey, we perform. We work. We do our homework. We put in overtime. We exhibit enthusiasm for the company. We conform. We observe ourselves, work on ourselves. We repair the damages done by a system that is slowly murdering us.

A life of compliance is a life of denial. We deny the body. We feel sick— yet we go to work. We feel hungry—yet we don't eat. We deny feelings— for the jail requires that we suppress our emotions, especially our anger and our rage that might lead to rebellion.

Obedience has its cost: the destruction of the self. To be good is to be a slave, unfree. When we comply, when we aid the system in its ultimate disregard and destruction of us, we hate ourselves. We know that we have been stupid, blind, weak. And so we cannot comply all of the time and live. At times, we must rebel.

Becoming aware of how and when we comply can help us act consciously. I suggest the following questions as an aid in the process. This is the first of a number of exercises for groups and individuals that you will find throughout this and the following chapters.

QUESTIONS ABOUT COMPLIANCE

Consider these questions in individual meditation, journal writing, or group rounds:

1. When in my life have I complied or obeyed when I didn't want to?
2. How did I feel at the time? What was I thinking? What choices did I perceive?
3. What other choices actually existed? What might have happened had I taken them?

REBELLION

Doreen has spent most of her twenty-three years in institutions. When she was thirteen, her mother, unable to care for her, placed her in a mental hospital. She graduated into juvenile hall and intermittent terms in the county jail.

Now she is trying hard to improve her life. She has a nurturing relationship with a woman lover. She is part of a supportive feminist community. She goes to AA meetings and comes to me for therapy.

One night she goes with her lover to a concert. During a break Doreen
steps outside to smoke a cigarette. When she tries to return, the woman
who takes tickets stops her.

"Where's your ticket?"

"It's inside—you saw me go out."

"I never saw you before in my life."

"Let me get my purse—it's inside with my friend."

"Hell no, bitch. You pay to get in."

Doreen becomes deadly angry. "Nobody calls me 'bitch.' "

"Oh yeah? You rather I call you fat girl?"

Doreen, in her mind, is back in jail, where the shreds of her self-worth
are so fragile that not to defend them is to die. She lunges at the ticket
taker, and in an instant they are yelling and fighting and kicking at each
other in the street. Women are screaming as Doreen pulls out her last
defense—her knife. She has just enough presence of mind to throw it away
when the cops come.

We rebel to save our lives. Rebellion is the desperate assertion of our
value in the face of all that attacks it, the cry of refusal in the face of
control. The jail has taken all that was ours; and we must assert what
belongs to us or disappear. Doreen, speaking about jail, once told me,
"Sometimes I had to get in trouble just to prove to myself that I existed."
In rebellion, the future disappears, consequences become meaningless under the immediate, explosive pressure of our rage. So we lash out with
noise and whatever force we can muster.

When we comply in our own punishment, the self knows and hates us
for it. When we rebel, we feel, even for a moment, powerful and free.

But that freedom and power are false, for rebellion, unless it can transform itself into resistance, inevitably becomes self-destructive. When we
rebel without challenging the framework of reality the system has constructed, we remain trapped. Our choices are predetermined for us.

The ticket taker's insult has immediately constructed for Doreen a certain reality of limited choices. She sees only two possibilities: submit to
abuse or attack back. Of the infinite potential responses to the ticket taker,
her experience of life, shaped by the jail, has taught her only these alternatives.

The ticket taker herself, who, it turns out, also has a history of jail and
institutionalization, inhabits the same limited reality in which challenge
must be responded to with verbal or physical force. Had she met someone
who responded out of a different set of choices, the whole incident would
have progressed differently.

When rebellion does not challenge the choices predetermined by the system, it cannot lead to freedom. For the choices the system presents us with inevitably increase the system's control. The system needs those who suffer the stick as much as it needs those who reach for the carrot. In order to retain control, the system needs to punish, and it needs to single out some individuals for more intensive punishment to serve as an example and warning to the rest. Rebellion provides the system with its excuse, its rationale, for punishment. Without transgressors, there would be no one to send to the worst place, no way to intimidate the good into being good.

When the system defines our choices, it channels rebellion into modes that it is prepared to control, into acts that harm the rebel, not the system. Prison guards know how to handle troublemakers; they are constantly on the alert for the belligerent, the instigator: such people can be quickly removed to serve as a warning to the rest. The schoolchild who rebels, refuses to study, harms her or his own future, not the educational system that functions, at least in part, as a winnowing device that removes those not temperamentally suited to obey from the tracks leading to the higher echelons of the hierarchy.

The culture of punishment also offers us channels for rebellion that destroy us slowly without challenging the power of the system at all. We can choose from a broad array of addictions that offer us the chance to rebel and administer our own punishment in a single act—for when we smoke, abuse alcohol or drugs, when we literally attack our own bodies with substances that harm us, we are affirming punishment's essential message: "You have no inherent worth, you do not deserve to live."

We find such addictions very hard to break because we identify them with being bad, rebellious, disobedient, unenslaved. The image sold to us by the media is that addictions represent freedom. They take us to Marlboro country. And we need to do something bad, for to be too good is to be dead. I had a cigarette: I'm bad (free); I denied myself a cigarette: I'm good (slave). We become addicted not just to the substance but to our failures to quit, which comfort us by confirming the existence of some small bit of the self that cannot be controlled.

But the badness of addiction does not buy us deeper, broader, more extended life. It too kills us, quickly or slowly. We enact upon ourselves the murder of the self, in our desperate attempt to keep alive some kernel of freedom.

Insanity can also be seen as an extreme form of rebellion, and is sometimes romanticized as such. "It's not that I'm not in touch with this reality," says James, a young man in the midst of what is clinically described as a schizophrenic break. "I defy reality!"

But to defy reality, alone and isolated, is not the same as to change it. To go crazy means to become the most vulnerable to control, to be isolated, locked up, subject to physical restraints, chemical, electrical, and even surgical punishments, all administered in the name of therapy. The insane serve as a warning to the rest of us of what will happen if we go too far, get too strange, challenge too much.

The punishment for rebellion is to be singled out, isolated, made strange. The price of being bad is to be outcast, cut off even further from the circle of worth.

Rebellion also cuts us off from the information we may need for survival. When we need our addictions to substitute for freedom, we lose the ability to feel what is really happening to our bodies. When we defy reality, we cannot see what range of choices reality may present us with.

Rebellion is our very life asserting itself, willing to settle for nothing less than freedom. But if our rebellion is to have any hope of achieving that freedom, it must transform itself into resistance.

Resistance challenges the framework of reality defined by systems of punishment. Rebellion can be the first step toward resistance, but we must avoid the sidetracks of self-destruction along the way.

Resistance differs from rebellion because it embodies a reality incongruent with that of domination. We do more than defy reality: we present its alternatives, communicating our beliefs and values.

Power-over is maintained by the belief that some people are more valuable than others. Its systems reflect distinctions in value. When we refuse to accept those distinctions, refuse to automatically assume our powerlessness, the smooth functioning of the systems of oppression is interrupted. Each interruption creates a small space, a rip in the fabric of oppression that has the potential to let another power come through.

The authorities can handle rebellion without stepping out of role. But when we speak not to the role but to the human being behind it, when we refuse to automatically defer to the power of a role, we challenge the basic assumptions underlying all hierarchies: that our worth is determined by our role and status. The philosophy and practice of nonviolence as a means of social change is rooted in the premise that all of us have inherent worth. To resist domination, we must act in ways that affirm value—even in our opponents.

We can begin by valuing ourselves, refusing to administer our own oppression, refusing to poison ourselves or numb the pain with substances that soothe but incapacitate, preventing us from making any serious trouble for the system.

We can also refuse isolation. To connect, to build bonds of caring and community, to create structures of support that can nurture us and renew our strength, are powerful acts of resistance.

QUESTIONS ABOUT REBELLION

Consider these questions in individual meditation, journal writing, or group rounds:

1. When in my life have I rebelled? How? With what success? At what cost?
2. What choices did I see that I had? Were other choices possible? What?
3. What might have been different?

WITHDRAWAL

"The only way to make it with the bosses is to withdraw into yourself, both mentally and physically—literally making yourself as small as possible."[12]

There are many women in the jail who are neither compliant nor rebellious. Instead, they have retreated to their cots and sleep out the action, or sit quietly in a corner. Withdrawal is another way to respond to an intolerable situation.

Camp Parks, June '82. We are meeting with our legal team, who inform us that the gym in which we are held has been used for many years for experiments with radioactive substances. No one is yet sure exactly how much danger we may be in.

I am standing on the outskirts of the group. I listen to the arguments. I say to myself, "I cannot deal with this while I'm in here. I can't think about it." And I don't.

Denial is a form of withdrawal, for when we withdraw, we shut out information. We may withdraw to conserve our energy and resources. Shutting out what we cannot cope with may give us time to adjust when we are thrown into a reality sharply different from what we have known before.

Victims and survivors of the Nazi concentration camps most commonly first responded to their ordeal by entering a state of shock, undergoing an "emotional death." "Entry into the camp world was characterized by an overriding sense of *nightmare* and *unreality*—two words which appear constantly when survivors refer to their first days and weeks."[13] In the camps, the Nazis literally created a different reality, one of such extremes of horror and cruelty that for most people it seemed to have no connection with their former lives. The camps could be comprehended only as a terrible dream.

Withdrawal cushions us from feeling the full impact of our situation. But it is ultimately dangerous, for wrapped in our cushion we are cut off from information and observations vital to our survival. "It was deadly to remain within the dream. Prisoners unable to shake off their sense of unreality could only drift as one drifts in dream, defenseless and stupid."[14] Those who did not succeed in waking became the so-called " 'Musselmanner,' the 'moslems' or 'walking dead,' for whom time ran out before they were able to shake the sense of nightmare and wake to their predicament. They starved, they fell sick, they stumbled into situations that got them killed. . . . They died inwardly, and as their spirit withered their outward aspect was terrible to see."[15]

"They behaved as if they were not thinking, not feeling, not able to act or respond. . . . Typically, this stopping of action began when they no longer lifted their legs as they walked, but only shuffled them. When finally even the looking about on their own stopped, they soon died."[16]

Those who survived the camps somehow found the strength to awaken and name the nighmare real, to turn and continue turning "from passivity to action—from horror to the daily business of staying alive."[17] Survival, itself an act of ultimate resistance, required paying "sharp attention, not to the horror or to their own pain, but to the development of objective conditions which had to be judged constantly in terms of their potential for life or for death."[18]

Unless we can grasp the reality in which we find ourselves, we cannot change it. When I refused to comprehend the reality that I and my friends were locked up in a place that might be contaminated with radioactivity, I tacitly accepted that we were powerless to do anything about our situation. Because we were only in jail for two days, the situation was not critical. Had we been held there for weeks or months, our acceptance of our powerless position could have led to damaged health and reduced life. Withdrawing, we were unable to act. Had we faced our situation, we might have been able to change it.

When we withdraw, our gifts, our perceptions, our energies are lost. The realities of domination go unchallenged.

To resist is to engage reality, to act. Awareness, emotion are not enough. Resistance is only real when it is expressed through action.

In turn, the action we take nourishes and strengthens us, for acts of resistance against systems that destroy us are ultimately acts of survival, creation, and nurture.

We often think of resistance as negative. "I don't want to focus energy on resistance, on the negative," people say. "I want to be positive, creative." But resistance is the refusal to be negated by systems of control. When we are embedded in negative systems, only acts of resistance and refusal can move us in positive directions. Only by refusing to withdraw, to blank out and disappear, can we become present in the world and begin to create. And creativity itself may be an act of resistance, the ultimate refusal to accept things as they are.

QUESTIONS ABOUT WITHDRAWAL

Consider these questions in individual contemplation, journal writing, or group rounds:

1. In what situations have I withdrawn? What happened? How did I feel?

2. What information did I not receive? What was going on that I didn't know about? What choices did I have that I didn't perceive? What action could I have taken?
3. When did I awaken? How? What sparked my return to awareness?

MANIPULATION

"I sorted some of the morning's mail—piles of forms which had to be routed to each engineer for initials before they were filed in several file drawers. . . . I stuck the stack of the papers way in the back of the filing cabinet, and I was done. Somebody's boss was watching, so I read my TempRite magazine."[19]

While some comply, some rebel, and some withdraw, there are some who figure out the system and how to best it. When we manipulate the system, we have the illusion of being in control. We can keep the rewards of the system while believing that we are not really complying.

But we are still accepting the system's terms, unspoken rules, and values, including the lack of value it accords to us. Women in traditional roles supposedly achieve power, money, and status through manipulating men, but such achievements do not challenge the low value placed on women.

When we manipulate, we may become sensitive receivers of information about the system. When we put on the mask of deception we feel conscious, not blank. But in reality our ability to see what's going on is still severely limited—by the limits of the system itself. We may know everything about how the jail functions and how to get the most out of it for ourselves, but that doesn't change the fact that we are still in jail.

"He came over to my desk, put one of his thick hands on my in-box, glanced at my tits, and gave me a smile. 'Well, that's okay, then, Kelly. We're glad to have you pitchin' for us even if you *can't* make coffee. Now why don't you sprint down to the corner and get me a cup of the *real* stuff.'

"I don't like to get coffee. 'I wouldn't mind going out, but I have some Xeroxing to do for Toole,' I told him, sweetly."[20] In this story from the radical office workers' magazine *Processed World*, "Kelly" knows how to avoid tasks she doesn't want to do—not always successfully (she does, in the end, get coffee) but more often than any of her bosses suspect. She can look sweet while arranging matters so that she has some small control over her work—more than the system allots to her. But the millions of minor acts of sabotage performed by secretaries and workers at the lower levels of the hierarchies do not change the essential structure of the working world.

Manipulation also does not challenge the low value the system places on the self. For in order to manipulate, we cannot be ourselves, express our true feelings, or share our real perceptions. We literally mask ourselves. "Kelly" must smile sweetly; were she to say to the boss "Get your own goddamned coffee, stop patronizing me, and go to hell!" she would simply lose her job. She would have moved from manipulation to rebellion. To move further, into resistance, would require organization and support.

Manipulation may garner for us some of the system's rewards, or it may drag at the system's wheels as they turn, but it neither liberates us individually nor changes the collective reality the system creates.

Resistance challenges the system's terms and categories, counters its assumptions, and communicates other values. Resistance speaks its own truth to power, and shifts the ground of struggle to its own terrain.

QUESTIONS ABOUT MANIPULATION

Consider these questions in individual meditation, journal writing, or group rounds:

1. When (whom) have I manipulated? How?
2. How did I feel about myself? What parts of myself did I have to conceal?
3. What happened?
4. What other choices did I have? Did I perceive them?

CHOOSING OUR RESPONSES

Responses to punishment systems are similar to the roles children adopt in an alcoholic family. The Hero, the good child, complies. The Scapegoat, the bad child, the delinquent, rebels. The Lost Child, the quiet one who disappears into the woodwork, withdraws. The Mascot, the child who clowns, entertains, manipulates.[21] All are responding to a situation in which power is experienced much as it is in any system of punishment: as arbitrary, inconsistent, capricious, violent. All follow the unspoken rules of the alcoholic family, which are the same as in prison: don't talk, don't trust, don't feel.[22]

The roles, and the rules, are strategies we adopt in order to survive. None of these responses are necessarily bad or wrong. At times, any one of them may be the best possible choice. We play the roles open to us, sometimes one, sometimes another, and in facing systems of power they may seem to be our only options. We need not blame ourselves for following them, although the self-hater in each of us may leap to do so. But we can recognize that the roles, the rules, the strategies of the jail stay with us when we attempt to create something new. They undermine us.

So we must understand them, learn to recognize them. For these patterns carry over into many situations: relationships, families, working groups, businesses, affinity groups. Observing the simple and overt strategies of control in jail may give us insight into the workings of other sorts of groups.

Resistance is hard. We find it relatively easy to commit a single act of resistance, but to sustain that resistance over days, weeks, over a hundred minor issues and constant confrontations, requires a diligence and stamina far beyond what most of us possess. Our admiration increases for those who hold to resistance against greater threats, extremes of pain, privation, and fear, for months and long years. For we find that resistance demands enormous energy. We cannot resist all the time, in every area of life. We must choose our battles and the priorities of struggle.

But knowing that resistance is a possibility makes all our choices real choices. They become part of our resistance, not opposed to it. We can say, "I will obey right now because this issue is not where I choose to make my stand." We can say, "I will rebel not by harming myself but by making trouble for the authorities." We can say, "I will withdraw now to conserve my strength but I will return tomorrow with my eyes open." We can say, "I can use my ability to manipulate the system to prepare the ground of struggle." We can be conscious when we put on a mask that we are not wearing our true faces—and so retain the ability to take the mask off.

SELF-EVALUATION QUESTIONS

The following questions are for group consideration and feedback. Each person in the group should have a chance to consider these questions aloud and receive a caring response. Allow twenty to thirty minutes per person; in a sizable group, this process might take more than one meeting. If so, be sure that everyone is committed to completing the process.

1. Which roles do I play in the group? Which masks do I wear?
2. When? In response to what?
3. How do I feel in the mask?
4. How do others respond to me? (Ask for feedback.)
5. What other choices do I have? (Ask for suggestions.)
6. What choice would I make if I felt I had power?

The Descent of Inanna, I:
The Storehouse

You are trying to remember something
It teases
  your nostrils
  like desert dust
Take a breath
Smell the dry air
  and the mud
  by the irrigation canals
  and the moist earth
  under the date palms
Hear
  the play of water in the fountain
  in the courtyard
  where you walk
Remember your name
  Inanna
  Lady of the Date Palm
  Lady of the Storehouse
Its gate stands before you
From the doorposts
  streamers fly
It is your temple
  your body
This place
All comes here
  to be gathered, counted
  to be given out again
What is it you gather? What do you hoard?
What do you give?

This is a big place
You could get lost here
Searching through dusty corridors
  where everything that ever was
  still is
Whatever you have lost
  you can find here
  if you don't
  lose yourself
Take care

Call someone to watch for you
Who would come after you
   if you walked into danger?
Who helps you? Who cares?
Call
See that person sit beside the gate
   to wait
And if you know no one you can call
Ask the Mother herself to guard you
   to remember you
   and bring you back
Feel her hand touch your hand
Smell the breath of earth
   as you push the gate aside
   and enter

Inside, it is cool
You reach out your hand
   touch the stone
   smell the damp
   feel the air on your skin
   as you walk through dim corridors
Lined with oil jars, grain jars
   baskets of dates, figs
   pistachios, jars of honey
   all the land's produce
You are the storehouse
You walk through your own bowels
   room after room
Here are treasures
   carved and molded images
   precious stones, gold
Here is a loom and a tapestry
   and the tattered shreds of history
   to unravel and roll into yarn
What will you weave?
Feel the texture
See the colors
Here is the gathered up knowledge
   of the ancestors
   secrets piled like old bones
Search through them
   among them
   is the thing you need to know . . .

And here is a chamber that is yours alone
What do you find there?

There is still somewhere
  you are trying to go
You hear a rustle
A snake
  uncoils from a basket
  glides along the floor
You follow
Deep in the storehouse a chasm opens up
A crack leads down
  below
Listen
Put your ear to the crack
Do you hear a call?

Unraveling and Reweaving: Pattern and Ritual

I come downstairs to begin work for the day. The phone rings. It is a young woman I know slightly.

"I probably shouldn't be calling you," she says. "I'm getting messages that I really need to go through this alone."

"Go through what?" I ask.

"It's that I'm being told that if I don't finish school this semester I'll go crazy and end up in a mental hospital. I hear this voice and I guess maybe I'm starting to hallucinate. It keeps telling me that I shouldn't be talking to people on the phone and freaking out—I should just write. That I've wasted too much time."

I talk for quite a while with her. I recognize the voice she hears. It is my own voice, it is the voice each one of us hears in this culture, the voice of the self-hater.

I feel deeply sad for this woman, who is in pain. There is very little I can offer her at this moment: I am not taking on new clients, and she already has a therapist. Anyway, I'm not sure anymore that I'm the best therapist for someone like her, because my ability to be there for her is colored by rage at the culture-created demon, the monster thought form of authority. And she is so effective at tormenting herself.

"I've made mistakes. I've missed so many opportunities, and now there's no going back. If you miss an opportunity, you don't get a second chance. And now if I blow this one, if I drop out of school, I'll end up on welfare for the rest of my life, or in a mental hospital."

My rage wants to bash down that structure in her head that keeps her gnawing at her own vital spots.

"Have there been chances in your life that you've missed, and haven't been able to go back to?" I ask her.

"Yes."

"Did you grieve for them? Did you cry? Did you let yourself feel your sorrow?" This is perhaps the only thing I say in the whole conversation that has truly any chance of moving anywhere.

"No," she says. "I never did."

"Perhaps that's what you need to do. And you can't do that alone. You need to be able to grieve with someone."

"But what if it's too late?"

I could have done it with her. I could have said, "What do you grieve for? Tell me the missed chances, the lost loves, the pain. Cry, and I will hold you, crooning."

Instead, my rage leads me to argue with her, to offer her belief systems, theologies. "I don't believe that," I say. "I'm a Witch. I don't believe you fry in hell forever if you blow one chance. In Witchcraft, if you miss an opportunity, all that happens is that you keep getting presented over and over again with that same opportunity, until you're ready to take it."

Argument does not make for good therapy. I know better. But then I am not this woman's therapist, I am just someone she called in the middle of a Tuesday afternoon, someone who is herself struggling with her own voices. "You ought to be writing—you're not making enough progress on your book. You ought to be paying your bills today, washing the floor, doing the laundry. You ought to call your lover, make time to see her. You ought to call your other lover, make time to see him." The woman who calls is a fun house mirror distortion of myself.

The woman counters my theology. "What if you're hurting other people by missing those opportunities? What if I'm hurting you right now by keeping you tied up on the phone?"

"If you were hurting me, I'd tell you," I say, not quite honestly. If I were telling the truth I'd say, "I like to think I'd tell you to hang up if you were hurting me, but in reality if I felt that you were in greater need, I probably would allow myself to be somewhat hurt, and I'm not sure that's altogether bad." Besides, I may yet hurt her. It may hurt her that I take her pain and write about it, when her pain is bound up with her inability to write. But that is the chance you take, I tell myself, when you call up strangers who are writers on a Tuesday afternoon.

"And you know," I go on, "human beings are bound to hurt each other in our encounters, just in the nature of things. But I don't hear that you've done anything so awful."

"It's what I haven't done."

"You aren't working out at Livermore designing nuclear weapons. You aren't taking food out of the mouths of orphans."

"I've wasted money," she says. "That's taking it from the starving. I've wasted so much. I've never worked at anything."

"There're so many people who deserve to feel guilty," I tell her, aware that my rage has led me far away from anything that might actually be helpful. "There're people planning nuclear war. There're people using napalm in El Salvador. There's Ronald Reagan. Why should you use up the guilt that rightfully belongs to them?"

"I don't believe in limited guilt," she tells me.

PATTERN LANGUAGES AND POWER

In the dismembered world, in the landscape of power-over where guilt is an endlessly renewable resource, we face the self-hater. We hear the voice of the ruler who has become a voice inside us.

Power-over works like sorcery: it casts a spell on us. It changes our consciousness, clouds our vision so that we don't notice it in operation. It is the magician who distracts us with a rabbit as he saws the woman in half.

From a Witch's viewpoint, power-over is an entity, an independent being with an energy and life of its own, an ensouled thought form. Not necessarily intelligent or conscious, it may function like a great astral machine, in patterns that we can identify.

"At all times, in every human culture, the entities of which the world is made are always governed by the pattern languages which people use."[1]

"The patterns, which repeat themselves, come simply from the fact that all the people have a common language, and that each one of them uses this common language when he makes a thing. . . ."[2]

In these quotations, architect Christopher Alexander is discussing building, but the same concept applies to every aspect of culture. Culture provides us with a "language"—a set of internal rules and expectations for combining things and acts. The patterns that make up a house, for example, may in one culture produce a structure with solid walls and a peaked, shingled roof, while in another they may result in a round, collapsible tipi. The structure, in turn, determines what can be done inside it. A bay-windowed Victorian is not easily folded up for transport across the prairie, while it is hard to serve a formal dinner with china and crystal inside a tipi.

These patterns are never accidental; they are the concrete manifestations of a culture's deepest assumptions, structures, and power relationships. A Gothic cathedral, with its stone walls, lofty spires reaching skyward, and long, narrow spaces in which a huge congregation focuses all their attention on the priest at the altar, embodies a concept of God, and of power, quite different from a Sweat Lodge built on bent branches and skins on bare earth, in which a small group sits in a circle together.

Cultures have pattern languages not just for buildings, but for all aspects of life. In a traditional culture, the way food is grown, the way houses are built, the Gods that are served, the rituals that are performed, are all generated by a network of harmonious pattern languages. A living culture is made up of living patterns, each true to itself and to its interrelations with others.

Negative patterns are easily identified. The entities of control—the Conqueror, Orderer, Judge, Censor, Master of Servants—are patterns that generate languages, sets of unconscious rules of thumb, that determine our behavior and the structures we create. Jail, for example, is made up of patterns generated by the Judge and the Avenger. We could call them Restriction of Movement, One-Way Observation, Minimal Sensory Stimulation (Ugliness), and so on.

The patterns in our minds reflect the patterns of power in our culture, as surely as our architecture, clothing, and work reflect those patterns outwardly and visibly. Power-over reproduces itself inside the human psyche. The structure of our inner being is like a landscape peopled with events, beings, plots, and stories that we take in from the culture around us. The patterns of patriarchy become literally embedded within us. We are possessed.

Earth-based, shamanic traditions have always taught the techniques of a different sort of possession. In the Craft, we "draw down the moon," become the Goddess. In the Yoruba-based Afro-Caribbean traditions, initiates may fall into a trance during ritual and become possessed by one of the orishas—the Goddesses and Gods.

Sacred possession serves several functions. It is an ecstatic state, and ecstasy reminds us that the sacred is immanent. When the great powers are moving through us they also bring knowledge, abilities, and healing that go beyond our ordinary limitations. Equally important, the knowledge of how to become possessed is also the knowledge of how to become unpossessed. Ritual gives us the boundaries that let us choose what powers to court, how to call them in and how to send them away, how to become aware of what state of consciousness we are in.

In the culture of domination, we are possessed without knowing it and without knowing techniques to free ourselves. When the self-hater whispers its poisonous dialogues, there is no one to toss a white cloth over our heads and whisper our true names into our ears.

The self-hater that possessed the woman on the phone is the root pattern in a society based on power-over. Although an abusive or authoritarian family will strengthen its grip, it is no anomaly produced by a particular family constellation. The self-hater is the literal embodiment of structures of domination. In this culture, it possesses us all.

The self-hater is not, however, an archetype in a Jungian sense, not some innate constellation of the generic human psyche. It is a culture-created demon, born in a recognizable historical era, thriving only in a particular psychic environment—that of power-over.

Clearly, what happens to us in childhood is important. A loving environment in childhood can give us a firmer ground of self-esteem; an unloving or abusive environment can implant in us the self-hater in its most cruel forms. But in a culture shaped by the needs of war, where the self-hater's lies are reinforced by almost every institution and interaction, all of us are susceptible. If we were raised in a toxic physical environment (as, more and more, we are) those of us who were given good nutrition in infancy might be less susceptible to disease than those who were starved or fed junk food. But we would not be immune. We could spend years

examining our particular childhood lacks and subsequent vulnerabilities—
but the environment would still be toxic.

So too with culture. When our major cultural structures destroy human
value and natural balance, we all are sick, regardless of the particulars of
what our family did or didn't do. There is value in looking at those particulars; in understanding our unique patterns of vulnerability and resistance. There is value in learning to feed ourselves better and reshape our
lives in the situations given to us. But a psychology of liberation is ultimately interested in changing those situations; cleaning up the poison, not
just strengthening our individual immunities.

RITUAL AND PATTERNS OF EMPOWERMENT

The pain within us is a mirror of the power structures outside us, yet
because that is so our task is simpler. For what can challenge the visible
oppressors outside us can also challenge the invisible oppressors within
us. We are creatures of situations; we must create situations in which we
can be healed.

"Create situations" was an anarchist slogan of the Paris student revolt
of 1968. When we understand how we are possessed, we know what conditions we need for freedom.

A primary insight of liberation psychology is that groups can be structured and society can be restructured in ways that foster liberation.

Many such situations, of course, already exist, and we can learn from
them. Some time ago, I gave up my practice as a therapist, in part because
I no longer felt that I knew how I expected change to come about. The
ideas in this book were in embryo; the theories—psychological, magical,
or practical—that I had learned or developed had begun to seem more like
articles of faith than true reflections of my own and my clients' experiences. I became interested in the question: what works? What really
changes lives?

I heard many answers. Sometimes traditional and nontraditional forms
of therapy work; sometimes they don't. Some people find growth and
healing in feminist consciousness–raising groups, support groups, ritual
circles, covens, affinity groups formed to do civil disobedience, Alcoholics
Anonymous and related Twelve-Step Programs, such as Alanon and Ov-
ereaters Anonymous, based on the twelve steps to recovery pioneered by
AA. I began to see some common factors in these groups and to suspect
that the changes that occur in their members have less to do with the
groups' stated purposes and more to do with their essential structures.

All the situations that foster growth restore to their participants a sense
of immanent, inherent value. They are structured in ways that undermine
each aspect of the King's possession, and reclaim what is positive. In restoring true value, they deflate false glory. They provide protection and
safety, they evoke mystery, they meet needs in ways that are balanced and

sustainable, they break the silence of the Censor, and they offer freedom from the Judge's discipline and punishments.

These factors can become the warp and the weft of the new tapestry we weave. As we unravel the threads of the fabric of control, we can use even the cords that bind us in new ways. For when everything is interconnected, nothing is wasted.

One of the great tools of the weavers of culture is ritual. In the dismembered world, we live in a vicious circle of killer patterns. Ritual can help us regenerate a culture of life.

Ritual is a way of marking and intensifying value. The moon waxes and wanes, and we may barely notice. But when we mark her changes with ritual, we identify with her cycles. We are reminded at the new moon of our own power to begin. At the full moon, we remember and intensify what it is in our lives that we are bringing to fulfillment. As the moon wanes, we let go. The moon cycle takes on a new depth of meaning, and the changes in our own lives become integrated with the flux of the forces around us.

Ritual is the way culture enacts and affirms its values. The transitions a culture marks with ritual are considered important; those that go by unmarked become nonevents. In this culture few women are given any positive celebration to mark their first menstruation. Coming into womanhood becomes a time of shame or embarrassment, not of pride, but were we to celebrate that passage, we would profoundly affirm the value of a woman's inherent, body-rooted power.

Ritual can become free space, a hole torn in the fabric of domination. The traditional Craft phrase "between the worlds" takes on a new meaning: we stand one step beyond the institutions of control, not wholly in the otherworld of the mysteries, astride them both, a bridge that brings through into the world of the everyday a sense of the sacred. And so the everyday changes, deepens, until the sacred, like an underground stream, wears away control from below.

The making of living patterns is not foreign to us. It is a simple and common ability. "The power to make buildings beautiful lies in each of us already. . . . Imagine the greatest possible beauty and harmony in the world—the most beautiful place that you have ever seen or dreamt of. You have the power to create it, at this very moment, just as you are. . . ."[3]

Ritual and myth are like seed crystals of new patterns that can eventually reshape culture around them. The visions we share, the acts we create, make tangible our immanent value.

We live infused by the great life-sustaining powers, sucking them in and spitting them out like sea creatures feeding on ocean water. In certain moments, we can feel the great tides moving through us. The purpose of ritual is to create the situations in which those moments may happen.

Ritual is patterned action. The traditional forms and processes of ritual are the rules of thumb that resolve the problems inherent in opening to the great forces of life.

The patterns of ritual together form a language that can be named and described much as are the patterns of architecture. Just as a building needs an entrance, so do we need a transition to enter ritual space and time. Witches do this by grounding, cleansing, and casting the circle. In the Yoruba traditions, we might "open Alegba": call the Trickster, who is the power embodied in gates and crossroads. Other cultures have other specific traditions, but all take us across the boundary, out of daily concerns into the realm of mystery.

When we practice ritual over time, we develop a repertoire of patterns. They will be different in different traditions, yet not at odds with each other, for they are different ways of solving the same problem. None is more right or wrong except in how right each feels in the moment.

The patterns of ritual establish the conditions needed for healing and freedom. In ritual, we value each other for our inherent being. We see the Goddess, the Gods, alive in each one of us. Ritual itself gives value to any change or transition that it marks.

In ritual, we create a symbolic space of protection and safety, in which we break the Censor's dominion and express freely whatever comes. We let go of judgment, taking each other's offerings as gifts, not performances to be critiqued. We are equals in the circle, serving only the energy that renews us as it moves through us. Ritual sustains us as it marks the cycles of birth, growth, decay, and renewal that sustain our lives.

Ritual can be handed down from past generations, and it can be designed, created, critiqued, and revised to fulfill the needs of our community and our time. When what works in ritual is repeated, over time it takes on a power of its own. To plunge naked into the ocean on the Winter Solstice, once, is to be touched by the wildness of the elements. To plunge every year, in community, is to gather that wildness and weave it into the strands and cycles of our own lives so that it becomes a living part of our history, as each year, in the shock of the cold, we remember what it was we let go in the years before: the wedding wreath given to the waves when the marriage died, the title page of the novel that never got published, the fears. We remember, also, the powers we called forth, and the changes we've made, and the changes of the elements around us: the year it poured rain, the year the sun set in splendor, the year I was in Nicaragua, sneaking off from the Baptist church with friends to plunge into the warm, phosphorescent Bay of Corinto.

Even within one tradition such as Witchcraft, rituals vary. They also change, grow, and develop, take root in particular places and reflect particular moments in a community's history. Ritual that is alive does not become frozen in form. When we write ritual down, we risk killing it. What I present here are forms and techniques that have developed in my own community or out of my own work. They do not represent Witchcraft as a whole, but my own idiosyncratic views. They will remain alive if you take them as suggestions, a framework meant to spark imagination; they will go dead if you take them as unchangeable, universal, or definitive.

Tradition does preserve useful insights, tools, and techniques. Witchcraft teaches us an overall pattern of ritual, each element of which is itself a pattern. The rituals in this book are not specific to Witchcraft, but they do follow the underlying structure of Craft rituals.

A Craft ritual begins with an entrance transition: a cleansing and grounding. Next, we create sacred space by casting a circle. Into sacred space, we invoke aspects of power, Goddesses, Gods, ancestors. We work magic; that is, through chanting, story telling, dancing, meditation, drumming, or visualizing, we change consciousness, raise power, travel in the imagination. Usually, we end by feasting—sharing food and drink as tangible expressions of mutual nurturing—and then make a transition of return, opening the circle.[4]

To understand ritual, we must also understand the magical concept of energy. We imagine energy as a force that flows through our bodies in patterns we can learn to identify. Energy, what the Chinese call *chi*, the Hawaiians, *mana*, the Japanese, *ki*, flows through all living and nonliving things. In ritual, we raise it and shape it into patterns that set in motion forces that can bring about what we envision. Although energy is less tangible than matter, we can learn to be aware of it, to sense it, sometimes to see it, and to consciously direct it. We can allow each of these patterns to become situations that foster freedom.

ENTERING THE RITUAL

Any ritual is an opportunity for transformation. To do ritual, you must be willing to be transformed in some way. That inner willingness is what makes the ritual come alive and have power. If you aren't willing to be changed by the ritual, don't do it. Don't go through motions, for they will remain empty—if you are lucky. If you are unlucky, the energy of the ritual will work its transformation anyway, against your will, and not gently.

CLEANSING

Take time before the ritual begins to let go of concerns, anxieties, or preoccupations that might keep you from being fully present in sacred space.

Cleanse with water: take a bath; plunge into the ocean, a stream, lake, or river; take a sauna, or meditate on a bowl of salt water.

Cleanse with fire: burn sage in a shell and waft the smoke over your body, or do the same with a stick of incense or the light from a candle flame.

Cleanse with movement: stretch, breathe and let your breath move your body, tense and release each muscle, do yoga, or dance.

Cleanse with sound: breathe deep, let yourself become aware of any tensions or blocks in your body, and make sounds that release them. Experiment with sound: let it resonate in your belly, your heart, your forehead, your crown. Learn some simple voice exercises. Make big sounds. Make a sound you are not supposed to make.

GROUNDING

To ground means to connect with the earth, with our own centers, with the forces around us and the people who share our ritual. To be grounded also means to be in a particular energy state, calm and relaxed yet alert; aware of both your own internal energy and the group's energy. When you are grounded, your energy literally flows in a treelike pattern, up from the earth, through your body, and back to the earth. The following meditation establishes that pattern.[5] This meditation is one that I do every day and before any ritual work.

Notice your own energy. How do you feel in your body? In this space? In this circle? How connected or disconnected? How tired? How excited? Just observe your energy; don't try to change it.

Now imagine that you can extend your inner ears, as if you could listen to the energy of the group as a whole. Or imagine that you can feel it, smell it. How does the group feel? Is the energy, the excitement, high or low? What color would it be if you could see it? How would it sound?

Now take a deep breath, down into your belly. Place your hands on your belly. Feel it expand as you inhale, becoming round like the moon.

If you haven't stretched, do so now. Notice how your energy changes as your breath and body change. And notice how the energy in the room changes.

Now imagine your breath sinking down through your hips, your legs, your feet. Imagine yourself as a tree, rooted in the earth, with your breath sinking down through your roots. Feel your roots push down through the living soil. Let them connect you to this spot on the earth; let them tell you what it is like to be rooted here, to be linked to the plants, the animals. Let them tell you about the weather and the seasons.

Breathe deep, and feel your roots push deeper, down through rivers of clear, healing water. Let your roots push down through time, through bones and fossils and the memory of those who lived here before us. Ask their permission to root here in their land.

Breathe deep again, and let your roots push deeper, down through the bedrock, down into the core of fire at the heart of the earth. Feel the fire as pure, transforming energy. If you still carry any energy you'd like to let go of, let it go into the earth, to feed the earth, like compost. Let it go with a sound. Let yourself make a bigger sound.

Notice how your energy feels, and how the energy in the room feels. How did it change with your sound?

Now, breathing deep, draw energy up from the fire. Breathe it up. Feel it come up through the bedrock, through the bones and fossils. Feel it come up through the water, through the living soil of this place.

Feel it enter your body, with each deep breath. And each part of your body becomes relaxed, yet very alive, as the energy moves up through your feet and legs, up through your hips, up through your genitals and into your belly. Breathe it up into your heart and feel your heart expand; breathe it up into your arms and down through your hands. Bring it up through your neck and throat, and into the third eye in the center of your forehead. Breathe the energy up through the top of your head, up like branches that reach up to touch the sky and then sweep back down to the earth again, creating a circuit, a circle.

Notice how you feel in that circuit. You can make your branches as thick as you need them. If you need your own private space in this circle, imagine them thicker, like a protective filter that can screen out what you don't want and let in whatever you do. Or, if you feel disconnected, thin them out. Extend tendrils out to connect with others.

Notice how you feel now, and notice how the energy of the circle changed as we each adjusted our own. Reach out now, take hands. Feel the energy move around the circle.

Now feel the air on your leaves and branches, notice the energy of the sky. Feel the moonlight (or, in the day, sunlight; or, in the dark of the moon, starlight) shining down on your leaves, and breathe it in. Soak it up, eat it like a tree feeds on light. Bring it down through the top of your head, down through your heart and your hands and your belly, down through your legs and feet, down through all the layers of the earth until it reaches the core of fire at the center of the earth. Feel how the earth's fire and the sky's fire meet in you, how you are the link, the bridge between them. And notice how your energy feels now, and how the energy of the group feels.

Now let's breathe together, breathing in and out. Letting our breath become one breath, letting ourselves become one living, breathing organism.

And as you feel that sense of oneness, that link between us and earth and sky, gradually let it become a sound that carries our connection on your breath into the center of the circle, that lets our linked power rise up like a fountain and splash back on all of us.

(The group makes sound, which rises and eventually falls.)

Now ground the energy by touching the earth with your hands, or by lying down on it. Imagine letting the energy go back to the earth, for her healing and renewal.

Know that when you ground energy, you don't lose it. It is always there; you can draw it up again in an instant with a breath, but you don't have to carry it all yourself. Let the earth carry it for you.

Now notice how you feel, and how the energy of the group feels. What has changed?

CREATING SACRED SPACE

Ritual takes place in space and time marked off from the everyday. Established religions build churches, cathedrals, and temples to mark sacred space architecturally. Ancient earth traditions built stone circles or identified sacred groves.

Our rituals take place in a field or on the beach, in public halls or our living rooms. Rarely do we have the luxury of celebrating ritual in a space designed for our forms. The rituals itself must transform the space it is in.

PREPARING A SPACE

We might begin by asking, "What do we need to do to this space to make it feel like ours?" Maybe we want to open the windows, or turn off the fluorescent lights. Maybe we'll hang banners or scarves, or if we're outdoors, create altars in the four directions from stones or sand. We could carry incense or smoldering sage around the room to smudge it in Native American fashion, or sprinkle it with salt water.

BUILDING AN ALTAR

An altar is a place for sacred and symbolic objects: stones, shells, cloths, statues, mirrors, pictures, bones, crystals, feathers, candles, and whatever else you want. We can put altars in the four directions, and spend hours or days arranging altars that cover the entire periphery of the room. But my favorite way to build the altar is very simple.

Ask each person who comes to the ritual to bring something for the altar. Lay a cloth in the center of the circle, or if space is cramped, lay it in the north or east. Ask each person to place her or his special object on the altar, and perhaps to tell the group about it. Hearing the stories that go with the objects, we learn about each other's lives, and building the altar becomes a ritual in itself.

DRAWING THE CIRCLE/BANISHING

Witches traditionally "cast a circle": we draw a circle, usually with a wand or ritual knife, visualizing an energy boundary taking form. I generally see it in my mind as a barrier of blue flame. The circle symbolizes our equality. Everyone can see everyone else; there is no head nor tail, nor is attention focused on one speaker. Everyone can speak in the circle, and attention can move easily and naturally around.

The circle contains the energy we raise, so that it can stay focused and reach greater intensity. It also establishes protection from unwanted energies or entities, which can, in fact, be banished from it.

We might, for example, walk around our ritual space clockwise, the direction in which the sun moves and so the traditional direction for drawing in good influences. We can draw a circle, touching each of the walls and corners. Then we can say something like: "This circle has become a free space. All you voices, telling us what we can't do or be, what we should think or say, telling us we're bad or wrong or stupid or crazy—leave right now! In this circle we are each the Goddess, the God, the open channel for the moving energies of life. We are all fools together. Some of us may bring power through in noisy and flamboyant ways, and some of us may bring it through silently, in stillness. We honor both ways. Now, all you energies we don't need or want, begone!"

To increase the power of this banishing, accompany the words with shouts, yells, foot stomping, movement in counterclockwise direction (traditional for banishing), and/or drumming.

CALLING THE FOUR DIRECTIONS

When the space is formed and clear, we invoke into it the powers and qualities of each of the four directions, and the center. The pattern of the quartered circle, with each direction corresponding to elements, qualities, times of day, animals, tools, and powers is common both to Celtic Witchcraft and Native American and other earth-based traditions, although specific correspondences vary even among Witches, for they derive from the qualities of specific places. The correspondences acknowledge our basic life-support systems of air, fire, water, and earth.

I was taught that East corresponds with air, sunrise, and the mind; South with fire, noon, and energy; West with twilight and water; North with midnight and earth. In San Francisco, identifying the West with water makes sense; on the coast of Maine, the opposite might seem right.

To avoid religious wars over these issues, I like to call the directions in the following way. One person may lead, or the group may try this in ensemble fashion.

Begin a drumbeat or a clapped rhythm. Everyone turns to the East. The leader says: "Let's call the East. Breathe deep, open to the energies of the East, let them come through. And when a word, or a sound, or a movement, or a rhythm comes to you, call it out! Do it! Give it to the circle!"

People call out images or qualities: "Sunrise!" "Air!" "New beginnings!" "Change!" "Wings!" They dance or chant, make bird sounds or animal cries, just as they feel. The images that emerge may or may not fit with traditional correspondences; what matters is only that they express the energy of the moment.

When energy begins to die away in the East, the leader says, "Welcome, powers of the East!" Everyone then turns to the South, and repeats the process, going then to the West, the North, and the Center.

Because the powers of every direction like to be entertained, we often finish by chanting and dancing.

INVOKING

When we invoke, we name what we value, name it as sacred, and call it to us.

Religion, conveyed by images of the sacred, stories, myths, songs, ritual, is a powerful shaper of our internal patterns. Religion, of course, reflects the patterns and power relations within a culture, but it also translates those patterns into imagery and symbolism that move directly into our inner landscapes and give us the characters of our inner dramas. Religion makes visible the flow of power. When power relations change, so must mythology. New Gods and demons are born, who may then recreate our inner beings in their image.

The Goddesses, the Gods, embody the repeated relationships and actions of a culture. They are associated with colors, with animals, with places, plants, qualities, stories, all of which further describe the pattern.

For example, in the Yoruba traditions, Yemaya is the Goddess of the ocean, the great mother, nurturing, mysterious, fierce, giving, deep. She teaches us that powers that generate life are like the ocean. The birth force, the nurturing force, ebbs and flows, is sometimes placid and light-sparkled, sometimes powerful and imperious, sweeping all away; it has great mysterious depths; it is moved by the moon; it is unbounded in its power to create and unbounded in its power to destroy.

Historical Goddesses and Gods should not be confused with Jungian archetypes or mere psychological symbols. Nor are they innate structures of the human psyche. Jungian scholars are fond of using Greek Goddesses, for example, as givens of woman's nature. But all written history dates from late in human history, from transitional or clearly patriarchal times, when the major patterns of culture were already those of war. The God-desses and Gods reflect their cultures. Aphrodite, Hera, Athena embody ways of adapting female power to patriarchy. Only if we could recover their most ancient forms might we learn something about female power flourishing untrammeled.

The Goddesses and Gods are real forces: if you call them, they will come and rearrange the patterns of your life. They are bigger then you, although not separate from you; be prepared to change. For they are the mysteries that cannot be known intellectually but only through ourselves becoming what they are. They flow through us; we flow through them. We are generated by them, and generate them in turn. And when they become real in us, they also change with us, because we too are real. Our powers are not separate, and we continually renew the Gods.

To invoke the Goddess is to in some sense become possessed, moved by a deep pattern that reorganizes our being and actions. Suppose we invoke the Maiden, the New Goddess, young and wild. We may find ourselves beginning something new, giving birth to a project or under-taking that we've put off for a long time. Or we might invoke the Mother, the Full Moon, who is not necessarily the mother of children only, but also of culture. We may learn about sustaining and nurturing what we begin. And eventually, we will invoke the Crone, the Old Moon, the wise one, who knows about age, decay, and death, about letting go of what we have brought to birth so that something new can be born.

For the mysteries are always about the full circle, about grief and loss as much about ecstasy and creation. The lament for the dead is the coun-terpart of the song of the vulva. All that burgeons, swells, rises, sprouts, blooms, flows, and trembles in the growing time must later shrivel, wither, shrink, fall to earth, dry up, die, and decay. But it is that death that feeds the earth, that nourishes the seed, that covers the root from the frost, that makes way for something new to be born.

Or imagine that we invoke the God as food, as the seed that sprouts and reaches for sunlight; we learn what it is to stretch for new possibilities. The seed flowers and fruits and then gives itself away to be consumed, to feed; only so can its power be realized. When we call the God as grape or grain, we can expect to learn what it is we have to offer; to learn how to allow ourselves to be eaten. And when the new seed forms it goes underground, to wait in the dark earth until the sprouting time comes; so the Old God will guide us into the realms of the dark, where we learn patience, and silence, and that every end is followed by a new beginning.

Birth. Death. Rebirth. That is the pattern that shapes our lives today, amidst the computers and the VCRs, as it shaped us as wild animals on the open savannahs and as gardeners among the date palms of Sumer. It is the cycle of the wheat and the rose. It is the core of every ritual, which must itself begin, live, and come to an end if it is to fulfill its purpose.

We invoke in many ways: through poetry, song, chanting, drumming, quiet meditation, dance. But let us consider how to invoke the Goddess, the God, who is immanent in each of us, who is our inherent value, our right to be. This invocation can be very simple.

NAMING INVOCATION

Stand or sit in a circle. One person begins by singing her or his name to the circle. The circle sings it back. As we sing each name, we look at the person, honoring her or him as the embodiment of the sacred.

WORKING MAGIC

The heart of any ritual is work that realizes the purpose of the ritual. The work is carried out by directing energy through images. We create a mental image that represents the forces we want to generate or harmonize with. We might also find or make a physical object that somehow can carry those forces. Then we "raise power": we draw the vitality, the energy of earth, sky, and our own being up and imagine it filling, "charging," our image or object.

Many techniques exist for learning to sense and move energy. Here is one of my favorites.

ENERGY DANCE

One person can lead this ritual. Unless she or he can drum and talk at the same time, someone else should drum. Or if you don't have a drummer, use a long piece of music. Keep the rhythm or music continuous throughout.

Begin in pairs. Find someone you feel comfortable with. Stand together, and look into each other's eyes. Place one hand on your partner's belly. Breathe together. (Allow time to pass.)

Now bring your hand up to your mouth, and feel your own breath. Feel the very edge of your breath, the place where it stops. It's a very subtle boundary, a delicate shift—maybe only a sense of heat or moisture. Find it.

Now, continuing to breathe deeply, feel the edge of your partner's breath. Again, sense what a delicate edge it is.

The edge of your breath is very close to the edge of your aura, the body of energy that surrounds you. Now, still breathing deeply, move your hand and explore the edge of your partner's aura. Again, the boundary may be very delicate, may feel like heat or electricity or a slight tingling, may feel different to each one of you. Explore with both hands. Move around. (Allow time for exploration.)

Now imagine that you can pass the energy back and forth between you. Play with it: let it become a shape, a motion . . .

And when you feel the energy moving between the two of you, expand your group to include another pair. Play with the energy between the four of you, until it becomes as strong as it was in your pair . . .

And now expand your group to include another group of four. Play with the energy among the eight of you, until it becomes as strong as it was in your original pair . . .

And now expand your group so that it includes the whole circle. Play with the energy among all of you, until it also becomes as strong as between your original pair. (Let the group move and dance together.)

Now create a form together out of the energy. Imagine a tree in the center of the circle—the tree of life, rooting you all in the earth, carrying you up to the sky. Form the tree together. (People may use their hands to shape the trunk, branches, leaves.)

If you know someone who needs healing, or if you need energy for something in your life, imagine that person or that thing hanging in the branches of the tree. See it, feel it, imagine you can touch it there.

As you breathe, direct the energy with your hands and your voices into the tree. Imagine power flowing through you; imagine the tree glowing with power as your breath becomes sound.

(Let the sound grow, swell, peak, and die away. As it peaks, drums should stop. Taped music can be gently faded to let voices take over.)

Now touch the earth and ground the power.

CONE OF POWER

The more a group's energy can harmonize, can come to a single, focused point, the more powerful the work will be. In the Craft, we traditionally think of this process as raising a "cone of power." In building and charging the tree, you have just raised a cone of power. You can raise a cone to charge any image, object, or intention.

In the circle, hold hands. Breathe deeply, draw power up from the earth. Let it become sound, a long, sustained, wordless note. Imagine the energy circling around your feet, your bodies, rising even higher, circling and spiraling up ever tighter. Let it go until it reaches a peak, and as it peaks, hold the image in your mind.

(The energy will move in its own time. Don't push it. When it peaks, let it go. Imagine shooting it off as an arrow.)

Now ground the energy, reaching down and letting it flow back to earth, for her healing.

Always ground the energy whenever you raise it. If you don't, its power will dissipate and you will be left feeling irritable, incomplete, and fuzzy.

When a group becomes experienced at raising power, generally it will begin a cone with a chant and possibly free-form or spiral dancing. When the energy is high enough, the chant will spontaneously turn into wordless chanting and focused power.

GOING PLACES

Another aspect of the magic we do in ritual is exploring other dimensions of consciousness and going on journeys into other dimensions of reality. I used to call this pattern trance, but the word sets up troublesome expectations. People expect trance to be a state of mind totally discontinuous with the ordinary. Actually, trance is any state of consciousness when we are focused inwardly rather than outwardly. I am in trance writing this, as I would be if I were watching a movie, or jogging on the beach. My six-year-old friend Vanessa once said, "Trance is easy—you just go someplace in your imagination."

Story, myth, drama all take us into the collective landscape. What we often call guided meditation or guided fantasy can perhaps best be thought of as a particular form of storytelling, an improvised, oral poetry that creates a collective story we tell together. The stories that introduce each chapter of this book are an attempt to put on the page a story I might tell in ritual, with drumming and chanting and all of us moving, dancing, and weaving words together.

I used to suggest elaborate cautions and complicated inductions for trance work.[6] Over the years, I have found them unnecessary and often obstructive. The more we tell ourselves or someone else that the process is going to be safe, the more we subliminally suggest that we are embarking on a dangerous activity.

Now I begin by saying, "This is a story we tell and create together. We can take it any way we want to, change it, make it our own." People can speak, dance, move, yell, draw, and still remain in the story. We are not aiming at levels of trance so deep that we become unconscious, although occasionally we get them. (Don't worry—when the story is over, even those who are snoring will wake up.) Instead, we aim for levels of consciousness where our imagination flows freely, where we can invent and pretend as children do, and play. I also often tell people, "If nothing comes to you, make something up."

Some people experience the world visually, others take it in through hearing or kinesthetic feeling. Sound and movement make the story more vivid and put it into our bodies.

Two practices will assure safety and smooth transitions in and out of the story. The first is to "go places" from a physical location that is protected from dangers or sudden interruptions, and secured by a magic circle making it sacred space. The second is to come fully back from the story by undoing whatever it was we did to get in. If we took three deep breaths and imagined floating on the ocean waves, we take three deep breaths and float back. We also allow time to rest quietly and return fully to this reality. Saying your own name out loud and eating are also helpful.

The places we go may be our own internal landscapes of emotions and images, the realm of dreams and fantasies. With practice, we can go into the energy realms that move beyond the personal into the collective. What we create in the landscapes of the otherworld affects how energies move and what is ultimately created in the physical world.

To learn to travel safely in other worlds, we need landmarks. We find them by creating them, creating places of power and safety. Here is a story for creating your own personal place of power.

PERSONAL POWER PLACE

You may want to do this lying down, by taping the following story or asking someone to read it or tell it to you. Or you may find that you experience more intensely when you are standing up, moving around, drumming, shaking a rattle, dancing to music you like. Experiment—find what works for you.

Remember a time when you felt empowered. Breathe deep. Remember how you felt. How did you move? How did you breathe? Where do you carry that feeling in your body? Breathe into that place, let your breath carry you down like waves, flowing in and out, and let yourself rock on three deep waves, going deeper into yourself.

Feel the flame you guard. Feel the spark at the core. Enter into it.

It is like a landscape you can travel in. It is place of power alive in you. Breathe here, feel your power. This is your place—make it real.

Breathe deep—and turn to the East and notice what you see and hear and feel and sense, and what is there for you, in the East . . .

(Repeat to South, West, North, and Center.)

Look . . .

In the center of this place, your place of power, is a gift. Feel it, touch it, hold it, look at it. This is your gift, the gift you bring to the people. Feel how you move with it, dance with it, carry it in your place of power . . .

Your gift can sustain you. Your gift can heal you. Know how to use it.

Take your time, explore this place, find what is in it for you. (Allow time without words being spoken)

When you are ready to leave, return to the center of your place.

Breathe deep—and turn to the East and say goodbye and thanks. (Repeat to South, West, North, and Center.)

And say goodbye and thanks to anyone you have met here. Remember your gift and know how you will carry it back with you. And remember what is at the center of your place of power so you can find it again just by breathing and remembering.

Feel your breath now, like waves flowing in and out of that place in your body where you carry power. Feel yourself ride the waves. Say goodbye, and come back on three deep breaths, coming back, bringing back knowledge and memory and gifts, and feel yourself fully present again in this circle, in this room.

Breathe deep, move, stretch, open your eyes, and say your own name out loud.

Sharing with others what we find in our journeys creates strong connections. Take time to talk about your story. Write it down, or draw a picture of it. These stories, like dreams, fade quickly, so record anything you want to be sure to remember.

FEASTING

No ritual is complete without food and drink. Raising energy and going places makes people hungry. Providing food for each other is one tangible way of caring for each other and affirming our value.

Groups might want to discuss whether some or all of your rituals should be alcohol-free. When people are struggling with addictions, we can show caring for them by not providing temptations.

Feasting time is also a good time to offer thanks, to express gratitude for what has happened in the ritual or in our lives. Libations may be poured or offerings made. Food and drink that is shared can be blessed.

TRANSITION OF RETURN

Every pattern must have its completion; every boundary its opening. When the ritual is over, we must return to ordinary space and time. Food, drink, socializing, flirting, and kindly gossip help begin this transition. We might also take time to express commitments and name ways we will bring the magical work back into our daily lives. To make the transition complete, we must formalize it by saying goodbye to all the powers we have invoked: to Goddess, Gods, elements, and directions. This can be done, again, with poems, songs, chants, or improvised speeches. Or a group can develop a standard litany. The one I use to dismiss the elements and open the circle is an amalgam of a traditional Faery invocation I learned from Victor Anderson, a traditional Craft greeting, and a few lines I added myself:

> By the earth that is Her body,
> And by the air that is Her breath,
> And by the fire of Her bright spirit,
> And by the living waters of Her womb,

The circle is open, but unbroken,
May the peace of the Goddess go in your heart,
Merry meet and merry part, and merry meet again.

In the rituals that follow, when I say "open" or "open the circle," I mean to complete a transition of return and to say goodbye to all that has been invoked.

Our challenge is to bring the Goddess back to life, to envision, create, and inhabit the re-membered living body of the earth. The values and perceptions that arise from that reality are incongruent with the systems of domination. When we speak and act from those values, our behavior no longer fits the expected patterns of power-over. We might chant when the guards expect us to scream; we may say no when the boss assumes we will say yes. And we may say yes to patterns, to rhythms and visions we have been taught were impossible. We may make an alliance with someone we are supposed to fear. The Solstice may find us plunging into the ocean; the full moon may find us dancing on military land.

No one of these acts is, perhaps, very important; certainly no one act is enough. But their accumulation, their repetition, sustained over time, will change what the system expects, and the system will have to change in turn.

The Descent of Inanna, II:
The First Gate

When you hear the call
   from the Land Below
   it sounds both strange and familiar
Like the chorus of a song
   whose words you can't remember
Like the promise of a lover
   you don't completely trust
Like a dare
It frightens you
Entices you
All the treasures of the Upper World
   sunwashed groves
   sky-mirroring fountains
   hillock land, well-watered furrow
   and the moon's narrow boat
All of that seems so shallow
You have heard the call
   from the deep

You follow
Take a deep breath
   and go down
   feeling the weight of your body
      shift
   as you descend
   and the cool stone closes around
      you
Feel the heaviness of earth
   above you
And the snake guides you
Down
Down and down
   following the path
   that leads
   to the Land Below . . .

And at last you come
   to the first gate
Look at it
   see what it is for you

that walls off the depths
and blocks your way
What does it look like? Feel like?
What's there for you?
In front of the gate stands the
Guardian
   and you breathe deep
      and walk forward . . .
And the figure of the Guardian
   becomes slowly clear
You see what it is for you . . .
   human, animal, or some other
      creature?
You begin to see its body and its
      limbs,
   how it is clothed, its color
You begin to sense its size
   smell its odor on the air
You walk closer
Now you see its head, its face, its
      features
You can hear its voice, you look
   into its eyes
The Guardian speaks to you . . .
Breathe deep, and hear what it says

The Guardian says
      Who comes to the gate?
You answer
      It is I, Inanna
      I want to go
      to the Land Below
The Guardian shrugs
      Impossible
      You're not worthy
      You're not qualified
      You don't have the right
         credentials
      Who do you think you are?
You say
      I am the Queen of Heaven
The Guardian replies
      You're in the wrong place,
         then

So you set out to convince
   the Guardian

that you are worthy of this
  journey
You list your achievements
Your skills
  what you have produced, what
    you have accomplished
  what you have stored in the
    treasure house
  what's owed to you
The Guardian looks bored
The gate stays shut
And everything you name
  seems hollow
Behind you
  the way back has disappeared
At your feet
  even the snake looks dead, torpid
  her eyes glazed
You were stupid to come down here
  arrogant
  foolish
Now you're stuck
Your great achievements
  all the things you do
  to prove your value
  the emblems of your position
  mean nothing down here
They all drop away
  clatter to the ground
The snake rubs her belly on them
Her skin splits
She sloughs it
  sliding free
It lies in a heap like an old rag
She has shed
  as you have shed
The gate opens . . .

Beyond the first gate
  you wander
  light, unburdened
  with the simple confidence
  of a cat, or a child
That your life is worth something
Everything you pass, touch, see
  is outlined in the clear light

of wonder
that it should be
what it is
You need only be what you are
All that is, has its being in you

Go down
Continue
Down and down

The Sacred Spark: Reclaiming Value from the Judge

To heal the world, and heal ourselves in the process, we must understand both how we internalize domination and how we can foster freedom. We must understand how we internalize each aspect of the self-hater and develop techniques for ridding ourselves of internalized domination. We must envision situations of liberation so that we can create them.

In this and following chapters, I will examine each aspect of the self-hater in turn, along with rituals and ways to organize groups and structure relationships that undermine its power. To mount actions of resistance or create positive alternatives, we must organize, so I have focused on small groups, because they are in many ways ideal situations in which to foster change. A group becomes a community that can embody new values and strengthen us to change ourselves. In a small group we can each be seen, known, and valued as individuals. These insights are also relevant to families (another form of small group), child-rearing, and love relationships. In the small groups I discuss, everyone has equal official power, but these principles can also be adapted to hierarchical situations, where they can alleviate the worst abuses of power-over. These processes and rituals are not meant to be instant "cures" but to stir up emotions and energies and begin the process of change.

Power-over takes shape within us as the self-hater. The particular forms in which the self-hater may possess us mirror the five roles of the king: Judge, Conqueror, Master of Servants, Censor, and Orderer of the Universe. Each aspect carries with it an obsession with its own issues and a view of the self and the world. Each brandishes its own weapons and threats and makes its own particular offer, which presumably we cannot refuse. Each deludes us in its own way, and each contains some positive value we must reclaim.

POSSESSION BY THE JUDGE

The King is lawgiver and judge. When we are possessed by the Judge, we experience the self as an object to be judged, and we identify with the Judge and judge others.

The Judge demands obedience, allotting or withholding value according to how we meet imposed standards. In its possession, we are obsessed with questions of good and bad, right and wrong, purity and impurity. The delusion it perpetuates is that we have value when we meet the standards the Judge imposes.

Judgment implies a punishment system. The duty of the self as subject, like the duty of the law-abiding citizen, is to act so as to avoid being punished. Judgment can imply rewards, but they are generally of lesser importance. Law codes, for example, are not written to spell out "right-doings" and their rewards, but to list wrongdoings and their punishments. For example, from the Babylonian law code of Hammurabi, c. 1800 B.C.E: "If a hierodule, a nun, who is not living in a convent, has opened (the door of) a wineshop, or has entered a wineshop for a drink, they shall burn that woman."[1] Or, from the Bible: "He that smiteth a man, so that he die, shall be surely put to death" (Exod. 21:12).

The weapon of the Judge is punishment, inflicted upon the guilty, and the Judge determines our guilt or innocence. To be possessed by the Judge is to be possessed by guilt.

To instill guilt, immanent value must be destroyed. The body becomes a thing to despise. For value is embodied; we feel it in our physical being, in the pleasure inherent in taste and touch and movement, in the erotic tides that flood us, in the simple acts that assure survival.

To restore immanent value, we can begin by affirming the body, not denying its needs or desires. Pleasure, humor, laughter, fun, art, sex, food, and beauty are our liberators. Spirit is not seen as separate from matter. When the sacred is embodied, spirituality, the means we use to connect with the sacred, takes us into the body, not away from it. Traditionally, Witches quote the Goddess as saying, "All acts of love and pleasure are my rituals."[2]

Guilt is internalized hate of the self, instilled through fear of punishment. Guilt is the way we punish ourselves. The internalized Judge sustains the power of every coercive institution. Because punishment becomes self-administered, because it is a voice within us that is telling us we are bad, we are not aware of being externally controlled, and so we are helpless to challenge that control.

Guilt does not encourage us to change, to redress mistakes and act rightly; instead, it paralyzes us. When we believe that mistakes are irreparable, we cannot act, for no one can grow without making mistakes. We step aside from the responsibility of taking action.

Freedom from guilt alone, however, does not necessarily mean liberation. It can become simply a license to exploit. Relationships based on exploitation destroy immanent value. If I can feel comfortable living well when someone else suffers, I value that person's life less than mine. But the moment anyone's life is subject to rating on a scale of worth, we have all been devalued, for either each being has a value inherent to itself, or none do.

Between guilt and exploitation lies responsibility. When we know our own power-from-within, we become enabled to act. Instead of punishing ourselves we can ask the questions that lead to responsible action and constructive change.

JOURNAL MEDITATION ON GUILT

For a day, notice when you feel guilty, and about what. Ask yourself:

1. Who does this guilt serve?
2. Is there some real responsibility I need to take?
3. Is my guilt preventing me from taking action? How? From doing what?
4. What judgments am I making because of guilt? Are they sound? Unsound?

Think of a time in the past when you felt guilty.

1. How did you act? What did you do? What choices did you make? What responsibilities did you take? Fail to take? What happened?
2. If you could do it over again, how would you change what you did?

If guilt is the Judge's first weapon, observation is also part of the arsenal, another way of devaluing the self. A prison is constructed not only to confine its inmates, but to ensure that they can be continually watched. Foucault describes a model prison: "Each individual, in his place, is securely confined to a cell from which he is seen from in front by a supervisor; but their side walls prevent him from coming into contact with his companions. He is seen, but he does not see; he is the object of information, never a subject in communication."[3] The most effective surveillance is unverifiable: "The inmate must never know whether he is being looked at at any one moment; but he must be sure that he may always be so."[4]

We are aware that at any time we may be observed by a myriad of agencies and institutions devoted to rating, comparing, and keeping an eye on us. God has been portrayed to us as the Big Judge, always watching us, knowing our every sin. Even Santa Claus knows when you're awake, if you've been bad or good (so be good for goodness' sake).

Observations follow us in the form of records: school records, credit records, criminal records, IRS records. They may or may not actually determine the parameters of our lives, but when we believe they do, our fear keeps us controlled. "I can't write to my congressperson—I'll get my name on a list." "I cannot run naked into the ocean—the park police might see us." Because the possibility of surveillance, of sanctions, always exists, we have no clear way to know whether our fears are realistic or inflated. We protect the self in its vulnerability by hiding—but hiding always involves restriction. So we punish ourselves before we even have a chance to commit our crimes.

Surveillance is not limited to jail. Under the Judge's rule, we mount surveillance on ourselves, carefully noting any failure to meet the standards, any extra ounces on the thighs. "I looked down at parts of my body—at my wrists, at my ankles, at my calves. There was always something wrong with them, something that could be improved or perfected. How could I know then that the time would never come when I would regard myself as sufficiently slender? How indeed could I possibly imagine that one day I would weigh less than ninety pounds and still be ashamed to go out in a bathing suit?"[5]

The nasty magic of domination is done with mirrors. What is not mirrored in us, what is not seen, tends to disappear. To be constantly watched, not so our organic individual can be celebrated and nurtured, but so that we can be judged on how closely we approximate the rule, is a form of murder. What is murdered is what is unique in us, what does not conform. We see ourselves as we are seen: I am a size 16, I look in the mirror and cannot see my own flesh and gain any conception of its real curves and forms, cannot call them beautiful. Anorexia, like cancer, is a warning signal of the unhealthiness of the environment we are all subjected to.

SEEING AND VALUING EACH OTHER

To be valued, we must first be seen. In a nurturing family, children are seen and valued for being who they are, not for fulfilling their parents' desires or fantasies. Groups that restore immanent value provide a process by which we can be seen and known for who we are, not for the roles we play or the achievements we can count.

Hearing each other's stories is a powerful way of valuing each other. Sharing experiences, telling our stories is the basic change-sparking process of support groups, consciousness-raising groups, of Alcoholics Anonymous and the other Twelve-Step programs. Devoting time in a group to talk about our lives establishes that our lives are of interest, of value, to each other. In families and intimate relationships, mealtimes or bedtimes can become organic check-in times, when each person tells the story of her or his day without being judged or interrupted. Some families do this naturally, in the course of conversation. Others may find establishing a formal process helpful.

In Twelve-Step programs, immanent value is reinforced by anonymity. Participants are known only by first names. Originally this policy offered protection, since to be known publicly as an alcoholic or addict might be detrimental. But in practice, the impact of anonymity is far-reaching, for it takes the focus of the group away from members' positions in the world of status and hierarchy. Instead, each person can only be valued for who she or he is in the moment, and for the life experiences she or he brings to the group.

Oral traditions tell us that Witch covens' members had special names used only inside the group, and may or may not have known each other's outside identities. Anonymity was protective: you couldn't reveal your fellow coveners' identities under torture if you didn't know them. In actual practice, Witches who lived in small towns and villages, where everybody knew everyone else probably did know each other's identities, but formal anonymity did away with class divisions and roles, leaving all equal in the circle.

The following processes can help people feel seen.

CHECK-IN

Begin each meeting, or a family dinner, by going around the circle, giving each person a chance to share how she or he is feeling, what important events have occurred, and so on.

In larger groups, break down into small groups, pairs, or threes. Or check-ins can become symbolic. For example, you could ask: "If the way you feel now were a state of the weather, what would it be?" (Cloudy, calm, sunny and bright, stormy, and so on.) "If the way you feel now were an animal (or plant, color, place, something to eat, and so on), what would it be?" Or check in nonverbally—with a gesture, a dance, a movement—or draw or paint your check-in.

Ritual can also help us see and be seen. One of the patterns of ritual that affirms our unique value is naming.

Naming affirms value. When we name ourselves, or take on a new name, we may be seeing an aspect of our power that is new. My own name came from a dream about a hawk who turned into a wise old woman and took me under her protection. The star came from the card in the Tarot that symbolizes hope and the deep self. Taking on the name Starhawk for me meant taking on a commitment to the Goddess and to new levels of my own power-from-within. The name itself became a challenge.

A new name can affirm a new beginning or a transition. Names can be taken on for a temporary occasion: for a particular ritual, for a season, for an action.

SELF-NAMING

At a time of transition, let a name choose you. It may come in a dream, or a meditation, or suddenly pop into your mind. In sacred space, announce it to the four directions. Encourage your friends to use it. If it's right, it will stick.

GIVING NAMES IN THREES

When a new group comes together, break into groups of three. Tell stories about yourselves: what brought you to the group, what your journey has been, what race or class or religious background you come from, what transition you are undergoing. Each person in the triad should have a protected time to talk without being challenged, questioned, or interrupted. Five minutes each is a surprisingly long time. Then take a few minutes to discuss what common threads and differences you hear in your stories.

Now, two of you focus on the third member of your group. Choose a name for her or him, or choose an epithet, something to add to her or his name, as in "Catherine the Great." When you finish with the first person, recombine and do the same for each member of your group.

Bring the whole group back together. Go around the circle. Each person sings her or his name, stepping forward into the circle and expressing its power with movement or dance. The group sings the name back.

THREE-WORD DESCRIPTIONS

The name-giving can be varied by giving each person three descriptive adjectives instead of a name. The adjectives should be followed by *woman* or *man,* so that a person might step forward and say, for example, "I am Carol, a brave, sensual, searching woman," or "I am Bill, a curious, cheerful, funny man."

LITANIES

A similar process can be used to build a personal litany. Give each person a line of praise that reflects her or his story and begins with the words *I am* . . . or *I* . . . . When the circle comes together, say or sing the lines in turn so that they create a litany: the Goddess, the God speaking.

"I am facing my own fears."
"I weave with words."
"I am the one at peace with herself."
"I am turning my rage into my power."
Over time groups might come back together and tell the stories of their

ongoing changes, and receive new lines so that each person develops an individual litany.

"I am stepping back on my own ground and finding myself."

"I live in the present as if it were the future, and love carries me through."

"No one can stop me from doing what I need to do."

"I drum the living heartbeat of the earth."

STORY AND MYTH

Storytelling is the heart of ritual. When an experience becomes a story, it is passed on, given away, made sacred. The story intensifies the value of the events that have passed. Pain and rage can be released, isolation broken, triumph and ecstasy celebrated. What was a singular experience becomes woven into a larger context.

TELLING PERSONAL STORIES

Whenever possible in ritual, incorporate the telling of your personal stories. This can be done in many ways.

Go around the circle, or break into threes, giving each person a protected time in which to talk. You might choose a particular topic, as feminist consciousness-raising groups do, perhaps looking at the list on page 288 for suggestions.

Ask one person, or several, to prepare a story for a particular ritual that reflects focus of the ritual. For example, for a ritual of healing for AIDS victims, someone who has the disease or who has lost a lover might tell his or her story.

People can respond in many ways: through silently listening with deep attention; with sounds of appreciation, release, and power; or by drumming, chanting, and dancing, or enacting the story as it is told. Storytelling thus becomes collective improvised theater.

TALK-STORY

The whole group drums or claps to create a sustained rhythm. The story is told over the rhythm, and can easily move back and forth into chanting and dancing.[6]

Telling our personal stories in ritual also moves us close to the realm of myth. When we identify with a mythic character, the events of myth become paradigms that can carry us through times of danger and trouble, and that link the events of our lives to processes that go beyond the personal. Thus, the journey of the Israelites to the promised land became a mythic metaphor for the journey north to freedom of slaves on the Underground Railroad. The slaves that fled saw their journey as part of a great project of human freedom enacted again and again throughout history, in which they had allies even in the roots of the very religious tradition invoked to justify their enslavement. Today, the Underground Railroad, the bravery of Harriet Tubman—called Moses—and the dedication of those who offered sanctuary take on a mythic dimension that is drawn upon by the sanctuary movement for Central American refugees.

Myth gives us a set of organizing symbols that places our own lives and events in a context that stretches back to the past and forward to the future, that links us to a broader community and deepens the meaning of our lives. Our personal stories can become the ground of the new myths we need in order to create the world anew.

PERSONAL MYTH

Tell your own story as if it were a myth. Which Goddess, which God are you? What challenges have you faced? What powers have helped you? Held you back? Talk-story your tale, and let the group chant, drum, and dance with you. Let the story change as you tell it, give it a life of its own. Maybe it ends differently; maybe you see possibilities you never suspected.

Over feasting, others can share what they identified with in your tale, and what differences they see.

Afterward, you might want to write your story down, draw pictures of it, or express aspects of it in some other creative way.

MYTH STORY

Tell a myth as if it were a personal story. The group may want to prepare for this by reading a variety of myths and discussing them. Choose one that seems to fit the transformations people are going through. Change elements if they don't feel right. For example, I often tell the story of Persephone's journey into the underworld not as a tale of rape and abduction, but as a tale of exploration, in which she chooses to go to the world of the dead to learn what is there. (This version is probably true to the earliest versions of the story.)

The stories of Inanna that link chapters in this book are other examples. They can be adapted and used in the process described next.

In sacred space, one person may begin the talk-story. Others might drum, chant, or make rhythms. (Taped music can be used if you have no drummers in your group.)

Some of you may be tale-tellers, some musicians or singers, some dancers. You may decide these roles ahead of time, or let inspiration flow spontaneously. You might make masks for different characters, that can be left on the altar to be picked up, worn, and put down as inspiration strikes and wanes.

Tell the story in the second person: use *you*, not *she* or *he*. Leave enough spaces in the telling so that people have a chance to experience the events described, to visualize and feel them. Encourage people to make sounds, to move and dance. Let energy rise and be sure to ground it. Have a clear way to bring people back out of the story, as often this work induces a trance state. (Some people may even fall asleep, go so deep they cannot remember anything about the story. They may feel disappointed afterward, but they may have been experiencing the story on a deeper level. Or it might not have been the right story for them at this moment.)

MYTHMAKING

Use the process just described, with a tale you create collectively that expresses your challenges and transitions. Let new myths evolve.

To be disconnected from our past, our history, is to be disempowered. In consumer culture, we consume time and forget what has gone before. We do not value the stories, the experiences, of the elders. But when we devalue their lives, we devalue our own, for at best, we can hope to some-day become old. The elders may offer us perspectives we need in times of change.

One of the most powerful rituals I have experienced was not meant to be a ritual at all. In June of 1983, hundreds of us were again in jail for blockading the Livermore Labs. We became locked in a solidarity battle with the presiding judge, and what we had expected to be a short stay became a prolonged seige. By the fourth day, morale was dropping. We were cold, hungry, and beginning to fear that we would lose.

Many older people had blockaded with us. That night, in our women's section (men were held separately), a group asked the older women to speak to us. One by one, the old women got up and told their stories to the assembled crowd. One said, "I'm a lifelong Republican; I've never done anything political before. But when I look at my grandchildren, I just had to do something. And I'm not leaving here until we win this one!" Another, a lifelong activist, told us stories of labor organizing in the thirties. As one woman after another spoke, we began to see our situation differently, not as an isolated event but as part of a long, ongoing struggle, a continuous history of which we were the latest chapter. The spirit of the group changed and commitment deepened.

TALES FROM THE ELDERS

Include older people in actions, rituals, and communities. In times of stress, trouble, or lack of clarity, ask them to share their stories (which is different from asking for advice).

Collect the stories of your own grandparents, older friends, of people whose lives inspire you and of those whose lives serve as a warning. Preserve them in some way: tape-record them or write them down, or simply remember them.

In sacred space, tell a tale told by your grandmother, bake your aunt's favorite recipe, tell your grandfather's favorite joke. During rites of passage or children's celebrations, at birthday parties or at bedtime, tell them the elders' tales. Teach their songs; preserve their struggles.

Cultures can effectively teach their values to children in two ways: by example and through stories. Children love stories; the most hardened TV addicts listen to them enthralled.

CHILDREN'S STORIES

Make a ritual out of the traditional bedtime story. You and your child can together create a sacred space. Your child might enjoy making an altar to keep special things on. But don't stress the forms; if it's not fun, forget it.

Put your child to sleep with stories. It's the best possible magical training. Some ideas might be:

Make your child the main character, under another name. Tell about her or his day, or some major life change, as if it were a myth or fairy tale.

Tell traditional myths or stories about the Goddesses and Gods as if they had happened to personal friends of yours.

Tell an ongoing story, with a chapter each night that ends in a cliff-hanging predicament.

Let your child finish the story, or ask her or him to tell you a story.

Include children in ritual by telling them the story of the season. Create special stories for special times, with props: for example, to describe how day and night are balanced in length at the spring equinox, one Pagan mother paints an egg half black and half gold.

VALUING EMOTION

No army can function if its soldiers are fully conscious of their fear, if they break down and weep in grief at the destruction of their comrades or in sorrow for the wounds of their enemies. Nor can the structure of obedience withstand open expression of rage or irritation at commands from above. And so the Judge must control our emotions, especially those, such as anger and rage, that might undermine our obedience. Anger is a force within us pushing for our liberation, but it is seen as being a mark of our badness. Women have had to learn to value our rage and not be deterred by the labels and judgments of a system interested in suppressing us.

To value each other, we must affirm each other's feelings, the nice ones and the nasty ones. Our thoughts may be confused, our analyses flawed, our conclusions faulty, and our reasoning warped, but our feelings are always valid. If you feel something, the feeling is real. We can acknowledge each other's feelings, even when we might argue with the assumptions upon which they are based or the actions that spring from them.

Valuing emotion does not mean, however, saying in a calm expressionless voice, "Yes, I can understand how you might feel that way." It means creating an atmosphere in which people can cry, laugh, yell, scream, become ecstatic, or express despair. It means being willing to change or at least to reconsider behavior that makes someone else feel bad. It means asking questions that evoke feelings, and understanding that often we feel several contradictory things at once.

Rage is survival. It arises in us when life is threatened or attacked; it gives us amazing energy. At this time in history we are always under attack, from the systems outside us that would control us, from the self-hater within us. Every city is literally a target for missiles. To find liberation, we need to awaken our anger. We need rituals of rage, and we need the support of others to grieve our losses.

But rituals must not leave us stuck in rage and grief. When the great energies are unleashed, they need transformation, for rage carries with it the potential of passion, ecstasy, creation. So ritual becomes a catharsis, a cleansing that unlocks our potential for renewal.

ANGER RITUAL

You can do this alone, but it is most powerful in a group.

Begin with a personal meditation.

When you are furious, or when you are depressed, numb, whiny, or feeling dull, ask yourself:

1. What am I angry about?
2. In what ways am I under attack? Threatened?

3. What losses have I suffered? Am I faced with?

Write out the answers.

As a personal meditation, you might simply read the list over each night for a week, saying, "I am angry about———, and I have a right to be angry." What do I want to change? Again, read the list over for a week, saying, "I have the power to change———." Do something, no matter how small, to set that change in motion. For example, if you are angry about nuclear war, tell yourself, "I have the power to change the threat of nuclear war," and then write an angry letter to your government representative.

For a ritual, the group should first find an outdoor place where you can make noise and dig a pit. Collect stones. Also bring to the circle a shovel and a bowl of small fruit such as grapes or berries. If you cannot find such a place, you can do this indoors with small pebbles in a large pot, or with pellets of paper and a fire.

Create sacred space. (In these rituals, when I say, "Create sacred space" or "In sacred space," I mean that you should do whatever seems appropriate to cast a circle, call in the four directions, invoke the Goddess, Gods, or whatever powers you want to work with.)

One person picks up a stone and says to it, "I am angry about———and I have a right to be angry." Start in a low tone of voice, and repeat the phrase until you can shout it out loudly and powerfully. The group encourages the person by drumming, clapping, shouting her or his name, or calling out "Say it louder! Say it stronger!" When your rage is running freely, throw the stone into the pit.

Then someone else takes a turn. Continue as long as the need lasts and the energy can be sustained.

Go around the circle again. One by one place a shovelful of earth on the stones, saying "I have the power to change———." (If you're using a fire, place a twig of cedar or a sprig of sage on the fire.) The circle responds, "We bless your power."

When all have spoken, dance, chant, and raise a cone of power to give each person strength to make changes.

Ground. Pass the bowl of fruit around. Each person takes a piece of fruit, and shares an image of change. Say it as if it has already occurred. For example: "The earth is at peace; I see my children playing in the yard and I feel happy and confident for their future"; "I am friends with Laura again, and we can laugh about this fight"; and so on.

Eat the fruit. End, and open the circle.

EXPRESSING CARE

To be cared for establishes immanent value when care is offered without judgment. Groups that restore value offer care not dependent on members' performance or achievements. One example is Alcoholics Anonymous, whose success rests on its refusal to play Judge. The principle that "any alcoholic is a member of our society when *he* says so" gives power and immanent value back to the individual. It lays the only possible basis upon which a person can willingly give up the false power and release from pain that a drug affords.

"At one time, every AA group had many membership rules . . . beggars, tramps, asylum inmates, prisoners, queers, plain crackpots and fallen women were definitely out. Yes sir, we'd cater *only* to pure and respectable alcoholics. Any others would surely destroy us. Intolerant, you say? Well, we were frightened."[7] The rules changed because "experience taught us that to take away any alcoholic's full chance was sometimes to pronounce his death sentence, and often to condemn him to endless misery. Who dared to be judge, jury and executioner of his own sick brother?"[8]

Care is most meaningfully expressed in concrete ways. Sharing resources equally, whether money, attention, time, or food, is a tangible expression of care. In a coven, participation in ritual is a form of care. In a business, participation in profits may be how care is expressed. Pay scales, benefits, job security are all clear measures of how each individual is valued. No verbal expressions of equality can outweigh or disguise unequal economics.

Money is always a highly charged issue; for a group to handle money in ways that are liberating, members need to openly discuss how to share both responsibilities and remuneration. I belong to a collective in the San Francisco Bay Area called Reclaiming, that teaches magic and ritual, puts on public rituals, and publishes a quarterly newsletter. At one period in our history, teachers were paid from the class fees they collected, and donated money to cover the printing costs of the newsletter. Eventually, the people who worked on the newsletter became very angry because they were not getting paid anything. Over months of discussion, we hammered out a new money policy, by which all members of the collective shared all the money taken in each quarter according to how many hours each of us had worked. The policy was cumbersome, and pay was only a token at best, but the policy made the necessary statement that all collective members were equally valued.

Giving each other gifts is a ritual way of expressing care. Gifts help mark points of transition and changes of state. Traditional times for giving gifts are at entry into a community, at initiation, at the year's transition points such as the Winter Solstice, as part of rites of passage, at ending and beginning times.

Each Christmas season we experience how gift giving deteriorates in a consumer society into the grossest form of materialism. To reclaim gift giving as a sacred act, we can give gifts of power, which may or may not be material. Generally, they are not consumer goods but things whose value is symbolic rather than measurable in dollars: rocks, shells, curious found objects, food, acts of consideration, children's drawings, bones, flowers, herbs.

GIFTS OF POWER

When someone you care about is undergoing a transition, taking on new responsibilities or power, and perhaps doubting her or his abilities or value, give that person a power gift. In sacred space, put her or him in the center of the circle. Each person in the group can give a gift, which may be simply a symbolic statement, an active wish: "I gift you with the ability to stay grounded under pressure in your new job."

Something tangible may or may not accompany the wish. "I give you this special button to carry in your pocket for your first day at school. It came off Grandma's coat, and I want you to remember how much she loves you."

Chant the person's name, hug, and feast.

GIFTS FOR THE NEWBORN

A similar ritual forms part of a welcoming ceremony for a newborn baby. The child is held in the center of the circle, and each person expresses gifts of qualities she or he hopes for the child. These are most powerful when they reflect some quality the giver has. So before beginning, allow some time for reflection. One person might say, "I give you the quality of perseverance against difficulties." Or, "I would like to give you the benefit of all my experience in rotten relationships—but I know I can't, so I give you the hope that you can always remember to love yourself."

A candle is passed around to be held as each gift is expressed. Later, snuff it (don't blow it out—that dissipates the energy) and save it to burn during future celebrations in the child's life, or when she or he is in danger.

GIFTS OF CHANCE

When a group is undergoing a transition, especially when it is dissolving, one way to ease the parting is to give gifts. Each person brings one gift, something symbolizing what she or he has been given by the group. In sacred space, they are placed on the altar. At some point in the closing ritual, each person in the group takes a gift at random, without knowing who it is from. As you feast, people can acknowledge their gifts and tell what they represent.

By giving up control, letting randomness reign, we invoke a mystery. The gift becomes a "reading"—something that gives us information about our state and the forces around us. It forges a special link between giver and receiver.

CHOOSING STANDARDS

To refuse to play judge does not mean a group cannot have standards or expectations. The Judge, by casting everything in terms of good/bad, valuable/valueless, actually prevents us from making sound judgments. The Judge's own real interest is not in improving quality but in establishing superiority. Possessed by the Judge, we act in subtle ways to keep others inferior. The presence of the Judge's standards is a sure guarantee that people will not do their best work, solve problems effectively, or allow their creativity to flourish.

When we accept that each person has an inherent value, then we can choose what standards or expectations make sense for a group's purpose. A family may expect children to wash dishes and clean their bedrooms. A support group for incest survivors may expect members to respect confidentiality and to attend meetings every week. A computer software marketing collective can expect members to carry out projects responsibly.

We are so accustomed to systems of punishment that we find it hard to imagine how to impose standards or protect our concerns without sanctions, threats, or moralizing. The Judge's language is the first that leaps to our tongues when we need to offer criticisms or complaints. But when we speak with the Judge's voice, we actually complicate situations and subvert our chances of resolving difficulties. For whatever the Judge seems to be saying, the underlying message is always "I am superior to you."

Consider the difference in the following two statements: "The bathroom floor is dirty again! You're just not a responsible person—I don't understand how you can consider yourself an adult when you ignore filth."

"The bathroom floor is driving me crazy—it just makes me feel sick when I walk in there. I hate living like this!"

The first speaker uses the condition of the bathroom floor to justify the underlying message, "My value is more than yours." The second speaker, who might be equally as loud, is vulnerable rather than self-righteous, and conveys a different message: "This is a problem that is causing me great distress."

We rightfully feel resentful when told, however subtly, that we are of lesser value than someone else. We tend to fall into our usual patterns, either complying resentfully (and often reverting quickly back to our usual sloppy habits), rebelling, manipulating, or withdrawing. None of these tactics will get the floor cleaned consistently: they will, however, consistently confirm the first speaker's sense of superiority. And so the game goes on.

In contrast, we mostly do not enjoy causing other people distress—and we feel good when we can solve problems. The second speaker admits her or his inability to control us, and by so doing empowers us to empathize and commit ourselves to solving the problem. Our incentive to clean the floor is increased when we can do so without feeling that we are knuckling under to someone else's control.

I am not suggesting that we merely change how we phrase complaints. What needs to change is not just our words but our emotional need to prove ourselves superior. But of course, we can only let go of the need to be above others in a context in which all of us as equals have inherent value. As we strive to create that context, our usual postures and moralizing will begin to sound incongruent, out of place. We will begin to hear the Judge's voice, instead of not even noticing its presence because its tones are so familiar.

In families, adults do have power over children: we control their resources; we are bigger, usually stronger, and if not smarter generally more knowledgeable about the world. We also need to impose responsible limitations that children may not understand. We know why a two year old should not run into the street, and why a twelve year old should not experiment with cocaine. They may not, and letting them learn by experience may leave us with only a corpse to value.

Authoritarian patterns have been our models for child rearing. When child rearing is conducted on authoritarian principles, the Judge takes possession early, often before we learn speech. Because judgment is imposed by those who presumably love us, and whom we must love if we are to survive, it is much harder to resist than direct, visible oppression from outside. If someone hates us and judges us as being of lesser value, we can hate back and reject their value system. If someone is kind to us, gives to us so that we become dependent, and judges us negatively, we are very vulnerable to that judgment.

Psychoanalyst Alice Miller, in *For Your Own Good,* examines the authoritarian underpinnings of child rearing and their destructive effects. "Since training in many cultures begins in infancy . . . this early conditioning makes it virtually impossible for the child to discover what is actually happening to him."[9]

Miller quotes a succession of "experts" on the best means for training children to respond to the voice of the Judge: "It is quite natural for the child's soul to want to have a will of its own, and things that are not done correctly in the first two years will be difficult to rectify thereafter. One of the advantages of these early years is that then force and compulsion can be used. . . . If their wills can be broken at this time, they will never remember afterwards that they had a will, and for this very reason the severity that is required will not have any serious consequences."[10]

The horror of the "poisonous pedagogy" she describes is that those who administer it are not exceptionally sadistic, abnormal parents. On the contrary, it has been considered not only the norm but the ideal, the standard of aspiration, in child rearing. And the patterns of domination we first experience as children are repeated, confirmed, and mirrored by the shape of every institution of society we find around us.

A different principle upon which we might base both interactions with children and adults is the realization that actions have consequences. What we do or fail to do affects how others feel and how they respond to us. If we don't wash our dishes, the people around us become angry and distressed—and when the people around us are unhappy they make our lives unpleasant.

We do children a favor by teaching them this lesson early. For part of our personal power is our power to affect others. Unless we realize that what we do has an impact on others, we cannot truly be free, for freedom is never the complete absence of restrictions but rather the ability to make the choices that will best serve our interests. Any choice is also a limitation, for it eliminates other possibilities.

We can empower children—and adults—by giving them choices whenever possible and by being clear and direct about how their actions affect us and what the real limitations of choice are. There is no moral or safety reason why seven-year-old Jeremy should not constantly quack like a duck, but if he is, in reality, driving me crazy, I can clearly offer him a choice: "Make your duck sounds somewhere else, or stay with me and make conversation." If all feelings are valid, so is my irritation. I am not suppressing his creativity by asking him to be quiet; I am teaching him that he is a powerful person, that the way he uses and directs his energy affects others, that some ways of using energy will draw people to him and others will drive them away, and that he can make choices about what he wants.

We also empower children by treating them with the respect and consideration we want in return. We don't call them names, or make fun of them, or denigrate their abilities. We don't tell them they are awkward, ugly, clumsy, stupid, or otherwise attack their self-esteem. Nor do we harp on our own superiority to them. Children notice that we are larger, more skilled, sophisticated, and generally more solvent than they are, and these facts are already a source of great frustration to them. We don't have to rub it in.

When the Judge is internalized, we may hear all feedback about our impact on others as attacks on our worth. "We are so used to perceiving everything we hear in terms of moralizing rules and regulations that sometimes even pure information may be interpreted as a reproach and thus cannot be absorbed at all."[11]

A woman and man are making love. She says: "Gently, lightly, and a little lower down." He says, "Goddamn it—you always have to be so critical! Nothing ever pleases you! Well just forget it, then! I'd rather go to sleep." Variations on this sad theme are played out continually between lovers, friends, partners, coworkers, members of groups. The Judge distorts our hearing, makes us respond to the suggestions, needs, and wishes of another as to attacks on our worth. When we lash out in response, communication becomes impossible, and our partners are left with the frustration of not being heard. Such frustration can indeed lead them to form negative judgments about us—confirming what we suspected all along.

We also have a responsibility not to let ourselves fall passively into the role of the Judged. We do not have to accept others' evaluations of our worth, nor are we obligated to believe in their superiority. Whichever role we are assigned, we can stop the game by refusing to play our expected part. When someone suggests that our recent behavior has undone our right to exist, a useful question to ask is, "What do you want? What can I do to make the situation better?" This often reduces the Judge's voice to silence, because what the Judge really wants—but cannot admit—is to make you feel bad, not to get the floor clean. When we feel secure in our inherent value, we do not have to argue about our worth as human beings. Instead, we can attempt to solve the problem.

The Judge must also attack creativity, for the artist threatens the rule of the King. Art asserts the immanent value of things: color, shape, form, the space and flow and tone of music, the rhythm, sound, and meaning of words, the process of creation itself.

But in this society, art has become a commodity, and so the power of the Judge comes into play, wielding the carrot of praise and the stick of blame. The work of art becomes valued for its success as a commodity. Artists are only taken seriously if they achieve the tokens that mark success—money, recognition—and then are sometimes taken seriously far beyond any semblance of reason.

The adulation and praise heaped on the few successes maintains the myth that everyone can make it, that if you don't the flaw is in you, not the system. Esteem, like capital in Marx's vision, becomes concentrated in fewer and fewer hands.

Creative artists are forced to compete for esteem as they do for material rewards, and at the same time may judge themselves harshly for feeling competitive. An artist client of mine described how she felt when her friends were sharing their work. "I saw Anne's slides—and they were good. I guess I felt competitive. And I felt really bad about myself—I don't want to be jealous of her work. But my work seems worthless to me." In a society ruled by the Judge, to be a creator is to live by praise or blame. "If my work is good, then I am okay, worthy to exist, to create. If my work is bad, or mediocre, or simply not 'great,' if I am to be not one of the few stars who make it into the history books—then I am worthless."

What needs to be reclaimed from the Judge is the ability to make choices and decisions, without each judgment becoming a pronouncement of our inherent worth. When we have inherent value, then our work may be more or less effective, moving, or powerful, without calling into question our own right to be. Only then can we ask ourselves the questions that help us truly improve our work and our lives.

As a writer, I continually question my own work. When I began writing many years ago, the voice in my head kept up a running commentary of judgment: "This is good. This is lousy! People will hate it. People will love it!" I often found myself blocked, depressed, exhausted. Now, when I write, I still hear "voices," but their comments are in the more productive form of questions: "Is this what I really want to say? Is it clear? Does it flow?" As I hear them I feel my own power-from-within, my ability to use words effectively. Yet when I was held by the Judge's voice, I literally could not ask these questions. I could see the work—and myself—either as wholly good or bad, worthy or unworthy, and anxiety attached to the judgment made editing and rewriting an excruciatingly painful process.

CREATIVITY EXERCISE

Choose some creative activity that appeals to you: writing, painting, dancing, and so on. Set aside some time to do it.

Notice what judgments you make about your own work. Are they helpful? Do they deepen the work? Block it? What do you fear? Write the judgments and criticisms down as they arise. Periodically burn the paper. Keep creating.

ROUNDS FOR GROUPS ABOUT JUDGMENT

In a group, give each person protected time in which to speak to the following questions:

1. What judgments do you imagine others are making about you? Ask for feedback.
2. What are the spoken or unspoken standards of the group? How do you judge yourself?
3. Share the results of your creativity meditation. What internal dialog does the Judge whisper to you? Ask the group to suggest questions that would actually be helpful to your art. Write them down.

PRIDE RITUAL

Create a ritual circle. Each person should bring something to share that you have created or that represents something you have done.

One person at a time goes to the center of the circle, and describes what she or he feels proud of. The group can show its appreciation in many ways: singing your name, chanting, drumming, clapping, anointing with scented oil, and so on.

Celebrate by feasting. Like Pagans of old, pass around the ritual cup (which may hold juice or water if people in the group prefer not to drink alcohol), and take turns boasting. Notice how you feel when you allow yourself to be proud without judging yourself negatively.

If anyone in the group finds this impossible to do, encourage the person to write out or say the negative judgments that arise. Shake rattles. Waft smoke of sage and cedar over her or him. Splash the person with cold water. Burn the judgments in the fire, and keep on until the person is able to share pride.

RESTORING AN ETHIC OF INTERCONNECTION

Dethroning the Judge does not mean throwing away ethics. The ethics of immanence are based on the recognition that all is interconnected. When the earth lives in us, as we in her, our sense of self expands until we can no longer believe in our isolation. When we practice magic—the art of seeing the connections that run deeper than the visible surface—we know that no act is out of context. If we participate in a Native American sweat lodge, we are obligated to aid their struggles for land and treaty rights and their battles against forced relocation. We have sunk a spirit root into the living soil of their community. They have fed us. But to be fed without feeding, to take without contributing, is not a road to power-from-within. We cannot grow in strength through being parasites. If we adopt ritual trappings without concern for the daily realities of those we learn from, we become spiritual fungi.[12] But power-from-within derives from integrity, from our recognition of the context of every act, from a consistency between what we say, believe, and do.

We must reclaim justice from the Judge. The immanent value of the individual cannot be separated from a concern for social justice. For that concern to root itself in reality, it must be expressed in action.

Any group that claims to offer liberation or spiritual growth must at least be concerned with minimizing the harm it does. It will not support itself by investing in South African diamonds, nor will it instigate financial pyramid schemes. With the Judge's attacking voice stilled, we can face and ask difficult questions: How do our acts affect the poorest third of humanity?[13] How do they affect the health of the environment? The lives of other creatures? The answers will guide our struggles for justice and lead to acts of healing.

Value is embodied not just in the individual but in the greater earthbody, the complex organism in which all creatures are cells. Immanent value cannot exist out of context, as individuals cannot exist outside of the web of beings, elements, and relationships that sustain life. We cannot truly value our selves, our lives, unless we value what supports life.

To restore our own value, we must work to restore value to the earth and to the animal, plant, and human communities that are a part of her. When we take action in support of our ideals, we find our sense of worth deepens. For immanent value is embodied in the whole context that supports the diversity of life. We cannot liberate ourselves unless our lives and our work are directed toward sustaining the balance of life.

The Descent of Inanna, III:
The Second Gate

The Second Gate is fear
When you go down far enough
  it arises
  wearing a helmet, armor
  wearing an enemy face
  carrying weapons
  it blocks the gate

Fear says
      Go back
And you hear what it threatens you with
  if you go on

Fear says
      Turn around
And you hear what it offers you
  if you obey

Fear says
  something you alone can hear
  and you know what it is

Choose

To go on
  you must take off your clothes
Lay down the cloak that keeps out the
  cold
  and the shield that turns the spear
  and the armor that turns the arrow's
    point
Take off your breastplate and helmet
Fear doesn't go away
  but you walk toward fear
  naked
And the gate opens

Past the Second Gate you dance
  fearless in the open
  your skin one living organ
  that embraces air

Risking the Boundaries:
Dethroning the Conqueror

What we value, we attempt to protect, including ourselves. We cannot be free when we live in fear. To feel valued, we must feel safe.

In the dismembered world, however, our model for safety and protection has been the king as war leader. We could call this entity the Conqueror. The king justifies his conquests as defense, so the internalized Conqueror could also be called the Defender against Enemies, or the Avenger.

The king's primary purpose is to defend the realm against enemies, to avenge hurts and right wrongs. Without an enemy, there is no king. When we are possessed by the Defender, we see enemies everywhere, and any difference, any disagreement, becomes the occasion for defining the other as the enemy.

Clearly, the personality structure that is shaped by the Defender/Avenger is a useful one for soldiers in war. It is deliberately instilled in men in basic training should they somehow have failed to catch it from the culture. "My military father began constructing the face of The Enemy within my mind quite early. As a boy in the Panama Canal Zone, he warned me about the head-hunters. He even showed me a shrunken head. Man, I wasn't about to go outside the gates into that world! . . . A few years ago. . . , I ventured back to Panama. I asked a Panamanian historian how the head-hunters were doing. He laughed. . . . That's what they tell U.S. children to control their natural curiosity about our people. We don't have any headhunters. But we are black."[1]

Soldiers, who like the rest of us have been taught since childhood that killing is wrong, must be trained to kill. "The basic aim of a nation at war in establishing an image of the enemy is to distinguish as sharply as possible the act of killing from the act of murder by making the former into one deserving of all honor and praise," writes J. Glenn Gray in *The Warriors*, his book on World War II.[2] Gray distinguishes different images of the enemy. He notes that soldiers in past centuries saw the enemy as a fellow professional doing a job worthy of respect. This image has changed as war has been extended to civilians and whole populations.

"Increasingly, we cannot fight without an image of the enemy as totally evil, for whom any mercy or sympathy is incongruous, if not traitorous."[3] "Most soldiers are able to kill and be killed more easily in warfare if they possess an image of the enemy sufficiently evil to inspire hatred and repugnance."[4]

The enemy may be seen as nonhuman or subhuman—especially if he or she is of another race. "My platoon and I went through Vietnam burning hooches (note how language liberates us—we didn't burn houses and shoot people; we burned hooches and shot gooks)."[5] Or the enemy may be seen as the devil, demon-possessed, the enemy of God. The image of the demonized enemy is the foundation upon which are built the psychic structures of racism, women's oppression, pornography, religious oppression, homophobia. Those patterns of domination in the culture in turn shape our internal landscapes.

POSSESSION BY THE CONQUEROR

When the Defender rules, our first response to difference is fear.

"My phone went out," an older woman client says, "and you know who the phone company sent to repair it? A black man and a Mexican in a sombrero! I was afraid to open the door!"

The woman in question has been a lifelong supporter of civil rights. Now she lives alone, and feels vulnerable. When we feel weak, unsupported, vulnerable, we are most susceptible to the Defender's threats and promises.

The Defender paints the world around us as dangerous, and threatening. Death, violation, humiliation await us unless we comply. Fearful, we believe the Defender's vision.

Certainly, the world today is not a safe one, and we may have many realistic reasons to be afraid. No one can blame a woman alone for being fearful. But fear entraps us, removes the possibility of help, distorts our vision. We respond to the shape of a hat or the color of skin, not to the intuitive scent of real danger. We lock out the repairman, yet would open the door wide to admit the world's most dangerous creatures—white men in business suits.

The Defender offers to protect us by destroying the enemy. The price of that protection is that we condone, comply with, and participate in the brutalization of the other.

In the political realm, this unholy bargain can be very clear. The woman who fears the repairman has always believed in equal opportunities for all. Yet, because of her fear, she would be happier if the phone company did not hire men of color.

Her fear arises, in part, out of the stereotype of the black rapist, which was perpetrated in the American South after the Civil War at a time when the lynching of black people became a white political weapon. Black men were credited with a "rape instinct," while the rape of black women by white men was quietly accepted. Angela Davis writes, "Before lynching could be consolidated as a popularly accepted institution, however, its savagery and its horrors had to be convincingly justified. These were the circumstances which spawned the myth of the Black rapist—for the rape charge turned out to be the most powerful of several attempts to justify the lynching of Black people."[6]

Conquerors wreak destruction on the enemy, but their own people also pay a heavy price for protection. For a white woman in the Reconstruction-era South, the price of white male protection was her own submission to white male authority. The cost of the Defender's protection is also high; it is our freedom, our ability to truly defend ourselves, our capacity to feel. Writes Susan Griffin, "When a living soul allows herself to act from fear. . . another sort of suffering takes place, which is deeper than even fear itself. For a woman who does not act from her own will has by that failure again become an object, a thing.[7]

The Defender's protection is no protection, for in seeking it we have already lost ourselves, and become complicit in our own destruction. When we are possessed by the Defender we are equally possessed by the image of the enemy. We, ourselves, become *both* rapist and slave woman, conqueror and victim, protector and threat. The outer war can be waged on other people's bodies, but the war within is waged on ourselves.

In complying with brutalization, we brutalize ourselves. We experience ourselves, or parts of ourselves, as the Enemy.

"Breathe deep," I say to Betty, a woman in her late twenties who has come for help. She feels depressed, uneasy in groups and fearful of people. "Follow your breath down to the place where it begins, to your place of power. Look to the center, to your own core. What do you see there?"

Betty begins to cry. "I see a monster. It's ugly and cringing and sniveling. I hate it. It's me."

"What do you want to do with it?"

"Kill it. Hide it. I'm afraid people will see it. If I let anyone really know who I am, they'll find out I'm the monster."

The enemy self becomes in us something we try to destroy or contain, and at the same time, something we fear for and protect. We hate the monster and yet carefully protect it from exposure behind the barriers we erect, like the walls of ancient citadels, to guard us from the world. Whatever is in us that we have been taught is bad, wrong, unacceptable—our anger, our intense feelings, our sexuality, our bodies—becomes monstrous.

The Defender's core issue is safety. In a world of enemies, how can we be safe? Betty was always afraid that people didn't really like her, that someone would attack her. She wanted intimacy but found it terrifying, for if she opened up to someone, they would see the monster. And of course, the more fearful and hypersensitive she became, the less people were drawn to her.

Part of her healing process was learning to fraternize with the enemy, to get to know the monster. We created a ritual together, for which she made a monster mask and came dressed in red and black, the colors she associated with the monster. In a large room lined with mirrors, she became the monster, and we talked, danced, fought, and played together. Later, she made a monster doll, of old socks stuffed with rags, button eyes, yarn hair. At home, she played with it every day for several weeks—sometimes screaming at it or beating it, sometimes holding and rocking it.

Eventually, the monster became familiar, friendly. Betty began to experience the monster's rage and rebellion as her own ability to defend herself, as creative and erotic energy. For those aspects of ourselves that the Avenger demonizes are often precisely the qualities we most need to resist domination and fight for our freedom. To win free of the Defender's control, we must learn to know and accept those aspects of ourselves that we have seen as the enemy.

At the end of our work together, Betty made a new doll, embroidered with moons, stars, and spirals—symbols of power, protection, and integration.

Our softness and vulnerability may also become the demonized enemy. Another woman, Cathy, identified a "Little Person" inside herself. "What does she look like?" I asked.

"She's very thin, slight, almost a little girlish—she looks like me when I first married my ex-husband. I can't stand her. She's so fearful and cringing. She's just a weak sort of person. Why can't she stand up for herself?"

The Conqueror despises the conquered. When we submit to domination, we hate ourselves for complying even though we cannot help ourselves resist. Self-hate becomes a self-reinforcing system.

Cathy brought in photo albums of her wedding and married years. Together we pored over pictures of her as the Little Person, talked about the events they recorded and her feelings. Over time, the Little Person grew up, became more solid, strong, able to assert herself. Cathy, in turn, became better able to change conditions in her life.

Individual meditations or group rituals can help us transform the internal image of the Enemy.

SELF-HATER STORY

Put on some soothing music. Relax. Let your breathing be slow and even. Read through the following story slowly, letting the images form

for you as the words suggest. Or get someone to read it to you and use it as a guided visualization.

Begin by going to your place of power. (See page 110.) In your place of power, begin the story.

In the center of this place, your place of power, you can hear a call, a sound soft as a breath of flame. Find the direction it comes from.

Breathe deep, and begin to walk in that direction . . . following a scent, a hint of something, feeling the ground beneath your feet and the weight of your body shift from foot to foot. And feel the air on your skin, noticing what you feel and hear and see and sense along the way . . .

And you come to your own border, that place that separates what is within from without; your boundary enclosing your living power, your protection. Look . . . feel . . . What is that boundary for you? How does it appear . . . what does it do for you? And do you like it? Do you want it to be that way? Here, in your power place, you can make it thicker or thinner, stronger or more flexible, more solid or more permeable, however you want.

Breathe deep, draw power up from the earth; become a shaper, make magic, change . . .

And when you have changed, listen . . . for the call remains, luring you out of yourself, into the world, across the dismembered lands. Across that border lies the dismembered world, the corpse lands of the kings, the rulers. And you breathe deep and call the earth's power to you as you cross. And notice how you walk here, and how your body feels, and how you feel the ground beneath your feet, and how the weight of your body shifts from foot to foot, and how the air feels on your skin and smells in your nostrils. Notice what you see and hear and feel and sense in the country of the rulers.

Always following the whisper call, following your path as it twists and winds and climbs . . . until you see, far in the distance, someone is waiting for you . . . someone who hates you . . . someone blocks the path . . . someone stands in the way . . . one of the rulers of this land. And you breathe deep and walk forward. And the figure of the ruler becomes slowly clear. You see what it is for you . . . human, animal, or some other creature? You begin to see its body and its limbs, how it is clothed, its color. You begin to sense its size, smell its odor on the air. You walk closer. Now you see its head, its face, its features. You can hear its voice, you look into its eyes, the ruler speaks to you . . . You breathe deep, and hear what it says . . . You answer . . .

Choose. Draw power from the earth, from breath. And know what it is you must do to move forward. Look into the eyes of the one who hates you.

Where is your power? Breathe deep. Listen. Look. Look so deep that you can see your own eyes stare back at you and feel the rhythms of survival in your breath . . . Draw up power from beneath your feet. Feel it rise on your breath, in your voice . . . Give voice to it and draw it back from the voices around you . . . as you face the one who hates you. Fight. Love. Change . . . Transform the one that hates you. See how it changes. What is it now? What has it become? What does it say to you now? What gift do you find in it? And when you are ready, say good-bye. Thank it. Walk back. See how the lands have changed around you. Find your way back to the boundary. What is it like now? Has it changed? Return to your place of power.

Say good-bye to your place of power, and everything in it. Return from the story.

Groups might wish to go through the story together, and then discuss what you each saw and heard. What was common, what different? What have you learned from it?

You may need to go through the story several times before you succeed in transforming the self-hater. Ritual can also help make the transformation.

MONSTER DOLL

After working with the self-hater story, make yourself a doll that represents the self-hater. Or find a doll or stuffed animal that seems appropriate.

Take some time each day to talk to your doll. Do whatever you feel like to it. Allow yourself to be violent toward it, if that feels right, or to be tender or nurturing. Keep this up for some time—at least one full cycle of the moon or longer.

When you feel ready, decide what you want to do with the doll. You might burn it or bury it, reshape it, dress it differently, embroider new features, create a companion for it, give it away to a child.

Again, sit down, relax, and reread the story. Notice what has changed.

MONSTER PARTY 1

Have everyone bring monster dolls to the group. Set out a doll's tea party. Introduce the monsters. Let the monsters proceed to have a tea party, acting in their most monstrous fashion.

MONSTER PARTY 2

Make monster masks. These can be very simple, drawn on paper plates or paper bags, or elaborate.

Come to the group dressed as your monster. Bring your mask. When the mask is on, become the monster. Introduce your monsters to each other. Have a party. You can alternate wearing the masks and wearing your own faces. Or you can let someone else wear your mask, and fight, dance, play, yell, or reason together. Invent your own dramas.

At the end, hold a ritual demasking. Sit in the circle. One by one, take off your masks. Each person holds up the mask, faces it, and speaks to it, saying what you have done in the past under the self-hater's rule, what you will do differently in the future, and what you will do with the mask itself.

After each person speaks, have the group empower her or him. Sing the person's name, chant, say something in blessing: "We bless your power." Or simply applaud and yell.

At the end, feed each other.

FINDING PROTECTION IN SOLIDARITY

At the core of the Defender is a quality that we need to reclaim in a positive way: protection. We do at times have real enemies and need defenses.

To liberate ourselves from the Defender, we need to find situations in which we can be safe and valued.

We often have unclear or unrealistic expectations of what safety means in a group. We want to be assured that no one in the group will ever hurt our feelings or make us feel bad. But no group offers perfect acceptance, and in any genuine relationship, we encounter conflict, anger, and differing needs.

Safety in a group is not a matter of niceness or politeness. On the contrary, the nicer we are expected to be, the less safe we are to reveal the core parts of ourselves that are not so nice. No group can eliminate risk. But a group can establish safety by assuring that risks are shared, that boundaries are clear, and that power structures and hidden agendas are brought out into the open. We cannot eliminate risks, but we can face them with solidarity.

Solidarity is based on the principle that we are willing to put ourselves at risk to protect each other. Nothing makes a more powerful statement of the inherent value we give to each member of a group than our willingness to risk ourselves in each other's defense. Groups that do civil disobedience and practice solidarity in facing physical risks create strong bonds, for the drama of action cements our trust. However much members of my affinity group might annoy me or hurt me, I know that in the moment of danger they will be concerned for my safety, not just their own—as I with theirs. And so we can trust.

Soldiers develop enormously strong bonds when they face battle together. To end war, we cannot just deplore its destructiveness; we must understand its appeal. Human beings have the ability to develop comradeship so deep that it enables us to readily die and kill, and that fact should actually give us hope. For if we can learn to create those powerful bonds without also needing to create demonic enemies, we will have created a strong base from which we can reshape the world.

Bonding together against an enemy is one of the easiest ways for a group to form, but it cannot bring liberation. Real wrongs and grievances exist to be redressed, but we need to beware of ideologies that turn some group into the enemy or the other, even when that group has historically been our oppressors. For casting them as the enemy locks them into the oppressor's role, while approaching them as potential allies shifts onto them the responsibility to change.

Safety in a group is not found by avoiding danger, but by facing it together. For freedom is dangerous, inherently unpredictable. Whatever truly challenges systems of domination involves risk, for those systems will exert power-over to defend themselves. Danger is not necessarily negative: an encounter with danger can be an encounter with mystery, a descent into the heart of crazy chance, the wild card, the odd thread in the pattern that alone makes freedom possible. Change involves risk, and when we risk we know what we are: vulnerable, mortal, alive.

Groups may face many different kinds of risk, from the physical risks of action to the emotional risks of breaking the Censor's hold and telling our truth. We risk our time, our confidences, our work and commitment, and can feel safe doing so in a context in which everyone is at risk. If, for example, a support group forms for battered women, the women in it must all be willing to share their experiences. If a facilitator were to prescribe advice but not share her own pain, the group would not feel safe.

Healers who are effective have always themselves been wounded. Our wounds, our illnesses, our mistakes, our pain are our roads to a healer's power, for unless we ourselves have been vulnerable we cannot approach someone in pain as an equal. Healing that empowers and liberates springs from a sense of mutual struggle with the forces that hurt us all. When we start believing that we are "more together" than someone else, we use our healing power as another way to establish our own superiority. We become the Judge. From that position, we can only administer the mechanics of aid.

When solidarity is not present, a group cannot bond, for its members cannot truly trust each other. For example, a group of social workers worked together in a large agency. Early in the year, the head of their branch of the agency was precipitously fired by his own protégé, who had recently joined the governing board. The man who lost his job was overbearing, and strongly disliked by most of the other workers. They all felt that his departure would actually benefit their clients, although they also felt he had been unfairly treated. Members of the group grumbled to themselves, but no one was willing to complain to the board or take action in his behalf. So he was forced out.

Months afterward, the group found itself having great difficulties working together. They had many complaints and grievances, but could not agree how best to proceed. They tried to build trust: they held potlucks, started peer discussion groups, brought in outside consultants for encounter sessions. But the problem remained, because they could not, in reality, trust each other. No one could feel sure that her or his own job might not someday be threatened, should he or she cross wills with members of the board. Not one of them had any reason to believe that the others would take a stand in her or his behalf. No cosmetic changes could make them feel safe.

QUESTIONS ABOUT SOLIDARITY

Consider these questions on your group:

1. In what ways does this group agree to stand together and protect each other? What actions are we willing to take?
2. Does our solidarity extend to everyone in the group? Does it have to be earned? Can it be forfeited? If it is conditional, how do those conditions make us feel? What do they say about how we value each other?
3. In the past, have we supported each other? Failed each other? What effect does that history have on our ability to trust the group?

If real safety in a group is established by sharing risks, then ritual should make us deeply secure, for it poses continuous risks for us to face: the risks of expression, of bringing forth the energies and images that emerge in us, of connection, of caring for and sharing with each other, of experimentation, of trying out new ideas that may or may not work.

We can create a ritual specifically to evoke and face our inner fears.

TEAM CHALLENGES

Divide the group into two. Each plans a series of challenges and obstacles for the other. This works best in an outdoor setting where people can move through space. In a Reclaiming workshop, one group challenged us by ambushing each of us from behind a tree, holding a mirror to our faces and asking, "Who are you?" Later, we ambushed them as they walked out toward a wild headland above the ocean. Each one of us jumped out at a woman and said, "I'm your mother! You don't belong on the headlands this late at night. Come back home with me!" We continued on until our victim found a way to free herself.[8]

ESTABLISHING BOUNDARIES

To establish safety, a group also needs boundaries and continuity. We need to know who is in the group and who is not, and to have some sense that those whom we connect to and trust will not suddenly vanish.

The term *boundaries* is, I admit, psychological jargon, but I use it because it conveys a clear image. Somewhere a line of demarcation must exist, dividing the group from what is not the group. In Witchcraft, one of our magical tools, the *athame*, the knife, is used to make divisions. With it we draw the magic circle, which divides ritual space and time from ordinary space and time. A group, too, needs a circle around it to define it.

The *athame* is a powerful tool: it is double-edged to remind us that any separation cuts both ways. Boundaries contain our power so that it can deepen and intensify, and they may keep out what could threaten or disrupt our group. But boundaries may also exclude those who might benefit us or bring us power. A boundary is always, in essence, somewhat arbitrary and false: an island of separation carved out of the rippling whole.

Nevertheless, we cannot trust unless we feel safe from intrusion. Each member of a group needs to have some control over who comes in. Each group needs some sense of focus and purpose, which necessarily excludes other possibilities. A group needs a shape and an edge, a skin. Like skin, a boundary both separates and interacts with the world, keeping some things out, letting others in. Boundaries can be thick or thin, solid or permeable, fixed or elastic. But a group with no boundaries is not a safe place to be.

Families and intimate relationships also need boundaries. Every member of a household needs areas of physical and emotional privacy that are respected by others. With sexual abuse of children rampant, we need to teach children early that they have a right to refuse invasion and intrusion of all sorts. We commonly deny this right, in ways that seem harmless but undermine a child's sense of personal power. We grab a cute toddler in a big bear hug, instead of asking first, "Could I have a hug?" Asking would give the child an opportunity for choice; grabbing, even with affection, reinforces the idea that adults have the right to do what they want to with children's bodies.

Boundaries can be created by marking off times and spaces. In ritual, we cast a circle to create sacred space. In families, adults need private times, when the bedroom door is locked and children do not interrupt. Children, too, have the right to identify times when they can be free from adult demands, other children's intrusions, and interruptions.

We all also need some physical place that is ours alone to control; if not a room, then a corner, a desk, a special altar spot. We can give a young child a special box, saying, "This is yours, to keep whatever you want in it. I will never open it or look in it unless you tell me I can."

Ritual can help us create boundaries. To create sacred space is an act of protection. Ritual can create a "liberated zone" of the spirit, can change an atmosphere, make a space ours. It can become a political act: the Women's Peace Camp at Greenham Common can be seen as an ongoing ritual, reclaiming the space of the missile base for peace. Marches and demonstrations may also be rituals of this sort.

Ritual can also affirm a space that we make our own: a new home, a business, an office, a garden. It can establish an energy boundary, a circle of protection, and it can transform a space that is not ours.

At the end of the action at Livermore in June of '83, many of us ended up held in a barracks at Santa Rita County Jail. We were tired after ten days of the action, but in the barracks we felt exhausted, almost drugged.

My friend Pandora led a small workshop on ritual for those of us who could remain awake. At its end, we decided to do a ritual to cleanse the space. When we came in, we were handed lists of rules which we immediately tore up and folded into paper cranes, symbolic of peace. We walked around the barracks, sprinkling them with water for cleansing. Holding cranes, we then went "flying" around the room while singing a song about being free as a bird who builds her nest high in a willow tree. We hid cranes everywhere.

For the rest of our stay there, we were constantly catching sight of the cranes. Lying down in our bunks, sitting down in a corner, standing in line, we would look up, and one would be tucked into a cranny or perched atop a post. Each time we saw one, it would lift our spirits. The atmosphere of the barracks changed.

TO CLAIM A SPACE

Walk the boundaries of the space if you can. Cleanse it: use salt water, sage, incense, or whatever you have available. If appropriate, physically clean it. Establish its physical security: for example, in a new home, make sure the locks all work. Cast a circle around the space, and ask that it remain as a permanent circle of protection. Raise power, envisioning some image that speaks to you of the purpose for which you claim the space: a hearthfire, an image of peace. Fill the space with that energy, either using your imagination or some physical representation, as we used the cranes. Put up permanent emblems of the energy you have created: imagine it embodied, for example, in your favorite pictures. Or if you are reclaiming a missile silo, for instance, leave tokens of your presence: special stones, crystals, shells. Thank the powers you have invoked, and open the circle.

As a group changes over time, so do its boundaries. Most groups begin by being open to a wide variety of new members. Some groups remain completely open, which itself makes a statement of value: everyone has worth. Many Twelve-Step programs, for example, hold meetings that are open to anyone who comes. They establish boundaries not by limiting who comes, but by clearly focusing the group's purpose. Alcoholics Anonymous's Tradition Five states, "Each Alcoholics Anonymous group ought to be a spiritual entity having but one primary purpose—that of carrying its message to the alcoholic who still suffers."[9] A wide-open structure is appropriate for that purpose.

Nevertheless, not all AA meetings are open to the public at large. Closed meetings exist so that members can develop trust and intimacy. For we cannot instantly trust strangers. We may choose to share vulnerable parts of ourselves publicly (as writers do) because we feel our stories may have value to others and we feel strong enough to risk criticism or hurt. But willingness to risk is not the same as trust, which we can only develop by knowing people over time.

Political action groups that hope to mobilize large numbers of people also may need open structures. Boundaries of any sort may seem exclusionary and elitist. But when smaller groups need to work together closely and trust each other in action, they need tighter boundaries.

When wide-open structure is defined as the only "politically correct" structure, unrealistic expectations and severe problems can be created. Groups may be stuck with someone who does not fulfill responsibilities, whom nobody else likes, or who is, quite simply, a pain in the ass. If no process exists for asking someone to leave a group, what generally happens is that the productive, amiable members all drop out, one by one. The group dissolves, and its task remains undone.

About twelve years ago, I was first beginning to teach classes in ritual through an open university. At the first session, one of the students began asking hostile questions and making disparaging remarks. Being young and insecure, I first tried to placate him and soothe his objections. Finally I got angry, and asked him to leave. As soon as he walked out, the class breathed a collective sigh of relief.

"I'm so glad you got rid of him," one woman said. "If you hadn't, nobody would have come back next week."

When a group must function together at deep levels of trust, everyone in the group must have a voice in admitting any new members. We cannot feel safe if we must fear intrusion. If we value the members of our group, we must give their needs priority over others who have not yet made a commitment to the group or shared in its struggles.

Establishing limits on membership does not have to be done in a way that devalues outsiders. We can communicate clearly that the group is closing because of its own needs, not because others are judged inferior or unworthy. And groupness, fortunately, is not a limited resource. Established groups can help new groups to form.

Covens, groups of Witches who practice ritual together, are traditionally among the most tightly bonded and bounded of groups. Members are said to be "closer than family," and while this is sometimes more of an ideal than a reality, coven structure strives for that ideal. New members undergo a ritual of initiation, and are only admitted after a long trial period.

Ritual circles are somewhat more loosely bounded. They may be covens in formation, or they may function as spiritual support groups, lasting for a time and then dissolving. Members generally do not undergo a formal initiation process. Each circle decides for itself how open to be.

In my own covens, when we found ourselves beginning to be besieged by people wanting to join at a time when we were closed, we decided to teach classes and hold gatherings that would encourage new groups to form. We could offer help and advice, but we did not wish to sacrifice our own group by opening it at a time when we wanted closeness and intimacy.

Groups may be open in some aspects and closed in others. Our community sponsors a few rituals each year that are open to the general public. They create an opportunity for newcomers to experience ritual. Big rituals generate a lot of energy and excitement, but are less intimate than small ones and more vulnerable to disruption by onlookers, hecklers, drunks wandering around the beach, fundamentalists talking in tongues, men or women on the make, compulsive talkers, people having active psychotic episodes, bad drummers, and the police.

We hold other rituals to which we invite selected friends. At others, several covens join together, or we invite our close families, lovers, and households. (Some of the most bitter conflicts arise when a group member wants to invite to an intimate gathering her or his current lover whom no one else in the group can stand. Should you find yourself in this position, listen to your circle. They may have better taste than you do.)

Many times, needs conflict. On a major holiday, for example, such as Halloween, we want to meet with our coven to do strictly private trance work, and we also want to celebrate with our entire community and our families. The children want to go trick-or-treating.

A community that sustains its connections over time can meet all those needs—but not all at once. Some years, we create a huge, public extravaganza ritual on a night before or after Halloween and reserve the night itself for our intimate circles and deep magic. Other years, we let some other group serve the public, and focus on community ritual.

Political groups that organize civil disobedience need to be both open enough to attract large numbers of people, and closed enough so that trust can develop among members. The Abalone Alliance, which organized the blockade of the Diablo Canyon Nuclear Plant in 1981, and the Livermore Action Group attempted to balance these needs with a complex structure.

Participation in the large group was open to anyone. To blockade and risk arrest, however, individuals had to undergo nonviolence training: a one-day or two-day workshop that taught the philosophy of nonviolence, the principles of solidarity and consensus decision making. The training itself functioned as a boundary.

The groups also formulated a set of nonviolence agreements. Everyone who took part in an action had to agree to abide by the guidelines for the period of the action.[10] The guidelines were seen by many as establishing our basis of trust. Not everyone liked them—the first guideline, "We will be open, friendly, and respectful to all people we encounter," was perceived by some as instructions to placate authority. In retrospect, we might have found less rule-bound ways to establish boundaries and safety had we understood that the code was serving those functions.

The big, open action groups were also further organized into small groups, collectives that took on organizational tasks, and affinity groups, generally consisting of five to fifteen members. Some affinity groups formed shortly before an action and dissolved once it was over. Others saw themselves as ongoing support groups that might continue throughout many different actions and develop a strong sense of community. All of them, in order to bond and generate trust, needed firm boundaries.

Conflicts in groups often develop about boundaries, and generally masquerade as something else. In the case of the Livermore Action Group, our boundary conflicts surfaced as a series of conflicts around the group's structure. In LAG (as we called the group for short), some people loved huge general meetings to which anyone could come. Others wanted big meetings to be structured as affinity group spokescouncils, with one representative from each affinity group charged with speaking. The conflict grew heated, complicated by people's interpersonal problems and suspicions, long-standing feuds, and broken love affairs. In the end, we built a structure so complex that nobody (even those of us who participated in inventing it) clearly understood what it was or how it was supposed to work. The structure itself exacerbated other conflicts.

We might have resolved our conflicts more effectively had we understood that they were about the group's boundaries, and that our real needs conflicted. Some of us identified strongly with the need to keep the group open; others identified with the need to create intimacy and trust. Both needs existed and were inherent in our purpose: at its best, the group achieved a dynamic tension between them. We could have more consciously valued that tension, for dynamic tension generates energy. Our ultimate structure might have been more workable had we not demanded that it reduce irreducible differences.

When the Reclaiming Collective began, we were influenced by the style of organizing we had learned in civil disobedience groups. We envisioned a large collective, open to anyone, composed of smaller work groups that we jokingly called cells.

After a couple of years, however, we noticed that nobody seemed to be joining the collective. When we questioned likely propects, we found out that they didn't know how to join. Although we imagined ourselves to be open, in reality we had become a tight group of friends that newcomers found intimidating. Because, in theory, no one belonged or didn't belong to the collective, no one could figure out how to get into it.

Of course, in reality, some of us did belong and others didn't. This became apparent when someone who didn't belong came to a meeting. In spite of our ideals of openness, we didn't really want to spend a lot of time and emotional energy trying to argue our politics or defend our peculiar style. In fact, we didn't want to meet frequently and bond closely with people we didn't like.

Believing that the group *should* be open hampered us from building community with those we did like. People could not feel truly committed to a group when they weren't sure to whom they were committing themselves.

We realized that our structure didn't work for us, and closed the collective. The type of boundary we needed was more like a semipermeable membrane, containing the group but allowing people to filter in and out.

Boundary issues are not resolved quickly. For at least three years, one agenda item at every Reclaiming meeting was Who is actually in the collective? Another item was How does somebody join the collective? Newcomers did join; most often they were people who became lovers of someone already in the group. This phenomenon sparked running jokes about our "casting-room couch," but reflected a real truth about groups and boundaries: an intimate group, in which people have long mutual history and close connections, is hard to enter except by forming a close connection with someone in it.

Not all these relationships lasted, but the group was able to weather the breakups. Many years ago, in a pessimistic mood, I formulated what I called Starhawk's Three Laws of Small Groups:

1. In any small group in which people are involved sexually, sooner or later there will be problems.
2. In any small group in which people are involved, sooner or later they will be involved sexually.
3. Small groups tend to break up.

Today, in a happier era, I can add a Fourth Law:

4. If a group can survive one breakup, subsequent conflicts between lovers will be less threatening. When the group has survived several affairs, members of the group will feel very safe, and bonds of trust will deepen.

Continuity also creates safety. We cannot truly bond with someone if we don't know how long she or he will be around. Children need care from some person who can be there consistently over time. Even sensitive nurturing from changing figures will leave a child feeling unsafe.

When someone leaves a group, the people remaining may feel shaken, abandoned, threatened. (They may, of course, also feel relieved.) If many people abandon a group at once, the group may not survive.

Leaving a group makes an implicit statement that the group, or the people in it, are not valued by the one leaving. Of course, the person who leaves may not mean to make this statement: she or he may have a wide variety of reasons for going. Formal leave-taking or a farewell ritual can help the group to recover its integrity. Unfortunately, many people leave groups by simply drifting away, without ever voicing their anger, criticisms, or appreciation. If you do value a group, you owe its members a chance to say goodbye.

A group that needs to heal after someone has left, or after major conflicts, might create a ritual to do so, creating a chance for the members who are left to reaffirm their commitment and express their affection and appreciation for each other. (For an example, see page 263.)

Boundary issues may also center around issues of space and time. How regularly the group meets, how promptly people arrive at meetings, how often individuals skip group events, how protected the group is from interruptions, how precipitously meetings are changed, and how consistently agreements are kept also determine how valued people feel, and how safe.

QUESTIONS ABOUT BOUNDARIES

These questions are for groups to consider:

1. Who is in the group? Who is not in it? How do we know?
2. How does somebody get into the group?
3. How does someone get out of the group?
4. What metaphor or analogy would best describe how our boundary functions?
5. Are we comfortable with how closed or open we are? What needs do we have for expansion or containment? Are they being met? What trade-offs are we making?
6. How appropriate is our structure for our purpose?
7. How do we resolve conflicts around boundaries? Are any of our conflicts around other issues actually about boundaries? Are there dynamic tensions we might learn to appreciate?
8. How much continuity is there in the group?
9. How much regularity do we have, and how much do we want, in

terms of our meeting times and places? How do we protect the group from intrusion or interruption?

10. What agreements do we keep? Not keep? Why?

ACKNOWLEDGING THE REALITIES OF POWER

We also cannot feel safe in a group, a family, or any relationship unless we know what is going on. If the power relationships do not correspond with what the group believes about power, if real agendas are concealed, we feel uneasy. Whenever power is not perfectly balanced (which is always), we can establish safety by being clear about power, purposes, and expectations.

In nonhierarchical groups, our belief that the group should not have leaders must not keep us from being open about the real power relations. When *power* becomes a dirty word, so that no one can name it or talk about it, it becomes most destructive. The flow of power must first be made clear before we can strive to make it truly equal.

When leadership cannot be acknowledged, but nevertheless exists, a difficult burden is placed on those who exercise it. In order to make their skills and knowledge available to the group, they must somehow pretend not to be influencing the group. They must construct false fronts, which, in contrast to those on Main Street stores, make them appear smaller, not bigger. The group becomes permeated with deceit.

When the group pretends that its leaders are not leaders, it cannot hold them accountable for their actions and decisions. Nor can they be expected to exercise leadership with any consistency. Others who might want to gain influence in the group cannot see how this is done. Power is concealed, and no one feels safe.

During the June '83 blockade, when we had been in jail for nine or ten days, one of the guards told a sympathetic nurse that the sheriff planned to have us bodily removed in the morning. She passed the rumor on to a friend she had among us, who shared it with a few others, including me.

We didn't know what to do. All of us knew that rumors generally cause only panic and distrust. Although we trusted the nurse, the guard might have purposely planted the rumor to sow fear. On the other hand, should the rumor prove to be true, we wanted the group to be prepared.

We were the unacknowledged leadership in the jail, but we had no official mandate from the group to withold or to spread information. We had no right to decide on a plan, but we could not call a large meeting without, in fact, spreading the rumor, and perhaps playing into the hands of the guards.

We did, in the end, make a good decision. We spread the word that we would conduct a role play, to explore possible scenarios around solidarity: "We've heard that some people have been spreading rumors that we might be dragged away tomorrow," we told the group. This was true, for in spite of all our attempts at secrecy, we had, in effect, been spreading the rumor ourselves. "Of course we don't think that's true, but let's practice what we might do if it did happen. We especially would like to invite the guards to watch." We suspected that once the guards knew we were prepared for forcible removal, they would abandon that plan if they had ever held it. We role-played being taken before the judge and refusing to plead, and answered the many legal questions that came up. Whether our strategy worked, or whether they had never intended to drag us out, we were not physically removed, then or later.

The hundreds of women who were not in our small meeting, however, never knew that major decisions had been made for them. We had, in reality, limited their choices: some might have wanted to bail out if they faced physical violence. Others might have wanted to prepare different sorts of resistance. Those not in our small group must have been left with an uneasy sense that power was being wielded somehow, without ever knowing how, where, or by whom.

I would do again what we did, but I would much prefer to have some leadership group, already chosen by the larger group, empowered to make emergency decisions and accountable for them. The real structure of power in the group would then have been clear, visible, and open to criticism and challenges.

In hierarchical groups, in which some people do have power to make decisions for others, safety is harder to establish. People cannot feel safe unless they have a voice in decisions that affect them. Yet hierarchies do not have to be destructive. In hierarchical situations, leaders can also empower others by being clear and consistent. When people know what consequences follow what actions, they can make informed choices. When expectations are clear, people can make choices about whether or not to meet them. The most destructive power is secret, capricious, and random.

We often believe that we need laws and rules to protect us against our unbridled impulses. In reality, what laws and rules do best is to impose limits on hierarchical power. For that purpose, they are invaluable. The Bill of Rights, for example, is an instrument designed not to control the people, but to control the government. It outlines what laws Congress shall *not* make.

In hierarchical systems, people need laws and rules that protect their rights. They feel safer when they know what those rules are and how to implement them, when the structure of the organization does not place anyone under someone else's arbitrary control without some procedure for appealing decisions, and when they know clearly who is responsible for decisions.

In hierarchies with an essentially benevolent purpose, such as classrooms or loving families, protection is established less through rules than through clarity of expectations. Teachers may have the power to give grades, but they can empower students by stating clearly on what basis work will be judged. Parents may control a child's allowance, but they can make clear what the child is expected to do in order to earn it.

Hierarchies are most destructive when we cannot choose to leave them. Children are extremely vulnerable in families, for they have no way to get out of them. If jobs are scarce so that the risk of leaving threatens survival, workers are at the system's mercy. No matter what laws protect them, or how clear the system's expectations, they cannot feel protected.

Also unsafe are hidden hierarchies, groups that give lip service to equality but in which members truly do not have equal power. The atmosphere of equality encourages vulnerability, yet openness may have consequences it does not have in a truly equal situation. "I want to hear what you're feeling and thinking," says the head of a university department, but when one member admits to criticism of the department head, she finds herself passed over for tenure.

When we are struggling to loosen the grip of the Defender, to cease seeing enemies everywhere and begin establishing openness and honesty in relationships, we may forget that we cannot act in hierarchical situations in the same way we strive to act among equals, any more than we can wear the same clothing in a blizzard that we would on a tropical beach. Some situations call for more protection. Before you ask your boss to go through a mediation to resolve your communication problems, consider that she might prefer to simply get rid of you, and has the power to do so. In your personal relationships, you may be trying to learn to be more vulnerable. You should not, however, let your competitor at work know all of your weaknesses and insecurities. And a man who is learning to cry may find that it is still unsafe to practice his newfound skill on the job.

QUESTIONS ABOUT THE REALITIES OF POWER

Individually, write out answers to these questions:

1. Who has power in this group? What kind?
2. How much power do I have?

Collect the answers, read them aloud, and discuss:

3. How much do our perceptions of power in the group agree? Do those people know they have it?
4. Do some people think they have more power than they do?
5. How are decisions made in the group? Who has the power to make them?
6. How is information shared in the group? What information is private? Who keeps it? How is it made available to others?

Again, write out individual answers to these question:

7. What skills knowledge, or experience do I have that can benefit the group?
8. How much of it can I share?
9. What stops me?
10. What response do I get? How does it make me feel?

Compare and discuss the answers. Consider these questions:

11. What use are we making of each other as resources in the group? Are we squandering our gifts? If so, how? What might we do differently?
12. What do people need to bring more of their strengths to the group? How can we create the atmosphere that brings them forth?
13. Who do we respect in the group? Do we abdicate power to those people? If so, how?
14. In what ways do we comply, withdraw, manipulate, or rebel?
15. Is this group really safe?
16. What expectations exist in the group? Are they clear?
17. How does someone gain power or respect in this group?
18. If this group is hierarchical, what controls, laws, rules, or other factors limit the use of power? Are they effective? If not, can we make them more so?

SAFETY FROM ATTACK

Finally, to feel safe in a group we must know that we will not be attacked, physically or verbally. We do not want to be made into an enemy, scapegoat, or victim, nor do we want to be judged when we share vulnerable feelings and private experiences.

Kings are necessarily two-faced. To their own people they appear as protectors; to the enemy, they are the conquerors. They are benevolent to their own, ruthless to others.

When we are possessed by the Defender, our friends, lovers, family, and coworkers can suddenly become for us the enemy whenever we feel insecure or frightened. We may find ourselves suddenly attacking those we love. So the battering husband beats his wife when she threatens to leave him, because he needs her so desperately and fears that she will go. Ironically, the Defender, whose own conflicts center around issues of safety, is not safe to be around.

Issues of safety often feel like conflicts of life or death. When we're in the Defender/Avenger mode, safety is the crucial concern we feel. Will I be safe? Will someone attack me? Any criticism feels like an attack, and we fight back. The more powerless we feel, the harder and dirtier we fight, or we may, like kings of old, build strong, defensive walls.

When we fight to the death to defend our powerlessness, we may not realize how powerful and frightening we appear to others. We may feel weak and vulnerable, yet wear the face of the Conquerer.

At a conference I helped to organize between white women and women of color, we held a speak-out. In this process, the women of color sat together and the white women sat together. First, the women of color spoke of what they were proud of about their heritage. Then they told the white women what they never wanted to hear again from a white woman. The white women then told the women of color what they had heard. Later we reversed the process. The white women spoke of our pride, and of what we never wanted to hear from a woman of color. I spoke of my pride in my Jewish heritage, in the Jewish passion for justice and the Jewish sense of humor.

When the time came for the women of color to tell us what they had heard, Leila, a Palestinian woman, stood up. She began what sounded to me like a diatribe. At first, I couldn't understand her well because of her accent, but finally I realized she was speaking to me, saying, "How can you speak of the Jewish passion for justice when you know what the Jews are doing in Israel!"

I felt myself go into almost a state of shock. I had thought the ground rules guaranteed safety, that we could speak from the heart and have our truth understood and acknowledged. Instead, I was attacked. I felt powerless to interrupt her or answer her.

"I can't just sit here and listen to this," I remember thinking. "I've got to defend myself."

Suddenly I jumped up and screamed at Leila, "Fuck you!" I went on to call her anti-Semitic and to tell her that she'd better goddamned well hope Jews did have a passion for justice. The mediator told us both to sit down. Leila left the room, and some women followed to support her. Others came over to offer me support.

Both of us, separately, spent a rough night. I felt angry, violated, and at the same time, deeply ashamed of myself. I had spent months organizing this conference to bring women together across the barriers of our differences, and I had gotten into a public brawl. I was supposed to be a nonviolence trainer, an expert in process, known for my skills at conflict resolution and mediation, and there I was publicly losing control. How the hell could we expect armies to make peace if two women couldn't even talk?

I lay awake for a long time, going over and over what had happened, realizing how hard it was for me to defend myself, painfully reliving all the times and relationships when I had sat quietly under attack, being sympathetic or withdrawing or smiling politely while sustaining damage. And I knew it was time for that to end.

I couldn't regret confronting her. But I did deeply regret the way I had done it, my sense that I had hit her with forces not really meant for her, that the power I couldn't muster in the past to challenge my husband, or my lover, or my mother, or my friend had come bursting forth on Leila like a fragmentation bomb. "Your anger was really meant for a German woman," a friend, herself a survivor of the Nazi Holocaust, suggested to me later.

In the morning, I went to find Leila. I dreaded meeting her, but I wanted to try to move beyond the conflict. A woman who was friends with both of us offered to mediate. Both Leila and I were calmer. We sat in her small dormitory room, close to each other, and I told her that I was sorry for yelling and screaming at her. Leila told me that when I jumped at her, she had literally seen me as an Israeli woman soldier, someone who had the power of life and death over her. Her immediate thought was to protect herself against physical violence.

I was shocked. When I jumped up, I was not conscious of our difference in size. I am a big woman; Leila is slight. If anything, I thought of her delicate frame with envy—she is so thin and elegant and very beautiful. It had never occurred to me that my physical presence conveyed power. Nor had I ever imagined that anyone would find me physically threatening. I think of myself as a marshmallow.

When I let myself imagine seeing myself through Leila's eyes, I felt ill. I had become the image of what I most did not want to be as she had become for me, I realized, every stereotype I had ever heard of the fanatic Arab terrorist. We had not seen each other at all. It was as if neither of us had been there at all: two phantoms had fought it out on the conference floor while two flesh-and-blood women hid, hoping it would all be over soon. The more afraid we felt, the harder we lashed out at each other.

In a group, the Defender may strike hard whenever we feel powerless. Since very few people enjoy being subjected to abuse, this behavior will not make us popular, nor will it deepen the group's sense of bonding and commitment.

The group has a choice. It can collude or challenge us. It can try to be understanding, sympathetic to our unhappy childhood or current stress. Or it can be honest.

If the group accepts our attacks, it is really confirming our sense of powerlessness. As in other relationships, when we let ourselves be battered, we are doing no true kindness to the batterer; we are saying, "You are too damaged, too powerless, to act like an ordinary, decent human being."

No one wants to die in an unimportant battle for a minor cause. We want the risks we take to be important ones. The Defender must paint every battle as crucial, every cause as central. And so the Defender is like a magnifying glass. Through its eyes, everything becomes blown up in importance: slights and insults, issues and decisions. Every disagreement becomes a battle, and every battle seems crucial, a life-or-death situation.

A collective business is in trouble. Its members have many disagreements, which I am attempting to mediate. Much of the conflict centers around one man, Larry, the newest member of the group. When I arrive, hc keeps me and the others waiting for half an hour while he talks on the phone. This behavior diminishes my hopes for a successful mediation: it is a nonverbal way of saying, "Fuck you." After our first go-around, I ask the group: "Tell me—do you all really like each other? If you could choose any people in the world to work with, are these the people you would choose?"

With question so baldly stated, the answer is clear and unanimous: no.

"So why are you together?" I ask. The reason shortly becomes evident: because nobody is willing to be the one to quit.

Larry has the least investment in terms of time or involvement. Since the conflict centers around him, he seems the logical person to go. And clearly he is not happy, nor does he feel safe, in the situation. Yet he becomes entrenched in his position: "I'm not leaving because I'm a gay man and why should a gay man be forced out by a group of white heterosexual men? This is a battle I'm fighting for all gay people."

The magnifying lens of the Defender obscures our ability to see what is really going on. Larry cannot really know whether his coworkers dislike his gayness, something he cannot and should not attempt to change and might rightfully defend, or whether they dislike other aspects of his behavior that he might even benefit by changing. The solidity of his defense keeps him, also, stuck in an unhappy situation.

The world is full of real dangers. Even paranoids, as the saying goes, have real enemies. People really may discriminate against us unfairly. But when we need to see every conflict as a cosmic one, we lose our ability to judge how dangerous any given situation really is. When Reagan calls the USSR the "Evil Empire," for example, we should all tremble for our national safety, for we know that our government—with all of its secret sources of information—has absolutely no way of knowing how dangerous Russia really is. In demonizing the Russians as the enemy, we can no longer see them. Their real aims, motivations, and resources are completely invisible to us, and real dangers we might face from other sources could take us completely by surprise while we fix our eyes on the Communist Menace.

When we need to see enemies, we may alienate potential allies. When our only response to conflict is to battle to the death, we lose the possibility for resolving conflicts in creative ways.

And so the Defender does not really keep us safe. Its very insistence on seeing enemies creates enemies and keeps us locked into battle. The prime example is the nuclear arms race, where the more weapons we develop to assure our safety, the more unsafe the world becomes for us all.

Attack is not the same as criticism. We need to be able to offer criticism in a group, and we need to be free to make judgments. The differences may seem subtle but are very clear when we experience them. Criticism can be a gift that acknowledges value. Empowering criticism points out what can be done better, and what is interfering with the full power and potential of a work. When I was a young art student, some teachers would give helpful criticism. "Paint different parts of the canvas differently," one professor used to say. "Let there be variation." Others, however, were attacking.

"What are you doing?" asked the woman graduate student who was teaching her first class.

"At the moment, I'm just sort of playing around."

"There's no room in this class for people who are 'playing around.' If you don't take your work seriously, I don't have time for you. You girls, you're all alike—just marking time until Prince Charming comes along. Well, don't think you can do it here!"

Support groups, in which people share very intimate and sensitive experiences, often need to establish agreements and processes that assure safety, such as the agreement that whatever is said in the group will remain confidential. Processes that allow people to speak without being interrupted help people feel safe from judgment. Facilitators can also set a nonjudgmental tone by their underlying appreciation of the value of others.

A group can be clear about when responses or judgments are appropriate and when they are not. People can say, "I want to share this story and I feel very vulnerable about it—all I want to hear right now is support." If a group embarks on a process that is supposed to be nonjudgmental, everyone in the group must agree to suspend judgment.

In hierarchical situations, attacks are especially damaging when they are directed from above downward (which is, of course, how they usually are directed, for people are less likely to attack someone who has power over them). A teacher who ridicules students, a supervisor who verbally abuses a worker reinforce the implicit statement the structure of hierarchy makes: some people are less valuable than others.

When someone in a group is attacked, the group can support that person in defending herself or himself. The group should not, however, take over that task. To feel safe, we must learn to defend ourselves.

QUESTIONS ABOUT SAFETY FROM ATTACK

Consider these questions in your group:

1. How do we offer criticism in the group? How do we feel when we receive it?
2. Do we succeed in setting a nonjudgmental tone? If not, what could we change?
3. How do we respond to attacks? To defense?

Some helpful agreements:

1. Everything said in this group will remain confidential, unless we have clear permission to speak of it.
2. We accept all feelings as valid, even if we cannot accept all actions or assessments.
3. We will suspend judgment of each other for this process.

DEFLATING FALSE GLORY

The Defender may also seduce us by offering us a falsely inflated sense of value. Soldiers go to war for defense, but also for glory. Glory is a form of value not rooted in the idea of the immanence of the sacred, or in a sense of connection with all of life, but in the sense of specialness, of set-apartness, of disconnection that removes the hero from the common ranks. Glory is the value of the "enduring name" of the death-dealer. When we are in conflict, when we have enemies, we feel important.

The false glory of the Avenger is addictive. In war, the foot soldier is expendable. In the realm of the Defender, ordinariness equates with death. Without immanent value we have no inner assurance of survival. On the battlefield, where death becomes the norm, survival is only for the special.

War desecrates the body; war can only be conducted by those willing to violate the body of the enemy and risk the violation of their own bodies. Soldiers are required to ignore pain, discomfort, cold, hunger, fear. They are not valued as beings, but as objects, just as the women who are carried off as slaves and prizes become objects. In a culture of war, the body cannot be sacred, held to have an inherent value.

"To be made an object is in itself a humiliation. To be made a thing is to become a being without a will. . . . But to this degradation, the reduction of a whole being with a soul to mere matter, we must add the knowledge that matter itself is despised, and hated in its very essence. We read, for instance, in the phrase 'to feel like shit,' the quintessence of humiliation. For in the pornographic culture, humiliation emanates from the material."[11]

Nevertheless, we are bodies, and through our bodies we experience the immanent value of life itself. When the body is devalued, the self is stripped of inherent value. We starve for some substitute. The Avenger offers us disembodied value as a replacement for the worth culture has stolen from us.

The Defender confirms its kingship, its uniqueness, by destroying. William Broyles, Jr., in his article, "Why Men Love War," writes of his discovery during the Vietnam War of the body of a Vietnamese that the men of his company had obscenely desecrated. The dead soldier was "propped against some C-ration boxes. He had on sunglasses, and a *Playboy* magazine lay open in his lap; a cigarette dangled jauntily from his mouth, and on his head was perched a large and perfectly formed piece of shit."

The corpse is an icon of the Defender's mentality: the enemy is reduced to the denigrated body, corpse, pornographic icon, excrement. Broyles goes on to record his own reaction: "I pretended to be outraged. . . .I kept my officer's face on, but inside I was . . . laughing. I laughed—I believe now—in part because of some subconscious appreciation of this obscene linkage of sex and excrement and death: and in part because of the exultant realization that he—whoever he had been—was dead and I— special, unique me—was alive."[12]

In a war, soldiers must kill or be killed. The Avenger offers us the killer's glory—an addiction we can't give up, because relinquishing it feels like death.

To free ourselves from the Defender, we have to give up our attachment to the glory of the monster. We have to realize that our particular disease does not set us apart, that our individual healing and liberation is part of a common struggle.

When we are addicted to our sense of set-apartness, we fall prey to the delusion that we are the King. We believe that the enemy is outside us— to be conquered, feared, destroyed. The more we identify with the glory of the King, the more we feel set apart from others, the more we are also disconnected, alien, lonely. For it is the essence of the King's glory that it can belong only to one person. The King has no true peers, no comrades, only subjects. The King cannot ask for help or trust the helper. Pride in dealing death can never compensate for lack of joy in life. The more we depend on glory for our sense of value, the more we lack true connections, the more we need outside acclaim, and the emptier we feel inside. The more we need adulation, the less we can afford to see how others really perceive us.

I am giving a workshop in ritual at a healing center. Among a group of twenty women, there are two men. One is quiet and says little. The other, Bob, is effusive, subtly patronizing, and full of tales of his own exploits. Several of the women come up to me separately to tell me that they don't feel comfortable around Bob. His presence spoils the circle for them. Later, he approaches me himself.

"You know," he confides, "I think a lot of women in this workshop are attracted to me, and don't want to admit it."

I murmur something polite, and escape. Later, I reflect that I have once again fallen into the female role of protecting male delusions of glory, instead of saying to him honestly, "You couldn't be more wrong." The tragedy for Bob is that he is so cut off from real connection with others that he mistakes distaste for attraction. Had I been honest, and had he been able to hear me, his glory would have been severely dimmed. He would no longer have been able to see himself as extraordinary, as special. But he might have opened up the possibility of real relationships with the women present.

For those defined by the hierarchy as superior, the lure of glory is often

irresistible, especially when there are few other models of power and connection around. For men in a male-dominated culture, so many opportunities for glory and status line the road that only rare men pass them
by to continue the search for power-from-within.

If the possibilities of acclaim by others are limited, we may still be
strongly possessed by the King, who is both defender and demon/enemy.
We may become the King of the Conquered, the Prime Victim, made
special, set apart by the magnitude of our defeats. We can derive false
value from our very oppression, the depths of our suffering, the intensity
of our martyrdom. So we may cling to our victimization, for from it we
derive the only worth we know.

I am not saying that there are no true victims in the world, or that those
who are victims or survivors of oppression have somehow chosen or created their own suffering. I am not interested in any form of blaming the
victim, only in understanding how some of us, some of the time, remain
powerless when we could take power.

When we are possessed by the Defender and addicted to our own specialness, even supportive groups become dangerous and painful places.
Instead of contributing to the group's strength, we may find ourselves
undermining its purpose and even destroying it.

Generating safety and restoring value in groups is relatively simple to
do. What is difficult is to challenge the false value we have each acquired
as the consolation prize of power-over. False glory must be deflated if we
are to build true value, but to do so is tricky, for how do we undermine
the only value someone may have without attacking her or his already
low self-worth?

The Twelve-Step programs, again, give us one model. In Alcoholics
Anonymous, the first step is admitting powerlessness. "We admitted we
were powerless over alcohol—that our lives had become unmanageable."[13]
By giving up the illusions of control and the grandiosity that alcohol gives,
there is hope of recovery. "Only through utter defeat are we able to take
our first steps toward liberation and strength. Our admissions of personal
powerlessness finally turn out to be the firm bedrock upon which happy
and purposeful lives may be built."[14]

This step, which at first reading seems painfully humbling, works because AA provides a structure of immanent value, in which both group
and individual support is offered. AA offers each member a sponsor who
offers counsel and support. Sponsors are themselves recovering alcoholics
who have gone through the twelve steps to sobriety and so can counsel
without playing Judge. Group support comes through meetings, which
prevent the grandiosity of drink from being replaced by the glory of the
King of Victims, who whispers, "You are the most awful (and therefore
special) person in the universe. No one else has fallen so low. Only you."
The sharing of stories in meetings makes clear that the problems of individuals are not unique, but follow a common pattern. At the same time,

meetings offer models of those who have overcome problems to build better lives. By joining AA a person is given value and given hope at the same time as she or he makes the admission of defeat.

Only by breaking down the delusions of glory can we break down isolation. The ending of that loneliness is the motivation for undergoing the painful process of giving up delusions.

Because grandiosity and denial are such strong components of addiction, deflation is strongly stressed in the Twelve Steps of AA and related programs. Steps Four through Ten are also devoted to deflation of false glory: The complete Twelve Steps are as follows:

Step One: "We admitted we were powerless over alcohol—that our lives had become unmanageable."

Step Two: "Came to believe that a Power greater than ourselves could restore us to sanity."

Step Three: "Made a decision to turn our will and our lives over to the care of God *as we understood Him.*"

Step Four: "Made a searching and fearless moral inventory of ourselves."

Step Five: "Admitted to God, to ourselves, and to another human being the exact nature of our wrongs."

Step Six: "Were entirely ready to have God remove all these defects of character."

Step Seven: "Humbly asked Him to remove our shortcomings."

Step Eight: "Made a list of all persons we had harmed, and became willing to make amends to them all."

Step Nine: "Made direct amends to such people wherever possible, except when to do so would injure them or others."

Step Ten: "Continued to take personal inventory and when we were wrong promptly admitted it."

Step Eleven: "Sought through prayer and meditation to improve our conscious contact with God *as we understood Him,* praying only for knowledge of His will for us and the power to carry that out.

Step Twelve: "Having had a spiritual awakening as the result of these steps, we tried to carry this message to alcoholics and to practice these principles in all our affairs."[15]

(The Twelve Steps reprinted with permission of Alcoholics Anonymous World Services, Inc. Opinions expressed here are, of course, the author's and not those of Alcoholics Anonymous.)

The searching moral inventory is bearable because the process is self-initiated and controlled. Nothing is easier than to make a searching moral inventory of somebody else, but then we become the Judge. To look at ourselves, to admit the worst, and still find acceptance, is hard but empowering.

Acceptance is unreal unless the admission of the worst about ourselves is real, and so amends must be made. Instead of torturing ourselves with guilt, we take responsibility for the harm we have done, and that expectation is itself empowering, for the assumption behind it is that we have the power, the ability, to repair some of the damages we may have caused. And if damages are irreparable, we still have the power to act differently in the future. Accepting responsibility generates hope.

Supportive deflation seems like a paradox. How can we do it?

First, we must establish a context that restores immanent value and creates safety. Like the Twelve-Step programs, we can encourage self-reflection and expect people to take responsibility for mistakes.

Having created that context, a group then has three powerful tools available for challenging false value: nonparticipation, questioning, and reframing.

When we are possessed by the self-hater in any form, what we think, say, and do is not spontaneous and free but preset in predictable patterns. We know those patterns and respond to them, for the most part, as predictably as the mesh of gears in a well-maintained transmission. John offends Joan, so she runs out of the meeting and Jean follows to placate her hurt feelings. Jean will not criticize John directly but complains about him to Joe. Joe agrees with Jean and then tells John that Jean doesn't like him. And so it goes.

As we identify patterns of oppression, we can refuse to perpetuate them. Groups often come to grief with the King of Victims. We want to be nurturing, but find more and more of the group's time and energy taken up with one person's problems. The person seems to use the group to confirm her or his stuckness. The group can never do enough, and when people express resentment or boredom, they simply reinforce the person's King Victim stance. Pointing this dynamic out does no good at all. We may be accused of blaming the victim, or may find ourselves speaking in the voice of the Judge.

Anne Cameron, in her novel *Daughters of Copper Woman,* tells the story of a women's society among the Indians of Canada's Northwest Coast. If a woman came to the group with a problem, others would listen, offer advice and help. If she came back again, they would listen a second and a third time. But if she returned a fourth time with the same problem, and hadn't made changes, they would all get up, walk away, and sit down somewhere else.[16]

Nonparticipating can be done verbally, and directly: "Joan, we talked about your problem last week and the week before. Now I feel it's draining my energy, and I don't want to talk about it anymore until you've done something about it."

Such tactics may provoke attack, expressions of hurt, or defensiveness. Joan may stomp or flounce out of the room. The temptation may be strong to follow, to try to bring her back and offer comfort. Resist the temptation, for conflicts will not be resolved by allowing one person to manipulate the group. I used to be a flouncer myself, resorting to the tactic as a way of dramatizing the intense hurt I was feeling. I learned quickly not to when the tactic became ineffective. One night at a meeting of my affinity group, we were arguing about who could come to a particular ritual. I was intent on bringing my then-current lover whom the rest of the group didn't like. (Not without reason.) I ran out of the room in tears and my closest friend Rose followed, not, as I expected, to comfort me and let me cry on her shoulder, but to scream at me, "Get back in there, you bitch! How dare you walk out just because you aren't getting your way!" I remember feeling quite surprised. It had never occurred to me that my desperation could be interpreted as manipulation, and yet manipulation it was. I came back, and haven't tried the great walkout since.

I suggest as a rule of thumb for surviving the dynamics of a group never to walk out in the middle of a fight (unless you are about to inflict or suffer physical damage). Never follow someone else out or try to coax anyone back. The worst that can happen is that the person will not return. If she or he is gone for good, perhaps the time or the chemistry simply was not right. And the group may be relieved of a draining problem.

This advice may sound cold, but sometimes people need to deeply experience the loneliness of King Victim before they are ready to face the painful task of giving it up. A group that expresses support when members actually feel used and resentful creates an illusion of connection that holds back the process of change.

Current thinking in some circles is that there are no problem individuals in groups, only problem dynamics, that getting rid of one person only means that someone else will become the scapegoat. I have not found this to be true, except in that so many of us automatically play scapegoat, that often when one leaves a group another jumps into place. A group that is willing to play ear to King Victim will usually find someone to take advantage of its sympathy. But when a group stops allowing itself to be manipulated, the difficult person will either change or leave. Groups may carry on after a leave-taking with renewed energy, vitality, and humor.

We can also refuse to collude in manipulation or avoidance of conflict. Joe can tell Jean, "Don't bitch to me—tell John what you're feeling." Or, "Hey, Joe's my friend too. Anything you say to me about him, I'll probably repeat to him." We can encourage people to bring conflicts directly to the individual involved, or to the group, and offer our support. "Look, if you feel afraid to face John, let's go to him together. Or let's find someone else to mediate."

Identifying other people's delusions and false value for them places us in the position of Judge. We cannot do it supportively. We can, however, ask questions.

Questions leave us open to mystery and surprise. When we ask a question, we want a deeper knowledge or understanding of a person. We test our assumptions instead of leaping to conclusions about others' motivations and meanings.

In the grip of the self-hater, we communicate in a cryptic code, patterned and predictable. We respond not to what's actually happening, but to what the self-hater whispers. We use words as screens, to keep others from seeing and knowing too much. And when we encounter the barriers others put up, we tend to politely back away. We don't ask ourselves, "Do I really understand what Jane means? Does what she say match what I intuit she is feeling?"

Jane is sitting huddled in a corner of the room, silent and withdrawn. Everyone can feel the misery she radiates.

"What's wrong?" Susan asks.

Inside Jane's head, the self-hater is whispering, "Everyone else is going to the hot tub afterwards when you have to work. They don't care about you or your problems. Nobody does. But that's okay, don't say anything about it. Don't spoil their good time."

"Nothing," she replies.

The group can accept her answer and go about their business, knowing full well she is unhappy. They will thus confirm her self-hater's basic premise: that nobody cares about her. Over time, some of them may begin to resent her silence and depression, and may truly not want to have her around, further confirming her self-hater's evaluation.

They can attack: "Goddamn it, don't lie there like a dying squid—tell us what's wrong!" This approach will not augment her self-esteem, nor deepen the group's bonding.

Or, they can refuse to be stopped by the barrier of her answer, and test their perceptions.

"That's odd," Susan might say. "I thought you looked unhappy. Are you unhappy about something?"

Embedded in Susan's question is a supportive statement: "I care enough about you to notice how you are feeling, and to be concerned." Her question has itself challenged the self-hater.

The group might have to go through several rounds of specific questions: "How are you feeling?" "Have we hurt you somehow?" They are also entitled to give up, if Jane is determined to cling to her unhappiness in private. Their questions will, nonetheless, have posed to Jane an alternative to the self-hater's version of reality.

"It's nothing," Jane finally says. "I guess I always feel left out when the group makes plans and I have to work."

The group might respond defensively, as if Jane had attacked them. "We can't run our lives around your work schedule." Or they might react apologetically: "I'm sorry—I guess we weren't sensitive. Let's not go out if Jane can't go." Either response will convince her that she was a fool to open her mouth.

A more empowering response would be to ask the question, "What can we do? How can we make it better?" The question implies, "We care about you—we want you to be happy." The group might come up with suggestions, but they do not rescue her. For the responsibility of naming what we need is itself empowering: it implies that we have the power to know what we want, ask for it, and get it. The question takes Jane out of the role of passive victim and challenges her to take an active role in securing her own happiness.

In counseling, I would find myself asking, over and over again, "What do you mean by that?"

"None of my lovers stay with me," a client might say. "They all say I'm too intense."

From the tone in her voice and the expression on her face, I sense that she finds this evaluation somewhat flattering.

"What do you mean by 'intense?' " I ask.

"Oh, you know—*intense.*"

"But I don't know," I say, because I suspect that what she means is something she does not want to admit. "Do you mean angry? Needy? Do you want too much sex?"

To answer my question, she must let go of the false specialness offered by the self-hater, and consider her real feelings. If she can take that risk, and find one place in which her rage, her need, her passion can be valued, she can never again be quite so isolated.

Feelings, perceptions, decisions, and actions are often tangled together like embroidery threads. We may translate an emotion into a decision, which seems to relieve the pain of feeling. When others respond to the decision, the emotion gets buried or ignored, and we end up feeling worse. Asking the right questions can sometimes help separate the strands.

I have asked my mother, who lives in another city but who co-owns our collective house, to apply with us for a new loan at a lower interest rate, and she has agreed. She calls me up late at night, angry.

"I'm not going to fill out this form!" she announces. "It's an imposition on me. The print is too small—I can't see it! I'm not going to do it!"

Once I would have taken her statement at face value, gotten angry, and we would have had a rousing fight. But I have learned, instead, to ask a simple question.

"How can I help you?" I say. I know my mother well enough to intuit her internal dialogue, which I suspect went something like this: "I don't want to fill out this damn form—my eyes are bad and I feel helpless—nobody's around to help me. I'm angry that I don't have help! I'm not going to do this!"

Asking "How can I help you?" cuts into the middle of the chain, countering the self-hater's message that no one can or will help. I follow up by actually providing help and explanations of aspects of the form that are confusing. My mother feels cared for and loved, instead of used and put-upon, and together we are able to complete the form without prob-lems.

Under the domination of the self-hater's messages, we act in ways that cause responses that confirm the self-hater's premises. When we do not believe that help is possible for us, we react to the pain of helplessness by screaming loudly, "I'm not going to help you!" Rarely are others sensitive enough to hear the underlying cry, "Help me!"

QUESTIONS TO CHALLENGE FALSE GLORY

Certain questions are particularly useful in challenging the delusions of power-over. Here is a short list:

1. What are you (we all) feeling?
2. What does *(word)* mean to you?
3. What do you need? What do you want?
4. What can we do? How can we help you?

Reframing is a term psychologists use for an old magical concept: that the way we describe and define reality determines the way in which we experience it. When we are possessed by the self-hater, domination frames all of our experience in the assumptions and terms of hierarchy. Reframing is an act of resistance, a posing of an alternate reality and value system by which to describe experience—one that affirms rather than attacks our sense of worth.

While I was still a student intern therapist in graduate school, I had a client who heard voices. He had been sexually abused as a child, had very low self-esteem, worked as a busboy for extremely low wages, and could have been diagnosed as "borderline" or "schizophrenic." Most of the ther-apy I did with him involved forming a relationship that affirmed his im-manent value. (At the time I couldn't have articulated that. I thought I was just improvising.)

I could not believe that Joe's voices were actually real beings but I also knew he probably would not be helped by my telling him, "Joe, you're just hallucinating. Those things don't exist. You're crazy." Magic provided a helpful framework, that offered tools for his condition and a less negative label for his problem.

"Joe," I said, "Something's going on with you and I don't know exactly what it is. I suspect you're very psychically open—but you've never had any proper training. You're like a radio that tunes into any old station out there with no way to sort out what's coming in. You may have entities buzzing around you, you may just be picking up on any old astral garbage that happens to be floating around."

I worked with him on developing psychic skills: learning to ground, to sense energy, to journey in trance states into other realities. Had I been further along in my psychological training, I probably wouldn't have dared to use those techniques, which are considered by most psychotherapists to be contraindicated for clients whose grasp on reality is shaky. But I felt that teaching him ways he could affect his own state of consciousness might make him feel less helpless.

The work with Joe was long, sometimes difficult, often rewarding, and too complex to describe here fully. But one day, he came into my room, sat down, and said, "You know, I've been thinking about those voices. If they really are entities directing my every move, they must be the most overworked and underpaid spirits on the astral plane." We both laughed. To make that admission, Joe had to let go of the sense of importance that the voices gave him—but he opened up the possibility of breaking out of his isolation. Although he still had problems, the voices were no longer among them.

As a sad footnote, Joe, who was gay, came to see me long before the AIDS crisis became known, in that period of time when the virus was circulating but the disease was not yet widely identified. Many of his "delusions" centered around fears for his health, belief that his blood was somehow "tainted," that he had acquired the "taint" by using drugs, especially through injecting heroin, which he had done in the past, that he had sores in his mouth and throat that were cancerous. I lost contact with Joe after our work ended, and don't know what happened to him. I hope he is well, but he was doubly at risk for AIDS, and if he himself has remained healthy, he has undoubtedly seen many of his friends fall ill. His "hallucinations" may have been ultrarefined perceptions of the state of his body. Our reframed description of reality was true; he was psychic, not paranoid.

A group can also reframe experience. We can define a setback as a failure, or as a stage in growth. We can define a success as a culmination, or as a first step in a long process. The way we frame our experience determines what we will learn from it and where we will go with it.

QUESTIONS OF FRAME

1. How are we naming or defining this event/experience/problem?
2. Where do those terms or definitions come from? What assumptions do they embody? How have they been used politically in the past?
3. What choices do our terms delineate for us? What roads do they open or close? What tools do they offer?
4. What alternative terms or ways could describe this event/experience/problem?

5. Which framework best serves us?

Ultimately, the structure of the group itself best challenges the false glory offered by the self-hater. When we are valued for our real selves, and feel safe to be who we are, the patterns of domination lose their force.

The Descent of Inanna, IV:
The Third Gate

The Third Gate is silence
Earth eats sound
The Dead have no voices
And somewhere
   you have lost yours
Words arise in you
   songs, chants, poetry
   pushed upward like fountains
   by the shifting weight of
      continents
   but find no outlet
Springs dry up

What keeps you silent
   is a voice
   that has stolen your voice
   and sings continuously
   in a low drone
   that you are, indeed, alone
Even the snake has disappeared
   anyway
   the damn thing only hisses
   sssssssssssssssssssss
To pass this gate
   you must sing
Emptiness echoes around you
No one will hear you
But you breathe deep
   and call
Your breath becomes a sound
   that tries to fill the echoing
      caverns
   and fails
   and tries
   again
Sing your own name
Sing the names
   of helpers, lovers,
   ancestors, children
   names of power
Keep on singing, keep on making

noise
even as your sound dies away
in the dark
and your throat hurts
from the stranglehold
of silence
Keep calling
Until at last
your call is echoed
from Below
And something comes through you
that blasts silence into pieces
they lie on the ground like
discarded jewels
The gate opens
You pass through singing
You have found your voice
and all that lives
sings through you
Beyond the Third Gate
Music weaves the fabric of the world

Finding a Voice:
Breaking the Censor's Silence

When we are free, we can speak the unspeakable and think the unthinkable. To liberate ourselves, we must challenge the internal Censor and find the voice that will let us express the power that comes from within.

The Censor makes its presence known as a voice whispering in our ears: "Don't say that! You don't really think that. You're the only one that feels that way—don't tell anyone." Or it appears as a figure in the internal landscape where we wander in dreams or venture in trance.

Notes from a trance to face the self-hater:

The West, the direction of water, is dry, but the air is pregnant with the coming storm, with foreboding. Alice heads into the storm, searching for that part of herself that demands perfection. She finds no place where she can stand, can root herself.

"Root yourself where you are, then," I suggest.

She breathes deep. She draws energy up from the earth, centers, and calls upon the creature to appear.

From the open space appears a huge, inflatable dummy. Made of plastic, she bounces and laughs and cannot speak, though Alice learns her name is Rhonda.

"What does she want?"

"To show me that there's nobody stopping me really, just something I imagine."

"Where does she come from?"

"The head."

"What part of the head creates her?"

"She can't talk."

"Can she show you?"

"No. Her arms are just painted on."

"Ask your head, then."

Alice begins to cry. "I'm scared. I'm scared to be all alone. I want someone to make sure everything's okay. I'm scared my own ideas aren't good enough."

"Is Rhonda smarter than you?"

"No, she's just someone there that keeps me blocking myself. I'm afraid to break away from blocking myself, afraid of what I might do."

"Let yourself look into the pool that you find at your feet. Let yourself see what you might do if you weren't blocking yourself."

Alice looks. She cries. "I'll be too happy. I won't be able to talk to people about my insecurities. I won't be able to relate to the same people anymore."

POSSESSION BY THE CENSOR

The King controls speech as well as action. War is always accompanied by censorship, and people are most easily controlled in isolation. The Censor keeps us from reaching out, from making connections. It reinforces the delusions of all the other aspects of the self-hater: that we are uniquely bad, that there is no help, that our personal suffering is not connected to the suffering of others. So Alice cannot trust her own ideas and thoughts. She is allowed to seek intimacy in certain patterned ways, by establishing a mutual litany of insecurities and self-doubts to ward off aggression. But Alice fears that if she lets her strength, her joy, her power show, she will be punished by being isolated. When the Censor rules, the self becomes like Rhonda: plastic, not real; inflated, not solid and grounded; unable to speak or to act.

The issue that obsesses us is that of isolation and connection. Can I connect? Will I be heard? How much of myself must I conceal to be accepted? But the acceptance we buy through concealing ourselves leaves us feeling even more isolated, sure that should we reveal who we really are, our worthlessness will show.

The Censor stops us from revealing both our real pain and our power. The delusion that the Censor imposes is that pain will go away if we keep quiet. As long as we say nothing, as long as no one notices anything, as long as what is happening is not named, it is not real.

"Don't talk" is one of the unspoken rules in alcoholic families.

"Thirteen-year-old Steve said, 'I thought I was going crazy. I thought I was the only one in my house who knew Dad was an alcoholic. . . . No one else ever said anything.' . . . I asked his mother and older sisters why they hadn't talked with Steve. They responded, 'Because he hadn't said anything, and we hoped he hadn't noticed.' "[1]

In the Censor's delusionary world, we discount other people's ability to see and hear. We blame those who refuse to close their eyes for "making a scene," while the victimizer is ignored, sympathized with, or forgotten.

"What might it have meant in practical terms if Freud had remained true to this insight [that emotional suffering in adults often stemmed from early sexual abuse]? . . . It is not hard to imagine the rage and indignation that would have greeted the facts. . . . The indignation would not have been directed against this form of child abuse per se but against the man who dared to speak of it. For most of these refined people were firmly convinced from an early age that only fine, noble, valiant, and edifying deeds (subjects) ought to be talked about publicly and that what they as adults did behind closed doors in their elegant bedrooms very definitely had no place in print. Satisfying sexual desires with children was nothing bad in their eyes as long as silence was preserved, for they were convinced that no harm would be done to the children unless the matter were discussed with them. Therefore, the acts they performed were shrouded in silence, as if children were dolls, for they firmly believed a doll would never know or tell what had been done to it."[2]

The Censor has a powerful weapon in shame. We keep silent because we feel ashamed of a situation, or fear shame if others find out. Incest victims are exhorted not to talk for fear of bringing shame on the family. And often the one who attempts to bring an abuse to light is shamed and blamed. Sandy Butler, in her book on incest called *Conspiracy of Silence,* tells the story of Margaret, who attempted to get help when she discovered that her well-respected husband was abusing their children. Her husband's family told her she was overreacting, imagining things. Eventually she was hospitalized with a "nervous breakdown." School authorities and police ignored her pleas. Finally, she turned to "her personal source of solace and refuge"—the church. She discussed her problem at a meeting, asking for help. "The people around her—people whom she had known, worked and worshipped with even before she was married—first expressed openness, then horror and disbelief, and finally masked their feelings behind expressionless faces. Margaret finished by asking for suggestions from anyone present as to what else she might try to do. She was answered by a muffled cough or two, the sound of bodies moving uncomfortably about on wooden chairs and nothing else. The next day Margaret was visited by two of the church's trustees. They told her that the church board had met that morning and had decided unanimously to recommend that she not attend any further church functions until she got things 'straightened out at home.' "[3]

Another victim said, "You come to believe that you're the crazy one and take all the responsibility for what is happening. . . . You try lots of different ways to tell, and nobody is listening. So you stop trying and come to the only conclusion that is left to you. That it's you that is bad, and that if you hadn't been so bad, Daddy wouldn't have had sex with you."[4]

Silence makes the victim culpable. A young woman I spoke with who had worked at a workshop center for a variety of Eastern yogis in the seventies told me of being "chased around the kitchen" by a succession of "spiritual masters" who preached and presumably practiced the strictest celibacy. "At first I felt so bad," she said. "I thought I must be really dirty and awful to bring that out in this holy man. I felt so ashamed—I didn't want to tell anyone about it. But finally some of the women started to talk—and then we realized it had been happening to all of us."

Women have always experienced the underside of patriarchy: the fist, the bottle, and sexual abuse. But with all our knowledge, women remain powerless against hypocrisy, rape, and abuse as long as we keep silent. The power of the Censor must be broken before we can become empowered. So the revival of the women's movement in the late sixties and early seventies was centered around the consciousness-raising group: small groups in which women broke years of silence and spoke to each other about our experiences.

CREATING CONNECTIONS WITH OUR STORIES

To be silenced is to be kept isolated. When we attempt to create intimacy and support, telling our stories becomes a central act. We have seen how telling and hearing our stories restores value. The stories we tell also create connections and break our isolation. When we can speak of our experiences, no matter how painful, we can make contact. And when our real selves can be seen, mirrored, affirmed, we can know, perhaps for the first time, that we are valued.

When we tell about our lives, we give shape to the events we have lived; they take on a pattern and new dimensions of meaning. Experience changes in the telling. When we talk about what has happened to us, we may feel what we could not feel at the time: hurt, sadness, rage. Or we may find that old scars have healed, that what was painful or humiliating has become funny. Telling our stories is an act of healing, the core of all forms of psychotherapy, the beginning of all forms of systemic change.

In Alcoholics Anonymous and the other Twelve-Step programs, the Fifth Step explicitly counters the Censor: "We admitted to God, to ourselves, and to another human being the exact nature of our wrongs."[5] Such admissions cannot be made without support, and even then we resist.

"Certain distressing or humiliating memories, we tell ourselves, ought not to be shared with anyone . . . yet . . . this is actually a perilous resolve. [Those who try] will tell how they tried to carry the load alone; how much they suffered of irritability, anxiety, remorse, and depression. . . . What are we likely to receive from Step Five? For one thing, we shall get rid of that terrible sense of isolation we've always had. . . ."[6]

Isolation is one of the great weapons of the self-hater. Breaking silence releases us. When others know the worst about us, and accept us, we can believe we are truly valued.

Telling our stories is a political act. "Women's stories have not been told. And without stories there is no articulation of experience. Without stories a woman is lost when she comes to make the important decisions of her life. She does not learn to value her struggles, to celebrate her strengths, to comprehend her pain. Without stories she cannot understand her self. . . . She is closed in silence."[7]

The feminist consciousness-raising groups of the late sixties and early seventies were safe places in which women could tell our stories. When we began speaking from our own experience, valuing those aspects of our lives that male authority had trivialized or rendered invisible—rape, battering, sexual abuse, abortion—we found that none of us were alone in our experiences, and that all of our experience had a political dimension. We developed analyses and actions that sprang from the reality of our lives. For the first time, we could see our lives in their full context.

Oppression can be so embedded in a system that we literally cannot see it. The new context created when we tell our stories makes oppression visible, and challengeable. When I joined my first consciousness-raising group, I was a twenty-year-old art student at the University of California at Los Angeles. At that time, almost no professors were women. Few women painters were studied in our art history classes; nor were black artists noted outside of courses on African art. Yet I was aware of discrimination only as a vague sense of uneasiness. Rarely were the real underlying prejudices against women given voice, and when they were, I did not hear them as evidence of systematic oppression. One of my favorite professors once admitted that he was less likely to devote a lot of time to women students or recommend them for graduate school, because "all you women are interested in is getting married and getting some man to support you." My inner reaction was: "Yeah, all those stupid, uptight, straight housewives—I'm not like them." Until I sat with other women, heard their stories, shared my own, became conscious of the ways that systems discriminate, I could not see that my professor's attitude did, indeed, affect me.

The stories of the oppressed are not told under systems of domination, and telling them can be a revolutionary act. William Hinton describes how a Communist party organizer in a Chinese village during the Revolution posed to the villagers the question of who lived off whom. He urged each member to tell his or her life story and to figure out for himself or herself the root of the problem.

" . . . This [story] reminded poor peasant Shen T'ien-hsi of the loss of his home. 'Once when we needed some money we decided to sell our house. We made a bargain with a man who offered a reasonable price, but Sheng Ching-ho, who lived next door, forced us to sell our house to him for almost nothing.'

"Then poor peasant Ta-hung's wife spoke up. 'You had to sell your house, but my parents had to sell me. We lived in a prosperous valley but we owned no land. In the famine year we were starving and my parents sold me for a few bushels of grain. . . .'

"Story followed story. Many wept as they remembered the sale of children, the death of family members, the loss of property. The village cadres kept asking 'What is the reason for this? Why did we all suffer so? Was it the "eight ideographs" that determine our fate or was it the land system and rents we had to pay?' "[8]

Breaking silence becomes political when our shared experiences become the ground in which theory and practice is rooted. We tell stories in the context of broader questions. We reflect on what is common in our experience, and what is different. From those reflections come our analyses, and our directions for action.

JOURNAL EXERCISE TO BREAK THE CENSOR'S SILENCE

List the subjects you could not or cannot talk about, notice, think about, or things you could not or cannot say, in:

• your childhood family
• school
• your present family, couple relationship, and/or household
• your job
• among your friends
• with your lover(s)
• with particular individuals

Decide whether or not you want to say them. Try saying some of them—and see what happens.

(I do not accept liability for consequences of this exercise!)

UNCENSORING EXERCISE FOR GROUPS/FAMILIES/COUPLES

Notice when you are bored, when the dull fog of the Censor creeps in. Ask: What is not being said here? What am I not seeing/saying/ doing? What do I want to do? What do I fear?

Some good general questions to ask periodically:

1. What can we not say? What can we not question?
2. What subjects do we avoid talking about? Shift away from?
3. When have any of us felt foggy, bored, distanced, or stifled?
4. When have we felt isolated?
5. Does each of us participate as fully as she or he would like to? What stops us? What changes could help us?
6. Do some people dominate discussions? How do others feel?

7. What beliefs and values do we hold in common? Are they stated or unstated? Can we question them?

CONSCIOUSNESS-RAISING ROUNDS

For each meeting, choose a topic. Give each person in the group a protected time to speak. Set a time limit, if need be. Allow no one to interrupt, ask questions, or challenge the speaker. (Time can be allotted for questions after each speaker finishes. A group larger than eight should consider subdividing to allow individuals more time.)

After all have spoken, discuss what common threads and differences emerged. What has the group learned? What directions for action, for change, emerge?

TRUTH OR DARE

The game of Truth or Dare is an antidote to the Censor. In a situation of enforced boredom (locked up in a holding cell, for example), the game's power to provide endless entertainment is unparalleled. We play it in two ways:

1. One person is it. Anyone else in the group is free to ask that person a question, which must be answered with the truth. The more embarrassing, the better. For example:
   —What is your most politically incorrect fantasy?
   —Who in this room would you most like to have sex with?
   —What question are you most afraid I'll ask you?—and answer it.
(To which my friend Max responds, "That one—and I just did.")
   If the person doesn't answer with the truth, she or he has to take the dare—which is even worse.
2. A question is thrown out to the group. Each person takes a turn to answer it. This version is often played more seriously to aid group understanding and bonding. For example, when our collective household was forming, we played rounds at house meetings with questions such as:
   —What issues are you especially sensitive about?
   —What are the open wounds from your childhood that we should be aware of?

THE ROUGH GAME

This game should be played on soft ground—a grassy field or sandy beach are best. A room with a carpet or smooth wood floor will do. It is a rough game, and people sometimes get hurt. That's a warning. Play at your own risk.

Remove eyeglasses and rings and put in some safe place. Take hands in a standing circle. Ask yourself, "What does the self-hater say to me? How does it attack me?"

One person gets in the center, and says out loud what the self-hater says. The group repeats it, shouting, screaming, taunting, while holding tight to each other's hands. The person in the center has to break through the circle. (Somewhat like the children's game "Red Rover.")

The game may become fierce and lively. Shouts ring out. "You'll never do anything right!" "Stupid!" "You're fat and you're ugly!" "Take care of me! You're so selfish!" To stand in the center, hearing your worst inner dialogue screamed at you from ten or twenty people, at first seems overwhelming, but as you gather courage and strength to break through, and the shouts change to cheers and applause, you feel elated. The tighter people hold to each other, and the harder it is to break the circle, the more power you feel at the end.

After each person succeeds in breaking free, she or he chooses the next victim.

At the end, discuss what was common and what was different, and what you learned. Check how each person is feeling. Usually, groups find this game creates immediate bonding. Everyone now knows the worst—so what is there to fear?

MAKING DECISIONS BY CONSENSUS

The decision-making structure of the groups we create is also expression of the value placed on each member, and can itself challenge the Censor. Groups that use consensus process make a powerful statement of value.

People either love or hate consensus. I have seen large groups run entirely on consensus in which each member felt empowered by the process, and I have seen consensus meetings become long, boring, frustrating, and nasty, and the process used to keep a group from wrestling with real conflicts or moving forward with controversial actions.

Problems arise with consensus because groups often don't clearly understand what it is. Consensus is not so much a decision-making process as a thinking process of the group mind. It is a way to consider problems, not just a way to choose between alternative courses of action. The stronger a group is as an entity in itself, the better consensus works.

In organic communities, tribes, and villages, consensus, formal or informal, is the way decisions are made. Issues are talked over until a general community sense is reached. Discussion of the community's affairs is considered not an onerous duty but a social pleasure, an empowering responsibility that lends status and prestige to those who take part in it.

Decision making can itself become a ritual. Jill Roberts from New Zealand described to me a Maori meeting to decide on important questions about use of their tribal lands. "The whole village met in a special hut. They began with ritual, and they all stayed until the decision was reached—even though it took days. People left to eat, but they slept right there, and discussion went on all night long. It didn't matter to them if you were awake or asleep—as long as you were there."

In small, closed communities, where people cannot simply leave when conflict develops, the cohesion of the group becomes more important than any single decision or plan of action. Consensus process furthers the bonding of a group, and affirms each member's value above the importance of any single issue.

Those of us who love consensus process see it as a spiritual practice rooted in the idea of each person's immanent value. The North American peace movement adopted consensus from the Quakers, whose religion recognizes the Inner Light of the spirit as immanent in each human being.

Many resources exist for learning consensus process.[9] I have observed that consensus works best with less formality and more humor, so I will describe it loosely here, as follows.

CONSENSUS PROCESS

A topic or issue is discussed by a group, and everyone's opinion is sought. Eventually, someone suggests a plan of action—makes a proposal. If response is enthusiastic and support is general, people are asked to state their concerns. The proposal is gradually modified until concerns are met. The plan is solidified when everyone agrees that it best meets both the circumstances and the needs of the group. Consensus is reached. Often, the plan is formally stated or written down; otherwise, people tend to forget their agreements.

When consensus works well, it becomes a creative process. The group examines all facets of an issue without becoming polarized into opposing positions. Aspects of an idea that one person might miss are seen by others. Proposals synthesize previous discussion and then are further refined until the best possible plan is made.

Of course, people don't always reach total agreement. Individuals may express reservations, or "stand aside"—not participate in a particular plan. An individual who has a strong moral objection—not merely a disagreement, however sharp, but an ethical concern—can actually block the group from carrying out a plan.

For example, last year I was part of a small group that planned a Summer Solstice ritual for our extended community. Two of the planners wanted to incorporate a fire walk, a ritual in which people walk barefoot over hot coals, presumably without getting burned. I was frankly scared, but I trusted the woman who wanted to lead it.

On the night of the ritual, about seventy people met at the beach. We cleansed ourselves in the ocean, and then discussed the ritual plan. The fire walk was explained as an act of empowerment. "Once I did it," one of the leaders said, "I felt I could do anything." We were then given some time to talk in pairs about our fears.

When we regathered, Deborah, a woman in my affinity group, stood up. "I have some very strong feelings about this," she said. "I can't participate in it, and if you're going to do it, I'll have to leave the ritual."

"Why? What's the problem?" we asked.

"I don't want to walk on fire. To me, it's like showing that we can triumph over nature, and that's not what being a Witch is about. Being a Witch is about being part of nature, not having power over it. It's like trivializing the millions of Witches who were burned, like saying they wouldn't have been hurt if they'd only had the right attitude."

We discussed her objections. Some of us agreed, some disagreed, but none of us felt like going ahead with the fire walk without Deborah. No ritual can work if the group does not feel wholeheartedly right about it. Trying to walk on hot coals when we felt divided in spirit seemed an especially bad idea. Deborah had, in effect, blocked the group.

Other people felt disappointed, so we came up with another plan: to hold a separate fire-walking ritual on another, more appropriate night (the Fourth of July) and to continue on with our Solstice ritual. We celebrated our own fire ritual, drumming and chanting and dancing as we burned a flower-decked effigy of the Year-God to symbolize the decline of the sun, the life that gives itself away so that life can continue. At the end, we felt complete, and tired, and very glad not to have to walk on fire. We had originally planned to put far too much into the ritual. The group mind, through Deborah's objections, had perceived what we planners had not.

The possibility of a block exists in the consensus process out of the realization that a flaw in a plan may at times only be apparent to one person. But blocks are, in practice, used rarely: generally, extremely strong objections are brought forth in discussion and the plan is either modified or dropped. But the potential to block shapes and limits discussion. An underlying premise of consensus is that if a group's course of action cause someone extreme distress, it's probably not worth doing. It will cause too much resentment and undermine the group's cohesion. The block becomes an unspoken expectation of how much power each person is entitled to wield.

Deborah knew that she had the right to stop the group from doing something she felt strongly it should not do, even if she were the only person who felt so. She overcame the inner Censor and spoke. Once she spoke, we found that many people shared her feelings, but had kept quiet because they did not feel entitled to speak. Had Deborah also not spoken out, the group would have gone ahead with the fire walk, never knowing those concerns existed and they might have undermined the ritual with disastrous results.

We are trained to have little to say in the decisions that affect us. We may hesitate to voice our objections or to go against what others seem to want or believe. But consensus only works when we do voice our own truth. Often, when we risk speaking out, we find that others share our concerns.

Over time, we become accustomed to shaping decisions. The sense that we are entitled to power becomes ingrained and strengthens our sense of worth. Consensus can function as a healing process and as a radicalizing process, for when we get used to being heard and valued, we become less and less patient with systems that invalidate us.

Consensus is not always the most effective or appropriate decision-making process. Holding rigidly to strict consensus process when it becomes painful and frustrating ultimately undermines a group's willingness to stay with the process at more fruitful times. There are some situations in which consensus may become more trouble than it's worth.

WHEN NOT TO USE CONSENSUS:

When there is no group mind

A group thinking process cannot work effectively unless the group is cohesive enough to generate shared attitudes and perceptions. When deep divisions exist within a group, or when members don't value the group's bonding over their individual desires, consensus becomes an exercise in frustration.

When there are no good choices

Consensus process can help a group find the best possible solution to a problem, but it is not an effective way to make an either-or choice between two evils, for members will never be able to agree which is worse. If the group has to choose between being shot and hung, flip a coin.

When a group gets bogged down trying to make a decision, stop for a moment and consider: Are we blocked because we are given an intolerable situation? Are we being given the illusion, but not the reality, of choice? Might our most empowering act be to refuse to participate in this farce?

When they can see the whites of your eyes

In emergencies, in situations where urgent and immediate action is necessary, appointing a temporary leader may be the wisest course of action.

When the issue is trivial

I have known groups to devote half an hour to trying to decide by consensus whether to spend forty minutes or a full hour at lunch. Remember, consensus is a *thinking* process—when there is nothing to think about, flip a coin.

When the group has insufficient information

When you're lost in the hills, and no one knows the way home, you cannot figure out how to get there by consensus. Send out scouts. Ask: Do we have the information we need to solve this problem? Can we get it? (If the information is not available by other means, consider an oracle: Tarot cards are what I use.)

In May of 1985, I participated in a walk with women from the Greenham Common Peace Camp in England. We walked from Silbury Hill, one of the ancient power places of the British Isles, across Salisbury Plain to Stonehenge. The walk began on Beltane, a major holiday of the Pagan year, and ended with an illegal ritual in the stones on a night of a total lunar eclipse. The plain is currently used as an artillery field and military base; through our walk, we symbolically reclaimed it.

For me, participating in decision making with the Greenham Common women brought on culture shock. In contrast to our West Coast style of consensus, involving facilitators, agendas, plans, and formal processes, their meetings seemed to have no structure at all. No one facilitated, no agendas were set; everyone spoke whenever she wanted to and said what she thought. Where we valued plans and scenarios, they valued spontaneity, trusting in the energy of the group and the moment. Instead of long discussions about the pros and cons of any given plan, those women who wanted to do it simply went ahead, and those who didn't, did not participate.

I found a delicious sense of freedom and an electricity in discussions unhampered by formalities. The consensus process I had known and practiced seemed, in retrospect, overly controlled and controlling. Its rules and procedures seemed to impose the Censor under a new form.

At the same time, the Greenham-style process also has drawbacks. The group's preference for action rather than talk produces an inherent bias toward more extreme and militant actions. With no facilitation, louder and more vocal women tend to dominate discussions. Women who have fears, concerns, or alternate plans often felt unheard.

Each group needs to develop a decision-making process that fits its unique circumstances. The balance between planning and spontaneity, between formal processes and informal free-for-alls, is always alive, dynamic, and changing. No one way will work for every group.

Here are some suggestions for processes that may be helpful or appropriate at various times.

ROUNDS FOR DECISION MAKING

Examine a question, tell stories, or give opinions by going around the circle, giving each person a protected time in which to speak without being interrupted or challenged.

Alternatively, try a web: speak in any order, but allow no one to speak twice until every person has spoken once.

Having a formal time period allotted in which to speak helps people who may feel uncomfortable talking in groups. Each person can choose to pass a turn, so that there is no pressure to talk. If, however, the group wants to exert such pressure, decide that if someone does not speak during her or his time period, the group will sit in silence until it passes.

This process works best in small groups. It can defuse a volatile disagreement—but it can also be used to keep real conflicts in the group from being thoroughly aired. If a round reveals splits, it is best followed with free-form discussion.

FACILITATION

Groups do not always need facilitation, but clarity and brevity may often be served by having someone recognize those who wish to speak, keep the group focused, and help move discussion through the agenda. Facilitators can help equalize participation by calling on people who tend to speak less, or by seeking out opinions from those who have not spoken.

Everyone in the group is also responsible for equalizing participation. Any person can say, at any time, "Let's hear from someone who hasn't spoken yet." Or: "Stella, that's the fourteenth time you've spoken in the last half hour."

Participation is never absolutely equal, nor would we want it to be. People have different strengths, skills, and temperaments, as well as good days and bad days. But giving attention to those who speak up less readily affirms the group's commitment to the empowerment of each member.

PASSING A WAND (RATTLE, SHELL, OR OTHER SACRED OBJECT)

Choose a sacred object, and allow whoever holds it to speak. When she or he is done, the object is passed to the next speaker.

This process slows discussion and gives it a ritualized character. I find it works well for certain subjects: for example, when I ask students to speak about their experiences of God or Goddess. But when it is used in general discussion, or as a means to contain conflict, I find it irritating.

BRAINSTORMING

For a specified, short period of time, have the group throw out suggestions or solutions or creative ideas, the wilder the better, without criticizing them. Later, evaluate the ideas, and choose a few to be developed further.

This process can be stimulating but can also lead to frustration. It has a tendency to generate long lists of things to be talked about at some unnamed future date. It is a disaster when used, for example, to collect possible items for an agenda. Be strict with the time limit: five minutes, ten at the very most, is more than enough time for a brainstorm.

WATCHING THE ENERGY

Whenever a group is together, energy is generated, and its level rises and falls with the level of excitement of a group. When we expect meetings to be grueling, we ignore signals of discomfort. But boredom is a signal that something is wrong. Often it tells us of the Censor's presence. Watch for it. Observe your own feelings, and the expressions and body language of others. When the energy in a group drops, ask:

1. Are people in physical distress? Do we need a break? Is the room airless? Are the smokers suffering nicotine withdrawal?
2. Are certain individuals dominating the group? Repeating themselves? If so, you do them a favor by cutting them short before everyone begins to hate them.
3. Are underlying conflicts not being discussed openly? If so, name them. Boredom will disappear fast.
4. Have we done too much talking? Do we need to shift into some nonverbal activity? Do so. For example, a group of women were becoming frustrated discussing plans for a ritual. They began moving, picking up sticks, dancing, drumming—and out of the physical motion new ideas evolved.

5. Does this subject interest everybody? Can those who are obsessed with it continue the discussion outside, or later? Is it really our business?
6. Are we talking about something we can actually do anything about? Are we being forced to take actions we resent? What choices do we have?
7. Are we having fun yet? How long has it been since we last laughed?

CHANGING THE ENERGY

When the energy gets low, dull, sleepy, or bored, some ways to quickly raise it are:

Physical movement, stretching, dancing, running around, playing games such as Hug Tag. One person is it. "It" tries to tag the others, who are safe as long as they are hugging each other. They can hug in pairs or promiscuously in groups. "It" can at any time count to five, at which time everyone has to scatter, run around, and hug someone else.

Dancing to loud music with a strong back beat.

Humor. Saying or doing something funny. (Some people have a natural talent for this and others never quite seem to get it right. That is not my fault.)

Saying something you are not supposed to say. Anytime the Censor's grip is broken, the energy will rise.

Sex—mentioning it, commenting on it, flirting with someone (but only, of course, in the most politically correct way).

Singing or chanting.

Drumming.

Expressing anger (not necessarily toward someone in the group: anger about a current situation, frustration, for example). Again, if the Censor has been repressing anger in the group, bringing it out will raise energy.

Taking a group nap for fifteen minutes.

If the energy of a group is too high, nervous, anxious, or frantic, you can calm it down by:

Running wildly around the room chanting:

> "When in worry, when in doubt,
> Run in circles, scream and shout!
> Eeek! Eeek! Eeek!"[10]

Sitting down and breathing together.

Doing a grounding meditation.

Chanting a single tone together.

Giving each other shoulder rubs or neck messages.

Singing, chanting, or drumming a slow rhythm.

Staying calm yourself.

EMPOWERED LEARNING AND ORGANIZING

Valuing experience and breaking silence establishes a model for learning, influenced also by the theories of Paolo Freire and adult learning theory.[11] The nonviolent preparers in the San Francisco Bay Area, those who took on the responsibility of preparing people for civil disobedience, searched for ways to teach the theory, history, and practical applications of non-violence that fit our commitment to equalizing power. We developed a style of training we called "empowered learning." We drew on students' own abilities to reflect and analyze, by asking them to share past experi-ences, and by creating experiences through role plays. The group could then reflect on what happened and draw conclusions and directives for actions. If, in a role play a woman lost her temper and began screaming at a "policeman," we could later discuss how the incident made us feel and what results it had. Over the years, our trainings, which originally had involved long lectures, became almost entirely a series of role plays and reflections. They were more effective preparation—and fun.

To break silence, we must feel safe. The commitment to undoing the Censor must be clear in every aspect of a group's interactions. We cannot encourage people to share their stories freely, and then discourage criticism of the group. We cannot ask others to reveal their true feelings, and then condemn them if those feelings are not "politically correct." Our ideas must arise from our real experience; we cannot constrain our experience to fit our ideology and become free.

Groups do tend to develop unspoken rules that govern what can be said and what cannot. Such rules can be deadly, undermining all the group's efforts to establish value and safety. A group that fosters liberation cannot afford "correct" or "incorrect" lines, dogmas, or deceits.

Nor can a group undo the Censor unless everyone is encouraged to speak. If the group allows a few articulate members to dominate discussion and decision making, others will be silenced. Processes such as rounds can help shyer people to win their struggles with the inner silencer, and help those who dominate discussion to learn when to be quiet. For when the Censor's silence is broken, we can recover the power to choose silence, to know when to speak and when to shut up.

A friend and I were discussing our experience of the Diablo Canyon action of '81, the first time either of us had been immersed in feminist consensus process.

"I come from a working-class background; I'm the child of an alcoholic; I don't speak up easily in front of groups. But I always felt that my opinion was valued—that I could speak if I wanted to," she said.

"For me, it was the opposite," I said. "I've always been verbal—all through school I was usually the one who had the right answer. But when I got into the action, suddenly I was no longer valued for always being the one to say the right thing. I learned to shut up and give other people some space. At first it was somewhat devastating. I hadn't realized how much of my own self-worth was based on feeling superior. But it was actually a relief to let that go."

I could change in the context of the group's commitment to what we termed feminist process, by which we meant group process committed to challenging unequal power relations. I was expected to temper my skills and abilities with restraint and awareness of the balance of power in the group. At first, I found the process ego-shattering, but later, I discovered through it a deeper sense of security. Feminist process took me out of a role that was isolating and lonely. People can give up power-over and superiority in a context in which they feel empowered and valued.

TAKING RESPONSIBILITY FOR OUR TRUTH

When the Censor possesses us, we are also obsessed with issues of responsibility. The Censor threatens that what we name, we will be blamed for. The implied promise is that we are not reponsible for what we don't name.

So the Censor stops us from speaking of our pain, for we fear being shamed and blamed for what has been done to us. Silent, we remain isolated, unable to connect with others. Isolated, we may accept the false compensation of "specialness": of being set apart by our very wrongness. For to connect, we must take the terrifying risk of speaking our truth, revealing our real and vulnerable self.

The Censor also stops us from revealing—and knowing—our power. For power-from-within arises as spontaneous action, movement, expression, joy. In war, of course, spontaneity is not allowed. Soldiers need to obey, to follow orders, not to act on impulse or intuition. Like good soldiers, we are trained by the Censor not to speak or act without first getting permission. On a thousand subtle levels, we scan the atmosphere before we speak. We ask ourselves: Am I allowed to express anger? Disagreement? Pleasure? What am I not allowed to say?

A group of women is going on a trance journey together. As they gaze into a crystal, each speaks of what she sees until together they weave a landscape, a road to travel. The terrain is lovely, full of green fields and flowers. The women dance together in the spirit world, trailing colored gauzelike clouds.

When they emerge, they discuss what they saw. "I'm really angry," one woman says. "That trance was disgusting—it was like Disneyland. I wasn't seeing all those flowers and butterflies. I kept seeing bones and pools of blood but I didn't feel I could say anything because you all were seeing rainbows."

"That's funny," another woman says. "I was seeing bones, too. I wasn't seeing the flowers, but I didn't want to say anything because you all were in such a positive space and my vision was so negative."

As we go around the circle, I begin to wonder who was seeing flowers and rainbows for every woman seems to have had a more grim but more powerful vision. Yet every woman was waiting for someone else to give her the permission to say what she really saw. No one took the dare—to tell the truth, whether or not it was "allowed." Each is ready to blame the group for somehow failing her, instead of taking responsibility and taking her own real power. Every one of them could have spoken. There were, in reality, no rules, no sanctions, no threats to prevent them. And had any one woman spoken out, the others would have taken her example as permission to also speak.

If we wait for some authority to grant us permission to take our power, we will wait a long time; it is not in the interests of authority that we become empowered. Responsibility means being responsible to our own power. To take power is to be willing to speak the truth that rises in us, whether other people approve of us or not. When the sacred comes alive in us, we become responsible to the truth we alone can tell, to that facet of the great vision we alone can see. That responsibility overrides any obligation to please. As a model, we might take Alice Walker's praise of her daughter: "She spoke her mind in no uncertain terms, and would fight back when attacked."[12]

In ritual, energy moves from person to person, striking first one, then another, with inspiration. Your body begins to move; you want to dance wildly. If you do, you will bring power into the circle, a gift to everyone. Some will feel your dance as inspiration and join you. Some will witness, watching and appreciating. Some will be caught in their own movements but will feel the freeing of the energy as you spin.

But when the Censor intervenes, you feel the urge and cannot act. "Dance!" your body says, and the Censor says, "Don't make a fool of yourself. Nobody else is jumping into the center." So the impulse is stifled, but not destroyed. It remains, like a stone on the cover of a well, weighing down the energy of the group, preventing any new impulse from arising until you release it. Instead of inspiring or entertaining or outraging the circle, you become a neutral or even deadening force. No one may notice you at all, but the ritual will be less exciting, less powerful, than it could have been. And as in ritual, so in other groups, in life. The tragedy of the Censor's rule is the loss of the life, the color, the wildness, the power, the humor, the passion, that might have been.

When Witches say someone "really knows how to move energy" or is "good in a circle," we mean that person is open to the moments of power that come. To move energy is to be courageous in expressing what spontaneously arises and to be fearlessly still when the impulse to move or speak has passed. For as well as keeping us quiet when we have a truth to speak, the Censor can also keep us talking when we actually have nothing to say. "Say something!" the voice whispers. "Show the teacher how smart you are. Show the boss how on top of it all you are. Keep talking—don't let there be a silence that might reveal the real emptiness here." In ritual, the Censor whispers, "Don't notice that the energy isn't really in what's happening—and whatever you do, don't mention it."

The following processes and rituals are for helping inner power find its voice.

A DANGEROUS MEDITATION

For a day, let yourself be aware of the impulses you have for self-expression. What happens when you act on them? What happens when you suppress them? How do you suppress them?

Choose a day when you can be free of responsibilities and devote it to acting on whatever creative impulses arise. Write in your journal about how you feel, what changes, what happens, what fears arise, what surprises develop.

SINGING NAMES

Easy version: One by one, people in the group sing their names, as creatively as each person can. The group sings them back, as a way of affirming each person.

Challenging version: The challenge is to sing your name in a way that reveals your power to the group. After each person sings the first time, the group responds with criticism and encouragement:

"Come on—I know you're more powerful than that."

"Go ahead, let it out."

"That was good—but you can be stronger."

Repeat the process a second time, and then a third. After the third time, if the group is satisfied that the singer has really shown her/his power, they sing the name back, perhaps adding applause and drum rolls.

POWER DANCE

The group sings, drums, claps, makes rhythm, and chants in a circle. One person jumps into the center and dances to reveal her or his personal power to the group. Or each person might say something about where she or he finds power. The group may affirm each person with a song, a chant, by singing names, or shouting "Ache—acheo!" (the Yoruba word for personal power—shouting it out is like saying, "More power to you!").

When each person leaves the center, she or he chooses the next person to go into the circle and dance.

SCARF DANCE

This ritual is helpful in enacting the way power and inspiration move from person to person. In the center of the circle, place a pile of colored scarves. Within sacred space, drum and chant or put on some high-energy music. Whoever is moved to grabs a scarf and begins to dance. When the inspiration passes, she or he passes the scarf on to someone else (who may or may not want it—but that is how inspiration works). Continue until the energy for the ritual passes.

Over food, discuss how the energy moved and flowed. Did you want the scarf when you got it? Did you take it when you wanted it? Did you let it go when inspiration left? How did you feel, what did you hear in your mind, when you made each choice? How big, how loud, how wild did you allow yourself to get? What helped you or blocked you from being wilder?

BREAKING THROUGH THE FOG

The Censor does not always prevent us from talking about pain. We can talk about past pain, old pain, childhood pain, generic pain endlessly. In times of healing, the events of the past become illumined with the energy of the present: we feel the old hurts anew and can mourn and rage and do the undone work that remains to release ourselves. At other times we recite a litany of stale sorrows when no real emotional power moves through them. But the pain we cannot express is the pain going on at the moment, the pain clamouring to us to change something here and now.

A man and a woman are making love. He is stroking her vulva when suddenly he turns over on his back and withdraws into himself.

"Why are you stopping?" she asks.

"My hand is tired," he says, "and besides, I'm bored."

"That's sort of insulting," she says.

He is a man who prides himself on sensitivity. He has been through support groups, therapy groups, co-counseling groups, men's consciousness-raising groups. He knows the proper phrases with which to deflect conflict.

"Yes, I can see how that might seem insulting to you," he says. "If you need to express your anger, I want to hear it. You have my permission to get angry at me."

She could, at this point, make several honest responses, variations on the theme "Get out of my bed, you turkey."

Instead, she begins to cry. She cries for all the rejections of the past, all the buried pain of her childhood, all the lovers who have hurt her, all the disappointments. The pain of the moment begins to seem insignificant by comparison; she has all but forgotten it. She can even ask him to comfort her as she weeps; she can be open to him, vulnerable, excruciatingly honest about all her past mistakes. But the Censor keeps her mouth firmly shut about the pain he is causing her at that very moment. For to own that pain would be to become responsible for acting out of it. She would have to rebel.

Instead, she withdraws, goes to sleep, says no more about the incident. In the morning, they go out to breakfast, talk about the headlines in the newspaper. She is bored now. She wants him to go away, and he soon does.

Boredom is a nearly infallible signal of the Censor's presence. For the Censor's realm is gray and dull. When we are possessed, we do not necessarily feel great pain or shame or guilt. We become numb. Numbness may be preferable to great pain, and the dullness of not feeling may be the benefit we obtain by obedience to the Censor's strictures. But, of course, when we deny our pain we also lose the potential for changing the conditions that are hurting us.

The Censor appears in the inner landscape as fog, dullness, the blankness of nothingness, of shutting down. Elisabeth went through a series of trance journeys in which a recurring theme was the arising of fog that would inevitably block or dissipate whatever power she had gathered.

She goes to the forest, in the west, where nothing grows on a plowed field, and the air seems misty, chilly. She has a hard time seeing clearly, as if a film keeps her one step removed. It makes her angry.

She breathes her anger up. "I want to rip open whatever's between me and the forest." She makes sounds, screams, then stops.

"I'm tiring. There's no resistance, nothing to push against. I keep forgetting I'm angry. I'm floating, I forget that I'm on the edge of the forest. I have to pull back, be aware of whatever's blocking my sight."

"How do you feel?"

"I have an image of a lion prowling, pacing at the edge of the barrier, clawing, tearing, bellowing . . . it's a part of me, a powerful uncontrolled part . . . it feels like it's gathering energy, pacing back and forth—it's a big lion . . ." Then silence.

"What's happening?"

"I'm losing touch . . . I'm trying to draw up fire from the center of the earth—it gets into my body, and dissipates."

"What's blocking it?"

"Fog. Creeping fog."

The Censor's fog can take hold of a group, a relationship, a life, as a feeling of deadness, weariness, boredom. The Censor's presence is felt as an absence—of feeling, passion, energy. At other times the room may echo with screaming, but nothing is really moving. We can easily mistake noise for emotion, creating dramas that function like the illusionist's mirrors, distracting the eye from what is really going on.

When I was practicing as a therapist, my dog Arnold always lay on the rug in my office. Half Australian sheepdog, half husky, he appeared with his mottled coat and different-colored eyes to be six-year-old cubist's idea of a wolf, but he was infallibly empathetic and not easily fooled. Clients could dramatize their emotions, could scream, yell, and throw things, and he would lie quietly at my feet. But whenever someone was in real distress, whether they were crying aloud or sitting absolutely silent, he would jump up, nuzzle them, and try to comfort them by licking their faces. He would do the same for me whenever I was upset, comforting me when I was pretending to myself that everything was fine.

We can't all have Arnold to help us. We can, however, learn to be aware of our own inner response to the Censor's presence. When someone is emoting, and we find ourselves feeling bored, some truth is not being said. We may be censoring our own pain, tension, or anger. Or the real issue causing pain may still be hidden.

What is helpful at such times is to stop and ask: What is going on here? What are we not saying? Why do I feel confused? Why am I not reacting in the way I think I should? Opening the process up to mutual questioning, admitting the fuzziness and unclarity of our feelings, undermines the Censor's grip. Beware, however, of jumping into the role of the Judge, telling other people what they are really feeling.

Asking questions is a useful tool, but the Censor can turn our tools into new strictures and forms of control. Many excellent group processes and aids to expression of emotion have been developed by feminists, the radical psychiatry movement, the reevaluation co-counseling movement, and others. But when the tools become formulas, they reinforce the Censor's underlying message that feelings are not okay in their raw state. For example, I-messages can be helpful when expressing anger. Saying, "I feel angry when you forget to do your dishes," will cause less hurt than saying, "You asshole! How many of your goddamned cups do I have to wash?" But when a family, a group, or a couple has a spoken or unspoken rule that the only acceptable way to express annoyance is with I-messages, they have reinstalled the Censor in a new form. Now the person who is mad becomes "bad" for being angry improperly—but anger's very essence is that its energy moves beyond what is "proper" or permitted. The more jargon we must use to confront each other or express ourselves, the more formal our processes for "feeling-sharing," the less we can simply and clearly say what we mean.

In a group, a family, or a relationship, we can, however, expect people to take responsibility for what they do say, to stand behind their words and work through any hurt or misunderstanding they cause. If you call someone an asshole, you'd better be willing to stand there and finish the argument, not run off to your room and sulk. If you are trying to work with people who are different from you in their culture or history, who may have different associations with words or tones of expression, you might choose your words carefully. If you consistently hear from others that the way you express yourself hurts them, consider changing. For the power we reclaim from the Censor is also the power to contain our feelings, and the clarity to know when to speak and when we might be wiser to keep silent. When we know what we are feeling, we have a choice.

The only rule I would propose for groups is, Say anything you want, in any way you want, but take responsibility for it. Consider the impact that what you say and how you say it have on others, and then tell the truth.

When we risk expressing our feelings, and take responsibility for our actions, we can also see clearly what we are not responsible for. The fog rolls away. We can know how we have been hurt and know that we do not cause our own victimization by protesting it or by expressing our pain. We can take action to hold accountable those who have and do hurt us.

We can also assess the situation we find ourselves in and predict possible consequences. For the power to keep silent is one of the traditional four powers of the magician. (The others are to know, to will, and to dare.) Openly expressing our feelings does make us vulnerable—and being vulnerable is not always a good idea. Where power is unequal, the person with less power who expresses vulnerability risks getting eliminated. When we don't have to conceal our own feelings and perceptions from ourselves, we can make decisions about what to say and whom to trust.

Not everyone is trustworthy. Just as the Defender prevents us from seeing who our real enemies are by painting everyone as a threat to be conquered, the Censor prevents us from seeing who we can or cannot trust with our feelings. Without the possibility of silence there can be no true intimacy or trust. We need to know that confidence can be kept, that our secrets can be respected, that we, not someone else, will choose to whom our story is revealed.

Each of us has something unique to bring into the world. Powers exist that only you can bring to life; a perspective exists that is yours alone. No one else can speak your truth for you or give birth to your vision.

When we reclaim our responsibility for our own gift, our own truth, we also reclaim the ability to connect. For the acceptance that comes when we share our true selves, the good and the bad, the pretty and the ugly, becomes the real love that can warm and shelter us.

The Descent of Inanna, V:
The Fourth Gate

All that singing has made you thirsty
All the shedding has left you hungry
Down here
You find no food, no water

The Fourth Gate is need
You are ravenous
   inside you is a cavern
   that cannot be filled
   bottomless
   immeasurably
   empty

This is the Gate of the Give-away
Pass through here to be
   recycled
To make way for something new

When you are empty
   you have nothing to give
   but yourself
Give yourself away
Say good-bye
   to the body
   soft touch of skin on skin
   smell of wet earth
   birdsong, drumbeat
   sunlight, color
Good-bye, good-bye

You can bring nothing through here

Rip open your skin
Throw it over your shoulder
Carry it through
   the open gate

Past the Fourth Gate
You follow a river
   that flows backward and forward
   at once

Creating Sustainable Culture:
Serving No Masters

Immanent value is literally embodied. We know it in our physical beings. To be free, we must be able to sustain our lives, our culture; the society we create must meet our needs, and we must see it extending into the future. What we value, we tend and preserve.

Our sense of inherent value is rooted in the body's ability to care for itself and in the direct ways we can provide for our own physical needs. When making money becomes a substitute for foraging, gathering, hunting, planting, we lose important sources of power. The zucchini I buy in the store with money is entirely different from the one I pluck off the vine in my garden. The store-bought squash is an object, a dismembered part of the dead world, while the one in my garden is a whole process in which I have participated, from the composting of my garbage to the sense of wonder evoked when I find the vine still producing in November. I am not suggesting that we all turn to subsistence farming, but that our sense of self-worth is dependent on some direct contact with the broader cycles of birth, growth, death, decay, and renewal that do, in reality, sustain our lives. For even Hostess Twinkies are made of flour made of grain, and time still moves in its cycles and seasons even when tracked by a digital clock.

To heal ourselves, to create a sustainable culture, we must consider how we meet our needs: the needs of the individual body and of the larger earth-body that encompasses us all.

THE MASTER-SERVANT MODEL OF MEETING NEEDS

The dismembered world gives us only hierarchical models for sharing and caring: models in which one person's needs supercede another's. The King is the master of servants, the owner of slaves, the one set apart, whose needs are ministered to by others whose own needs are not taken into consideration. Marduk creates humans to serve the gods:

"I will form *Lullu,* man.
Let *him* be burdened with the toil of the gods,
that they may freely breathe."[1]

In war, of course, it is necessary to define the larger class of men, the ordinary soldier, as having no inherent being or value. Soldiers are by nature expendable. They are also servants to the officers, to those who make decisions, whose value is higher, and distance between the classes is reinforced in a hundred ways symbolic and concrete: separate quarters, differences in dress, salutes, food, and so on. The divisions are maintained for a reason. Explains Paul Fussell, infantry officer, World War II: "You've got to keep distance from [your soldiers]. The officer–enlisted man distance helps. This is one of the most painful things, having to withhold sometimes your affection for them, because you know you're going to have to destroy them on occasion. And you do. You use them up; they're material."[2]

Officers make decisions; ordinary soldiers comply. Officers issue orders; ordinary soldiers obey even when those orders, those decisions, may cost their lives.

But, of course, the officer is also a servant. Except perhaps for the top commanders, officers too are expendable. In recent wars their casualty rates in fact have far exceeded those for enlisted men.[3]

The Lord of Servants expects service as his due, not because he has inherent value, but precisely because he does not. He knows underneath it all that he is expendable, that his being is erased by his role. Service is false compensation for the loss of self, but it may seem like the only compensation available.

War and the mythologizing of the structures of war set the pattern for a human society in which some classes of people are served by others, and in which males are served by females. Under patriarchy, men are taught to identify the self as lord in relation to women, although the same men might be servants in relation to other men. Women have been conditioned to see themselves as servants of men, although the same women might be masters in relation to other women and men of the lower classes. But in a male-dominated society, women's status is determined by the status of the men to whom they are attached as wives, mothers, sisters, daughters, girlfriends, slaves. Women become dependent on men for status as well as sustenance and economic security, and are valued even less than men.

Having destroyed our inherent value, the Master offers us a substitute sense of worth in receiving service. Alternately, our service may be valued, while we, the servants, are as nothing. The unspoken promise of the Master is that we will be taken care of. If we ourselves take the role of master, servants will tend our needs. If we play the servant's role, the master will protect and provide for us. It is the identical promise a male-dominated society makes to the wife, the "good woman": serve a man, and he will take care of you. You will not have to take care of yourself.

The threat, the counterpart to the promise, is that if we fail to play our proper roles, we will not be cared for, and will be unable to care for ourselves.

A hierarchical society limits the options available to those of the wrong class, race, or gender to roles and occupations of service. Throughout much of history, a woman's choices were to serve a husband, serve God, or remain as an unpaid servant in the home of her birth family. Opportunities for independence were not available. Even today, women abound in the service professions: domestic work, child care, teaching, nursing, social work, and of course, the business of offering sexual service—prostitution and pornography. Fully 80 percent of women working outside the home in the United States do clerical work, servicing the papers, forms, accounts, and telephones of others.[4] Secretaries are often treated as servants, expected to wait on their bosses, serve coffee, run personal errands, and provide "wifely" emotional support, while their organizational skills are undervalued. People of color, people of poorer classes, are also relegated to servant roles and service occupations—"woman's work" or equally low-status hard physical labor.

We may earn our living by serving others without being possessed by the Master of Servants. When our own people provide us with a culture of resistance, when we are valued by family, community, friends, when we have networks of support, when we can sit together on the park bench or the back porch and discuss the oddities of white folks, rich folks, management, men, when we can organize to protect our own interests, we can sometimes escape internalizing the Master's image of our low value.

Under patriarchy, men are trained to be masters, women to be servants. Even in male-dominated cultures, women fare better where women's networks provide support. "One of the crucial functions of networks lies in providing women with a context in which they can share feelings and problems. The validation they receive from each other is a tremendous influence on the degree to which they accept and internalize male values and thinking."[5] One of the gifts of the feminist movement of the late sixties and seventies was the revelation that women could identify as *women* and support each other. For we are often isolated, expected to compete with other women for men, or to identify with men.

The soldier is not valued for individuality, but for his stock qualities, which allow him to be counted on, in planning and strategy, as a replaceable part. The soldier's own being is invisible. To the master, also, the servant is invisible as a person. The servant is not a separate individual, but one who fills a certain role.

"Presently she looked up and inspected the girl as if a new servant were no more than a new bonnet, a necessary article to be ordered home for examination. . . .

'Your name?'

'Christie Devon.'

'Too long; I should prefer to call you Jane as I am accustomed to the name.'

'As you please, ma'am.' "[6]

The servant is entitled to no name, no being of her own. Women take their husbands' names, losing even their own first names in formal correspondence to become "Mrs. John Doe." In Bangladesh, a woman who gives birth to a son becomes known by his name, as "Mother of ———."[7]

When we identify with the Lord, we cannot see the being of others. When we identify with the Servant, we lose our own being.

The officer is entitled to expend the lives and bodies of his men in their mutual service to the war effort. The master of slaves literally owns their bodies and can use or abuse them as he pleases. In the early patriarchal family, fathers held the right of life or death over their offspring, particularly their female offspring, whom they could choose to expose and kill or let live.[8]

SEXUALITY IN THE REALM OF THE MASTER

Patriarchy was established through the institutionalization of warfare, and war meant rape, the capture and enslavement of women who became war's prizes. Power became sexualized, and sexuality became tied to violence and power-over. Male sexuality became identified with aggression; female sexuality with submission. The Master/Servant roles haunt our fantasies in the dismembered world. They are reflected in the images of violent pornography, in which women's bodies are literally dismembered. They are enacted in the role plays of sadomasochism and dreamed over in the pages of romantic fiction.

Those possessed by the Master see the Servants' bodies as territory they are entitled to control and conquer. A company's rules may prohibit executives from demanding that their secretaries sleep with them, but the same company will expect their lower-status women employees to dress attractively, adorn themselves, make up their faces, and present an appearance that is pleasing and seductive. The guru may preach celibacy, the evangelist fidelity, yet expect sexual service from their followers.

Sexuality is a mystery, beyond analysis or control. We can only wonder at the depths and intensity of pleasure possible through the touching of the body. The erotic is humbling; in deep pleasure we become the body, animal, moved and shaken by the great forces of biological life. We cannot maintain our sense of being set apart; as the waves break we are no different from a cat in heat or the androgynous, coupling worms. Inherent in the erotic is a sense of letting go, of giving way. When the sacred is immanent, in the body, in the living world, that letting go becomes a doorway to connection and union with all that is.

Like all mysteries, sexuality is a paradox, for also inherent in the erotic is art, the pleasure of feeling power in our impact on another, the sense of our own skill in bringing the whole living universe to a singing, throbbing response.

When sex becomes not merely good but great, the two impulses move through us and between us, we give and receive pleasure, let go and at the same time devise new movements and rhythms of giving, feel our power-from-within in the giving way to the power flooding through.

But in the dismembered world, we make love not to the living body of the Goddess but to her corpse. Power becomes sexualized. When all power is cast as domination, we can only feel our power through dominating another, and can give way only through our submission to another's control. The Master colonizes our orgasms.

The norm for heterosexual relationships has been one of domination and submission. Psychiatrists and experts of all sorts have been advising women on how better to be sexually submissive since they began advising women at all. I don't have the heart—or the space—to quote even a representative sample. I will content myself with one quote from Freud: "The development of sexual inhibitions (shame, loathing, sympathy, etc.) proceeds earlier and with less resistance in the little girl than in the little boy. The tendency to sexual repression certainly seems here much greater, and where partial impulses of sexuality are noticed they show a preference for the passive form. . . . In respect to the autoerotic and masturbatic sexual manifestations, it may be asserted that the sexuality of the little girl has altogether a male character. Indeed, if one could give a more definite content to the terms, 'masculine' and 'feminine,' one might advance the opinion that the libido is regularly and lawfully of a masculine nature, whether in the man or in the woman."[9]

Here Freud smoothly appropriates libido—sexual energy—and any active seeking of clitoral pleasure as "masculine." Even Gilgamesh at least still termed lovemaking "the woman's art"; Freud has defined the erotic as inherently male, and has made female sexuality, in contrast, inherently passive. The "female" woman responds to the male, does not initiate or actively seek her own pleasure. Freud never explains how female genitalia can be masculine; nevertheless, his theories molded psychiatric opinion and advice to women throughout this century, so that, while women have been having sex for millions of years, the normality of the clitoral orgasm was not popularly admitted in North America until the feminist movement made it an issue in the late 1960s.

When passivity is defined as the norm for women, then a woman in a relationship with a man is required to fit her sexual responses around his needs and desires. She cannot ask for what she wants or define the rhythm, the timing, the pace, the techniques of lovemaking. (Freud goes on to warn of the "dangers of fore-pleasure.") Even the most loving relationship becomes one of sexual service.

Battering, incest, and sexual abuse are endemic realities in the dismembered world. The Master becomes the abuser, rapist, molester, who hurts others because he does not see them as having an independent and valid existence of their own. The father or stepfather who molests his own child sees the child as a servant, someone who is there to meet the father's needs. The child's own being, own needs, are invisible. Offenders, and even the professionals who treat them and their victims, have often tried to excuse their abuse by blaming their wives for failing to provide them with sexual satisfaction, love, warmth, time, understanding—the "services" women are supposed to offer men. "It was depressing, my job and all, and [my wife] just wouldn't give me any sympathy or encouragement at all. . . . And I would come home feeling so low, and it would be a big fat zero. A man's home is supposed to be the place where he gets the love and attention and the caring he needs. Not in my home, I can tell you that."[10]

Comments Sandy Butler, "Most men have been socialized to believe that they should occupy positions of power in this society and expect to be loved and cared for by parents and wives as they go about making their mark on the world. But what if they fail to achieve the power and attention they expect will be theirs? When some men feel themselves to be powerless in the outside world, they become, while they are in their homes, utterly despotic. As our culture has taught them, their homes are indeed their castles, and they are the unchallenged rulers of that domain."[11]

Incest and sexual abuse are no more anomalies in the patriarchal family than rape is an anomaly of war. Abuse is the logical outcome of a system in which power is sexualized and men have power over their families.

The Master of Servants, like the other forms of the King, clouds our perception. We become encased in psychic blinders that make whole aspects of reality utterly invisible to us. We do not see that a child is a child, that a woman who says no means no, that others have beings and perceptions of their own. When we see others as servants, they become invisible.

Yet the matter is more complex. Many of the offenders themselves are victims of incest and abuse. They, too, began life as servants to the needs of others. Their own being, own sense of self, was assaulted at an early age. Their needs were denied; they were invisible to one who should have cared for them. Their history does not excuse their acts as adults, but it allows us to see how the pattern is perpetuated.[12]

Just as the Defender is also Enemy, and the Orderer is also Chaos, the Master is also Servant: one who is dependent on others to meet needs he cannot fulfill for himself.

The delusion of the Master is that others exist to serve our needs. The delusion of the Servant is that we exist to serve the needs of others. Either way, we cannot take care of ourselves. For to care for ourselves would be to affirm the value of being, the immanent value we have lost. So the father, denied his wife's sympathy, turns to the next most available source, his little girl. He has never made contact with the wellsprings of nurture within himself. His own value has been destroyed. No one will ever sing of his cock that its rising makes the desert green and the grain spring up from the fields. He lives in the dismembered world, where the soldier pats first his machine gun, then his crotch, chanting:

> This is my rifle,
> this is my gun
> One is for fighting,
> one is for fun.[13]

He has himself become a weapon that has no needs except for periodic servicing and is ultimately expendable, whose value is that of a thing, an object, a possession.

CHILDREN AS SERVANTS

Children who are sacrificed to the needs of adults become good servants, caring for their own parents: "[My parents] beat the shit out of me and they sexually abused me and my father gambled and I mean it was crazy. They had no control. It was like they were the children and I was the parent."[14]

Children may be subordinated to their parents' needs in many ways. Abuse, sexual and physical, is perhaps the most extreme. Alcoholic families or families suffering any extreme loss or stress may openly or subtly "parentify" children. But even in seemingly normal, functioning, loving homes, what is loved in the child may not be the child's self, but her or his capacity for bringing glory to the parent.

A family is gathered for Christmas dinner. Three-year-old Lisa, the first grandchild, is being shown off to the assembled aunts, uncles, and cousins.

"Lisa, show Uncle Fred how you can count," beams her smiling mother.

"One, two, three, four . . ." the child obediently begins.

"She's very bright," her mother says. "We had her tested—she's well into the gifted range."

"Lisa," her father interrupts, "show Cousin Lee your baby. Where's Lisa's baby?"

The little girl runs to get her doll from the sofa. She begins to rock it and croon to it.

"Isn't she a little mother!" beams her mother. "Lisa, sing Cousin Lee the rock-a-bye song."

"Rock-a-bye baby," she sings. Her mother takes the doll out of her hands. "Let me show Cousin Lee the dress I made dolly."

Lisa begins to scream, "My doll!"

"Don't cry," her dad says. "Lisa, stop that crying! Be a good girl! You can share your dolly with Cousin Lee. Come here and sit on my lap and sing Uncle Fred the alphabet song . . ."

And so on. No one would accuse Lisa's parents of being abusive. No harsh word has been said. Praise has been heaped on her. Yet her parents remain serenely oblivious to her. They praise her achievements and accomplishments and possessions, not because of the joy Lisa might get from singing or rocking her doll, but because her parents' status and glory are increased by possessing a bright, talented, obedient child. Lisa never has a moment to follow her own interests. When she starts to enjoy the doll it is taken from her; when she becomes engrossed in one task she is interrupted by another.

In a society dependent on the tokens of status to replace the lost value of the self, all children become to some extent gratifiers of adult needs. Few models exist for parents wanting to nurture their child's true self. No standards exist for judging their success: their child's greater capacity for resistance to control may show itself as failure to fit into the institutions of domination. A child of freedom still has to live in the dismembered world of control, where all children are subject to the power of adults, where every institution—especially the schools—teaches us to place value in tokens of achievement and status, to conform to a hierarchy of winners and losers. So in growing up we inevitably learn how to serve and be served.

Children can, of course, meet some of their parents' needs. Naturally, parents take pride in their children's accomplishments and achievements. To value a child is to take pride in what brings them pleasure, growth, and freedom, knowing those things may be very different from what parents might choose or from what looks good on a school record or an annual letter to old friends. Contributing to the well-being of the family can be empowering for children when their tasks are suited to their abilities. When parents have expectations that they can state openly and clearly, that come from seeing the child's developing capacities, and that have some inherent usefulness that can be seen and understood, their demands help strengthen the child's sense of value. Children who help with the cleaning, cooking, gardening, and maintaining of the home, contribute in a real way to the family's welfare and learn to care also for their own needs. Lisa would be better off if her parents let her play with her doll according to her own whims, expected her to put it away afterward, and praised her for helping clear the table rather than showing off her cleverness.

POSSESSION BY THE MASTER

When we are possessed by the Master/Servant, we become obsessed with the question of need. Are our needs getting met? Who is meeting whose needs? For in the Master's realm, we cannot meet our own needs.

To serve, to give, to tend, to care for others, can make us feel good, needed, powerful, but not when our value is defined only in relation to those we serve. The Master demands enforced, coerced service about which we have no choice. When we are possessed by the Servant, we feel compelled to serve or we lose value and die. Such service can never empower us, for service can be empowering only when it is freely given, not when it becomes a substitute for value or a means of garnering false glory.

The service we get from the Servant is not the care we really want. It can never really restore our sense of value, for it is offered under duress, a tribute to our position or our role, not to our self.

The Servant is even more dependent on the Master, for survival, for food, for money, perhaps for life itself. Dependence may be our only option, or it may seem like an easy way out. We pay a heavy price, for we lose our freedom. We are expected to obey the one upon whom we depend—father, husband, state.

When we are forced into the role of Servant, we hide ourselves to survive. We act; we mime the master's expectations, as slaves on the plantations of the South pretended to be happy, stupid, slow, or content as a way of surviving. Hidden, our true selves may escape the master's attention. Our false persona can please, while secretly we plot escape or revenge. But the danger in miming and acting is that we may hide our true selves and desires also from ourselves. We become the mask we put on, and lose connection with our own real needs.

"Marilyn Monroe actually created a character, whom she called 'Marilyn,' and who she knew was not her*self*. . . . In Monroe's private life she rarely dressed anything like the self we know as 'Marilyn.' . . . Monroe would suddenly assume a 'simpering and sighing' attitude when she became 'Marilyn' for the public."[15] Her persona expressed the promise of sexual service men in power consider their due. Marilyn herself was molested as a child, trained early to be the servant of male desires. "Finally, she became the sex goddess of her age. Now she was the very image she had hoped so desperately to imitate. Yet, even *being* this image, she still *felt* empty. Inside this perfection was the same nothingness and the same numbness she feared."[16]

"But now we are at the heart of a female tragedy within pornographic culture. For within this culture, when a woman expresses her real power, this power can only be expressed through images which transform female power into an image of submissiveness."[17]

When the Servant possesses us we seek out masters, for we are dependent on being needed for our sense of value. We find ourselves in co-addictive relationships. We may become the classic alcoholic's wife, who runs the house and balances the checkbook in spite of his periodic binges, who gets him up in the morning and off to work, calls his boss with an excuse when he is too hung over to go to the office, tries to hide his condition from the children, humors him out of his bad moods, and forgives his rages and his violence, doing it all to "help" him.

The Servant does not truly value the Master's life or serve even his real needs. Instead she adapts to his whims and wishes while actually serving his destruction. The delusion of the Servant is that she is helping the one she serves. But the Servant is also the Master in disguise: she believes and expects to be cared for in return. When we are caught up by the Servant, we actually inflate our power, imagining that our love, our devotion, our sympathy, our eagerness for sex, can heal someone else. We seek out needy ones to nurture, who, of course, by definition, must be somehow lower, lesser than ourselves. Our "unselfishness," our negating of our own needs to focus on someone else, is really a way of maintaining power. But the price of that power is isolation, is to be always above or below, never equal.

RECLAIMING TRUE SERVICE

True service, real giving, is possible, and can be empowering both to the giver and to those who receive help. To serve without losing ourselves, we must first know ourselves.

In the Twelve-Step programs, recovery for both addicts and co-addicts involves service to others: "Having had a spiritual awakening as the result of these steps, we tried to carry this message to alcoholics, and to practice these principles in all our affairs."[18]

Service, however, is the *twelfth* step, not the second or third. It must be based on the individual's "spiritual awakening" to her or his immanent value, and upon solid sobriety. Warning is given of the dangers of "two-stepping"—jumping straight from the first step, admitting one is an alcoholic, to the twelfth, trying to help others, without undergoing the necessary "housecleaning" and breaking down of false glory in between. For without the searching moral inventory, the admission of faults and the amends made for harm done, service to others becomes another way of avoiding one's own problems and garnering the illusions, not the essence of value.[19]

In groups, in the family, when we play the Servant we may become the one everybody depends on for advice, the one who keeps everything running smoothly, patches up fights, manages conflicts to keep them from surfacing. We convince ourselves that our own needs aren't important, or that we have very few needs.

In reality, we do not know what our needs are, because we maintain our focus on the needs of others. Yet everyone has needs, and they will surface eventually, either overtly or covertly.

Individual needs are most easily met in a group when they are clearly stated. We are more likely to get what we want when we ask for it. When we are possessed by the Servant, the self-hater whispers, "Don't ask for

what you want—you shouldn't want anything. You don't need anything—
you exist to take care of others." Because the Servant is also the Master,
the voice behind the whisper tells us, "People should know what you need
without your having to ask for it. They should take care of you, and they
aren't. They don't care."

When we cannot ask, we may nevertheless resent others' not fulfilling
our wishes, of which they may be entirely unaware. If the group does not
meet our unconscious expectations of care, if they get tired of seeing us
as "above" them, we become resentful, angry, burned out. We complain
about the irresponsibility, the immaturity, the ingratitude of the group in
inflections similar to those of Victorian ladies discussing the sloth and
ingratitude of their maidservants.

We can only really be free to ask when others are genuinely free to say
either yes or no. If others know they cannot refuse our requests, they may
rightfully resent us for asking. A group can help undermine the self-hater
by encouraging members to state their needs directly, to give when they
want to and can, and to feel free to say no when they cannot.

To serve freely is to give, and a gift has a unique character. In a society
based on gift giving rather than commodity exchange, "whatever we have
been given is supposed to be given away, not kept. Or, if it is kept,
something of similar value should move on in its stead . . . the gift must
always move."[20] Service is empowering when it is the passing along of a
gift, but we must receive the gift first ourselves, and allow it to work its
healing transformation within us.

Lewis Hyde, in *The Gift,* calls gratitude "a labor undertaken by the
soul to effect the transformation after a gift has been received. . . . With
gifts that are agents of change, it is only when the gift has worked in us,
only when we have come up to its level, as it were, that we can give it
away again. Passing the gift along is the act of gratitude that finishes the
labor."[21]

A true gift supports our growth, makes us more than we were, rather
than confirming the giver's superiority. A true gift increases our power-
from-within, our ability to do, rather than keeping us bound and dependent. A true gift is sometimes harsh; it may be the withdrawal of the false
service that has enabled us to cling to our addictions or our limitations.

A stranger once gave me a true gift. My old Volvo died on the street
in a rainstorm, and I could not get it to start. The engine churned and
churned, but would not turn over. A man walked up, peered in the window, and said:

"You're flooded. Take off the distributor cap, dry off the points, and
she'll start right up." He walked away.

I got out of the car, thinking, Whatever happened to the good old days
when men just fixed cars for you? To hell with all this feminist bullshit!
I don't like cars! I don't like engines! I don't even know if I can recognize
the distributor cap. I found a rag, opened the hood, and remembered just

enough information from the one auto mechanics course I had taken to find the distributor cap, undo the clips, dry off everything I saw on the theory that something must be the points, and put it back together again.

Much to my shock, the car started.

A few years later, I was in a car with a group of women who attended a peace conference in Rome. We were being driven to the airport in a heavy rainstorm, and we were late, when the car died in the middle of a flooded and crowded intersection. Around us, horns were honking and irate Italians were shouting. Our driver was trying to flag a taxi, when I said calmly, "I know what's wrong." I jumped out of the car, pulled off the distributor cap, dried the points, put it back, and the car started. Dozens of Italian men were left standing in astonishment as we sped off to catch our plane. It was a perfectly satisfying moment. Yet had the man on the street fixed my car, rescued me instead of giving me the information I needed to take care of myself, I might still be stuck in the mud.

What needs to be reclaimed from the Master/Servant is the ability to identify our true needs and real desires and to care for ourselves in ways that bring us closer to others rather than separating us. When we allow ourselves to face our desires, then we can begin to find ongoing sustainable ways of meeting everybody's needs. The conflicts we have will be clear and open ones, not covert and insidious. Removing the masks we wear to please others, we can begin to know and value ourselves.

MIRROR MEDITATION

Spend some time each night staring into your own eyes in a mirror. Let your breathing become slow and even. Ask yourself, Who am I? What do I really want? Do this regularly for some period of time that feels right—a week, a month.

DECISION MEDITATION

1. For a full day, let yourself be aware of each choice you make, and ask yourself, Is this what I really want? When you wake up in the morning, when you make your breakfast, if you go to work or go to the beach or clean the house or walk the dog or make love, continue to ask yourself, Is this what I really want? What do I really want? Don't necessarily change what you do, but notice your responses. Keep notes.
2. On a day when you can do this without suffering irreparable consequences, begin with the meditation above and this time do exactly and only what you want.
3. Before making any important life decisions or commitments, before

promising to do someone a favor or take on a responsibility, again stop and ask yourself, Is this what I want? Make this a regular practice. If need be, enlist a friend to help you, someone you can call or who will check in with you.

TAKING CARE MEDITATION

Every day, think of something you can do as a conscious act of caring for yourself. Do it. You may choose something you do anyway, such as brushing your teeth, but instead of making it an automatic act, use the time to affirm yourself and your ability to care for yourself. Take a walk, take a nap, take a long hot bath. You might take care of yourself by doing something you need to do but have been putting off. Have you been driving for the past six months without a license because you have been avoiding getting it renewed? Have you not worn your favorite shirt for weeks because you haven't had time to iron it? Are collection agencies hounding you because you lose all your bills before you get a chance to pay them? While you are waiting in line at the Department of Motor Vehicles, repeat the affirmation, "I can take care of myself."

You can expand this meditation to take care of yourself in ways that make demands on other people or institutions. Of course, you take the risk of not getting what you ask for, but the act of asking can be an act of self-care. For example, my friend Carol realized that she had been suffering from neck and back pain ever since she changed offices and desk chairs at the bank where she works. She could ask for a better chair in her new office.

When caring for yourself becomes a habit, care for your neighborhood, your land, your environment, and the larger life of the earth. Expand your self-care into the political realm in some way that feels right to you: write a letter, work for a candidate, vote, march in a demonstration, sit down in front of a nuclear weapons plant, start an organization, go to a meeting, while silently repeating the affirmation, "I am caring for myself."

DECISION-MAKING CHECK

In groups, before making any group decision or agreement, stop and check with each member. Ask, "Is this what you really want? Is it what we want?"

THE SERVANTS' MASKED BALL

In the group, make a mask that represents the face you wear to please others. Talk about it as you make it. For each mask, find a one-line phrase or sentence that represents the essence of what the mask says: "Stay covered up," "I'm sweet, don't hit me," "I won't ask anything of you," and so on.

Put on the masks, and play some music. Dance, saying your phrases to each other. Periodically stop the music. Interact with the person you face. Then exchange masks and phrases. Try on someone else's persona: speak in someone else's voice as the music resumes and the dance continues.

To end, hold up the masks. Dancers ransom their own back by saying or doing something that reveals their personal power.

Talk about how it felt to wear the different masks. Then decide what to do with them, perhaps creating a ritual for their destruction, perhaps keeping them as reminders of the game.

When we begin to win free of the Master and refuse servitude, we need support. If we are survivors of abuse, incest, or addicted families, we absolutely need support. Resources such as Alanon and Adult Children of Alcoholics groups, and groups that meet around abuse and incest issues, are excellent ways of confronting the Master/Servant within. Groups that form to work or live together, ritual circles, and worship groups can also be fruitful places for working together on these issues.

Storytelling, consciousness raising, and ritual are all tools we can use to offer support. Healing can happen in many ways. Here is one technique.

HEALING RITUAL

The healing we give each other is a tangible way of nurturing and caring for each other. Ritual itself creates a healing space. But at times we may wish to focus a ritual specifically on physical or emotional healing.

A simple approach to healing is to create a healing image. The person in need of healing thinks of an image that represents the energies she or he needs. The process of deciding on this image is itself part of the work of healing, and of learning to identify and ask for what we need.

She or he tells the group what the image is. The group may focus on it as a visualized image, or create a physical representation: a picture, a charm that brings together colors, herbs, stones, or objects that represent what is needed. The person is then placed in the center of the circle. Group members may place hands on the person's body, or, if that does not feel appropriate (and it is important to talk about this first), place your hands a little above the person's physical body but still within the sphere, the aura, of her or his energy.

Ground, and begin to breathe deep, imagining energy coming up from the earth and down from the sky. Be sure to imagine the energy coming through you, not originating in you, or you will quickly exhaust your personal stores of vitality and get tired. Hold the persons' image in mind, and imagine energy coming through your breath and hands to fill it. Some people like to imagine the energy as fire, or as light, or as a fluid like water. Find a symbol that works well for you. Chant the person's name, sing, or make wordless sounds to charge the image with power.

For example, suppose Rose is in the center of the circle and she has pneumonia. She wants us to imagine sunlight drying up the fluid in her lungs. You breathe deep, close your eyes, and visualize a sun shining down on her chest. You might lay a hand on her heart, or take her hands, and imagine your breath and voice becoming a golden, liquid fire, filling the sun, making it shine more brightly, giving off healing warmth. You sing her name. The energy peaks, and then you ground it by touching the ground and letting it fall back to earth.

Be sure to ground the energy after a healing, and to shake off your hands so that you symbolically rid yourselves of any energies you might not want to pick up.

Sometimes this process gets spectacular results; sometimes nothing much seems to change, except that the person feels loved, cared for, and valued, which is healing in itself.

RITUAL FOR HEALING FROM ABUSE

We can create ritual to help us heal from abuse and violation. Begin with the Anger Ritual on page 127. Go back to some protected place, and soak in a ritual bath: any bath in which salt has been added to the water with the intention of creating a substance that can cleanse and purify. (A plunge in the ocean or any very cold body of water also works.)

With a friend as companion, meditate in the bath (or meditate first, then plunge into the just-mentioned cold water), letting yourself feel the sense of violation, rage, helplessness, sorrow, or whatever emerges. Make sounds to help release the energy. Let your friend comfort you.

Empty the tub, and let other members of the circle wash you with water mixed with honey, cinnamon, protective herbs, and flowers. Use whatever herbs feel right or are in season: rosemary, sage, lavender, comfrey, and rose petals would be my choice. They murmur praises of your body, your self, and hopes for your empowerment and protection.

The washing continues until an image of power comes to you. Tell your circle what it is. Let them use it as a healing image, channeling energy through it to you.

Afterward, the circle dries you off. When you are dressed, they give you a gift of power, something tangible to symbolize your renewed strength.

As you take the gift, name out loud what power you take with it. Show it to each of the four directions, naming and claiming your power.

Share an especially good feast, and open.

The following ritual for collective recovery evolved in a workshop I led in New Hampshire over a Fourth of July weekend. Both women and men were present. We had gone through story about facing the self-hater with drumming, chanting, movement, and dance. Afterward, no one wanted to discuss what they'd experienced. We went on to create a ritual for the Fourth of July. We invoked the Goddess, who appeared as one of the group members dressed as the Statue of Liberty. We lit a bonfire and cried and screamed and raged as we named the wrongs we felt our country was committing in our name, and then looked into the flames to evoke visions of hope and change.

It was not a great ritual. We listed every political issue and atrocity on the current agenda. Somehow we couldn't seem to go beyond slogans and cliches. Our chanting and screaming felt hollow.

Over breakfast, the room buzzed with conflicts. People were angry, frustrated. Some hadn't liked the Goddess as Statue of Liberty; they felt the symbolism was frivolous. Others liked both the humor and the meaning. Some had liked the ritual—others hadn't. After some time, a woman said, "You know, we had a powerful experience with the self-hater story yesterday and we never really talked about it. I wonder if all this conflict has any connection?"

We began to talk about what we had seen and felt when we faced the self-hater. People began speaking about intimate and painful things: the powerlessness they felt in their lives, the times they had been hurt or abused, the ways in which they had been victims or survivors. We decided to create a new ritual, of healing and cleansing. We took a long time considering carefully the words we would use and the structure we would create.

In the afternoon, we went outside and formed a circle in a secluded meadow. In the center, we placed a bowl of salt water. Both salt and water represent cleansing and purifying. We created sacred space with singing and chanting.

One woman began by going to the center. A second woman followed her into the circle and knelt by the water. She looked into the first woman's eyes and said, "In the past, I have denied my feelings and closed my eyes to what was going on around me in order to survive." The first woman then washed the second woman's face and hands with the salt water, letting the washing become a cleansing. When she was done, the second woman said, "Now I will open my eyes and face what is really happening."

They hugged each other. The first woman left the circle, and the woman who had been washed took her place and washed the next person who came to the center. One by one, each of us went to the water, spoke, and was washed, using the formula: "In the past, I have done ——— to survive." (Washing.) "Now I will do ———."

People cried, laughed, and expressed the deep emotion we had not been able to reach before. To enter the circle and say out loud and in public the ways in which we had hurt ourselves made them less charged, less shameful, because each one of us in that circle shared the same risk of vulnerability and exposure. The ritual would not have worked if I had imposed it on the group or if I, as "leader," had sat safely back and listened to others but not gone into the circle myself. Coming to the center as equals in the circle, feeling the touch of the cool water and the support and sighs of recognition from others as we each named our own pain, we could feel truly cleansed.

Afterward, we went around the circle, sang each person's name, chanted, shared food, and celebrated each other.

RITUAL FOR COLLECTIVE RECOVERY

In your group, read over the preceding description of our group's ritual. Take time to discuss it first, to change it or add to it so that it becomes truly yours. Be very clear that no one is pressured to participate. Each person should ask, Is this what I want to do? For some, the moment might not be right. Excuse them. But all who sit in on the circle must be willing to come into the center; otherwise, no one can feel truly safe. Do the ritual.

MEETING NEEDS SUSTAINABLY

We may come to a group or a relationship with the unvoiced hope that this time all our needs will be met, that we will be cared for as we have never yet been cared for, that we will be the one who is served, not the servant. And so we are endlessly disappointed, for no group, no person, can meet all our needs, for others have needs of their own.

When we consider how to balance conflicting needs, how to distinguish true gifts from false service, empowerment from rescue, we might borrow from the ecology movement the concept of sustainability. Can the gift, the relationship, the group, the movement, the patterns of interaction, be sustained over time? We are not used to asking this question, for a war culture is concerned with immediate victories at any price, not long-term survival. Native Americans ask how each decision will affect the seventh generation after us. Corporations do not. Our agriculture destroys thousands of tons of topsoil every year while poisoning the environment. Our economy is run on the nonrenewable resources of fossil fuels. Our projects too often demand that we work nonstop until we burn out.

The sustainability of the environment we live in is the ground of our sense of worth, yet it is rarely recognized as such by psychologists. "Do you ever hear a psychoanalyst talking about how we humans need a proper niche in a natural ecosystem, for the sake of our own mental health? Or how a lot of mental unease would go away if we could simply stop worrying about how well we fit into the natural world, and where our food and clothing and shelter is going to come from?"[22]

A psychology of liberation must also be a psychology of ecology. The environment tells the body how much our lives are valued. When the air we breathe is full of poisons, our lungs get the message that we aren't worth much. And this is literally true. Somewhere, the decision has been made that our lives are not worth the cost of smoke-scrubbers.

Traditionally, psychology has focused on our early childhood experiences as the ground for self-esteem as if we were raised in an environmental vacuum. The assumption has been that environmental and political concerns are peripheral. Of course, what happens to us in childhood is important, but to disregard the impact of the physical and social environment on us every day of our lives is like looking through spectacles smeared with bullshit.

Our sense of worth is partly dependent on how well we were loved and nurtured in infancy, but is no less dependent on the situation we find ourselves in and the messages our culture delivers about value. A child can receive the most perfect nurturing, the most sensitively attuned and timed feeding, yet if the mother's milk is radioactive, that child's body will get the message: Die! When we grow up in a culture that assaults us continuously and threatens the annihilation of life, we can at best hope to grow up confused, suspecting we might be worth something even though the evidence of our senses tells us we are not.

We cannot be empowered by work that destroys the environment around us, or creates systems of inequality. No matter how our work is organized, it cannot fully empower us unless we believe in its purpose. Nor can a company or business be empowering if it is based on exploitation—of the workers who assemble the parts in some Third World country, of the consumers who buy a shoddy or faulty or useless product. Such a system must of necessity be rooted in denial, riddled with unspoken messages not to see, or talk about, basic realities of its existence.

Sustainable service is reciprocal. In a sustainable system, what goes around comes around. Bryce and Margaret Muir, describing informal barter networks on the Maine coast, stress that these networks "don't rely on trust, or the emotional bonds of friendship, for their durability. They depend on that old individualistic motive: mutual self-interest."[23] "Every good and service has a recognized fair value. Everyone knows how long it takes to time an engine. Everyone is keeping score. I know you owe me fifteen minutes of sweat and a bale of hay. Everyone's goal is 'balanced reciprocity'—tit for tat."[24]

A sustainable system is one in which the energy going out of the system is balanced by the energy coming in, and in which resources are preserved or augmented, not diminished. Reciprocity assures that nobody's resources are drained, and that nobody profits unduly at someone else's expense.

To know if a system is truly sustainable, we must take into account all its resources. For too long businesses have used monetary profit as the only measure of energy flow, ignoring what other resources, human and environmental, might be consumed in pursuit of profit.

Human energy is also a resource, derived ultimately from the fertility of the soil and the health of the environment. The human race has been described as a semiparasite or even a disease of the soil,[25] an unflattering but sobering way to look at ourselves. What wastes our energies and labors and erodes our lives also wastes the environment that supports us. A sustainable system does not take out of us more than it puts back.

Martyrdom is no model for an ecological society. Sustainability teaches us to cultivate an ecological laziness—getting the most results for the least energy expended, not by depleting scarce resources but by intelligently observing and joining with the larger patterns around us.

If a group is of value to the people in it, then sustaining the group's existence must be a paramount value. The needs of the group as a whole may take precedence over the needs of individual members. "Each member of AA is but a small part of a great whole. AA must continue to live or most of us will surely die. Hence our common welfare comes first. But individual welfare follows close afterward."[26]

Placing the group's needs first can, of course, only be empowering when all benefits are shared by all members. If one person reaps undue rewards and profits, then others are simply being used when they subordinate or compromise their own goals.

When the group's existence truly serves those who are a part of it, real solidarity becomes possible. We can choose to act in ways that may seem to be counter to our immediate self-interest, because we know that in the long run, preserving the strength of the group will benefit us. Unions, for example, require individuals to give service, attend meetings, take on responsibilities, even at times go on strike and risk their jobs. But those who belong to a union recognize that only by acting together can they gain any real power in an economic system weighted against them.

Groups must identify their collective needs and set limits on their collective giving. Many alternative organizations dedicated to bettering the world are notorious as terrible places to work, expecting long hours for little pay from their staff. We try to redress the exploitation of the economic system by exploiting ourselves.

If we are interested in victory, not martyrdom, we need to create structures that can be successful in our own terms. If those who develop skills, knowledge, and experience are forced to leave a group in order to reap the rewards of their work, the group cannot grow.

QUESTIONS ABOUT MUTUAL CARE

Think about or discuss the following questions in the group:

1. How do we take care of each other's physical needs? Assure each other's safety? Respond to limitations?
2. What is the wider context in which we exist? What ties do we have to our neighborhood? Broader community? The natural environment around us? What ties do we want?
3. How do our actions and projects affect the ecosystem?
4. How do our actions and projects affect the poorest third of humanity?
5. How do we offer care to each other? What is that care dependent on?

In a money economy, questions of sustainability involve the issue of money. Groups that offer services, entertainment, or products to the community are often under pressure to keep prices low or nonexistent, so that what they do can be accessible to all. And groups that are conscious of the economic inequalities built into our society do not want to exclude the poor from what they offer. So members may end up oppressing themselves. (Perhaps they could contract with the authorities to be paid for doing so?)

At the other end of the spectrum, some groups offer New Age catchwords such as "prosperity consciousness" and "manifesting abundance" as a rationalization for greed. Somewhere in between, the concept of sustainability can help us find a balance. If what the group is doing is valuable, it must be made sustainable; otherwise, the group will cease to exist, benefiting no one. It must also maintain an "option for the poor," an awareness that those who are economically disadvantaged also have a right to the benefits offered by the group.

The theory is easily articulated. The practice is more difficult in an unequal economic system. Because I make a large proportion of my own living offering workshops and lectures, I am continually faced with these questions. Money is one of the Dirty Subjects we are not supposed to talk about publicly: that silence, like all silences imposed by the Censor, perpetuates illusions and isolation. Some of the strategies I have found useful are:

1. *The Robin Hood approach:* Take from the rich and give to the poor. This can be done by using a sliding scale, charging, for example, three to fifteen dollars for an event, with a suggested income breakdown for paying different prices. A variation is to offer many different sorts of events, some of which are more expensive or lucrative (the two don't always go together), which then subsidize others that are free or low-cost.

2. *Spreading costs over larger numbers:* Larger classes pay better than smaller ones. Of course, smaller groups offer an intimacy that larger groups cannot. We have had many discussions in the Reclaiming Collective about the trade-offs between offering larger classes and making more money, and keeping classes small and co-taught by two teachers, which best reflects our commitment to egalitarian process. After considering the trade-offs, I find the strategy of doing workshops for large groups valuable.

3. *Subsidizing what doesn't pay with what does:* For a long time, Reclaiming attempted to subsidize our free newsletter with our small, nonlucrative classes. We saw ourselves as offering a service that, in an ideal world, should be free—the teaching of magic and ritual. We did not consider ourselves a business, nor was money our primary interest. (Nevertheless, we spent hours and hours in meetings talking about it.) Eventually, we realized that both classes and newsletters generally need to be subsidized by something else. Unblessed by endowments, or state support, we have decided to find other sources of extra funds: advertisements in the newsletter, paid subscriptions, and sales of tapes of chants.

4. *Asking for gifts:* Grants are occasionally available for projects and can be enormously helpful. However, if a group becomes dependent on grants it becomes vulnerable to outside control and may cease to direct its own destiny. Grants are perhaps most useful in developing new areas of activity or undertaking temporary projects, rather than for funding the group's basic activities. Individuals can also be asked for smaller gifts. I have known people who sent letters to all their friends asking for small donations to support them in an undertaking such as community networking.

Also helpful in thinking about sustainability are the insights we can gather from understanding how biological systems function. Lewis Quincy has outlined six principles of permaculture, an approach to organic agriculture that designs ecosystems in which each part supports and sustains the whole.[27] The same principles are useful in designing sustainable social structures.

1. Design patterns, not single elements.

The first principle teaches us to think not of isolated parts, but of the ways they are linked together. Elements are arranged so that they work using minimum amounts of energy. A classic illustration of this principle might be: In the country, place the woodpile between the back door and the outhouse, so every time you go to the outhouse you can bring in a stick or two of wood.

Groups, too, can be seen as patterns. What a group does, says, believes, and how it makes decisions determine the way people within a group will interact. Undermining internalized oppression may not be the overt purpose of a group, just as bringing in wood is not the primary purpose of going to the outhouse. But when a group is structured so as to restore immanent value, the self-hater is continually eroded in the course of the group's normal activities.

For such healing to occur, the group's normal activities must themselves be sustainable, and must run fairly smoothly. If we block the outhouse door with the woodpile, we have set the stage for an embarrassing accident. To be sustainable, a group needs to remain focused on its primary purpose, whether that be work, support, intimacy, magic, or whatever. If a group's energies are drained by people too needy to function collectively, they will not find the group a healing environment, nor will anybody else.

A group cannot be sustainable if its ideals, however fine, generate a structure so cumbersome that it interferes with the group's primary purpose. For example, a group may be committed to the equal participation of all its members. But participation in every decision demands time and energy that not all members may have to give. Requiring each member's involvement in every decision may seem to be most purely democratic, but it can also become exclusionary of people with full-time jobs or children to raise who cannot attend meetings several times a week.

Groups easily become identified with abstract ideals that become meaningless or destructive when we cease to consider how they function in a given concrete situation. For example, our group might say that we are committed to decentralization, when it might better serve us to ask, instead, which functions are best done by decentralized groups and which by centralized organizations. Centralization and decentralization are tendencies that exist as a dynamic polarity within a group. They are not moral absolutes; when we treat them as such we cannot design a system that best incorporates both.

Groups can combine to share resources. Often, for example, small, alternative organizations find that sharing office space cuts down on overhead expenses. They may form coalitions or consortiums that share certain functions.

A consortium of health care clinics might share a fund raiser or a bookkeeper. In Baltimore, several organizations providing job training for minorities share a loading dock and warehouse for supplies and construction equipment.[28]

Nationally, covens have joined together to incorporate as a church, the Covenant of the Goddess, which has held federally recognized tax-exempt status for over a decade. Individual covens remain autonomous in deciding their internal affairs, forms of ritual, times of meetings, and specifics of belief. Individuals' loyalties are to their small groups, not necessarily to the organization as a whole. But having one national organization saves us from having to incorporate each coven separately, and when national issues arise—such as discriminatory legislation—we can act together with resources and numbers that no individual coven alone could achieve.

2. Have multiple functions for single elements.

This principle explains how to do more with less, thereby conserving energy. In permaculturalist Susan Davidson's garden in British Columbia, the beans are planted so that as they grow tall they shade the young lettuce from the sun and their roots add nitrogen to the soil that feeds neighboring plants.

Groups function through meetings. If we can get as much from our meetings as Susan gets from her beans, our group stands a greater chance of being sustainable. A meeting can also serve multiple functions. It may be a place where business gets done, but also a place where our check-ins affirm each other's value and keep us in touch with each other's lives, where we might share food or music or ritual to aid group bonding and connection and build community. During warm weather, Reclaiming often holds general meetings outside, sometimes incorporating a gentle hike to some especially beautiful place. I like to bring needlework to meetings. Many of my friends do the same, which has inspired our affinity group motto, "Tatting for Revolution."

3. Plan multiple elements for single functions.

If your farm must produce cash, grow more than one cash crop, in case one fails. If your group needs money to survive, have more than one source.

4. Use biological and renewable resources that are actually renewed.

Weeder geese are better than herbicides. Human energy is potentially renewable, but a group must take care that its members are being replenished. Burning out group members is no moral improvement on burning up irreplenishable oil reserves. No system is sustainable unless all resources are renewed.

A group that produces or tolerates burnout undoes all its other efforts to restore immanent value, for we cannot truly value ourselves or others when we treat each other like Appalachian hillsides, to be strip-mined for what is valuable and then abandoned. When members of a group complain of burnout, the group must ask itself how it can:

Do less: What projects can we drop? Postpone? Which are vital? If we saw ourselves as existing for many years in the future, what would we do later?

Take in more: What do we need that we're not getting? Getting enough of? Money? Appreciation? Fun? Time off? A sense of effectiveness?

Do more with less: Is our structure too cumbersome? Are interpersonal conflicts draining our resources? Are certain aspects of the work more trouble than they are worth?

Recruit fresh energy: How can we bring others to this task? Is it exciting, important enough that new people might be drawn to lend their energy? How can we make them welcome?

Replenish members: Many tried and true ways exist: Rest, sleep, food, fun, laughter, movies, singing, drumming, ritual, rock and roll, dancing, hot baths, lying in the sun, group sports, trips to fun places, sex, parties, entertainment, games, nature, victories, adventures, empowerment. Human energy can, in fact, be replaced much more quickly than oil can form from plant debris or groundwater collect in diminished aquifers.

5. Value diversity.

Nature favors diversity, because in diversity is stability. A diverse system has a wider capacity of response to unfavorable circumstances. A sustainable group is also diverse, but "because interactions . . . are both beneficial and competitive, diversity in and of itself is not as important as the *right kind* of diversity."[29] In other words, some kinds of diversity strengthen a group; others can destroy its sense of common purpose. A support group for women might destroy its purpose by including men. Yet the women involved might, in a campaign to end domestic violence, find some men valuable allies. A group working to end war might strive for a diversity of membership in terms of gender, race, ethnic and class backgrounds, and political or religious affiliations; however, its purpose would not necessarily be served by including lobbyists for the weapons industry or agents of the FBI. Yet weapons manufacturers and peace activists might coexist supportively in a chapter of Alcoholics Anonymous.

Once a group is clear about its primary purpose, it can value and encourage the broadest kinds of diversity that support that purpose. For every difference expands our perceptions and broadens the ways we can think about problems and create alternatives. A group or a movement that lacks racial, gender, age, or class diversity is often handicapped by the limitations of its own perspectives.

In chapter 12, I write more fully about generating diversity in groups and about the challenges of building connections across the lines of oppression. In this context, we must simply understand that whether we come from a privileged or an oppressed group, bridging our differences is a task we undertake for our own survival.

A group that supports diversity may find that members' goals diverge from the group's. Some may leave to found new organizations. A group may thus develop influence that extends beyond its own boundaries. But if people are forced to leave in order to grow, the group may be too restrictive or rigid.

6. Plan for succession.

An ecosystem undergoes a natural progression through time, and good design plans for change and growth. While fruit trees mature, vegetables can be grown underneath them.

Groups also mature and develop. We can look ahead and plan ahead, realizing that solutions that work at a particular stage of the group's formation may need to change over time.

Groups have a life cycle. They are born, grow, flourish for a time, then die. Some groups may continue for decades, others are not meant to last long. But a group may meet its demise long before its useful life is over by failing to realize that its needs and goals will change over time.

A group may fall victim to factors that interact negatively. For example, a group that depends on volunteers will find that people will give service for a time, but few can continue indefinitely. Lives change, new demands arise, burnout sets in, and so on. The group may suffer a slow but constant attrition of those whose energy, skills, and experience help the group function.

At the same time, as a group matures it becomes harder for new people to enter. Like a climax forest, in which dense shade prevents new seedlings from taking root, the skills, experience, and sense of community in an established group may intimidate newcomers.

As an example, in doing nonviolent civil disobedience, we found that as a core of experienced blockaders developed, newcomers experienced less of an immediate sense of empowerment from the actions. During the Diablo blockade of '81, few people had blockaded before. Consensus, solidarity, meeting facilitation, all called forth new skills and generated a great sense of experimentation. The group's ideology—that we were all equal, that everyone should rotate responsibility for aspects of the group's function such as facilitating meetings or talking to the media—had a basis in reality, for the gaps in our levels of skill were not very great.

Four years later, I participated in a much smaller action at Livermore. Half the people were new, half experienced. Some had been through dozens of actions at that same place. The tone and feeling of the action were very different. For any problems that came up, we could draw on a backing of previous experience. When specific skills were needed, such as that of facilitating large groups, some of us were there who had practiced them hundreds of times. Newcomers felt a little like outsiders.

At Diablo, power-with, influence developed freely and spontaneously out of the group. If someone turned out to be great at facilitating meetings, we all felt empowered because that person represented the possibility that anyone could do the same. Four years later, when the same person was much more highly skilled, newcomers felt disempowered: "I couldn't do that—it requires lots of practice—I'd better let the expert do it." And, of course, their attitude reflected a new reality, for reaching a level of skill and experience equal to that of someone who'd been facilitating meetings for the past four years would, in fact, take time and practice. The group had more to lose by letting someone new attempt facilitation, because now the gap in skills was much greater.

Old-timers steeped in the ideology of equality often attempted to solve the problem by stepping out and not using their skills. But this strategy also resulted in a loss to the group. Instead of feeling empowered, people felt frustrated, manipulated, and abandoned. We often forgot that people can gain skills by seeing something done well.

We most successfully planned for succession by setting up trainings in skills we had learned and teaching strategies we had developed. Also helpful was having a variety of levels upon which people could practice. A new facilitator might start out in an affinity group meeting of ten people, later attempt to facilitate a cluster (a group of affinity groups) of thirty, and finally feel confident to try facilitating a spokescouncil of a hundred or so.

A group is an entity, a being in and of itself. A group that stays together over time develops a culture of its own, a shared history, a style of relating, unspoken rules, in-jokes. That culture can be very powerful, but from the outside can be hard to penetrate. It becomes a de facto boundary—often one that is invisible to those inside.

To be sustainable, a group must understand, anticipate, and plan for its own needs to change over time. The structure appropriate for a new group may not work for a group that is more well established. In the Livermore Action Group, our "leaderless" structure served us less and less well as the very stress on individual empowerment generated leaders. What we needed and lacked was a model of empowering leadership that could have eased our transition into another phase of growth.[30]

QUESTIONS ABOUT SUSTAINABILITY

1. What are our resources? Human? Material?
2. How well are our resources being replenished? Which are getting drained?
3. What service are we giving each other? The community?
4. What are we getting back? Is it enough?

5. How might we get more without losing sight of our primary purpose?
6. Whose needs are getting met in the group? How much time do we devote to the needs of each member?
7. Whose needs are not getting met? Who claims to have no needs? How can we renew the energies of those members?
8. Read through the six principles of permaculture. How well does our group meet each? Brainstorm possible changes.

The Descent of Inanna, VI:
The Last Gate

You come to the Last Gate
You have no senses left to see it, feel it
But you know it's there
You know what it is
And who sits before it
The Guardian says
    Who passes this gate
    Does not return
But how could you go back now
  anyway?
Nothing but bones and a rag of skin
What more could you possibly lose?
    Your memories
Says the Guardian
    Give them up
    Let them go
They fall out of you
  like ripe fruit
  old rotting meat
  grain and seed
  lie in the dust
  before the gate
Nameless, memoryless
You pass through

The old rag of skin
  they hang it on a meathook by the
  gate
The bones
  they are scattered, lost
This is the end of it all
All comes down to dead meat
  hanging on a wall
And below you march the Dead

They come in an endless procession
And some come old, eager for rest
And some come young, raging
And some come sick, and weary
And some come riding in battle
  formation

And some come screaming from
  wounds of torture
And some come empty-bellied and
  stick-legged
And some come burned
And some come in the great glut
  of war
The procession winds like a snake
They pass by you, every one
And there's not one damn thing you
  can do about it
You are the corpse on the gate

Your sister
  is Queen of the Dead
She is more powerful than you
You know that, now

She swallows them all
  the starved, the poisoned
  the bombed in their crowded hordes
They make her stomach hurt
She moans
    Oh, my belly, my heart
They are her children
She cries for them

Look into her eyes
They are your mirror
They are your own eyes

Feel your belly swell
  gorge unwilling
  until you think you'll burst
And still the killing goes on
  and they come
  the Dead in their endless lines

You have lost yourself
  but you are not lost
You have forgotten yourself
  but you are not forgotten
Somebody waits for you
  Remember?
If you have ever known help
  remember it now
  help is coming

If there is anyone
  who would follow you down
  to danger
  bless them now
  for here come two strange creatures
They have no sex, they have no
  gender
They approach the Queen of the Dead
  where she moans
    Oh my belly! Oh my heart!

    Oh your belly! Oh your heart!
They cry
She looks up, surprised
She does not expect sympathy
She is moved, she weeps
Her tears join the river
  that flows both ways at once
The Dead are flooded out
    Who are you? What do you want?
    Sweet creatures, I will give you
      anything!
Says the Queen of the Dead

    We want nothing
They say
    But the corpse on your gate

    Take that old rag, and welcome to
      it

You are lifted
You taste honey
  on your tongue, the Food of Life
  between your lips, the Water of Life

The Queen of the Dead gives a great
  cry
Her belly ripples like wheat in the
  wind
You are blown away
Swirling, spiraling
  around and around
You are eaten, swallowed
In her belly all souls dance
You dance too
  in rhythm with

the round of the stars
and the atom's frenetic beat
the swirling clouds, the rain
the running flying creeping crawling
  things
the swimmers and stalkers and
  shapers
all dance
  back and forth, in and out
  death and rebirth
You hear voices far away
They sound strangely familiar
  Bear Down! Push!
  Breathe!
The world contracts. You are shaken.
  Squeezed.
    She's crowning!
    Look! Here it comes!
You slide free

Beyond the Last Gate
  you are reborn

This is the mystery of the Round Dance
Birth. Death. Rebirth.
What you have learned is that no one
  escapes
What you have learned is that
  everyone returns
  and renewal
  comes as the Vulture
  taking all that has been wasted
  to feed
  what circles and soars

9

Evoking Mystery:
Restoring Organic Order

In my dream, the hawk soars overhead, twilight gleaming on pale breast feathers, red tail aglow. She approaches, wings outspread, looming larger. And then she is not flying, but walking toward me on the ground, her wings stretched out and trailing in the dust. I hold out my hands to her.

"Watch out," someone says. "It could be dangerous."

I know that she is wounded, or she would be flying. She is hurt or sick. She comes and lays herself in my hands. I know somewhere a place exists where she can find healing. Somewhere they rescue wild birds. I will take her there.

"Be careful," someone says. "She's wild. She'll bite you."

"No," I say, stroking her soft feathers, the down under the curved beak. She lays her head on its side and turns one eye up to me. "It's okay. She trusts me. I can handle her, because the hawk is my totem."

Mystery is what is wild in us, what is never entirely predictable or safe. Older and deeper than domination and control, it is the immanent value of the beating heart, blood, breath, survival, life. But what is wild in us is wounded. Where do we take the slow and shivering bird for healing? How do we teach it to fly again?

POSSESSION BY THE ORDERER

In the dismembered world, the King establishes order in the realm. He carves out the universe from chaos, parcels out the lands, determines who ranks high and who ranks low, makes the laws and enforces them.

The order established by the King is a rigid order, imposed on the natural world from without. It is a form of control that serves the needs of war.

"It is not necessary for Acme Carpet Sales or the Department of Motor Vehicles to regiment their employees and rigidly routinize every aspect of their work, for they operate in an essentially secure and predictable environment. The mail will be delivered each morning, the sales representatives will not be ambushed and killed on the way to their afternoon appointments, and the secretarial pool will not be driven to mass panic and flight by mortar rounds landing in the parking lot. Armies in peacetime look preposterously overorganized, but peace is not their real working environment.

"In battle, however, the apparent lunacies of orders given and acknowledged in standard forms, of rank formalized to an extent almost unknown elsewhere, of training . . . all find their justification by bringing some predictability and order to an essentially chaotic situation."[1]

In the realm of the Orderer, there is no room for the wild, for the mystery that cannot be analyzed, defined, contained. For the Orderer must maintain control. When we are possessed by the Orderer, control becomes our major issue.

The Orderer demands control of the self. We experience the self and especially the body as an object to be controlled, to be set in order. The body becomes a terrain to be carved and shaped, not a whole to be felt. Our size, our shape, our sexuality, our level of fitness become qualities subject to will rather than need, desire, health, or inclination.

In war, extreme order is necessary precisely to cope with the inherent disorder, unpredictability, and chaos of battle. Just as under the Defender's grip we are possessed by both Conqueror and Enemy, under the Orderer's power we are possessed by the dual image of rigid order and extreme chaos, by control that is essentially out of control.

The Orderer promises that we can gain value if we exert enough control. If we can only become thin enough, work hard enough, jog far enough, if we can only control our craving for sugar, for a drink, for sex, we will be worthy to live.

The implicit threat the Orderer makes is that we lose all value when we lose control. The Orderer perpetrates the delusion that all can be known and controlled. The dismembered body of the world becomes the Big Machine, the Cosmic Clock of seventeenth-century physics. We experience the earth as "a mere lump of dead matter," inert, lacking its own life, purpose, consciousness.[2] We experience ourselves as machines, programmable as this computer I write with, valued for our functions, not our being. So we idolize athletes who play on, ignoring injuries and pain, and except during periodic bouts of public righteousness, wink at the drug use that keeps them going. We admire the lightness and public grace of the ballerina who in private is driven to self-torment.

Prima ballerina Gelsy Kirkland describes her training at the hands of ballet master, George Balanchine: "I had an encounter with Mr. B. in class which underscored his demand for starvation. . . . He halted class and approached me for a kind of physical inspection. With his knuckles, he thumped on my sternum and down my rib cage, clucking his tongue and remarking, 'Must see the bones.' I was less than a hundred pounds even then. Mr. B. did not seem to consider beauty a quality that must develop from within the artist: rather, he was concerned with outward signs such as body weight. . . . He did not merely say, 'Eat less.' He said repeatedly, 'Eat nothing.' "[3]

Kirkland is metaphorically dismembered: "I frequently received verbal corrections addressed to each part of my body in isolation, figuratively dismembering me and dispelling any semblance of grace. It was as if separate strings were arbitrarily attached to my head, arms, and legs."[4] "Balanchine's conception of the human form was essentially mechanical. The body was a machine to be 'assembled.' "[5] Eventually, Kirkland is literally carved up through plastic surgery she undergoes in an attempt to achieve the perfect "look." She starves herself, purges when she succumbs to hunger, and neglects injuries that cause her constant pain.

To please the Orderer, we dismember ourselves, for in the Orderer's realm, we can never be valued as a whole self. Our size, our performance, our profile, our line and extension have value, not our joy in our bodies, or our connection to a living earth through touch, movement, smell, taste, sound, sight.

But, of course, we are not machines. We are not infinitely programmable, endlessly reshapable. The self has demands of its own, and the body has needs that cannot be denied. The Orderer's belief that all can be known and controlled is a delusion. This same delusion underlies our collective attitude toward science and technology. We place a nuclear power plant on an earthquake fault, sure that our technology is superior to the earth's raw strength. The accidents at Three Mile Island and Chernobyl are the Orderer's legacy.

The quantified knowledge, the control imposed by the Orderer are false. Just as the Conqueror's false protection keeps us actually unsafe, the Orderer's false knowing keeps us from seeing and understanding the true order inherent in our bodies, in nature, in the ways we interact. The anorexic looks in the mirror and perceives a skeletal body as fat. She can no longer see herself as she truly is.

What the Orderer demands from us is denial. We must close our eyes to the reality around us and within us, to feelings, to interactions, to the needs of the body so as to accept the Orderer's arrangements.

RECLAIMING THE BODY

What needs to be reclaimed from the Orderer is our own ability to create an order grounded in organic reality and connected to the natural world, the order of the body's own needs and processes, pains and pleasures. We need to give form to an order that is flexible and open to change, an order that recognizes its own limits and leaves room for wonder and mystery.

To counter the Orderer's control, we can begin by reclaiming the body, listening to its real needs and desires, praising it for the shape it is, pleasing it with touch and sensation and care.[6]

BODY MEDITATION

Prepare a luxurious bath for yourself. Lock the door. Scent the water with fragrant oils and herbs: rose petals, lavender, jasmine, mugwort, and comfrey are the ones I like. Light candles. Set out flowers or plants. Create an atmosphere.

Relax in the tub, and examine your body. Praise each part, from your toes on up to the hairs on your head. Think not just about beauty but also about function, strength, health, or, if you've been ill or injured, your body's miraculous ability to heal. Pay special attention to vulva, breasts, or penis. Touch and massage each part you name.

As you do this, you may find that negative thoughts surface. You may dislike parts of your body. Have pen and paper beside the bath, and write out the negative messages, or draw them as images. Then resume your song of praise. Pleasure yourself.

When you are ready, get out, clean up, dress, and collect your notes.

Repeat this periodically over time. I suggest once each quarter of the year—perhaps between equinox and solstice.

When you feel ready to complete the ritual, clean house. Go through your drawers and closets, find what you don't need, and give it away or throw it away. Save something small and burnable. Build a fire, collect your notes and your burnable object. Begin naming things you don't need. Start with physical objects: the clothes you will never really wear again, the old egg cartons that seem like they should be useful for something. Progress on to emotions and qualities: unwarranted guilt, responsibility for other people's feelings, unspoken anger, fears. End by reading aloud all the notes you've collected. Then burn them. Sing and dance, if you want to. (This part of the ritual also could be done in a group.)

Take another ritual bath. Linger over your own praises. If negative thoughts still come up, snap your fingers three times and say: "I no longer need you—the fire has consumed you—gone, gone gone!"

FOOD OF LIFE/WATER OF LIFE

Do this when you are feeling depressed, when everything is going wrong, when nobody likes you, and there's nothing to do but eat, drink, smoke, or do yourself in.

Read the Descent of Inanna story preceding chapters 4 through 10. Imagine yourself as Inanna, strung up on a meathook on the gates of the Land of the Dead, looking into the face of Ereshkigal, Queen of Death. Sing (to the tune of "Standing on the Corner, Watching All the Girls Go By"):

> Hanging on a meathook
> Dead to all the world
> Dead to all the world
> Dead to all the world
> Gone by . . .

(This chant was made up by Amber Khan-Engel, who warns that if you sing it for too long, you may start to decompose.)

Now think of someone who has been a helper to you at some time in your life. You may think of a living person or an inspiring figure from the past. If you can't think of anyone at all, imagine a faceless, sexless creature coming to you, bringing the Food of Life and the Water of Life.

Go through your refrigerator and pantry. Examine what is there. Ask yourself: Is this the Food of Life? Is this the Water of Life? Go through the garden, walk through the aisles of the supermarket, asking (silently): Is this the Food of Life? Is this the Water of Life?

Collect the Food and Water of Life, and make yourself a feast. Do not let your intellect make the judgment for you. If the Food of Life is Heath Bar Crunch ice cream, don't try to persuade yourself it should be grapefruit.

Keep this meditation up until you feel intuitively that you have been revived. Over time, you may well find that the Food of Life changes, and becomes those foods that do in fact further health and life. But don't try to hurry the process. Let it ripen in its own season.

FEAST OF LIFE

A group can turn the previous meditation into a ritual. Hold a group potluck, in which people prepare the Food of Life and Water of Life that is theirs, and serve it to the others.

Each person may also bring a place setting that represents herself or himself, which becomes a personal altar.

BODY INTRODUCTIONS

(I learned this one from Luisah Teish.)

Gather in a circle. One by one, introduce your bodies to each other. Introduce all your body's parts. Name what you like and what you don't like. Tell what your body has done for you, and its history.

After, discuss what is common to all, and what is different. What have you learned?

Follow with some form of body celebration.

BODY PRAISE RITUAL

Create sacred space. After body introductions, begin drumming and chanting, or put on some lively dance music. Dance freely. One person begins by dancing into the center of the circle. The rest of the group calls out praises and appreciations. When the first person has had enough, she or he returns to the circle and chooses the next person to go to the center. Continue until everyone has had a turn; then dance as long as you want to.

Many people are shy about dancing in front of a group, but part of the benefit of this ritual comes from doing it anyway, pushing aside all the voices that say, "You don't do it well enough. You'll look like a fool." The joy of the celebration comes from watching how people reveal some essence of themselves as they dance.

BODY CELEBRATION

Create sacred space in some congenial spot, ideally on a secluded beach or in a private, sunny meadow or a private room covered with soft blankets and pillows, lit by candles and graced with flowers, and provided with massage oil. Gather. Take off your clothes, and do body introductions.

One person gets in the center. The group massages the person, taking plenty of time and praising her or his body.

Give each person a turn in the center. Groups of up to five people work best; after that, the group may get tired.

End by feasting, and open.

ADDICTION, ANXIETY, AND DENIAL

In the Orderer's grasp, we are always creating illusory controls while denying our true needs and desires. We attempt to gain value by controlling what is inherently uncontrollable.

The terrain of the Orderer is that of addiction. In any addiction, issues of control are central. Alcoholism, for example, is at least partially a biochemical condition that makes alcohol behave as a physically addictive substance.[7] Alcoholics cannot control the way their bodies react to a drink, alcoholism is sustained by the belief that drinking can be and is being controlled.

One drinker recounted: "Always we'd emerge with a new formula for avoiding future trouble. 'You've got to space your drinks and take plenty of water in between' or 'coat the stomach with a little olive oil,' or 'drink anything but those damn martinis.' "[8]

One alcoholic and drug-addicted doctor prescribed pills to counteract the effects of his increasing drinking, and then other drugs to counteract the first pills, until in order to sleep he was injecting Pentothal intravenously. "I didn't feel I could lie in bed and squirt the stuff in my veins while my kids and wife stood around watching me, so I kept the drug in my bag and the bag in the car and the car in the garage. . . . I would put the needle in my vein and then try to figure out exactly how much medication to inject to overcome the pep pills while adding to the sleeping pills while ignoring the tranquilizers, in order to get just enough to be able to pull out the needle, jerk the tourniquet, throw it in the car, slam the car door shut, run down the hall, and fall in bed before I fell asleep."[9]

But the Orderer's control is inevitably broken. "I made promises to myself, my family and friends—and broke them. Short dry spells ended in heavy drinking. I tried to hide my drinking by going places where I was unlikely to see anyone I knew. Hangovers and remorse were always with me."[10]

The alcoholic, the addict, the binger, can spend years denying the reality of the problem, believing that the next time, control will hold. As a society we attempt to control addictions by imposing more severe punishments, more complete surveillance. So, as I write, Ronald and Nancy Reagan have instigated a "War on Drugs," and one of the major weapons they propose to use is mandatory urine testing in the workplace, bringing into daily life the surveillance of the jail. Of course, force, threats, and twenty-four-hour surveillance have never controlled drug use in prisons, nor can they on the streets or in the home. All they can do is further undermine our sense of inherent human value as we become judged, not for ourselves, but for our urine samples.

Yet drugs and alcohol attract us because they give us an illusion of importance. A few drinks, a snort of coke, and anyone can feel confident, cool. When we cannot exert our power in any other area of life, we can control our intake of substances.

The Orderer's world is one of anxiety. Chaos, destruction, is always on the verge of breaking loose. Caught up in denial, unable to face problems directly, we become nervous, for our problems, we intuitively know, will eventually catch up with us.

Once, driving in the country, I knocked a hole in my gas tank. A friend fixed it by the simple expedient of plugging the hole with soap. I drove home, two hundred miles, in a state of extreme anxiety because I was afraid to look under the car and see whether the plug was holding. I told myself I didn't want to know. Had I looked, I would either have been reassured, or I could have protected myself by pulling off the road and getting help. Instead, I spent three hours imagining that at any moment the car might blow up.

In beginning to face what we are afraid to see, the following meditation can be helpful.

SCRYING THROUGH DENIAL

Fill a dark bowl with water. Create sacred space. Sit comfortably, and gaze into the water.

Ask yourself: What do I know that I'm afraid to know? What might I see that I'm afraid to see?

Don't force answers. Let images or thoughts arise, and simply note what they are. When you get tired, open your circle and pour the water out.

Do this over time: nightly for a full season is best.

If disturbing information surfaces, find a supportive group or person with whom you can share. Members of a circle or group could do this meditation throughout the same period of time, and check in with each other about what comes up.

When the Orderer's control breaks, chaos ensues: "After my last binge I came home and smashed my dining room furniture to splinters, kicked out six windows and two balustrades. When I woke up sober, my handiwork confronted me. It is impossible for me to reproduce my despair. . . . I'd had absolute faith in science, and only in science. 'Knowledge is power,' I'd always been taught. Now I had to face up to the fact that knowledge of this sort, applied to my individual case, was not power."[11]

Control is also an issue for children of alcoholics and adults who grew up in alcoholic homes. The presence of a parent who drinks can create a climate of uncertainty equivalent to battle. "I remember, as a boy, coming home from school and seeing either the living room or the dining room furniture thrown out on the driveway . . ."[12]

Fights, physical abuse, and all forms of family stress create uncertainty. Children who don't seem harmed may become overly responsible, assert control in a way that later in life becomes rigid. "Everything must be in order in my household or it brings great anxiety to me. The orderliness probably stems from the chaos I felt in my adolescent years. My parents' house was always physically orderly, but human relationship-wise . . . CHAOS."[13]

Denial becomes a family characteristic. Claudia Black, writing about alcoholic families, describes the unspoken family rules as Don't talk, Don't trust, Don't feel. These are also the commands of the various aspects of the self-hater: Don't talk, says the Censor, don't trust, says the Defender, and don't feel, says the Orderer. Don't feel the body, don't feel your emotions, don't get out of control.

Clearly, denial is useful in war. Soldiers must deny their discomfort, their fear. Orders, routines, commands, regulations create an illusion of control, when in reality, no one knows when chaos might erupt.

Alcohol, in fact, has been the historic camp follower of battle. "The prospect of battle . . . seems always to alarm men's anxieties, however young and vigorous they be, rather than excite their anticipation. Hence the drinking which seems an inseparable part both of preparation for battle and of combat itself. Alcohol, as we know, depresses the self-protective reflexes, and so induces the appearance and feeling of courage. Other drugs reproduce this effect, notably marijuana; the American army's widespread addiction to it in Vietnam. . . . may therefore be seen if not as a natural, certainly as a time-honoured response to the uncertainties with which battle racks the soldiers."[14]

The Orderer creates anxiety by imposing a false picture of reality and then insisting that we hold to it. Order, control are held out as ways to relieve that anxiety, as are addictive substances, or patterns of behavior, or beliefs. But none of these solutions really alleviate our anxiety because they don't change the conditions that create it. In fact, they make it more difficult, if not impossible, to change conditions.

When we are caught in the bind of attempting to control what we cannot control, we are distracted from noticing how we are controlled by others and what is really destroying us, as drink distracts the soldier from realistic terror before battle.

There seems no way out of the dilemma. The more we try to exert control, the more out of control we get.

In Alcoholics Anonymous, the program most consistently successful in helping alcoholics get sober, the crucial first step is to withdraw from the control game. "We admitted we were powerless over alcohol—that our lives had become unmanageable. . . . We perceive that only through utter defeat are we able to take our first steps toward liberation and strength. Our admissions of personal powerlessness finally turn out to be firm bedrock upon which happy and purposeful lives may be built."[15]

Powerlessness may seem a strange foundation upon which to build power. But the sense of power and control alcoholics give up in AA is the false power of the Orderer, the illusory confidence offered by the drug. As long as we hold on to that false sense of worth, we are caught up in the Orderer's delusions.

Facing the reality instead of the delusion can be painful. AA, the other Twelve-Step programs, and similar support groups make the pain tolerable because they immediately restore a sense of immanent value. Each person who comes is valued for being—not for doing, not even for stopping drinking, but only for desiring to stop drinking. The group itself, composed of many others who have each had to face their own grim image in the mirror of truth, becomes a source of hope and solidarity. Others have been through the same journey and come out the other side. Liberation from the destructive cycle of control and chaos is possible.

Just as an individual can be possessed by the Orderer, so can a relationship, a family, a group. If anyone in a group is actively alcoholic or drug addicted, the Orderer will rule the group's interactions.

When the Orderer rules a group, questions of control will become central. But no matter what rules or agreements the group makes, what procedures are adopted, what new systems are tried, chaos will inevitably break out. The group will have covert rules about what subjects are taboo and what cannot be said aloud. Group members may find themselves starting to drink more, overeat, use more drugs, need more sleep, overwork, or may find themselves in a continual state of heightened anxiety.

Should you find yourself in a group ruled by the Orderer or shaped by someone's addictive behavior, remember the Orderer's first weapon is denial. The problem will not get better by itself. Unless the person involved is confronted, the problem will only get worse.

In a group in which members have equal formal power, they can confront problems collectively. In hierarchical structures, confronting addictions can be nearly impossible to do when the person who is out of control is in a position of authority. Suppose, for example, that Laura teaches in a women's studies program headed by Sarah, who is an alcoholic. Should Laura decide to confront Sarah, she may well get fired. Should she go above Sarah's head to the dean's office, the entire women's studies program may be jeopardized, for such complaints may be just what the dean has been looking for as an excuse to get rid of the program. At best, all her colleagues will see her as disloyal. She might, perhaps, succeed in getting the other teachers to agree to talk with Sarah in a spirit of group solidarity. Yet how honest can the women be, when none of them can know what reprisals Sarah might take?

As this example shows, hierarchical structures can reinforce any aspect of the self-hater, who is, after all, the internalization of hierarchical control. In many hierarchies, controlling behavior, even when erratic and arbitrary, would not be seen as questionable; it is a prerogative of power. Still, when we are caught in an addictive hierarchical system, we can at least break through our own denial, and then take what steps we need to protect ourselves. We may look for sources of support and advice, begin scouting for another job, or strategize with others about what concrete changes might make things better.

By contrast, in a circle of equals, the women involved in our example could speak honestly and with caring to Sarah about how her behavior hurts them. They could state what they need from her. Sarah might still not want to listen; however, she would no longer be able to get rid of her accusers.

What no group can do successfully is to control the drinker. If a group attempts it, whether through shame, guilt, or manipulation, the group becomes the Orderer and compounds the problem.

A wealth of resources, literature, and research exist on alcohol and drug problems. Twelve-Step programs such as Alcoholics Anonymous exist in every city and offer free services. Many other groups and programs also exist. If you have a problem with alcohol or drugs (and if you are wondering whether you do, you probably do), or if you are close to someone who does, get help. Any other work will otherwise ultimately become paralyzed.

OPENING TO MYSTERY

AA's second step is to open to mystery. "We came to believe that a power greater than ourselves could restore us to sanity."[16] Mystery frees us from the Orderer's grip, for to invite in the mystery, the deeper power, is to invoke an order that has nothing to do with imposed rules and laws, an order that regulates itself because it is rooted in the processes of life itself. To open to mystery is to acknowledge the body's true hungers, to seek for the Food and Water of Life that restore us when we hang on the gates of death. To open to mystery is to love the body, to marvel at the intensities of its pleasures, to allow ourselves to fully feel its sensitivity to pain.

Many tools exist to help us in that opening. We have already learned much about ritual. Myth, story, dream, and laughter are other roads that can take us to the enclosed chamber where the mysteries can be viewed. They are the transport. Mystery itself is what is common to us all: the pattern, the cycles of time, the body, the sense of place. It is the ear of corn; it is the stalk of wheat. It is the knowledge that through us move forces older and stronger than human will, that we are connected in ways we can barely suspect, that what is within us reflects what is outside us, and what surrounds us mirrors back what is in us.

In certain moments, we can feel the great tides moving through us. The purpose of ritual is to create the situations in which those moments may happen.

To evoke the mysteries means to call in forces that are greater than our expectations and designs, that move to their own beat and disrupt the most careful plans. Energy has its own rhythms; it can be shaped and directed, but never controlled.

WILD RITUAL

Every real ritual at some point goes out of control, breaks the plan, does the unexpected. Let it happen. Get out of its way. Get wild.

Scream, dance, yell, make noise, or find some other way to wildness that is uniquely yours.

Wild does not mean violent or insensitive. To be wild in ritual is to have energy pouring through you, to be at once a clear channel and deeply sensitive to the energy of the whole, because you have become part of the whole. We can whirl and weave through a crowd—and still watch our elbows and not trample the children.

Go to the wild. Experience the elements raw: jump in a river, roll in the snow, run naked into the wind. Bury yourself in the earth; decay like a seed to be reborn. Leap the fire; dance like a flame. Let go. Never settle for tame or lifeless rituals; never mistake boredom for spirituality. Practice ecstasy so you can get there without the drinks or the drugs that will keep you, ultimately, from making any real trouble.

In the mysteries, we touch rage and grief, just as we touch the source of joy and the origin of creativity. The sun rises and sets, the moon waxes and wanes, seasons change. The cycles of ritual connect us with the order inherent in the natural world. Mystery becomes embodied in the concrete, in a particular place, or story, or person, or time. Only in the concrete can we experience the pattern of the whole. So mystery is not abstract. It is about a particular worm in a clod of dirt in a particular garden. It is not about Woman; it is about Persephone, or Yemaya, or you.

The cycle is a thousand thousand cycles, each intricately different, linked to its own particular configuration of soil and weather, of the local combinations in the endless genetic dance, linked to place. To understand the mysteries is to know that a Monterey pine planted three hundred miles north on the coast will grow but become brittle as it ages, dropping limbs and cracking before its time. It is to restore a corner of Wisconsin prairie with sensitivity to the hundreds of varieties of grasses, shrubs, and flowers and the genetic treasure of their subtle variances from mile to mile. Or it is to plant, in a damp, sunless spot outside a north-facing window, one red-flowered abutilon that becomes a feeding station of the hummingbird.

Rooted in place, we might begin to celebrate rituals that emerge from the place where we are.

RITUAL OF RAINRETURN: A CALIFORNIAN FANTASY

When the first rain comes after the dry season, everybody runs out of their houses, takes off their clothes, and dances naked in the streets in the falling rain. Drummers go wild; people turn their stereos up full blast; the radio plays raindance music. Bowls, cups, and ritual vessels are set out to catch the falling rain, which is saved for the bathing of newborn infants, for washing the face after a hard cry, and for washing the first strawberries of spring.

NAMING THE MOONS

To connect more deeply with the cycles where you live, try renaming the months by some natural feature of climate or cyclical change. Here is my proposal for a San Francisco calendar, starting with the Witch's New Year on Halloween:

Ancestor Moon
Sunreturn Moon
Wet Moon
Fruit Blossom Moon
Leafy Moon
Rose Moon
Golden Grass Moon
Fog Rolls In Moon
Fog Sticks Around Moon
Fog Sticks Around Some More Moon
Rainreturn Moon
Greening Moon

Openness to mystery is incompatible with rigid ideologies and dogmas. We may acquire knowledge, develop skills, painstakingly work out analyses, but we can't know everything. When our guiding ideas evolve from our experiences, they must remain flexible, for we experience continual change.

A group that fosters liberation may or may not have a specifically spiritual focus or identity. It will, however, neither be closed to expressions of spirituality nor rigidly convinced that it alone has found the One, Right, True, and Only Path. Of course, religion and spirituality can generate dogma and encase the mysteries in concrete blocks of theology. Political theories are imbued with similar capacities. But our spirits can remain alive if we remember that the core of the deep connection we seek is embodied in wonder, not certainty. Humor, irreverence, and laughter open the gates of the mysteries; self-righteous pieties of any sort slam them shut. Liberating spirituality, whatever its denomination, is not about defining, confining, and controlling, but about passion.

FREEING OUR CREATIVITY

The Orderer also attempts to rule our creativity. As we have seen with Kirkland's story, the training of artists, dancers, and musicians in the culture of the dismembered world imposes form and discipline from without.

When my brother Mark was a child, he studied the piano with a fine classical musician. "Your brother is really gifted," my mother used to say. "But his teacher says he doesn't have discipline. I always have to make him work."

"What do you mean?" I'd ask. "He's always playing the piano!"

"But he isn't practicing," my mother would complain. "He's just improvising. He likes to make things up—but he doesn't like to *practice*."

Mark became a folk musician and songwriter, but he steered away from classical music. Now he finds himself remembering how his early teacher's judgment undermined his confidence. "I felt that I just didn't have what it takes to make it in the mainstream music world," he says thoughtfully, "but now I wonder . . . All that improvising—that was creativity. What if I'd had a teacher who could have appreciated it, even used it to teach the technical aspects? And why didn't it occur to anyone to wonder that I had original music coming out of me when I was eleven years old? Isn't that more of a gift than just being willing to play someone else's music?"

The tracks of the Orderer are recognizable everywhere once we know what to look for. The way we teach children; the grueling way we train doctors; the way we conduct the arts and sciences; the way we are expected to work, all fit us for the battlefield, not the open fields of freedom.

Creativity is a mystery: a work comes through the artist and takes on a life and often a will of its own. Alice Walker speaks of the characters in her novel *The Color Purple* as "trying to form (or, as I invariably thought of it, trying to contact me, to speak *through* me)."[17] She describes a creative process very different from the enforced discipline of the piano teacher.

"There were days and weeks and even months when nothing happened. Nothing whatsoever. I worked on my quilt, took long walks with my lover, lay on an island we discovered in the middle of the river and dabbled my fingers in the water. I swam, explored the redwood forests all around us, lay out in the meadow, picked apples, talked (yes, of course) to trees. My quilt began to grow. And, of course, everything was happening. Celie and Shug and Albert [the characters of her novel] were getting to know each other, coming to trust my determination to serve their entry (sometimes I felt re-entry) into the world to the best of my ability, and what is more—and felt so wonderful—we began to love one another. And, what is even more, to feel immense thankfulness for our mutual good luck.

"Just as summer was ending, one or more of my characters—Celie, Shug, Albert, Sofia, or Harpo—would come for a visit. We would sit wherever I was sitting, and talk. . . . The days passed in a blaze of happiness."[18]

That last sentence is a revolutionary statement. For in the Orderer's realm, to create, to serve as the voice of an order that comes from within, is an act of disloyalty. The artist defies the order of the authorities and so must pay through suffering. We expect artists to suffer, especially women artists, who are doubly rebels. Our heras are the suicides: Virginia Woolf, Sylvia Plath, Ann Sexton.

Alice Walker's words challenge our hatred of our own creativity. For an artist who is a great artist, a woman artist, a black woman artist, to write of her creative process that "the days passed in a blaze of happiness" is to counter all our expectations of how art should be made, and tantalize us with possibilities. How might Kirkland dance if her life were "a blaze of happiness"? What sunny fields might Van Gogh have painted, what rock and roll could Janis Joplin have belted out, what intricate visions might Bob Dylan have sustained in a culture where artists were not interned on Desolation Row? And what might we ourselves do, if we gave voice out of freedom to what is in us?

One of the gates to creativity is our dreams. Working together with our dreams is one way we can open to mystery.

DREAM CHALLENGE

Ask everyone to bring to the ritual a disturbing dream. In sacred space, form into small groups.

Take hands; breathe together. Then someone begins drumming or clapping a rhythm. Everyone joins in clapping until the rhythm becomes well established.

One by one, each person tells her or his dream to the rhythm. Members of the group then give each person a challenge that comes from the dream.

A challenge is *not* an analysis or an interpretation. We do not attempt to explain the symbols or apply some preconceived idea of what they mean. The challenge emerges when we allow the characters and the events in the dream to tell us what the person needs to do. For example, if you dreamed of your dog being hit by a car, I might say your challenge is to learn to protect your animal self. If you dreamed of a monster chasing you, your challenge might be to turn and face it.

When all have received challenges, form a large circle again. One person enters the center of the circle, tells her or his challenge, and the group cheers, shouts, drums, and chants her or his name for empowerment. Then the first person chooses another, and so on until all have been empowered.

Meditate on your challenge; see in what guises it appears in your daily life, and use it as the basis for a dream story.

DREAM STORY

Use your dream and challenge as the basis for a collective talk-story that the group enacts. Find out what develops.

Encourage children to tell their dreams as stories, or to act them out with toys. If a child has nightmares, encourage her or him to change the ending when the story is enacted. You might collect a special set of plastic figures and animals, to be kept in a special place, for telling dream stories.

THE DREAM GAME

(This game was invented together with Kate Kaufman and Patricia Witt of Madison, two inspiring women.) This game works best with about fifteen people. It requires one or two people to be "architects of the game." They should wear some identifying piece of clothing, such as a scarf. The game also requires a basket or box; a gong, bell, or something else that makes a distinctive sound; and a fair amount of space.

People are asked to come with a disturbing dream—perhaps one for which they have received a challenge. They write their dreams down, and they are collected in the basket.

The architects take some time to read over the dreams before the game begins. They may arrange them in a likely order, or trust to randomness.

The architects say to the group: "The purpose of this game is to gain power. The rules of the game are simple: We have all the power. We create your reality. You can try to change it. If you succeed, you win. If not, you lose. The only other rules are: no physical violence, and so that we all can hear what's going on, no shouting. Also, whenever you hear the bell, reality will shift. Now let's begin."

The architects then create a setting for the group that comes from one of the dreams. They pick individuals for certain roles, whispering instructions to them or taking them briefly aside. For example, to several individuals: "You are on a bus. You've been arrested after a big demonstration." To one other person: "Go aboard the bus and say: 'I'm the guard here. We've just been informed that nuclear war has been declared. The missiles are on their way right now.' "

People must then react to the situation. The group might panic, or might decide to get out of the bus, or to use magic to turn the missiles back, or invent some other scenario. The architects let the scene develop until people begin to get a sense of their power; then they ring the bell, and announce a new setting from the next dream, again choosing characters and assigning roles, but preferably without stopping the action for more than a moment.

As the game goes on, the architects may insert characters from one dream into others. At its best, the game itself takes on a chaotic, dreamlike character, and people discover ways to help transform each other's situations.

Continue until all the dreams are done, until the energy wanes, or the group becomes so empowered that the sense of challenge is lost.

The most important part of the game is the discussion afterward. Ask people how they felt in each of their roles, what they learned, what prompted choices each person made. Open up discussion of issues of power and resistance.

Every group needs a certain amount of order, and people have different levels of tolerance for chaos. The state of my office might drive you crazy, while your bare desk top might make me too nervous to work. In a group that values mystery, order arises from the group's real necessities. We might schedule meetings three months in advance, not because we like having our lives so planned, but because otherwise we cannot be sure of meeting at all. We might assign responsibility for tasks that otherwise won't get done. But we avoid creating an atmosphere top-heavy with rules and regulations.

QUESTIONS ABOUT CONTROL

Some questions about control that groups might wish to consider are:

1. What rules, spoken and unspoken, do we have in the group? Are they necessary?
2. How comfortable is each of us with the balance we have achieved between order and chaos?
3. How does each of us react when we feel things are getting out of control? How do we try to reestablish order? How do others react to our attempts?
4. Do we as a group hold to any belief systems, dogmas, political or spiritual ideologies? Have we ever articulated them? What are they? Are they open to question?
5. Are we having fun yet? Can we laugh at ourselves? Mock our own rituals? Do we know any good jokes?

PLAYING WITH THE TRICKSTER

Laughter is also an aspect of the mysteries: the trickster, the sacred clown exists precisely to keep us from taking ourselves too seriously. At home with mystery, we write parodies of our own sacred songs and make fun of our most esoteric secrets.

During my walk with the Greenham women from Silbury to Stonehenge, only the accidental performance of a scandalous toilet paper ritual created enough unity in the group to allow in mystery. Mystery is encountered in the dynamic tension between form and formlessness, honor and mockery, plan and spontaneity. Let me close this chapter with my letter home from the walk, which tells the story.

5/3/85

Dear Everybody,

Greetings from Salisbury Plain Women's Peace Camp, established on the edge of the artillery field. As I write this morning, I hear the rumbling of the artillery in the distance like a slow bass drum.

Yesterday was a thoroughly satisfying day. We got up in the morning and had a meeting, and it was quite beautiful to see how consensus could work, with no formal process, just everyone talking until the sense of the group became clear. I had expected we would divide into two groups—one to cross the artillery range and one to walk legally around the edge of the field, but as we were discussing that—wait. Let me describe how it was put out. Mary, who is organizing this action and more or less leading it (of course no one would admit that), would put forth a plan, and then say, "That's only a suggestion—let's hear other suggestions."

So someone said she thought the whole idea was for us to reclaim Salisbury Plain by walking over the Military Land, and why didn't we all go and do that? All that was stopping us was their red flag (and about fifty policemen). (The red flag is put up to warn the public to stay off the road that crosses the base because they will be firing across the road that day.) And we talked on for a bit and the general feeling was that we wanted to go in a large group straight through the barrier and down the central road (which had the advantage of being the only route through the field that is clear of unexploded shells). And that decision felt very strong and centered—so of course I decided to go. (We thought it unlikely that they would actually shell us with artillery, in spite of the red flag.)

Then we broke up, took some time to pack up and prepare. Some women gathered at the gate to the artillery field and began chanting, and police began gathering and little knots of us stood around talking saying, "This is impossible—we'll never get through" and trying to figure out other tactics.

Then we had another meeting, which got bogged down in a discussion of tactics, and we finally sort of agreed on doing what we'd originally planned, even if we did all get arrested—and I said, "Maybe we need to do something right here and now to center" so I led a short grounding and then suggested we make sounds. The chant started off very low and I almost thought it wouldn't happen—and then I did something I hadn't ever quite done before—I built an energy shell for the power to fill—and the power started to rise—and then it took off, and I felt the spirits of the Plain rise and they were *angry* at the military and the desecration of the plain, and they were with us. Then we grounded the power and everyone spontaneously headed up for the gate and began making rhythm and dancing in snake lines and then the lines ducked through the barbed wire at the side, went around the clumps of police, and were out on the field.

The police ran out to stop us and we stayed in snakes, holding hands, and our lines were pushing against their lines. The police linked arms and tried to contain us but of course we could always get around the ends of their lines. At one point a circle of police surrounded a circle of us—with a baby in the center. I thought we were trapped and then someone broke through and I heard a policeman say "It's impossible!" and I knew we had won.

We headed down to the road and some women had been arrested so we all sat down, and then a policeman came to talk to us, and everyone was singing and shouting to drown him out and he was saying that in five minutes they'd have a clearance for us to walk down the road. So they escorted the rest of us—about eighty women, five to ten babies and small children, and two dogs—all the way down the road across Salisbury Plain.

We had a lovely six-mile walk, and the Plain was beautiful—broad and open, unfenced grassland sweeping in low swells, marred only by a few tanks and gun emplacements and bomb craters. The sun was hot and the sky blue and gorgeous, and I had wonderful conversations with women.

Then we arrived on the other side of the field and camped by a woods owned by the Ministry of Defense. Camp was set up, the firepits dug, wood gathered, suppers cooked around campfires, and then women sang and played guitars into the night.

Now today's meeting begins.

Later

Today's plan is much less clear—we are three miles from Stonehenge and some women want to walk there, take down the barbed wire around it, and free the stones. We also want to do a ritual at Stonehenge for the full moon which will be a total lunar eclipse. Some of the women feel the stones have bad energy and/or patriarchal energy and/or male energy and/or all of the above, and don't want to go there. There's another place we're supposed to camp but it's nine miles away and we'd have to be driven back to the stones for the ritual which seems chancy. Women don't want to split up but they want to do different things. In the no-process meetings, the strong, anarchist, energy of the women from Greenham overrides the women who voice doubts and fears or even strategic concerns. No real plan has evolved except to walk on to Stonehenge and then do what we feel.

Then we started to talk about the ritual, and feelings came out about the Beltane ritual (which I had informally led on Silbury Hill when the march began on May Eve). Several women said they hated it because they felt too controlled and that they couldn't scream or yell or do what they felt (which frankly I felt was not fair—nothing was stopping them and I left lots of space with no direction—but it's definitely a different culture— what seems like total lack of control to me probably seems like complete bureaucracy to them) and other women said they liked the ritual and there were times when the energy fell apart and it was good to have someone bring it back together—some women said they didn't like the grounding this morning and left because they didn't want to do it—a lot of others said it felt really good and they needed it and didn't feel like we'd have gotten through the police lines without it—other women said they felt it was the spontaneity of our snake dance that got us through the line— others said they felt the snake dance built on the grounding—and so forth and so on.

I said I felt what we needed maybe wasn't a *plan* but more discussion about what different women's expectations about ritual were, and what we wanted—and everyone agreed that would be good.

5/5

Greetings from our new location—the auxiliary car park at Stonehenge.

So—we had a circle before we left, and this time I decided not to lead anything and just see what happened and it was very nice. Women started different chants and then a spontaneous spiral dance—with about a hundred police watching us. Then we got ready to go—and the police were blocking the path we wanted to go on so again we were forming our snakes and running around and walking through them—but this time they gave in more easily—I think we'd demoralized them—so we walked out onto the Plain, a peaceful army of women with kids and dogs and drums and flutes, laughing and grinning at each other and singing, "We are Witches, and we are walking, walking on Salisbury Plain."

The police offered us the car park to camp in. We set up camp, and some of us had a long discussion about matriarchy and patriarchy and about what to do in the stones. Someone suggested using menstrual blood and that seemed very powerful and someone else asked about menopause and we talked about the power of the Crone and about birth and women's mysteries and I never wanted the conversation to end. After dinner, women were singing at different fires—one fire sang the "Isis Astarte" chant and another fire began chanting the names of the women there to the same tune, just as we do, and then other fires picked it up. We did, too—it was beautiful to be singing around the fire and hearing the echoes in the night.

Then I wandered over to a fire in the center of camp, where a group of women were doing something strangely ritualistic with a roll of toilet paper. They were parodying a ritual in a very devastating and funny way. I couldn't help feeling that they were also parodying me in a devastating and funny way so I felt a mixture of—what? A sting, and also an attraction, because it was so much like our kind of humor. So I got right into it, and as we carried it on and on, connecting us all together with the toilet paper (bog roll, in British) making a web, chanting, "We are the pee, we are the flow," miming a collective piss around the circle, singing, "You can't kill the bog roll, it's like a mountain, soft and strong, it goes on and on and on . . ." (I guess you had to have been there) we actually raised power.

Then this woman came over from outside the circle and said that she didn't like what was going on, that it felt nasty to hear us ridicule the songs that had gotten her through some very hard times—and then she walked away and we had some serious discussion. It became clear to me that what had happened was quite amazing—that the women who had the most discomfort with ritual had started this off and had somehow attracted to the circle the women who were most deeply into spirituality, and Coyote had tricked us all into a very powerful experience and done some healing around what is a deep split in the group. And I also realize how instinctively right I had been to join in and not run away from it. I'll never forget one woman saying, "I've never been comfortable in ritual—but when we tore the bog roll into the web, and held it up to the moon—it was so beautiful!"

Sunday

It's pouring rain, so instead of getting up perhaps I'll finish this.

Yesterday we relaxed. A few of us walked down to the River Avon to get water for the ritual. We found a lovely spot with green banks where the river winds gently under overhanging trees—a perfect picture-book English river, and two of us took a plunge—which left me feeling pure if not clean. I squatted naked on the bank and sang a Yoruba chant to Oshun and a big white swan came drifting down and listened for a while. Then we collected our water and went back.

It wasn't clear how we were going to get into Stonehenge, with so many police around, but we had already done so many impossible things, we were feeling somewhat invincible. We had another meeting. Again we talked about structure and structurelessness. Thanks to the bog roll ritual, we felt clear and united about doing ritual in the stones. We decided what we wanted was to let everyone do what she wanted but to also do something together.

I talked about grounding and some of us formed a circle to ground but then the others just surged across the road, through gaps women had cut in the barbed wire and across the field and it was so beautiful! I was crying and laughing. We went to the stones and just stood there quietly as all the women arrived—in awe of the place and amazement that we were there. We started chanting "Return to the Mother" and danced around the stones and then came into the center and drummed and chanted and raised power, and I was in deep trance and the energy was amazing! Totally unstructured and indeed spontaneous, chants rising and falling, women drumming—Zohl up on a stone dancing with her breasts bare, rags red with menstrual blood on the stones, women's pictures appearing, two children beating the big drum, women wailing and screaming and chanting and at one moment when the power was strong I found myself crying with deep, deep sobs, and saying to myself "It's been so long! It's been so long!" As if I could feel the earth was so hurt and damaged, and the spirit of the stones was there to help us and yet it felt weak and tired and overwhelmed by the magnitude of the destruction.

And then the moon appeared, just a sliver left with the earth's shadow crawling on its face, and we watched the eclipse become full and the holy dark, and I could see the alignment of the moon through the great trilithons, and feel the power of the moon through those gateways and someone was singing Ferron's chant "By my life, be I spirit . . ." and then we began singing "You can't kill the spirit, she's like a mountain, old and strong, she goes on and on and on . . ."

And women joined us and we sang and sang as the moon grew back again and the clouds passed over her face and drew back and the chant waxed and waned with the light and went on and on . . .

So of course, I couldn't ground for a week afterwards—I just wandered around Batya and Danny's flat in London in a daze, alternately writing myth and bursting into tears, then somehow getting myself out to the talks I had scheduled. I feel like something very powerful has happened to me—that I've seen ideas and values I share pushed beyond where I can take them. I got pushed really hard to let go, let go of the energy, let go of directing it or making it safe or thinking I knew what it could or couldn't do, and trust it. And so in the stones I felt free, and I realized that I hadn't felt free for a long time, and might not tomorrow, but I was free then, in the middle of that place of power and in the balance point of sun and moon, and I began to suspect what the perfect counterpoint to the entities of control may be, and that it's not something we can define or create, but something we become by jumping for it and being willing to live on the line, in the open. And it's hard, but I feel an incredible sense of hope this morning—that we can do it, that we can create this thing we all want that we have no models for.

So—let's do it. Let's trust the energy. Let's keep it alive and keep challenging each other and keep honest but let's fuck the red flags and the bobbies–within and go for it! Let's all be wild and fearless together.

I love you—

Star

The Descent of Inanna, VII:
The Return

You slide free
  and float down the river
  that flows both ways at once
Your newness
  almost unbearable
  the colors of everything so bright
  each sound so clear
  each smell so sharp
The river carries you
  What has been born in you?
  What new thing do you bring back
    from Below?

The current washes you up on shore
On the bank you find
  baskets of old fruit, grain, seed, memory
Sort through them
  Which do you take back?   Which do you need?
  Which do you transform or discard in the river,
    food for the trout and the water strider?

Dive into the river, let it carry you again
Let the swirling water knead you into form
What form do you take? How will you satisfy your hunger
  now that you have tasted
  the Food and Water of Life?

Swim to the banks. Raise your voice. Hear its power.
What songs will you sing of your journey?
What words do you bring back from Below?

Look down
On the grass is a pile of armor, weapons, clothing
They were yours once
Do you need them now?
Which will you take back with you?
How will you protect yourself?
How will you clothe yourself when you return?

And your skills, your knowledge, your achievements
They line the banks like a litter of coins
How will you carry them now? What will they mean to
  you?

What new understanding do you bring to them?

The river twists like a serpent
Blink your eyes
The river is the snake
She has shed
She is new, iridescent
She emerges through the crack
You follow her
   leaving the passages Below
   coming up
   into the storehouse
Examine its treasures with new eyes
Is there a gift for you?
Something to bring to the people?
Walk past the corridors, the oil jars, the grain jars
   the baskets of dates, figs, seed
Place your hand on the door that opens out
Say goodbye
   and emerge
   into the sunlit courtyard
Someone is there to greet you
Thank your helper
Tell your story
Look at the courtyard with new eyes

The fountain in the center is the holy well
   of water from the river that flows both ways at once
The flame on the altar is the earthfire, hearthfire
The story woman winks at you
   and you remember
   that you are not alone

Stretch out your hand
Touch
Feel the living edge
Of another being
We have all descended
We have all emerged
The biggest things
In the universe
Are circles
   of light
Anarchist circles
They refuse to obey
   the laws of gravity

By those laws
  they should fly apart
  but they hold together
So can we

Touch
Link
Circle
Hold on

Holding together
  we can hold on
  to the memory of who we really are
  and no barrier can contain us

Holding together
  in the circle
We can bring the dead lands
  Water of Life
We become healers
The flame burns to warm us, feed us
  in the center of where we are

Where we are is the center

All our paths
  are spokes of the wheel

Toward Community:
Structure and Leadership in Groups

We cannot change the world alone. To heal ourselves, to restore the earth to life, to create the situations in which freedom can flourish, we must work together in groups.

The problem is that we ourselves have internalized power-over, and too often we reproduce it in the groups we form. We may join a group that promises political or spiritual liberation, only to find that it has simply changed the trappings of oppression, that our own sisters/comrades/compañeros/fellow spiritual seekers can still hurt us, disregard us, disrespect us. How do we live a different reality when the ways we perceive, feel, and react have been shaped by this one?

For a group to become a place of liberation, its structure and process must foster freedom. The ways in which we structure groups and perceive power determine what can happen in a group, how conflicts can be resolved, and how creative energies can be manifested.

Every group is an entity, a being in its own right. When a group comes together, jells, when the magic happens that turns an odd collection of individuals (or a collection of odd individuals) into something more, it develops a spirit, an energy, a personality of its own. In a group of equals, each person is responsible for the group's energy. Each member contributes to the group's overall character and mood, and helps set its tone.

A group can be collectively either more or less than its individual members. Groups can be places of strength or they can exaggerate individuals' weaknesses. The group mind can be smarter or stupider than any single person's mind. For a group to become a place of healing and liberation, each individual must see herself or himself as responsible for the group. We are all conditioned to let someone else take the lead, to expect someone else to be in control. But anyone who is part of a group is part of the group mind and spirit, and so influences and shapes the group.

GROUP PURPOSE

Groups have different purposes and functions and may have many different ways of fulfilling the conditions of freedom. We will consider four types of groups: intimate groups, task groups, support groups, and learning groups.

INTIMATE GROUPS

The primary purpose of an intimate group is *being:* being a group, creating community, forming long-term, ongoing relationships. Traditionally, Witches have been organized into intimate groups called covens: circles that meet for ritual and magical work and develop strong bonds, loyalties, and attachments. Families are intimate groups, as are households that aspire to familylike bonds. Task groups and healing groups sometimes develop into intimate groups. All intimate groups take a long time—years, not weeks or months—to develop. They demand long-term, open-ended commitments and a high degree of openness and trust.

A basic chemistry of attraction also needs to exist among members: it's pointless trying to be intimate with someone whose company you don't enjoy, although members do go through times of conflict. But over time, a bond develops much like that in a loyal family, when you know that no matter how much you irritate each other, fall in and out of love with each other or each other's lovers, damage each other's cars, or differ ideologically, you will still be connected. For this to happen, members need to live close enough so that they can become part of each other's lives. Many groups aspire to intimacy, but long-lasting intimate groups are actually rare.

TASK GROUPS

The primary purpose of a task group is to *do* something. It may center around a particular project—preparing for a blockade, running a collective grocery store—or it may have a more generalized focus of work that encompasses many projects—creating right livelihood for members, providing legal services for just causes. Task groups last, ideally, just as long as they need to last to do what they are trying to do. Groups may spring up and dissolve for short-term projects, or they may continue for years. Individual members may come and go.

Members may value each other's skills, experience, and knowledge because of the task at hand even when they are not very attracted to each other's personalities. Varying degrees of openness may be appropriate, and trust will focus heavily on whether or not individuals keep their agreements and commitments.

SUPPORT GROUPS

The primary purpose of a support group is *change:* insight, healing, recovery from external or internalized oppression. The consciousness-raising groups of the late sixties and early seventies are classic examples, as are Alcoholics Anonymous and related support groups. Change may be seen as personal, or as extending out and having social and political impact. Groups often focus on specific issues or situations: race, ethnic or cultural identity, surviving abuse, assault, or discrimination, recovering from addiction. Or their focus may be to generate the insights necessary for action: for example, the Base Communities of Latin America radically challenge dictatorships. Support groups may evolve into task groups, and over time become intimate groups that form true community.

Support groups may vary in size and degree of intimacy. A group for incest survivors may be limited to eight or ten, while an AA meeting might encompass hundreds of people. Groups may be set up with a limited time commitment or they may last as long as support is needed.

Support groups work when members are willing to be open and share even painful experiences. Trust is highly important; members need to trust that they will not be judged or condemned for speaking, and that their secrets will remain confidential. They don't necessarily have to socialize outside the group. People often expect support groups to be or become intimate groups, and occasionally they are. Often, however, people do not realize that true intimacy demands time, and grow impatient, expressing rage or disappointment at the group's limitations. Yet there may be advantages in *not* turning one's support group into one's intimate community, for often what we need to be supported *about* are the conflicts and struggles we're involved in with our intimates.

LEARNING GROUPS

The primary purpose of a learning group is to facilitate *learning*. Classes, workshops, training sessions, and study groups are all examples. One person or several may take the role of teacher, trainer, facilitator, or the group may direct its own learning process.

Size and expected levels of intimacy can vary greatly. Learning groups have a limited duration, and for the setting to be an empowering one, teachers also need to see themselves as learners. Students have the potential, over time, to replace the teachers or do without them. The teachers' job is to make themselves obsolete, while learning from their students, who also have valuable life experiences, skills, and knowledge.

Learning groups are often fertile ground for seeding other sorts of groups. Covens or ritual circles often start from classes or workshops.

CONFLICT IN GROUPS

All groups have conflicts. Conflict is not a sign of a group's failure, but a necessary and potentially healthy aspect of its growth. Groups conflict because needs, directions, and dynamic forces are not always in harmony. Through open conflict, needs can be balanced, changes can be made, and new directions forged.

Conflict is not the same as violence. In a group of equals, conflict means that my needs, desires, or ideas run counter to yours. We can each be empowered to argue for, work for, and plan for our goals, but neither of us has the power to force our purpose or perceptions on each other or the group.

Creative conflicts often surface in groups at times of transition. When the group is uncertain about its primary purpose, or when that purpose is changing, different people may be pulled toward different focuses. Such conflicts help each person in the group become more aware of her or his own needs and purposes.

Conflict in groups also arises from confusion about the group's primary purpose. Feminists have stressed the importance of not separating thinking and feeling, giving emotional support when we work together. Nevertheless, a group may still have a primary purpose that is weighted either toward feelings or productivity. The closeness and support we can generate quickly in a support group or learning group can be empowering but is not the same as the intimacy and trust that can only develop over time. Unrealistic expectations lead to dire disappointments.

For example, a group I was involved with struggled for months to form an intimate collective out of women who lived on both coasts and in the Midwest, some of whom also traveled incessantly. We were women of color and white women from a wide variety of backgrounds and life experiences, but those differences were not what kept us apart as much as the sheer physical separation imposed by geography. We literally could not meet enough, talk enough, connect enough to develop the level of trust we thought we "should" have, as proper feminists. Eventually, we came to see that a more task-focused structure made more sense for our organization.

Groups may also transform in the other direction. My long-standing affinity group eventually decided that we were also a coven. We had gradually changed from being a group in which personal relations supported our task, to a group in which intimacy is primary, and tasks emerge. We continue to do political action, but because we see ourselves continuing indefinitely into the future, we can afford to think and plan in long time periods, to devote a season to organizing and another to deepening our knowledge of ritual.

Here are some questions to help identify what kind of group you want to be.

QUESTIONS ABOUT PURPOSE

After reading this section, write out, individually and anonymously, answers to these questions:

1. What is the group's primary purpose (stated in one sentence)?
2. What do I want the group's purpose to be?
3. What are my expectations? Disappointments? Satisfactions? Unmet needs?

Collect the answers, shuffle them, and read them aloud. Discuss:

4. Do we agree on our purpose? On what kind of a group we are?
5. What differences exist? Do they broaden and strengthen the group, or are they dividing us? Are we in transition?
6. What expectations can we and can't we hope to meet? What needs are we meeting? Failing to meet? Do we want to meet them?
7. What kinds of trust do we need in each other?
8. What structure or purpose will best help each of us to realize our visions for the group?

These questions may open up a long process of discussion. If the group is strongly divided, don't rush to resolve the issue. The conflict may be fruitful, leading to new creative ideas or structures, or to a broadened vision.

When the group resolves its direction, some members may leave to pursue purposes of their own. The group has succeeded in being a spring-board for those individuals' empowerment. The Livermore Action Group, for example, found that throughout its life span individuals would leave the group to work on other related issues: Central America, apartheid, the homeless. The skills and experience they had developed working against nuclear weapons thus affected many issues.

Creative conflicts also surface around all the areas discussed in earlier chapters: how individuals are valued, how boundaries are established and safety is created, how power is distributed and influence felt, what can and cannot be said, how needs are met and the group is sustained. In creative conflict, opposing forces interact in a dynamic balance. One side does not destroy the other.

Groups handle conflict effectively when they see it as information about differing needs and recognize those needs as valid. Conflicts become dis-empowering when needs are judged or invalidated.

In a collective household, one person likes to play loud rock-and-roll music before dinner. Another person likes to sleep in the afternoon. If the group tries to judge whose need is more important or more valid, nothing but hurt will result. But if the group accepts both sets of needs as valid although contradictory, it can find many creative solutions that can strike a fair balance between noise and quiet. It might juggle rooms, or designate certain times or days as quiet times. Neither person will get her or his desires absolutely fulfilled, but when people feel valued and accepted, they can more easily compromise and accept partial fulfillment of their needs or wishes.

Conflict also evokes fear. Most of us have only experienced conflict in situations of power-over, in which to lose is to be hurt, physically, eco-nomically, emotionally. When conflict surfaces, fears arise. We fear that we will lose value if we push for our needs over someone else's, or if we allow someone else's desires to supercede ours. Lisa may fear that if she demands quiet for her afternoon nap, others in the house will resent her and think she is lazy and fussy. The group might encourage her to state her fears and ask for feedback. Perhaps others do resent being quiet for her; if so, that is important information she needs to know. Perhaps others also resent being subjected to the megadecibels of Deathtongue in the afternoon; if so, the group needs that information in order to come to a sound decision. Or perhaps Lisa, out of fear that people resent her, is walking around with a martyred expression that does evoke resentment, making her fears real. If so, she needs that information.

In a group that fosters liberation, conflict is always better handled when it is open. Concealed conflict cannot be productive, for it is concealed information that the group needs. Ignoring conflict doesn't make it go away. Hidden conflict creates an atmosphere ruled by the Censor, in which more and more cannot be said and no one can feel truly safe.

Most conflicts can be handled by the group itself. Some may require outside mediation between individuals, or mediation among the entire group. Sometimes only an outsider can be objective enough to help a group move through a conflict to a creative solution.

QUESTIONS FOR GROUPS IN CONFLICT

Some questions that may prove helpful for groups in conflict to consider are:

1. What information is encoded in this conflict about contradictions in our needs or real situation?
2. What needs, drives, or perceptions are being expressed? Are they valid? Can we acknowledge their validity?
3. What transformation is the group as a whole undergoing? Do our conflicts reflect these changes?
4. If we accept differing needs as valid, how can we best meet them? What compromises might be made?
5. What judgments are being made? Are they valid? Are they interfering with solving the problem?
6. What fears do each of us have? Check them out—get feedback from the group. Are they valid? Are we manifesting them?

A mediator might also ask: What's the dirt here? What's the gossip? The ancient history? What are people not saying?

When a group gets into conflict, rumors fly, telephone lines buzz with gossip, and some people don't know what's going on. In larger organizations, when many people are involved in a conflict and others are peripheral, the following process is useful.

A FIGHT IN A FISHBOWL

At the meeting, the facilitator asks those involved in the conflict to come forward. They sit in a small group surrounded by the circle of the larger group, who act as witnesses. The fishbowl may be closed or open to those who decide they want to join and speak. Or people can leave when they feel done with participating and one newcomer can replace each person who leaves. When the group is strongly divided on an issue, people should take care that both sides are equally represented in the fishbowl.

A time limit is set: generally not less than twenty minutes or longer than an hour. Thirty to forty minutes is often best—after that, observers get bored. Also, just as medicine can generate iatrogenic—doctor-caused—diseases, too much process can lead to process-caused conflicts, when people develop hurts and grudges over the ways other people acted in mediations.

The purpose of the fishbowl is not necessarily to resolve conflicts, which cannot be done in an hour, but to bring them out into the open so that the entire group knows what they are. Dirt, gossip, personal history, old love affairs, and feuds may be important aspects of the conflict and are better aired than concealed.

The fight can be conducted using one of the following processes:

No process: This works especially well in groups who have a history of letting process and politeness stifle and constrict argument. The presence of a circle of observers acts as a restraint on personal attacks and real viciousness.

Facilitation for balance: A facilitator acts only to assure that different sides of the issue are aired for roughly equal time periods.

This exercise requires a certain amount of trust. People will usually want to establish agreements that keep the arguments nice. This tendency should be resisted, for the purpose of the process is to undermine the Censor and get the dirt out.

Once all members of the group know the relevant information, the group can begin to solve the problem, asking the questions listed in the previous exercise. Problem solving may not heal the hurt feelings of the principals involved, who may need further outside mediation, but the group as a whole can move on.

People have an endless fascination with gossip but a limited tolerance for processing other people's conflicts. When the same conflicts reemerge again and again, when the same people get into the same fights, the group may suspect it is being manipulated. When people in the group begin to resent demands for more discussion of the same problems, when they have processed so much they feel like cheese spread, they are justified in giving up.

Some conflicts are best resolved by division: people may be better off not working in the same group if their needs or goals are irreconcilable. Other conflicts are resolved by letting go, and by time. What seems insoluble now may seem trivial a year from now. What seems impossibly painful may become something to laugh about. People change, and so do their needs, perceptions, and purposes. A group may decide, "We can't resolve this conflict; let's keep it alive, but move on to other things."

Letting go can sometimes be helped by a ritual like the following.

CLEANSING RITUAL FOR GROUPS

Establish a ritual space. In the center, place a large bowl of salt water.

One by one, come to the water. Breathe deep: imagine your breath coming up from the fiery center of the earth, through your feet and legs, through the base of your spine, belly, heart, down your arms and out your hands, past your throat, through your eyes, and out the top of your head, carrying with it the hurt, the anger, the mistrust that you have collected. Let it all come out through your breath: imagine it as a stream, muddy or flaming, or in whatever form works for you. Let it flow into the salt water.

Name aloud what you are letting go: the conflict, the hurt, the unmet needs. Don't be diplomatic. If you feel moved to do so, yell, scream, moan, gag. Pour it all into the salt water.

As you listen to others, you may find their words arouse further hurt, anger, resentment, pain. Imagine breathing all of that into the water, letting it pass through you.

When all have been to the water, take a lit candle and pass it clockwise around the circle. As you take the candle, name something positive you feel about the group or the people in it, something the group has done that has benefited others or realized your desires.

When the candle has been around the circle, whoever has been the most involved in the conflict takes the candle and douses it in the water.

Sit there in the dark and feel miserable for a while.

Then softly begin to chant:

Free the heart, let it go
What you reap is what you sow[1]

Let the chant build power and energy. Raise power: imagine it lighting a new candle, rekindling the group trust and spirit. When the power falls, ground it. Light a new candle and pass it around the circle clockwise. When you take the candle, say what it is you rededicate yourself to doing in the group, what changes you commit to making, what new hopes you now hold.

Pour the water out on the ground. Set the candle in the center of the circle. As it burns down, feast and feed each other.
Open the circle.

Unfortunately, not all conflict is creative or productive. Conflict may arise in groups because some people are extremely difficult to get along with. When we are possessed by one or another form of the King, we behave in ways that damage relationships and destroy group trust. Groups structured to foster freedom can sometimes minimize this damage and help us free ouselves. Sometimes, we need more help than the group can give. Some people so naturally divide and disrupt groups that they may be accused of being paid agents. Some may be; others might just as well be. If you are committed to work for social change but are continually harmful to groups you join, if you have few friends and find that, in general, people dislike you, consider that they might have a reason. Are you abusive? Continually needy? Do you try to be superior to others? Are you too good for your own good? Are you unable to join in consensus reality?

If you need more help than a group can give, if you are possessed by some aspect of the King and can't get out, if you exhibit any of the conditions I've just listed, you may need individual therapy. Although in this book I attack many of the theories upon which most professional psychotherapy is based, the practice itself can prove enormously beneficial. I have certainly found it so personally. This seeming contradiction exists because good therapists, whatever theory they ascribe to, intuitively create the conditions that foster freedom.

A good therapist—or healer, doctor, counselor, minister, and so on— affirms your inherent value, creates a safe situation with clear boundaries, and approaches each client not as a disease to be labeled but with a sense of wonder at the human mystery that can never be entirely revealed. Good therapists do not issue judgments but encourage the breaking of the Censor's rule and the speaking of the unspeakable, meet needs but take care of themselves, are aware of the enormous influence of their position, and wield it responsibly. Finally, a good therapist is able to deflate the false values we cling to while supporting what may be a fragile sense of immanent worth. Good therapists also make mistakes: expecting perfection may be your self-hater's way of entrapping you in the belief that nobody really can help you.

STAGES IN A GROUP'S GROWTH

If we think of a group as an entity, as a being with an independent life, we can also understand that a group has a life cycle and, perhaps, a natural life span. Groups and movements go through stages. In each stage, they have different goals, problems, and pitfalls.[2]

One model of group development is based on the four directions and the four elements of the Wiccan magic circle.[3] No group follows these stages in perfect order; they are merely a framework for thinking about group changes over time, as well as for identifying some of the dynamic polarities that exist in groups.

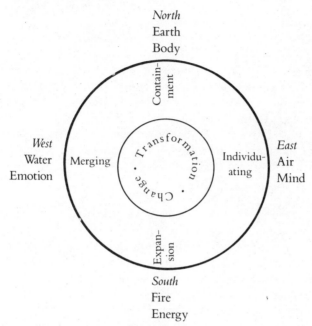

North
Earth
Body

West
Water
Emotion

East
Air
Mind

South
Fire
Energy

(circle labels: Containment, Merging, Transformation · Change, Individuating, Expansion)

AIR

The group comes together around a common vision or set or ideas. Air corresponds with East, the direction of the mind, of light, illumination, naming, differentiation. The group's first challenge is to establish an identity, focus on a primary purpose. Sometimes a group's purpose is clear; at other times it may shift and change, remaining fluid for months or even years. Purpose and direction evolve organically as the group congeals into an entity with a life of its own. The stronger that entity becomes as an independent force, the less amenable it is to any individual's control.

In the air stage, the group must attract enough people to secure its ongoing existence. For this reason, an open structure is often most appropriate. A new group is impressionable: strong personalities and powerful leaders can imprint their style on the group, creating a covert hierarchy. Either their roles should be openly acknowledged, questioned, and made visible, or the group should strictly adhere to rotation of responsibilities and processes that assure equality.

FIRE

Fire corresponds with South, the direction of energy, passion, courage, will, expansion. In the fire stage, the group often expands rapidly and begins to feel its power. Events move quickly. Conflicts are heated as people struggle around issues of power. As individuals in the group begin to feel their own power, they use it. New leaders may emerge; especially favored are those who have energy to drive the group onward, encouraging it to do more and more. Rage and anger can be creatively tapped.

The fire stage is a high-energy period, and groups may identify so strongly with it that they forget it is only one point on the wheel, not the whole circle. The challenge for the group is to openly and honestly confront issues of power.

The other challenge facing groups in this stage is to stay grounded—in touch with the earth qualities of limits, boundaries, and the finite capacities of the human body. Otherwise, growth can progress so fast that literal burnout results. As the group expands and takes in new people, older members may feel invaded and overwhelmed. While the group may enter the fire stage open and structureless, it must emerge with some boundaries and some ways to structure power.

WATER

Water corresponds with West and is identified with feeling, emotion, nurturing, sensuality, introspection. The expansion of the fire stage needs to be followed by time to replenish energies and renew sources of strength. This stage may at first seem like collapse, and may be identified as a time of failure, when the group suddenly lacks the driving energy it had before. In reality, this is an important stage of transition. With lines of power clarified, groups can focus on deeper feelings and connections, on developing real trust, on nurturing each other's abilities. The group needs time to turn inward, and may find a closed structure most appropriate for this period.

Members may resist new plans and projects. Influence shifts away from leaders who push to do more, toward those group members most at home with feelings, who can encourage others to express more.

The challenge for the group is to value this stage, to allow itself time for nurturing and reflection, to survive the sexual entanglements and disentanglements of members and to test the bonds of connection so that real trust can be built. The challenge may also be to shift the group's driving energy from rage at oppression to positive vision, to move from resistance to renewal. Groups need enough members and resources to carry them through this stage of turning within. If the group does not recognize the value of the water stage, and believes itself to have failed by not maintaining fire's expansiveness, it may indeed die.

While the group may enter this stage with formalized processes and structures of power, as trust is built members will find that structure and process may loosen up, become more intuitive and less rigid.

EARTH

Earth corresponds with North and represents growth, sustenance, the solidity of limits and boundaries, the ability to build lasting achievements. The group's task in this stage is to consolidate its gains and begin to win real victories and make lasting changes.

United by bonds of trust, members can work together to begin translating their visions of possibilities into concrete realities. The group may begin to expand again, this time moving perhaps more slowly, with a stronger sense of both its own power and limitations.

The leadership that emerges in the earth stage draws on a backlog of skill and experience. In a group that fosters freedom, however, leaders use their knowledge not to entrench themselves in their positions of power but to help nurture leadership in others.

One challenge now facing the group is to develop a structure that can bring new people in, while respecting the boundaries necessary to sustain trust. Structures of power and ways of working that are sustainable must be developed. The group will by this time have learned to do many things well, and have highly developed skills and resources. Its challenge is to not let what it does become institutionalized, codified, rigid, or dogmatic, to stay open to change, creativity, and new visions. For earth, also, is only one point on the wheel, not the stopping point. A living group keeps moving on to new visions, new times of fiery expansion and emotional introspection.

Air and water, fire and earth also form dynamic polarities. Understanding that dynamism can help us keep from mistaking it for opposition, for a group remains most vital and healthy when it values both poles.

THE AIR/WATER POLARITY

The air/water polarity is the polarity between identity and connection, separation and merging, autonomy and unity, decentralization and centralization, between the needs of the individual and the needs of the whole. A group that fosters liberation must value each individual's right to be independent, to hold to her or his own vision and follow the call of conscience even when it differs from the decisions of the group. Yet to act as a whole, the group needs a sense of common purpose, vision, agreement, action. To remain alive and vital, a group must find a dynamic balance, continually swinging in rhythm between these points.

THE FIRE/EARTH POLARITY

The fire/earth polarity is the dynamic tension between growth and limitation, expansion and boundaries, change and form. A living group must retain the drive and excitement of fire while not losing touch with the grounded practicalities of earth. Again, the challenge is to find a dynamic structure that acknowledges and incorporates both sets of needs and resources.

QUESTIONS ABOUT STAGES OF A GROUP'S GROWTH

1. Which stage of development is our group in? How do we know?
2. What is our current challenge and how are we meeting it?
3. Which of the dynamic polarities are alive for our group now?
4. What balance are we finding?

RESPONSIVE LEADERSHIP

Power is never static, for power is not a thing that we can hold or store; it is a movement, a relationship, a balance, fluid and changing. The power one person can wield over another is dependent on a myriad of external factors and subtle agreements. The power-from-within we can evoke at any moment changes too, sometimes diminishing as our abilities are attacked, sometimes increasing in conditions that encourage it to flourish. And power-with, the influence we can exert in a group of equals, our power to shape the group's course and shift its direction, is perhaps the most fluid of all forms of power. Responsive leadership is the art of wielding power-with in ways that foster freedom.

To empower its members, a group must not only be structured in ways that serve liberation; it must also be conscious of how power in the group moves and flows. It must somehow come to terms with the question of leadership.

Two basic myths exist about leadership. The first is that someone must always be in charge or nothing will get done. The second is that leadership is always oppressive. Although both myths contain kernels of truth, each is based on an essential confusion between power-over and power-with.

Power-over is decision-making power, control. In a hierarchy, it flows from the top down. In an egalitarian group, it remains broadly based. Decisions are made by the people most affected by them, and/or those who will carry them out.

Power-with is influence. Whose voice is listened to? Whose ideas are most likely to be adopted? Influence may never be entirely equalized. Some people do have experience or skills or imagination that a group finds consistently of value, and their opinions do carry weight. Influence can disempower others, however, when some people's ideas are adopted as a matter of course and others are not listened to at all, or when people give over their own decision-making power to experts. For example, in direct actions, when legal negotiations are going on, groups are often tempted to let their lawyers make decisions, even when questions are not actually about legalities but are political questions of solidarity and strategy.

Influence becomes destructive when it is not acknowledged. In "leaderless" groups, influence may become a dirty secret, like bad breath. Everyone knows who has it but nobody wants to mention it.

When we can identify influence and talk about it, we can evaluate it and challenge it. Those who have it can be acknowledged and validated. At the same time, the group can take more care to listen more closely to the ideas of others, and judge proposals on their own merits. Those who don't have much influence can begin to consider whether they want it and how to get it. The Censor's rule: Don't talk, Don't see what's going on, can be broken.

Influence also becomes destructive when exerted negatively rather than positively, when it comes not from respect for a person's ideas, but from fear of her or his reactions when crossed. When a member plays out any of the King's roles in a group, often our first instinct is to placate or comply. If we know that crossing someone will provoke a scathing attack or will evoke the Tearful Victim, we often avoid the confrontation. Ultimately, such avoidance stifles the group.

A group, as an entity with its own spirit and identity, needs a brain. It needs some people who are willing to look ahead, anticipate problems, suggest new directions, try out new solutions, keep track of information and decisions, who lead in the sense of stepping out in front and going first. Such leadership is a service to the group.

Leadership becomes oppressive, however, when individuals or cliques control group decisions and resources, institutionalize their position "in front," and use it as a way to accumulate greater status and rewards. Such leadership characterizes almost every organization and institution with which we interact and furnishes the model with which we are most familiar—the model that first leaps to mind when we say the word *leader*.

Groups that foster freedom need a way to envision and name the positive qualities of leadership that empowers. Otherwise, we too often simply react against the oppressive forms of leadership.

Perhaps the worst kind of leadership is hidden leadership, for leaders who are not acknowledged cannot be held accountable for their actions. Power that is visible, no matter how oppressive, can at least be identified, resisted, and sometimes avoided.

Covert leadership is also hard on the leaders themselves, for they cannot be supported by the group if they are not supposed to exist. Effective leadership is a service to a group, but offering such service becomes a thankless task when power is concealed and mystified because of an ideology that states "we have no leaders."

When we adopt any structure or process as an article of faith, we become unable to ask the questions about power that might help us develop sustainable and empowering structures. No one way of balancing power is applicable to all situations.

Leaderlessness is an ideal appropriate for some groups and situations. In covens or affinity groups, which are small and intimate, when people are relatively equal in relevant experience and commitment, know each other well, and have time to develop trust, power and responsibility can be shared equally and everyone can feel empowered. Such groups are not, in reality, leaderless, but rather "leaderful"—everyone in the group feels empowered to start or stop things, to challenge others or meet challenges, to move out in front or to fall back. Such groups function like a good jazz ensemble: now the saxophone wails out a solo, then takes a break to let the drummer go wild. But the energy can flow with no defined plan or leader only because everybody knows how to play music. If the drummer can't keep the beat, if the horn player can't hit the notes, the group will produce only raucous noises.

Leaderlessness also works well in direct actions. The law enforcement authorities often attempt to identify and remove leaders of civil disobedience, expecting groups to be rendered incapable of making decisions. At an action at Vandenberg Air Force Base in March, 1983, the military police somewhat arbitrarily removed one person from each busload of arrestees, inevitably choosing a man, and usually the largest and strongest-looking man in the group. "You're the leader here," they would say. "You tell your people that if we have any trouble with them, you're going to get singled out." No matter how much we protested that we had no leaders, the authorities did not believe us, for they could not conceive of an organization functioning without someone in charge. But because decision-making power was vested in each one of us and in the group as a whole, not in any individual, our decision-making process could not be disrupted no matter who was removed from the group. In fact, singling out individuals only made us, as a group, less cooperative.

Leaderlessness may serve us less well in larger organizations, when levels of skill, experience, and commitment vary. Hundreds or thousands of people cannot instantly develop personal bonds of trust. Communications, planning and long term strategy may be furthered by strategies that clearly designate responsibilities and draw on individuals' experience.

When power-from-within or power-with are used constructively, they become synonymous with responsibility. In Nicaragua, the word used by the Sandinistas for leader is *responsable*—the one responsible. Bill Moyer, one of the founders of Movement for a New Society, uses the term "nurturing leadership." I like the term *responsive leadership* to identify power-with or influence used so as to empower the group and individuals in it. I choose the term *responsive* because such leadership responds to the needs of the group and the opportunities in the environment, responds by feeling as well as by thinking and acting. A basic principle of responsive leadership is that power and responsibility work together. If you have power, you are responsible for using it in an empowering way. If you have responsibility, you need the power to meet it.

In an organization in which decision making is bottom-up, not top-down, that principle guides us in deciding who makes which decisions. If everyone has to make every decision, participation becomes tyranny. No one is free to act independently, and everyone is enslaved to endless meetings. The group might better determine areas of autonomy and responsibility. If one subgroup takes responsibility for the newsletter, they decide what goes into it, what type of paper it will be printed on, what type face to use, and so on. The group as a whole might give some broad philosophical guidelines: should the newsletter be an open forum in which we publish all opinions, or should it reflect a particular viewpoint? Or such decisions might be left to those who are interested in them. Autonomy requires trust, which can only develop over time. A group may find that as it matures, members function more autonomously and make more independent decisions. Leadership, like structure, changes as a group develops.

Rather than committing to any static dogma about leadership, a group would do well to periodically ask itself the following questions.

QUESTIONS ABOUT LEADERSHIP

1. What work needs to be done? What roles need to be filled?
2. How do we get people to commit to the work? To fill the roles?
3. How do we hold them accountable for their actions and decisions?
4. How can we support them? How can we nurture, replenish, and restore their energies?
5. How can they pass on their information, skills, and experience?
6. How can we as a group nurture each other to take on greater responsibilities?
7. Which decisions must the whole group make? Who is affected by them? Who carries them out?
8. Which decisions can be made independently? By whom? Who is affected by them? Who carries them out?
9. What power does each of us need to carry out our responsibilities to the group? Do we each have that power?
10. What responsibilities are implied by the power, abilities, or influence each of us has in the group? How do we meet those responsibilities?

GUIDELINES FOR RESPONSIVE LEADERSHIP

How do we know when leadership is exercised responsibly and responsively? Here are some guidelines, useful both for evaluating our own groups and others we might be tempted to join, not to mention public officials and heads of state.

1. Responsive leadership nurtures others. It sees itself as a temporary condition. Instead of using skills, knowledge, information, and experience to entrench ourselves in a position of power, we share them, try to spread them as widely as possible among others. Re-

sponsive leaders understand that people learn in many different ways. At times, they may provide models for others, showing how something can be done well. At other times, they might step back and challenge others to stretch their skills.

The roles and responsibilities of leadership rotate. Responsive leaders train others to take on the same responsibilities. An empowering group does not thrust responsibilities on people without preparation, but creates situations in which information, skills, and the knowledge gained by experience can be passed on. Responsible leadership also provides support when people are practicing new skills, and does not set people up for failure.

In a group with open leadership, everyone can see how leaders are chosen, and how they themselves can take on more responsibility and gather more power in the group. Power is not mystified.

2. Responsive leaders keep commitments. If they take on a task, they carry it through. If they are unable to fulfill a task, they take responsibility for finding someone else who will, and providing that person with needed information and preparation.

3. A responsive leader responds—listens to others, consults, hears others' concerns, acts as the ear of the group more than the mouth. Responsive leaders also listen to the mood, the energy, the underlying tone of the group as a whole. They can accept criticism and are willing to change.

4. Responsible leaders take responsibility for the decisions they do make, and account for them to the group.

5. Responsible leaders keep lines of authority, power, and decision making clear and visible. They name reality, rather than conceal it in the service of ideology. Their agendas and motives are open and visible, not hidden, and they are honest rather than pure or always "politically correct."

6. Responsive leaders think first about the interests and needs of the group, and give them priority. This is, however, another good reason for sharing and rotating leadership: for such service to be sustainable and not lead to martyrdom, resentment, or burnout, it must be passed around.

7. Responsive leaders don't expect special benefits, attention, release from a fair share of less desirable work or chores, adulation, or a more-than-equitable share of resources. A nonhierarchical group does not set up tokens of status that must be collected in order to advance, nor does it assume that the roles that carry most influence should be most rewarded materially.

Responsive leaders do, however, expect and deserve to receive support and nurturing from the group. When someone has worked hard in the group's service or is burdened with many responsibilities, some care and pampering may be in order. After a long ceremony in the Lucumi tradition, someone brings the drummers a plate of food so that they won't have to wrestle with the crowd at the table—not because they are a higher class of being, but because they have worked hard for the group, and people want to show respect and appreciation.

8. Responsible leaders do not play King—do not abuse or humiliate others, issue judgments, determine what can or cannot be thought or said, or attempt to use the group in battles with personal enemies.

9. Responsive leaders are self-disclosing; they express feelings and vulnerabilities, and give support to others. In a support group, in which people are expected to share deep emotions and painful experiences, responsive leaders do not set themselves apart, neither do they drain the group's energies and time by demanding that their moods be catered to.

10. Responsive leaders do not monopolize caring or care giving. In a nonhierarchical group, people should have many others to turn to for support. Leaders also need people to turn to for caring and nurturing and can find broader support when support is shared.

11. Responsive leaders make mistakes. An empowering group does not expect perfection from anyone. If leaders, or groups, are not making a fair share of mistakes, they are not taking enough risks. An empowering group does, however, expect mistakes to be acknowledged honestly, and expects people to learn from errors. Responsible leaders take responsibility for making amends and working to solve problems their mistakes might generate.

ADAPTING RESPONSIVE LEADERSHIP TO HIERARCHIES

We can create nonhierarchical groups, but most of us still work in and interact with hierarchies. Some of us find ourselves wielding power over others, and would like to do so responsibly. The principles of responsive leadership can be adapted to hierarchical structures.

1. In a hierarchy, those who wish to advance must also train and nurture others to take their places, seeing their own positions as temporary. Nurturing others' capacities, providing training and preparation, encouraging others to gain skills and take on new responsibilities can only strengthen an organization.

2. When we wield power over others, we have even a greater responsibility to keep the commitments we make and delegate tasks effectively.

3. Listening to others, responding to suggestions, and hearing complaints, criticisms, and concerns are especially important when we do have decision-making power, for even absolute authority does not guarantee absolute infallibility.

4. When we have the power to make decisions that others must live with, we must certainly be accountable for them. In a hierarchy, leaders are also ultimately expected to be responsible for the decisions they delegate to those under them.

5. In hierarchical organizations, people can still feel some control when lines of power are visible and clear. Secret influence, hidden agendas, and covert power are even more destructive when those making decisions have power over others.

   Power-over is also less destructive when it is bounded by clear limitations, when checks and balances exist, and when routes of appeal are available to challenge decisions. A responsive leader in a hierarchy makes sure that people know their rights, that channels of appeal function fairly, that people know how to use them, and that laws, rules, and agreements that bind power are kept.

6. Hierarchies often expect and demand that those serving them put the corporate interest before their own. But when we give priority to a group in which others have power over us, we may be acting against our own best interests. Responsible leaders in hierarchical situations take care of themselves and do not deny their own needs, nor do they expect self-denial from those under them. They are conscious of what demands they make on others' time and private lives, and are aware that people do have needs outside the organization.

7. In a hierarchy where control and influence are marked by tokens of status, such symbols become part of the reality of how power is distributed. We cannot change the realities of power simply by refusing the symbols and rewards of power. Responsive leaders, regardless of their ideals, retain their sanity and common sense. At the same time, they can suggest changes and fight for policies that more closely equalize rewards and give those of lesser status more of a share of resources and benefits.

   Responsive leaders also practice respect for others on lower rungs of the ladder. They do not assume that the secretaries, for example, exist only to serve the executives. They set up structures and policies that allow individuals as much control as possible over their own space and time, and respect those boundaries. Responsible leaders practice common courtesy and politeness. Manners, after all, evolved to cushion relationships of unequal status. The formal tokens of respect we give to others communicate how we rate their value. In a hierarchy, in which some people are valued less than others, those tokens become even more important as messages. When a secretary refers to the boss by his or her last name, and the boss calls the secretary by her or his nickname, their unequal status is reinforced. Responsive leaders are as respectful to those under them as to those above them.

8. Responsive leaders do not take a position of power-over as a license to abuse others—verbally, physically, sexually, or emotionally.

9. In a hierarchy, people can not be completely self-disclosing when the feelings or opinions they express might criticize, conflict with, or cause anxiety to someone above them. Responsive leaders create a climate in which feelings and emotions can be expressed, but are also clear and honest about the limits of safety. They don't pressure people to become vulnerable who are already in a vulnerable position, nor push people to make disclosures that might harm them or others.

   We cannot make an unsafe situation safe by ignoring its dangers. Responsible leaders may model self-disclosing, but will also protect themselves.

10. In a hierarchy, the person in power tends to become parent, judge, dispenser of praise and blame. A responsive leader encourages everyone in the group to participate in caring for each other, establishing an atmosphere that rewards cooperation rather than competition. Because praise and blame, reward and punishment, are the currency of hierarchy, responsible leaders know that they cannot simply withhold praise and starve those below them, or avoid all criticism and blame. Instead, they learn to offer criticism in supportive ways. They make their expectations clear, offer support or provide necessary preparation, and look on criticism as a mutual problem-solving process, asking, "How can we make this better? What support, what information of you need?" Specific, work-focused praise, thanks for extra efforts, appreciation of work well done can be a way of letting people know that they are seen and that what they do is valued.

11. Hierarchical leaders also make mistakes, which may be more devastating when their power has been unchecked. Responsible leaders admit mistakes and work to correct them. They accept the mistakes of others and encourage responsibility, not guilt; problem solving, not blame.

Hierarchies are different from groups in which everyone has equal formal power. Different structures, processes, and behaviors are appropriate. Concepts appropriate to one group do not work in another. Open and honest emotional encounters, for example, may be liberating in a group of equals, devastating in a hierarchy. Openness, vulnerability, self-disclosure, flirtations, love affairs, and open conflicts may bind a group of equals more closely together; in a hierarchy, they may reinforce oppressive power relations. Rules, laws, formal agreements, politeness, and fixed procedures may be stultifying in a group of equals, but liberating in a hierarchy where they limit abuses of power.

Hierarchical groups may be doing work of value, and many good reasons might lead us to choose to work in them, survival being not the least reason. Practicing and/or demanding responsible leadership in a hierarchy may not immediately remake the world, but it can remove some of the worst immediate abuses of power-over and alleviate the stresses that often make work situations painful and destructive. As a not inconsiderable side effect, it will also increase productivity and morale, for the better people feel about themselves and their situation, the more productive and creative they can be.

EVALUATING LEADERSHIP

1. How do I exercise leadership? How do I meet each of these criteria?
2. How is leadership exercised in our group? How does it meet standards presented here?
3. What criteria would you add to this list?
4. Apply these ideas, and your own, to your work situation. What changes would you like to see made? How might you organize to press for them?
5. Apply these criteria to your elected officials. How might we pressure for more responsive, and responsible, leadership?

LEADERSHIP ROLES

In every group, certain tasks need to be done and roles need to be filled if the group is to function. If we think of a group as an entity, a being in and of itself, it needs a mind, a heart, and a spirit; it runs on energy and generates emotion. These are the roles leadership must fulfull.

In hierarchical groups, all roles are filled by one person or a small elite, who are rewarded more highly than others. The leader, the "king," may be the brains, the mouthpiece, the drive, of a group. The various aspects of the King are aspects of hierarchical leadership: the Orderer determines the group's plans, the Judge makes decisions and establishes rules, the Conqueror defines the group's boundaries and establishes who its allies and enemies are, the Censor speaks for the group, and the Master of Servants demands that the other members of the group play a respectful, subservient role. Such leadership is bolstered by all the trappings and symbols of status and rank.

Nonhierarchical groups also have roles and functions that need to be fulfilled. In a group in which everyone has immanent value, fulfilling certain roles does not set one apart from the group or establish anyone as being intrinsically more valuable than others. The role we fill may be valuable and vital, and we may be appreciated for performing it well. But our inherent value does not depend on the performance of our role, and our leadership does not diminish anyone else's value.

The four directions and four elements of the magic circle are a useful framework for thinking about the roles and tasks of leadership. None of these roles are exclusive, and although they can be formalized when appropriate, they are not necessarily assigned to different people. Rather, they are aspects of power we each might assume at different times. The names I provide here are aids in helping us identify the powers that are needed if a group is to survive and grow.

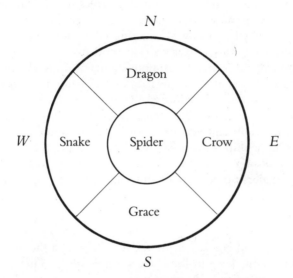

For the East, the direction of air, of the mind and vision, we have the Crows, who keep an overview of the group's tasks and progress. For the South, the direction of fire, of energy, we have the Graces, who help the group expand. For the West, the direction of water, of emotion, we have the Snakes, who keep an underview of the group's feelings and emotions. For the North, the direction of earth, of the body and finitude, we have the Dragons, who establish and guard the group's boundaries, who keep the group grounded. In the center, the place of spirit, we have the Spider, who weaves the group's connections.

These names are not sacrosanct. They were made up at different times and took on a life of their own, but they can be changed. Once when Reclaiming was restructuring itself, we talked about the need for a small group to keep an overview of what was going on, to play Crow. "How about an underview?" someone said. "Maybe we also need worms."

"That sounds like a bad combination."

"Snakes, then." The name was given. Later, we added Graces, originally derived from the task of welcoming and integrating newcomers at public rituals. A collective household called Cauliflower published a book on collective living, in which they recommended every group keep a Dragon—someone with a nasty temper—in the basement to get rid of those people who come to visit for a weekend and remain for a month, emptying the refrigerator and leaving their dishes on the table. Spider is a name I made up myself to name and articulate more clearly the role of the center. Groups may decide to use different names, or identify different roles. This model can help groups value contributions we don't ordinarily identify as leadership.

Some people most easily take on certain roles and avoid others. One person in the group may be a natural Grace, another may be a born Dragon. Groups may benefit by considering who tends to play which role, and by making conscious efforts to trade and exchange roles, especially as some tend to make people more popular than others. To be complete, we each need to move around the magic circle, not to remain stuck in any quarter, no matter how comfortable. And for leadership to be empowering, we must take on all of these tasks and responsibilities in ways that nurture the group and encourage others to develop.

Responsive leadership is exercised less by providing the group with answers than by posing questions for the group itself to consider. I will describe each leadership role more fully and provide examples of questions.

CROWS

Crows fly high and see far, from above. They take the long view, see the long-term vision, keep in focus the group's goals. They suggest new directions, make plans and develop strategies, and look ahead to anticipate problems and needs.

QUESTIONS FOR CROWS

1. What is our primary purpose?
2. Are we accomplishing it? Moving toward it?
3. What stage are we in?
4. Where are we going?
5. How do we get there—and by what steps, and with what timing?
6. What are our strengths and resources?
7. What are our weaknesses?
8. Is our structure working? How might it serve us better?
9. Who is with us and who against us?
10. Who are our potential allies? Opposition?
11. Who are we reaching? Who failing to reach?
12. What are the broader needs of the community around us? Are we, should we be meeting them? How?

13. What future needs can we anticipate? How can we provide for them?
14. What future problems can we foresee? How can we plan for them?
15. What details need to be taken care of?
16. What is falling through the cracks?
17. What can we learn from past mistakes? Successes?

The function of Crow is the one most closely resembling the role of hierarchical leadership. Crows often develop a lot of influence in a group. If one or two people are thinking about long-range plans, others may be likely to agree to them simply because they haven't come up with anything different. The group may benefit by considering together the Crow questions.

GRACES

Fire is the element of energy. Graces are continually aware of the group's energy, helping to raise it when it flags, and to direct and channel it when it is strong. Graces provide the group with fire: enthusiasm, raw energy, ability to expand. They make people feel good, generate enthusiasm about the group, welcome newcomers, bring people in. They furnish inspiration and generate new ideas.

QUESTIONS FOR GRACES

1. What does the group get excited about?
2. What inspired each of us to join the group?
3. What/who made us feel welcome? Unwelcome?
4. In what directions might we expand?
5. How do we bring new people in?
6. How do we help new people catch up on the information, skills, experience, gossip, and so on the group has developed?
7. Who is interested in joining the group? Why?
8. How do we appear to outsiders?
9. How do we interact with people outside the group? How can we help them feel welcome?
10. What resources in the larger community might we share? What needs might we help fill?
11. Where do we direct the group's energy?
12. Who do we want to reach out to—and how?

The role of Grace tends to make one well liked, but Graces must temper their enthusiasm with some of the grounding qualities of Dragons. Women are trained early to be good Graces. The role has been described as "what ladies do at parties": welcoming people, starting conversations, making introductions, being charming. But no one should be expected to be charming all of the time, and everyone can benefit by taking on the role some of the time. Again, the group as a whole might consider these questions, and take care that many share the role of Grace.

SNAKES

Water is identified with feelings and emotions, and also fertility and renewal. The snake is the ancient symbol of the Goddess and of life's renewal, for the snake sheds its skin and is continually reborn. Snakes cultivate an awareness of how people are feeling. The snake glides through the water, sees from below the surface, or burrows into the ground and brings up the dirt. Effective Snakes keep current with the group's gossip. They become aware early of conflict, and bring it into the open, where they may help to mediate or resolve problems.

QUESTIONS FOR SNAKES

1. How are people feeling?
2. What are people feeling that they aren't saying?
3. Who really likes and dislikes each other in the group?
4. What personal histories—known or secret—do people have? What sexual entanglements?
5. What secrets exist in the group?
6. What are the unspoken rules in the group?
7. What conflicts are people avoiding?
8. What do people grumble about privately and not say openly?
9. What do the smokers talk about when they congregate ouside the door of the meeting? (Perhaps this phenomenon is peculiar to California, where smoking inside a meeting is frowned upon. Often the conversation among the smokers expresses a very different and more negative perspective than what is openly expressed in the meeting. Does smoking lead to cynicism, or do cynics tend to become smokers? Whichever, the bitching going on outside the door is sometimes the most important interchange happening.)
10. What's the latest gossip?
11. What hidden agendas are operating?
12. Who's alienated? Why?
13. What conflicts are brewing? Unresolved?

Snakes violate the Censor, speak the unspeakable, bring out into the open what others may not see or prefer to keep hidden. The role of Snake can be an extremely uncomfortable one—and Snakes may become heartily disliked, but theirs is a vital role and the one that perhaps does most to undermine the King's attempts to gain control of the group. The mouth is the greatest organ of resistance. A group cannot function by avoiding conflict and not acknowledging feelings. The role of bringing conflict into the open is vital and valuable.

Snakes can minimize how much they are disliked if they remember to bring *questions* to the group, not analyses. An effective Snake might say, for example: "I feel tension in the room. What are other people feeling?" Rather than: "I know you really hate Mary and can't deal with powerful women, John, so why don't you admit it!" Being the Snake is no excuse for sliding into the Judge's role or playing group therapist.

If the Snake is truly aware of how others are feeling, she or he can help mediate conflicts by asking the questions that improve communication. It is also important to rotate this role. Someone who continually brings up conflicts may lose influence and eventually come to be considered a crank. A wise Snake occasionally turns enthusiastic or visionary.

DRAGONS

Earth is the element of nurturing, grounding, of the practicalities that assure our sustenance. Dragons keep the group grounded, in touch with the practical, the realistic. Dragons also live on the boundaries of the wild, guarding hordes of treasure with their claws and fiery breath. The Dragon in the group guards its resources and its boundaries and articulates its limitations.

QUESTIONS FOR DRAGONS

1. Is our work sustainable?
2. Are our resources being replenished?
3. Are people burning out? Why?
4. How can we better nurture each other?
5. What concrete skills and resources do we have? How can they be augmented? Passed on?
6. What concrete limitations do we have? Are we acknowledging them? Planning for them?
7. How much time can each of us really commit?
8. How much money do we have? Need? Can we really afford this?
9. Can we really take this project on, and do it well?
10. How many new people can we realistically absorb? In what time frame?
11. What boundaries do we need and want? How do we establish them? How do we protect ourselves from intrusion? Invasion? Distraction? From having our energies drained?
12. Who is in the group and who is out?

13. How do people leave the group?
14. How do we end relationships with people we no longer want to work with?
15. What practical tasks need to be done?
16. What are we going to eat? Who is going to shop, cook, clean up, and so on?
17. How can we better provide for our physical safety? Needs? Comforts?

Dragons establish boundaries that give the group a sense of safety, and limits that keep the group's service sustainable. They may be perceived as throwing a wet blanket on the fires of fresh enthusiasm, but they may win great appreciation from those in the group who are feeling overwhelmed and can't buck the driving force of the Crows and Graces. Nurturing Dragons may sustain the group for a time, but again, unless the role rotates even the Dragons will be drained.

SPIDERS

The spider spins a web that connects points across a stretch of empty space. Every circle needs a center, a way in which people feel connected. A group's center may be a spiritual heart, a common goal or vision, or it may manifest in a person. In hierarchical spirituality, the teacher or guru sits metaphorically at the center of the web. Each member of the group is connected to the teacher and through her or him to each other.

In nonhierarchical groups, one person may be perceived as being central: having information others need, being a point of connection for others. A person may volunteer for this task; or a group itself may serve as Spider for a larger community. For example, a group called Circle, in Wisconsin, is a center for networking for the Pagan community, keeping computer lists of contacts in outlying areas, so that if a person in Nebraska wants to find other Pagans, she or he can write Circle for contacts. (See the list of resources in the back of this book.)

In a group, when the task of Spider is not consciously assigned, the role may fall on someone who becomes the person everybody calls when they've misplaced the address of the meeting, the person people complain to and confide in. A Spider is most effective, however, not by monopolizing communication but by asking the questions that can create and strengthen a true and complex web of interactions.

QUESTIONS FOR SPIDERS

1. Who in this group communicates with whom?
2. How can we strengthen and expand those networks?

3. Why don't you talk to_____directly? Have you said that to her/him? Why not?
4. What is our common heart?
5. What can we do to bond more closely? To have more fun? To see each other more often?
6. What formal lines of communication would serve us?
7. What informal networks of communication do we have? Need?
8. What would serve to put them in place? A physical space? Time? Consciousness that we need them?

The Spider's role can be flattering, but can also lead to burnout. To be the one who receives everyone's complaints, the one whose phone is constantly ringing, is to be a form of group servant. Groups do better to create systems of communication that encourage shared responsibility and clear ways to transmit information. For the group's own security, important information should never become the property of only one person. And new people must have ways to find out information and learn history. The person with information is often perceived as the person in charge. The Spider will hear everyone's suggestions, complaints, fears, and questions, and needs support from the group and a way to bring problems and suggestions back to a body that can make decisions.

OTHER ROLES

Other, more formal roles exist in groups. Ideally, in a nonhierarchical group, they also are shared and rotated. The group may choose a representative to speak for it. In a nonhierarchical group, in which decision-making power extends throughout, the representative must know the answers to the following questions.

QUESTIONS FOR GROUP REPRESENTATIVES

1. Which decisions am I empowered to make independently?
2. Which decisions should I bring back to the group?
3. How do I bring them back to the group?
4. Who is my backup person? With whom do I share information?

The group should not expect to establish rules to cover every possible contingency, but discussing these questions ahead of time will help the group's representative develop an intuitive sense of the boundaries of her or his mandate.

Groups may also have a spokesperson—someone who represents the group to the public or the media, who acts as the group's mouth. The spokesperson for a group is often assumed by outsiders to be its leader and to have decision-making power. If the group wants to counter these assumptions, spokespeople should rotate frequently, although the group then risks losing the contacts and good will individuals may have established with the media. The spokesperson can be aided and the group as a whole can benefit from discussing the following questions.

QUESTIONS FOR SPOKESPERSONS

1. How do we want to present ourselves to the public?
2. Who are we trying to reach?
3. What are the most important points we want to communicate?
4. What myths or stereotypes do we want to counter?
5. What do we not want to say or have said about us?
6. What words do we want to use in describing ourselves? What names, labels, terms do we not want to use?
7. Who wants to be named publicly and credited for their work? Who prefers to remain anonymous?
8. What information do we want to share? What information do we not want to share?
9. How do I report back to the group? Who is my backup person? With whom should I share information?

Spokespeople and representatives receive attention, sometimes admiration and glory, that rightfully belongs to the group as a whole. The roles can be exciting, glamorous, and sometimes dangerous, as those who are publicly perceived as leaders may be singled out for special punishment in actions or harassment. Public spokespeople for a controversial group lose their privacy and the option of keeping their participation secret, which could bring repercussions to their personal or work lives. In an era that has seen the assassinations of Gandhi, Martin Luther King, Malcolm X, Fred Hampton, Karen Silkwood, and so many others, and the unjust jailings of Angela Davis, Dennis Banks, and Leonard Peltier, the position of spokesperson seems a mixed blessing. The vulnerability of movements built around personal charisma furnishes another good reason to share both the glory and the danger, to teach skills widely and spread responsibilities.

The roles of leadership also are found in our personal lives, for we each need to look ahead and plan, to grow and expand, to be aware of feelings and face conflicts, to stay grounded in praticalities and centered. Assessing ourselves in terms of the roles of leadership can be an insightful exercise. I, for example, tend to be a good Crow—planning ahead, following my visions, and making them happen—and a fine Grace, eager to expand, take on more and more, go new places, meet new people. I have learned,

painfully, to be a Snake, willing to bring up difficult emotions and conflicts, and am a disaster as a Dragon, having to struggle hard to admit I
might have limits, let alone identify what they are and stay within them.

Groups tend to reproduce the personality structure—and flaws—of their
leadership or those who have much influence. Reclaiming, for a long
while, was much like me. As a group, we had lots of visions, ideas, lots
of energy for expansion, but avoided conflicts and had no sense of boundaries or limits. After about three years many people were reaching burnout. At a retreat we decided to close the collective and establish boundaries, the only way we could truly build community. Also, we agreed to
turn inward, not take on any new projects for a season. These decisions
went entirely against all my natural inclinations. I was convinced that the
group would wither and die if it didn't continue to grow, but luckily, I
did not prevail. For those decisions were the healthiest we could have
made. In the long run, the group was strengthened.

The retreat was the first time we'd acknowledged the dread secret that
everyone knew, that I had a lot of power in the group. But once that
power was openly named, it could be openly challenged. The group could
move beyond my limitations—and so could I.

LEADERSHIP ROLES EXERCISE (This exercise was developed with the help of Liz Walker.)

1. For individuals:
On a blank sheet of paper, draw a large circle with a smaller circle
in the center. Divide the outer circle into quarters. Label them Crows,
Graces, Snakes, Dragons, and Spiders. (See my diagram.)

Reflect on your own strengths and weaknesses in each of these areas.
With a soft pencil or crayon, color in each quarter, making it darker
to reflect strength, lighter for lack of strength. You can also experiment
with different colors to reflect your feelings about each quality.

Meditate on the completed mandala. What does it tell you about
yourself? In which areas do you need to develop?

If one area is particularly weak, take time to focus on the questions
listed earlier for that area. Reflect on how they apply to your personal
life.

2. For groups:
Each person in the group should draw the same diagram as in the
preceding instructions for individuals. This time, reflect on the extent
to which you fulfill each role in the group. Color the chart accordingly.

When everyone is finished, hang up all the charts. The group may
choose to work with them in several ways.

Each person can identify her or his own chart, and ask the group for feedback. Does the group perceive you as filling the roles you see yourself filling? How would others color your chart?

Which areas are strong for the group as a whole? Which weak? What aspects does the group need to develop? You might wish to schedule time for discussion of the appropriate questions, or to work with ritual.

STARTING NEW GROUPS

Here are suggestions for beginning a group of your own.

1. Take time to reflect and meditate on what you want. Do you want a support group or an action group? A group to do rituals with or a circle to share both spiritual and political concerns? The more clearly you can define your purpose the more clearly you'll be able to express it.

2. Find like-minded people. You might begin by talking to your own friends. Lend them this book (or encourage them to buy their own copies!). Even one other person who shares your goals can be an enormous source of support.

   Look in wider circles for others. Put notices up in places where likely people may congregate. In one community, the best place may be a bookstore, in another, a food coop or laundromat. One woman in a rural town of six hundred told me she had started a coven by advertising in the local paper for people who wanted "to add more meaningful rituals to their lives."

3. Set a time and place for a first meeting. Encourage people to bring food and leave time for socializing. Plan an evening that gives people a taste of what you want from the group. If you want a group that does ritual, plan a ritual. If you want a group that discusses social issues, start a discussion.

4. After the experience, discuss whether the group should continue, how often it should meet, and so on. Set a time and place for those who are interested to return. If possible, get someone else to plan the next gathering.

Throughout Latin America, Christian liberation theology has encouraged the formation of small groups called Base Communities, in which people meet to study Scripture and respond to it from their own life experience. When I went to Nicaragua in 1984 with Witness for Peace, I was tremendously moved by the transformative power that had come from those small groups that combined spiritual and political concerns.

The movement in Latin America has led many North Americans to consider how we might organize in similar ways. Many of us cannot take our inspiration from biblical texts, yet we can still form groups that combine the power of spirituality, consciousness raising, and action. For when we see the Goddess as immanent within us, our own lives become our scriptures, the sacred text that brings liberation.

What follows is a suggested format for beginning a circle of liberation that might combine some simple forms of ritual with consciousness raising and storytelling, leading eventually to action. You can change the format, add to it, create your own rituals, or find your own topics. I have compressed it to fit one page for easy xeroxing—feel free to reproduce it.

SUGGESTIONS FOR STARTING A CIRCLE OF LIBERATION

Gather together with three to ten others. Expect to spend three or four hours together.

Sit in a circle. Breathe together. Feel your connection to the earth.

Make the space your own. Greet the four directions and the center. Acknowledge each person's presence in some affirming way.

Tell the story. Give each person a protected time to tell her or his own story, without interruptions, judgments, or challenges. If need be, set a time limit. Speak directly from experience.

Reflect together on the stories. Are there common themes? Differences? What do they tell us?

Do directions for action emerge from our stories? If so, what do we want to do?

Celebrate each other. Share food and drink.

Thank the directions and the center. Release the circle.

Agreements

What is said in the circle is confidential, unless we clearly agree otherwise.

Each of us has inherent value. All feelings are valid.

Responsibilities will rotate and be shared by all.

Subjects

Subjects you might tell stories about, in a suggested order for the first thirteen weeks, are (1) your experience of mystery (Goddess, God— whatever term you like); (2) your roots—ethnic, religious, racial, cultural; (3) your experience of power; (4) your experience of powerlessness; (5) Being a woman or man; (6) your experience of violence; (7) feeling/being different; (8) punishment and how you responded; (9) your body; (10) sexuality; (11) love; (12) work; (13) something you aren't/weren't supposed to talk about.

Other possible subjects are anger, loss, school, mothers, fathers, sisters, brothers, children, money, success, failure, conflict, enemies, guilt, fear, protecting yourself, need, meeting needs, addiction, hurting someone, obedience, being judged, rebellion, play, action, resistance, inspiration, relationships, jobs, creativity, or whatever subjects become meaningful.

Let shared experience suggest ritual, and generate theory and action.

Litany of the Holy Well and the Sacred Flame

Chant: Holy well and sacred flame! [call and response, three times]

Holy well
  waters of the Dordogne
  rivers of the ancient caves
  where the spirit herds   were dreamed into plenty
  water of the totems
  and the naked mother of flesh
Heal us with the memory
  of fifty thousand years
  we lived as animal with animal
    conscious   but still dancing
    awake   but still in dream-time
Brigid—we carry memory under the skin of our hands
  and in the bones' matrix
  deep in us
  deeper than all the years of spoiling
  no less deep
  in each designer   of neutron bombs or instruments of torture
  they too are human animal
  they crave survival
Brigid—that memory is your well
  may it rise!
  rise like the green blood of trees
  in your season
  may we remember our green blood
  and all that blocks its rising
  wash away!

Holy well and sacred flame! [call and response]

Sacred flame
  flame of the forge
  we have been tempered
  by red-hot rage   and love
  pounded
  shaped by blows   and noise   and pain
  heavy   and powerless
  as metal on anvil
Brigid—bring us out of the forge
  bright
  cool us with your waters

give us strength   and length
the form of a leaf
and a cutting edge
Brigid—we are willing to be   your edge
to be nicked   and bashed
and bloodied
but give us strength
not to break
and to notice when we lose   our keenness
strong tools also need to rest
to be rubbed   cleaned   sharpened
Care for us, Brigid
polish us
with soft cloth
and your skilled, tender hands

Holy well and sacred flame! [call and response]

Holy well
waters of Avalon
drawn from the lion's mouth
of Chalice Well   in Glastonbury
waters of the island
that is here   and there   and between
Teaching well
of the knowledge the churches
and the authorities   outlawed
knowledge of sun and moon, star and stone
the life that is in them
the voice
the language
the alignments between them
the mysteries
where these things can take us
   off the charts, outside the forms, beyond surveillance
   out of control
well of mists, fog, concealment
well between the worlds we move between
Brigid—let us look into your long well of vision
change takes time
prepare us
let us see   and know   that it will come

Holy well and sacred flame! [call and response]

Sacred flame
Fire of inspiration

help us see each other with the poet's eye
sharp to celebrate   textures and colors
to praise our differences
Brigid—let us savor your thousand names
let us call you Oya, Pele, the Mother of Volcanoes,
Changing Woman, Amaterasu
and so many more

let us learn all the old tales
sing the songs   dance

let us tell new stories
with no false enemies in them
and no lies that pass for history

stories about the four quarters of the world
red   yellow   black   white
about their different paths   and challenges
and how they finally learned   to come together

stories about love in all its disguises
passion, friendship, trickery, and common struggle,
laughter, heartbreak, and acts of courage

tales of a good crop, a living child, a clean river
tales of victory

Brigid—the fire on our tongues
burns through lies
we will speak truth   to power
and to each other

Holy well and sacred flame! [call and response]

Holy well
water of the ocean
that licks the mouth   of Diablo Canyon
clear running stream   ancient oaks
hills of ritual   where we made our secret way
again and again
slipping past guards   helicopters   dogs   horsemen
to stand above the plant and say   stop
Brigid—fire is a mixed blessing
it can warm or kill
we saw you on the hill   a year ago
cradling your well of fire
we swore fire would never burn
in the reactor
we were wrong

But Brigid—out of that lost battle   we forged a movement
   clusters of crazy, peaceful warriors
   weaponless but willing to go on
   again and again
   to Livermore, Vandenberg, to downtown San Francisco
   to Concord, Alameda, Bohemian Grove
   Nevada, Cape Canaveral
Brigid—we have made their jails our cauldron
   where we who are warriors
   who would rather be healers
   prepare our brew

Holy well and sacred flame [call and response]

Sacred flame
   fire of the hearth
   community
   a place we can make safe
   where we are welcome
   where when they come to take
     any one of us
   we circle   resist   protect
   until there is no longer need for protection
   where we burn strong together
   like the flames   of these candles
   we place together
   a home for us all
   a shelter
   a common granary
   a storehouse of each season's seed and fruit
   open to the hungry
   a fire to cheer the cold, the old
Brigid—this vision is possible   and simple
   you forge the plow as well as the sword
   and we would rather sow seeds
   heal wounds   weed the garden
   be the keen edge   of nurturing
   instead of struggle
Brigid—we've had failures
   but tonight
we claim this victory
that we are here together   in circle
learning   to work together
learning   to build to last

Holy well and sacred flame! [call and response]

Holy well
    waters of Corinto
    ocean water
    taken as the sun rose
        on the winter solstice
    after a night of fiesta
    in the port town of Nicaragua
    where the Virgin   a black-eyed statue
    extends her hands   to the tin shacks   and the dirt streets
    and the people
    who keep her nightlong vigil

    water from the harbor
    mined by U.S. ships

    in this land
    the Virgin's breasts
    hold wells of smoldering fire
    volcanoes
    watch the harbor
    saw the Contras ignite the oil storage tanks
    watch the children   who have no toys
    and the prostitutes   on their rounds
    there are no jobs   but they say
    the ships never fail us

    even the earth here   is volatile
    it shook down   Somoza
    and the people   love fire
    Solstice midnight   a man puts on the wooden
    frame of a bull   that shoots
    fireworks
    sparklers   Roman candles   fountains of light
    spout and gush
    the people shriek and laugh
    as he chases them
    exuberant in the war zone
Brigid—the ocean of Corinto
    is alive with fire
    sparks of phosphorescence   make stars
    as we plunge
We need that fire   in our water
    we will never make our revolution
    with guns   in the hills
    of Twin Peaks or Tamalpais
    but we need to know   that change

is possible
and can be defended
and can be lush   wild   intoxicating
a festival where we dance all night
Brigid—give us fireworks
and stars in the well

Holy well and sacred flame! [call and response]

Holy well and sacred flame
  the cauldron
  well of fire
  fire of hope
  the cookpot
  the broth that sustains us
  the brew that heals us
Brigid—you are a poet and healer
  as well as smith
  we chant to be healers   of wounds   in the world
  your cauldron
  in our nerves   our genes
  it is survival   it is life
We will not be walking dead
We are alive as the earth is alive
The running juices of our bodies
  are wells   we drink from them
  our tongues on fire
  to waken
  the call to life   in every body
  for under all we are animal
    as the earth is animal

May the animal rise in everyone!
May the voice of the earth   roar through us
May we sing   for stones   and stars
  and dance   as the flames leap and dance
May we rise!
May every well   be a fountain
  and break free
  a shower of sparks
  an all-night fiesta
We have the power to fight for our freedom
  to erupt   volcanic
  spouting new lands
  forging new tools
  singing new songs

We will not be walking dead
We are earth
  life is stronger
  we are survivors
  animals
  we are alive
  and life
  rises!
Holy well and sacred flame! [call and response, three times]

11

Ritual to Build Community

Ritual affirms the common patterns, the values, the shared joys, risks, sorrows, and changes that bind a community together. Ritual links together our ancestors and descendants, those who went before with those who will come after us. It helps us face together those things that are too painful to face alone.

A living community develops its own rituals, to celebrate life passages and ease times of transition, to connect us with the round of the changing seasons and the moon's flux, to anchor us in time. When we attempt to create community, ritual is one of our most powerful tools.

A culture of life would be filled with ritual: personal rituals, birthday parties, family and household celebrations, neighborhood rituals, street fairs, promenades, processions, fiestas, vigils, carnivals. As we begin to create rituals of community, we encounter new challenges and arenas of creativity. For ritual on a large scale draws together all the arts: music, dance, drama, mask making, decorative arts, and sculpture. Ritual is the original womb of art; its waters continue to nourish creativity.

CELEBRATING PASSAGES

Ritual affirms the value of any transition. When we celebrate life changes together, we create strong bonds of intimacy and trust that can generate new culture.

When we undergo a change uncelebrated and unmarked, that transition is devalued, rendered invisible. If we wish to restore value to the body, we can celebrate its changes with ritual. If we value a new relationship, we can publicly celebrate our commitment. When we finish a major project, such as writing a book, we can let it go with ritual.

We can create rites of passage for any transition. To give one example, my women's coven created a ritual for Bethany, the daughter of one of our members. We celebrated her first menstruation, her first blood.[1] First, we discussed the ritual with her to be sure she would feel comfortable with every aspect of it. This is a vitally important step for any ritual, especially one such as this: many young women would die of mortification at the very idea of such a celebration.

We prepared for months, making her a special robe upon which each of us embroidered some symbol of power. On the appointed day, we took her and her mother down to the beach. We tied them together with a silver cord, and asked them to run. They ran together as far as the mother could run; then we cut them apart and the daughter ran on alone.

We then went to a friend's house and joined other women in a hot tub. Thirteen of us, all women, spent the afternoon telling Bethany the stories of how we had become the women we were. Each of us gave her a special gift. We dressed her in her robe, formed a circle around her, and chanted her name to empower her.

Afterward, we went into the house, where the men in our community had prepared a special feast of red foods in her honor. We had wanted the ritual to be a women's mystery, but we also wanted Bethany to experience her womanhood being celebrated and affirmed by men. The men also gave her gifts, and we ended, as usual, by eating and drinking and enjoying each others' company.

In later months, some of the same men, who are in a men's ritual circle together, created a rite of passage for one of their sons when he reached puberty. The completion of his ritual was his celebration by both the women and men in the community.

A group of women in British Columbia celebrate a Croning ritual for each woman who reaches menopause. The ritual marks a woman's passage into a new stage of life: the Crone stage, in Witchcraft considered the time of life when experience and wisdom bring a woman into her full power. On one woman's farm stands an old, weathered gate. During the ritual, the woman who is becoming a Crone passes through the gate, and her circle sings, chants, and celebrates her reaching the other side.

Birth, too, can be a time of ritual. We can create a sacred space, whether at home or in a hospital room, for the sacred work of labor and birthing. The birth process itself has an energy and a rhythm of its own; the most powerful ritual simply respects that energy, supporting the mother and welcoming the child, assuring the baby that she or he is welcome, wanted, and loved. (A more elaborate ritual for welcoming a newborn is in chapter 5.)

Sophia created a ritual for her daughter Vanessa when she weaned her at the age of two. Sophia's mother had given Vanessa a special cup at her birth, in keeping with a long-standing family tradition. At weaning, Sophia gave the cup to Vanessa within a sacred circle. She poured dairy milk into the child's cup and her own ritual chalice, saying, "Now this will be your cup, and I will no longer be your cup. Now we can be sisters, and drink together."

RITUAL OF PASSAGE

Create ritual for times of transition: birth, weaning, puberty, commitments of love, separation, cronehood (aging or menopause), com-

pletion of major works or projects, recovery from illness, loss, death. Such rituals should include hearing the stories of those who have passed through the transition before you, symbolic acts to mark the changes, giving and receiving gifts, and sharing food as well as raising power.

When doing political action, or when facing any major battle in work, relationships, or any area of life, we undergo transitions that can be eased by ritual.

RITUAL TO PREPARE FOR STRUGGLE

Before gathering, each person who is to take part spends time in individual meditation and cleansing. You might plunge in the ocean, a lake, stream, or river, or take a long ritual bath in salt water. Burn sage, for purification, or steep sage leaves in the bath. Rub yourself with cedar boughs—used by Native Americans to draw helpful power, or with rosemary—a traditional herb of protection. Or use whatever herbs or incense seem right to you. Take time to feel your fears, doubts, any emotions that might cloud your judgment. Let them go into the salt water, not to be lost, but so that the energy locked up in negative images can be released and become available to you as clear power.

Those who are about to embark on an action, a struggle, a conflict gather with their community of support. Ground, create sacred space, and invoke the sacred powers.

Pass a crystal (or other sacred object such as a rattle, a stone, a shell, or something the group chooses) around the circle. As each person holds the crystal, (or whatever), clearly state your intention for the coming struggle. Why are you embarking on it? What do you hope to accomplish or gain? How do you intend to conduct the struggle? For example:

"I intend to go to Cape Canaveral and with my own body interfere with the testing of the new Trident 2 missile. I intend to act in loving nonviolence and maintain my sense of humor." Or: "I'm about to take the bar exam and I intend to pass it so that I can have the credentials I need to be a better fighter for justice. I want to stay calm, remain in touch with my sharpest intelligence and clearest memory, and retain my sanity."

Those who will offer support to the struggle tell what they intend to do.

When the circle is complete, those who will be at risk go into the center. Together, they hold the crystal. The group begins to chant, and raises power around them, while they focus on taking in that power and filling themselves with the love and protection of their friends. Each person may also create a personal image of power—a scene or an object to think of or remember in times of danger or stress. Visualizing the image of power during this time will help fix it in mind. Remembering it in tense moments, while breathing and grounding, will bring needed strength, calm, and power. A physical object can be used instead of a mental image and may be easier for beginners to work with.

Ground the energy. Affirm each person in the center—sing their names, hug them, bless them with power and protection.

Place the crystal in a pouch and bind the power as you close it up. Decide what you will do with it. Will you bury it on the Air Force Base? Place it on your desk during the test? Share food and drink. Entertain each other. Open the circle.

If you don't have a group to do this ritual with, adapt it to do alone.

RITUAL OF RETURN FROM STRUGGLE

Begin, again, with a private cleansing. This time, let yourself feel what was hard for you, what you want to release and let it go.

Gather with your friends. Ground, and create sacred space.

Going around the circle, tell the stories of the action. Go ahead, brag! Eat and drink.

Sense the energy. If people are still feeling rage, fear, or despair, light a fire. Move counterclockwise around the fire. Drum. Call out your rage and your anger. Let it build power until it peaks. Release it, and ground.

Go around the circle. Tell of your opponents—those you have faced in the struggle. If possible, name something you can honor about each one. If this strains imagination, imagine speaking to the sacred core within even your enemy's heart. Call to it. Acknowledge it in some way.

Now the group helps each person undergo whatever transformation is necessary. This will vary. At one time, it might be a healing for someone who caught pneumonia in jail. After one woman in our coven successsfully received her license as a Marriage, Family, and Child Counselor, we gave her a "weirding" by giving her sleazy clothing and helping her dye a streak of shocking pink in her hair.

Offer thanks—libations, more food and drink, to whatever powers, Goddesses, Gods, saints, spirits, ancestors, and living helpers have aided you in your struggle. Open the circle.

Again, if you must, adapt this to do alone.

COLLECTIVE TRANCE

Just as we can go places in trance individually, we can learn to trance collectively. The journeys we take together help strengthen our underlying connections, and the places we create help crystallize a group's identity.

GROUP PLACE OF POWER

Sit in a circle. Take hands; take time to breathe together and center. A leader might read the following story, or you could tape it and play it back.

Tell yourself this story: that you can feel your breath, flowing in and out, that it is the source of your life, the source you have never forgotten, for it has never been separate from you, never further away than a breath. Breathe deep, and follow your breath down, where it ebbs and flows in your body like a wave, like a wave of power. Remember your power. Tell yourself that you remember your power, the power that formed you and shaped you as a seed is formed, as a sprout, the power by which you shaped yourself, took form, grew. Breathe it in. Feel it, deep in you. Tell yourself that you can let that power go into the center of the circle, that you can feel it merge and blend with your companions' power. And feel the power swirl and flow and congeal in the center, like colors running together and separating out into form. Tell yourselves that your power can take form, and blend and solidify into a place, a landscape.

And now you begin to see that landscape take shape and to sense it and feel it. Turn to the East, and notice what you see and hear and feel and sense. And as the place begins to form for you, describe it. Tell the circle about it, share it so that it becomes real to us all.

And as we hear each other, our visions shift and change and merge, until they blend together into one place, one place of power for us all . . .

Members of the group say out loud what they see or sense. If their visions differ, they gradually change and modify them until they come together into a common vision. (We call this "enchantment by consensus.") Go to each of the four directions, and the center. Keep talking until you get a clear picture of each.

When your place is firmly established, you may wish to explore a particular direction or dimension. You may meet helpers or beings of power or teachers. You might hang out there in hot tubs having sensual feasts. Enjoy. Before you leave, find an image or an object you can use as a key, something you can visualize to bring you back to your place. Do not tell anyone outside the group what this key is. Also, go to each of the four directions and the center, and say good-bye. Then let the waves of your breath take you up. Establish a certain number of breaths to take you in and out of your place.

To return to your place, get together again, visualize your key, and breathe together. One person can "talk you down," or you can talk each other back. Always begin by looking to the four directions, and end by returning to the center and again facing each of the directions and saying good-bye.

This process gives us insight into the strength of a group. When it works easily, we know that members of the group have some underlying psychic unity. When it is difficult, the group may perhaps not be ready to bond. If one or two people never seem to be in the same place as others, the group might consider whether this reflects a level of emotional disconnection.

The place of power, group or individual, is also the beginning of deeper magic. An individual place lends itself to emotional work; a group place puts us more easily in contact with collective realities. In your place, you may find helpers or powers you can draw on. You will have adventures and discover images that you can weave into ritual, that become the basis of the new myths you collectively create. You can also create special places within your place for special purposes: for example, you might find a grove of trees in the west where you can be in touch with your healing power. Give that place its own key, and you can go there when you are doing healing work. You will find your ordinary abilities augmented. Just don't forget to come back out each time you go in; otherwise you will feel tired, dizzy, and slightly disoriented.

This process also helps to undermine the Censor, for its power depends on our willingness to say what we really do see, not what we think we should see or what others are seeing.

RITUAL FOR LARGE GROUPS

Small groups can build intimacy and trust that lend a ritual power and intensity. Large group rituals have a different function. They bind a larger community together; they introduce new people to the concepts and values the ritual represents; and they generate excitement, energy, and a wild beauty.

Large rituals are logistically demanding. Processes that are powerful in a group of ten are tolerable in a group of thirty and impossible in a group of a hundred. Passing a bowl of salt water around the circle for a cleansing meditation may take twenty minutes for five people and hours for fifty. Give careful thought to the physical problems of moving people in space, of passing objects around, of hearing and seeing. You can always multiply ritual objects: provide ten bowls, and someone to collect them. Or break into small groups, or groups of three, to share more intimately. Then find some way to come back together.

Keeping energy focused in a large group can also be a challenge. Especially if many people are new, or shy, energy tends to dissipate. You might:

- Learn to drum. The drum is the single most useful ritual object you can have. The drum unifies the energy of a group. It can raise the energy up or bring it down, and draw it together when it becomes scattered.

Drumming is an art, and fine drummers practice for many years. Fortunately, you can be a very minimally skilled drummer and be quite effective in ritual. Being able to keep a simple, steady beat is more important than being able to drum elaborate patterns or syncopated rhythms. Most important, however, is the drummer's sensitivity to energy. The drum must follow the energy of a ritual, not fight it. If the drum tries to override the energy's movement, if the drummer gets so lost in self-expression that she or he becomes oblivious to the flow of the ritual, a drum can destroy a ritual instead of unifying it. Also, once a drumbeat begins in a chant or story, it carries the energy. If the drum stops, the energy drops. Mosquitos may suck your blood, your hat may fall over your eyes and your tongue go dry, but if you value the energy of the ritual, you keep on drumming.

My drum is a *doumbek,* an hourglass-shaped Middle Eastern drum, traditionally made of ceramic. Mine, however, is metal with a plastic head, lightweight, portable, and extremely practical.

- Seed the ritual with more experienced people who know what to expect, can move energy, and can be models for others. When they get wild, others will follow. If they create an energy form, others will intuitively strengthen it. And when they ground the energy, it will bring the energy of newcomers back to earth with it.
- Appoint Graces, people to help greet newcomers, explain aspects of the ritual, teach songs, and make people feel welcome.
- Appoint Dragons, who will guard the boundary of the circle and deal with disruptive drunks, fundamentalists talking in tongues, police, and other distractions.
- Designate a few Crows, to keep the overall plan of the ritual in mind.
- Make sure that whoever leads the ritual is also a good Snake, who can watch the energy and be aware of the undercurrents.
- Choose a clear focus, a clear central image, and keep the plan simple.
- Try to avoid using terms or symbols that will make people feel uncomfortable, uneasy, or confused.
- Elements of performance work especially well in larger groups. Be dramatic, write poetry, compose music, create culture.

RITUAL TO STRENGTHEN COMMUNITY

When we face a collective task or undertake a new direction, ritual can help strengthen us and clarify our path. The following ritual evolved out of work I did with women of the WomanEarth Feminist Peace Institute as we attempted to bring together women of color and white women to consider issues of peace and power.

RITUAL FOR CROSSING BARRIERS OF DIFFERENCE

Create sacred space. Invoke the Goddess by the names of your mothers' lineages: "I am Starhawk daughter of Bertha daughter of Hannah." (If you wish, also invoke the God by naming your male ancestors of whom you are proud.)

Place a cauldron (any metal pot will work) in the center of the circle, ready to light with a mixture of rubbing alcohol and Epsom salts, in roughly equal proportions. This gives a smokeless fire that can be burned indoors. Breathe deep, ground. Drum, or put on music, and listen to the following story.

Breathe deep, follow your breath down into the caves of your body, into the belly cave where life originates. You are in a cave; it is the place of the ancestors. Feel it around you; sense its depths, its textures, the air on your skin. Explore it . . . (Allow time.)

And deep inside this cave lies a treasure, the treasure of the ancestors. Look for it, feel for it, find it. Know what is there for you, the store of knowledge and memories and wisdom, the gifts. Look. Feel. Touch. Sort through the treasure . . . (Allow time.)

Some of the gifts are valuable, and some of them may be harmful. Some things may have been valuable to the ancestors, but are not what you need. Some may have rotted underground; some may help you, some may hurt. Sort through them, find the ones you need and can use; find the ones you want to let go of . . .

And bring the gifts you no longer need, let them go into the fire, let them become the energy we need for change, let them transform. Bring your gifts to the fire . . .

Light the cauldron. One by one, each person comes to the fire and symbolically throws in her or his gifts, naming what they are:

"My ancestors gave me fear. They needed it to survive, but it blocks me, and so I let it go."

"My ancestors held slaves. They would like to give me the belief that some people are better than others, but I refuse to accept it. That belief ends here, now, with me, and I throw it into the fire."

"My ancestors gave me the warning not to hold my head up too high, or try to get above myself, and I toss that into the fire."

People may cry, laugh, yell. Hold each other. Let the flames of the cauldron burn it all away.

When the energy dies down, place in the center a bowl of honey. Continue the story.

Now breathe deep again. Look back at the pile of treasures. Find the gift that is meant for you. Take it, hold it, look at it. What is it? (Allow time to explore.) How do you use it? (Take time.) How can you take it with you back into your daily life? (Take time.) Now breathe deep, and bring your gift back with you as you come back out of the cave, following your own path, sensing the textures and the colors around you, feeling the temperature of the air on your skin, following your own breath up as you come back to your body, back to this circle, bringing your gift back with you.

And when you are fully back, say your own name out loud. And now bring your gift to the bowl of honey. Name it, add something of its sweetness to the sweetness that is there.

Each person comes to the center, symbolically adds something of her or his gift to the bowl, and names it, or names something she or he is proud of about the ancestors.

"My ancestors gave me the power to survive anything!"

"My ancestors gave me the power to keep my heritage intact, even when it has to be hidden."

"My ancestors gave me an irrepressible sense of humor."

When all have added to the bowl, chant and raise energy to charge it with the power of all the ancestors. Ground the energy.

Pass the bowl around from hand to hand. Each person dips her or his fingers in and smears honey on the lips of the next person, saying, "Together may we know the sweetness of life." End by feasting and opening the circle.

Ritual can also help us make a collective transformation, to confront problems and issues as a community that are too big for us as individuals.

THE BRIGID RITUALS

Early in 1981, after Reagan's first election, many of us in the feminist Pagan community in San Francisco felt despair. Most of us had been politically active in the sixties and early seventies, but had relaxed somewhat in the Carter years and taken time to explore spirituality. We felt that magic, ritual, and the earth-based spirituality of the Goddess were inherently political, but we did not quite know how to bring politics and spirituality together. So we decided to create a ritual of political despair, to try to transform despair into hope and energy.

Brigid is the Irish Goddess of smithcraft, poetry, and healing, the fire Goddess who is also worshiped at holy wells. Her festival, on the eve of February 2, is a festival of the waxing light, celebrated when the sun begins to grow stronger and the days begin to grow longer. Also called Candlemas, it is a time of purification and strengthening, and seemed an appropriate time for our ritual.

The heart of the ritual took place in small groups, which gathered around a bowl of salt water. We passed the bowl counterclockwise, and each person answered the question, Where in your life do you feel powerless? She or he breathed into the salt water, letting go of despair, and then washed with the water.

When the circle was complete, we chanted and raised power to transform the sadness and despair in the water into energy we could use for change.

Then we passed the bowl clockwise. Each person answered the question, Where in your life do you feel power? After each person spoke, the circle said, "We bless your power," and the person took back some of the water and washed again.

The answers became a litany: "I feel power when I go ahead and say something I'm afraid to say." "I feel power when I weave." "I felt power when I gave birth to my child." "I feel power when I write."

Then we poured all our water into a big bowl on the altar, and lit a huge cauldron. Each person had brought a candle, and individuals lit candles from the cauldron, and stated some commitment to an act of power. The room gradually filled with light, and we sang and danced with the candles until the power peaked.

Shortly after that ritual, we heard that people were organizing an action at Diablo Canyon. We decided to join, and so began a frenetic period of magicopolitical action. The questions we had had of how to link the spiritual and political were fully answered. By the next year at Brigid, we found ourselves doing a fire ritual in preparation for a blockade at Livermore. So began a tradition of doing political ritual on Brigid's festival.

Four years after our first political despair ritual, we found ourselves faced with the necessity of doing another one after Reagan's reelection. We reconsidered some of the logistics. Beautiful as the candle dance was, we found ourselves less than enthusiastic at the prospect of once again spending hours scraping wax off the floor. Of such mundane details is true magic made. Candle wax is an ongoing concern for Witches, just as celibacy is for Catholic priests.

To avoid the candle wax problem, we provided boxes of sand in which the candles could be placed. On the North altar, we had a large anvil. In the West, we had a well—(actually a punchbowl), filled with water, some of it collected from rivers, streams, and oceans all over the world.

I wrote the litany that opens this chapter, inspired by our collection of water. Roddy and Kelly wrote a litany of despair and led the small groups as people called out their own litanies of horrors, atrocities, and defeats, moaning, crying, and yelling. We moved out of small groups to dance around the cauldron in a writhing mass. The candles in the boxes of sand all melted together into blazing piles of wax. The litanies were spoken; wild power was raised, and the ritual worked.

This year, we could no longer feel despair. Although objectively, nothing had gotten much better, except for the coming to light of the Iran/Contra affair, we felt hopeful, filled with energy, ready for action. We decided to create a ritual for political momentum.

Again we had an anvil in the North. In the center of the circle, we had another holy well, with a smaller cauldron inside it, ready to light. We also had our collection of waters, which had continued to grow.

In the heart of the ritual, people formed small groups around leaders who brought a pitcher of water and a bowl and cups for each person. Kelly and I began to drum and talk-story. We said: "The people once knew a well of healing nourishing water, and once a sacred flame warmed them. But they lost the way to the well. They were the most powerful people in the world, yet they despaired. But never completely, for somehow, each of them found the way to the well." As we continued the rhythm, the group leaders asked, "How did you find the way to the well— what was the thread that brought you through?"

People spoke of what had given them courage and inspiration. And they drank. Then they were asked, "How do you replenish the well?" As they spoke of what they gave back to the community, each poured water into the bowl. When the circle finished, they held the bowl aloft, charged it with power, and then poured it into the central well to join the other sacred waters.

As the power rose, David began a spiral dance. As the groups formed into one twining circle, he lit the cauldron, which blazed from the center of the well. The energy became ecstatic, rising to a roaring, leaping cone.

When it was grounded, Jim began to beat the anvil. One by one, people went to the well, took water from it, bathed their faces, and made a pledge, which the anvil sealed. Their faces were lit by the cauldron's fire, and glowed warm and beautiful, as if that inner fire that warms and heartens had indeed come alive to blaze in each one of us from the center of the well of life.

Ritual also takes us collectively through the seasonal cycle, the round of birth, death, and rebirth enacted in the year's changes. As ritual is repeated year after year, as it grows, changes, and reenacts itself, takes on a richness of associations and nuance, and gives to our community a history.

THE SPIRAL DANCE

Halloween is the Witch's New Year, the time for honoring the ancestors, the beloved dead, for turning the wheel of the year. Three hundred people are gathered in a hall in San Francisco. Around the walls are built altars of crates, hung with old lace, holding dolls and skulls and ancient Goddesses, plates heaped with food for the dead, pumpkins, deer horns, pomegranates, candles.

The space has been made sacred, marked off from the circles of the world. The boundary has been drawn with wand and candles, with a procession of masked figures and beating drums. We have cast the circle, traded the safety of the everyday for this most ancient symbol of protection, the energy form that frees us by containing all the power we will raise here tonight.

We have grounded and sung to the elements; we have danced to air and fire and water and earth, as we do to begin every ritual. For the elements remind us of what sustains our lives, of the balance we must find within ourselves of mind, energy, emotion, and body; of the cycles of time: dawn, noon, twilight, midnight, spring, summer, fall, winter; of all progressions and returns.

We have called the Goddess and God as the great pattern of the mystery that runs through us and beyond us, as the powers that begin, sustain, end, as the green, the wild, the animal, the wise. In the repetition of this naming, ritual after ritual, year after year, we begin to restore that power within that knows itself to be bound to the pattern of birth, death, and regeneration, to be animal and wise, to grow and fade. Naming that self as sacred we restore its value and know its depths.

> For you can see me in your eyes,
> When they are mirrored by a friend—
> There is no end to the circle, no end,
> There is no end to life, there is no end.

We are sacred, within sacred space. And so we begin the calling of the dead. For Halloween, it is said, is the time when the dead walk, when our ancestors return, when the veil is thin that divides the world of the seen from the unseen. It is the time of mourning and reunion, when year after year we must remember the limits of control, remember that we, too, must die in time, and yet know that death is not an ending of the cycle but a part of the pattern that turns and turns around again.

The litany of the dead names our common ancestors of struggle, those whose names we do not know. In the Yoruba tradition, when you do not know your ancestors' names, you name them by the ways they died. And so we call them: those who died of hunger, who died on the slave ships, who were burned. Every year the litany grows. Now one person after another goes to the microphone (for this mystery does not disdain technology), and cries out a section, while we keen, tear cloth, rub ashes on our faces, and chant the response to the call "What is remembered lives."

We name the tribes who once called this place home, the dead of Auschwitz, Hiroshima, the disappeared of El Salvador, those gunned down in South Africa, the assassinated dead, the tortured, the poisoned, the AIDS victims, the war victims, the suicides, the burned Witches. With each section of the litany the moans become cries of anger and sorrow, rising together in a collective outpouring of rage and grief. In a city caught in the grip of the AIDS epidemic, as we each face fear and grief for our friends and our loved ones, this sacred space becomes a place where we can cry together, where the sound of our voices binds us together in the sharing of our hurt, our despair at the wounds and the immense task of healing.

Then we name our own dead. "I remember my grandfather who fathered eight children in India and dreamed they would come to America." "I remember my aunt, a closeted lesbian who loved me as her own child." "I remember my mother who died when I was too young to know her." The naming goes on and on: we hear the tragic deaths, the suicides, the car crashes, and the peaceful deaths. "My grandmother May, who died at eighty, the last of the great housekeepers." We cry together, hold each other, even laugh. "I remember Wally—he was my lover." "I remember Wally—he was my lover, too." I name my friend Anne, who would be thrilled by the ritual. And my father, wondering what he would think of it all, old leftist secular Jew that he was—would he prefer a Yizcar, or nothing? But he was an actor, too; if nothing else, he would have loved the drama of it. For this is the essence of theater: each death we name, each person we describe in a phrase or two, is another story, comic or tragic, and in the telling of these stories we become, all three hundred of us, one community, weaving together the different strands of these ancestors with those we have named in the litanies, so that they become our common ancestors, different races and religions and viewpoints not erased but linked. For in the public naming of our dead, we assert their value, which has not been destroyed by death. And in valuing them we value each other, the true histories of our lives, where we come from, who we are.

Morgan, who is only five, has a voice too soft to be heard above the crowd. I motion to her mother and whisper "shhhh" through the microphone. Her mother brings her up, and her voice sounds clear: "We remember Grandma Claudia." And I know, watching her, that this ritual has come alive, become a living tradition that for her will be how things are done, how the dead are mourned, a touchstone for her own identity. Months later, she tells a child in her preschool that she is a Witch. "You're not really a Witch," he says. "I am a Witch!" she asserts. "I called my Grandma Claudia at the Spiral Dance."

We grieve until we are empty. Then we let the ritual take us on a journey to the land of the dead, which is the place of beginning, the seed place of all potential.

The journey takes place by drum and voice and imagination; we form a ship, we sail, we arrive at the shining isle, we dance, we call into being all we envision for the new year:

> A year of beauty,
> Let it begin now
> A year of plenty
> Let it begin now . . .

As deep as we have gone into our grief, we go now into a great roaring wildness that leaps up and sends us whirling and singing and dancing together. The energy runs loose beyond our ability to contain or direct it—always it surprises us—breaking out into clapping and stomping and shouting rhythms, winding in crazy spirals that always go wild, into snakes and chains and free-form whirls and eddies of ecstasy; and the people dance, building power, building a vision that never confines itself to the poetry of the litany, but takes on a form of its own. Until at last the power peaks, in one rising cry of open throats; all our voices become one voice, one rising cone, carrying the vision and the wildness and the closeness out into a world where our rage and grief have opened a space to be filled by the passion for life.

When we let go, there is silence. We fall to the ground, returning the power to the earth. For the ritual, too, has its pattern, which is the mystery pattern, the cycle. The power we draw from the earth must return, what we raise must fall if it is to rise again. So we enact the cycle of the mystery, and, enacting it, we become united in it.

What the earth needs for her healing may be something we cannot see or even imagine, something that can only be brought to being by the unleashing of the wildness, the rising of the animal in us all.

When we return to the world of the living, we sing the names of the babies born this year. We give them a public welcoming, we acknowledge the sacred value of each one of them, for they are the continuance of life. The wheel of the year has turned. Halloween is the Witch's New Year, and now the lament for the dead gives way again to the song of life.

The Return of the Goddess

The Goddess, who is the soul of earth, of sky, of the living being in whose body we are cells, once was awake in us and all knew and honored her in women and men, in nature, in the turning cycles of the seasons and the shifting cycles of our lives, in the works of mind and hand we created, in the plants and animals, in moon, sun, and ocean, in tree and stone and the intricate dance all living beings do together. We lived in balance on the earth. Women were free, and men too, for we had not yet learned how to oppress each other. And because we lived in harmony with the earth, we understood the earth's ways and her mysteries.

But a time came—no one knows how or why—when in some places the people turned away from the Goddess. Men ruled over women, and over other men. They waged endless wars. The people splintered into rich and poor, free and slave, powerful and powerless. They rewrote the myths and the old stories; they took the old magic and twisted it to give them power over others.

Many of the people, especially the women, resisted. Many peoples of the world preserved the old cultures that held them close to the living earth. Those who held power waged war against them in many ways—sometimes subtly, through compromises and the promises of new religions and the twisting of symbol and ritual, but also openly. The Goddess was fettered, beaten, raped, tortured, burned, poisoned, and dismembered.

And so the earth herself nearly died. But though the Goddess suffered, she was never destroyed. And though her memory was denigrated and hidden, it was never forgotten.

In secret, some continued to practice the old ways. They passed on the mysteries. They were healers, midwives, shamans, benders and shapers of visions. In the West they were called Witches. The Witches were tortured, burned, and reviled. The word *Witch* itself was made synonymous with evil. And what was done to the Witches was done to the earth peoples of Africa, the Americas, Asia, Polynesia, Australia. Their old ways were called evil, their peoples enslaved, their lands stolen, their sacred places defiled.

Yet some also survived. In fragmented, tiny bands, they preserved seeds of the old knowledge.

And in the time when the final destruction of earth seemed probable if not inevitable, those seeds began to sprout. Women and men began to remember the Goddess, to cry out against war and destruction, to demand that it stop. The reborn dead walked the earth in new forms; the Witches arose and danced in the open. The peoples of the earth began to forge new links of friendship. They reclaimed the sacred places and with them the sacredness of the earth. And though the people had seemingly small power against the rulers, they learned again the ancient knowledge and the mysteries, and used that knowledge not to build weapons but to evoke the will to life of the earth herself that burns in every living being—even in the very blood and bones of the warmongers.

But the ending of this myth is not yet written. Has the Goddess re-awakened only to preside over the destruction of the earth? Or will our awakening come in time? For unlike other deities, the Goddess does not come to save us. It is up to us to save her—if we so choose. If we so will.

Resistance and Renewal

All over the world
the waters are breaking everywhere
everywhere
the waters are breaking . . .
JUDY GRAHN
(from the *She Who* poems)

We are faced with the task of ensuring that the collective story continues so that those who come after us can write their own chapters, so that the memory of those who came before us is not erased. We must preserve and renew the world, re-member Her back into life.

Every day we are surrounded by the culture of death. Its wastes assault our lungs and poison our waters. Its homeless die in our streets and its hopeless deal in the deserted parks for something to kill the pain. Its diseases attack our own bodies' defenses, destroying us from within. In our name, weapons continue to be made that can destroy the world. In our name, wars are begun, battles are fought, children are maimed by shrapnel and deformed by radiation before they are born. All of this goes on every day, and though we are the most powerful people in the world, we feel helpless to stop it, much less create something new.

To renew the world, we must become like the vulture, who feeds on waste, who is the aspect of the Goddess that eats the obstacles to love.

To create a culture of life, the vulture must take wing, to soar above the constrictions of the skyline and find a vision that reaches beyond the bars, to become the eagle, the great blue heron, the swallow and the gull. We need more than psychology, more than spirituality and community: we need an economics, an agriculture, a politics of liberation, capable of healing the dismembered world and restoring the earth to life. Most of all, we need to make a leap of the imagination that can let us envision how the world could be. Then we need to consider, step by step and in concrete detail, how to bring our vision about.

That project is beyond the scope of any one book and too big for any single person. I can offer only some tools with which we can collectively search for solutions. In this chapter I offer visions and suggestions that are meant to spark imagination. I draw on work that has been done by many groups and individuals. My intent is not to provide a new political platform but to suggest directions for exploration and at times push against the boundaries of what we believe is possible. We work magic by creating a vision and then directing energy toward it, removing blocks in our way, and generating the forces of change. We may not know how those forces will work themselves out, but we can see the end in mind, and begin the motion.

When our vision is clear, we can see the first steps we need to take. We cannot necessarily see how the ultimate transformation will take place. No revolution takes place as predicted, for change on the grand scale is a mystery, impossible to completely know or control. To open ourselves to that mystery should not make us passive, but eager to move forward, curious to see how events unfold. We move on as far as we can see the road; and from that vantage point a new horizon is revealed.

Our journey will necessarily encompass both resistance and renewal, acts that oppose the destruction and acts of creation.

Resistance challenges power-over by confronting it with speech and actions that embody a reality incongruent with that of the authorities. Resistance is rooted in the mysteries that defy the Orderer's control, and embodies the immanent value of our true selves that cannot be diminished by the Judge. In resistance, we violate the taboos and reclaim responsibility for our own truths and actions, finding safety through solidarity with each other. And effective resistance is sustainable, for we know that transforming culture and reshaping the world is a long project, a lifetime term of service.

The qualities that make resistance effective are also those upon which we can base the structures and acts of renewal: the immanent value of each living being, the interconnectedness and interdependence of all beings; openness to the unknowable and immeasurable, to wonder, ecstasy, and mystery; personal responsibility and mutual support; the solidarity of shared risks and benefits; and the creation of systems that are nurturing, healing, and sustainable.

What we can do, then, is clear. First, we can create structures of support, situations that by their inherent structure and function unravel the self-hater's bindings and embody a different reality rooted in freedom.

Nourished by that support, using the tool of ritual and the consciousness-changing skills of magic, we can take action in many ways to resist domination, to stop war, to envision and create ways of living that renew and sustain the richness and diversity of life.

In the dismembered world, war sets the pattern for every system, every institution of a culture based on power-over. To create a new society, we must stop war, or it will continue to shape our psyche in its image, to supercede all human needs and warp our desires, to replace love with its hierarchy.

Contemplating the system of domination that war generates can depress us; it can seem huge and overwhelming, a machine of enormous weight crushing the fruits of our lives. Self-propelled and self-maintained, with all the facets of oppression reinforcing each other with well-oiled precision, it seems invincible. Especially painful is the recognition that we are not separate from the systems of control, but a part of them.

But we need not despair. Blink your eyes; look again. War's very scope is the telltale evidence of war's fragility. The system of war encompasses all systems because only thus can war be sustained. If the whole world must feed war, then even a small decrease in sustenance can starve war. If war's weight is so great that many are crushed underfoot, then a little softening of the ground can sink the lumbering beast. If war is a towering edifice, then a crack in the foundation can bring it down.

Domination is a *system,* and we *are* part of it, and in that lies hope. For any system is always in delicate balance, dependent for its stability on the feedback of its parts. When the feedback changes, so does the system. At first it reacts to regain its stability, but if the new feedback is sustained, the system will be transformed.

Domination is not the creation of some evil force, but the result of millions of human choices, made again and again over time. Just so can domination be undone, by our shaping of new choices, by small and repeated acts of liberation.

To resist effectively, we must create, for resistance is not a mere withdrawal of energy, but a posing of a reality that challenges power-over. The choices we make, as we organize, as we struggle to support each other, as we confront systems of control, themselves create new situations.

Politics is a form of magic, and we work magic by directing energy through a vision. We need to envision the society we want to create, so that we can embody aspects of it in each act we take to challenge domination.

The edifice of war and domination is supported on three main pillars: our obedience, the construct of the enemy, and the enormous resources we devote to war. Each of these footings can be undermined. When our vision of what we want is clear, each act we take *against* an aspect of domination can become a positive act *for* the alternative we create.

A society that could heal the dismembered world would recognize the inherent value of each person and of the plant, animal, and elemental life that makes up the earth's living body; it would offer real protection, encourage free expression, and reestablish an ecological balance to be biologically and economically sustainable. Its underlying metaphor would be mystery, the sense of wonder at all that is beyond us and around us, at the forces that sustain our lives and the intricate complexity and beauty of their dance.

AFFIRMING IMMANENT VALUE

A society that affirms our inherent value must be just. If all of us are the Goddess incarnate, we can none of us be masters or servants, rulers or ruled. Instead, we must all be equals; equally entitled to society's resources and its fruits. Such a society must nurture and care for its members, assuring for all the means to a livelihood that makes a contribution to all, educating each of its members to further each individual's power-from-within.

In a society in which all are valued, decisions will be made by those who have to live with their consequences. We will foster self-reliance, yet admit our complete interdependence. A society rooted in immanent value will establish protection through peace and mutual cooperation. Its members will find ways to defend themselves that do not threaten the earth or reduce culture to a machine that feeds the omniverous mouth of war.

These values are not new. As schoolchildren, every day we pledged allegiance to a republic "with liberty and justice for all." But we have never lived these values. Our "Founding Fathers" preached liberty, and held slaves. They spoke of the inalienable right to life, and murdered tribes and nations of the native people of this land. They talked of equality, and denied a voice in their government to women. They fought for the right to pursue happiness, yet allowed economic conditions to condemn millions to misery.

Yet those good old "American values," the values we have always preached and never yet practiced, are still worth striving for. They are, perhaps, the magical challenge we have set ourselves, the illusion we now must make real. We must call to account our country, ourselves, to become what we say we are. If we have never yet lived liberty, maybe it is time to begin.

A society that truly recognizes the sacred manifest in the living world must go even further. For the earth herself becomes sacred to us, as do all her creatures: the animals, plants, all the intricate interdependencies, the oceans and marshlands, the fog-enshrouded forests and sun-glazed desert sand. Each is valued for itself, not for the profits that can be made, not even for the use it has to us.

Such values must transform every aspect of our lives. Our economic system, our agriculture, our industries that waste and our technologies that pollute would become intolerable. We would need a new science: one that sees itself as being taught by nature, not controlling nature. We would need a new technology, one that makes the best use of renewable resources and energies, one that can help restore damaged ecosystems.

REFUSING COMPLIANCE

Imagining a just society is easier than envisioning the strategies that will get us from here to there. The systems of domination that stand in the way of justice must be opposed. We must stop obeying, stop complying, refuse to keep silent, to lie, to not notice what is going on. We can develop a "bad attitude," one that questions authority.

Our individual attitude, however, will not alone stop war. To counter injustice, we must organize, and the groups and organizations we form must themselves embody the values we hold. Our "bad attitude" toward control must become a good attitude toward ourselves and those we work with. Resistance thus becomes a creative task. Forming groups to embody our ideals becomes a vast collective experiment; working together, struggling together we learn which of our ideals hold up in practice, we develop new skills, new tools, and new models.

Organizations can refuse compliance in many ways. To begin with we can identify those responsible for injustice, name them aloud, and hold them accountable. We can remember suffragist Alice Paul's principle, that the one who holds power to change a situation is responsible for it. If the president could allocate money to AIDS research and doesn't, he is responsible for thousands of deaths. We can speak out, write, demonstrate, to make that fact known.

We might consider campaigns to hold the superpowers jointly responsible for those situations they could jointly affect. When famine arises, or natural disasters occur, we might demand that the United States and the Soviet Union join forces to offer relief, that cooperation become normal and compassion not be used as a political weapon.

Refusal to comply means also refusal to remain within the constructs and confines of thought that are labeled acceptable. Instead, we can make our real values known. We can ask for what we really want. Our demands may be called unreasonable, but the "reason" our critics speak of means remaining within the value system of domination. When we oppose domination with values that are rooted in a different reality, our acts and demands will inevitably at first seem outrageous, shocking. But people become accustomed to outrageous proposals. Over time, they shape discourse, become "normal," make "reasonable" solutions seem conservative, reactionary.

Collective consciousness can be changed by new ideas only when they are brought to consciousness, put forth strongly and clearly. If our values are important to us, we must tell the truth about them, not water them down or conceal them in some attempt not to offend some mythical "general public." Such strategies are forms of manipulation, which confirms the power of domination. Ideas that seem normal to us today were once thought bizarre; we accept them now only because someone was once brave enough to state them clearly. Change can be hastened by articulating conflicts of value openly. Speaking our genuine truth may generate more forceful or vocal opposition, but that is a victory we should recognize, for whenever conflict is sharpened and clarified by truth we have moved a step closer to change.

War is always hungry; we can refuse to feed it, refuse to offer ourselves to its service or supply its resources. We can interfere with its operations by taking direct action. Nonviolent actions have delayed missile tests at Vandenberg Air Force Base and Cape Canaveral. Ongoing actions are currently being mounted at the Nevada Test Site, where nuclear bombs are tested. Weapons manufacturers and corporations that support military research or production can become the targets of demonstrations and nonviolent campaigns.

Sustained resistance forces the systems of control to use more and more resources to maintain themselves. Whenever we act against any system of control, we force it to exert more energy and use more resources to maintain fewer functions. We make visible the underlying violence that supports the system. We cause friction on the wheels, which eventually can grind them down. As resistance grows and spreads and becomes endemic, systems of control break down. To mount sustained resistance, we need communities of support, and we need to choose our struggles. None of us can resist everything all of the time. But collectively, we have the power to assure that no missile is ever tested without opposition, that no corporation produces weapons unnoticed, that no racist attack goes unchallenged, that no prisoner is abandoned and no refugee lacks sanctuary.

Understanding how the system of war permeates all systems of control means that whichever issue we focus on, whichever priority we choose, we are acting in concert with others. Instead of seeing ourselves as dozens of separate movements reacting against the latest particular horrors, we can recognize ourselves as one deep turning tide of change.

UNDOING THE CONSTRUCT OF ENEMY

A strategy to restore immanent value cannot be based on making any group the enemy. The heart of nonviolence is the recognition that every person embodies the sacred, that within each of us, even the torturer and the bomb maker, is a holy potential for change and growth. My own commitment to nonviolence is not that of a strict pacifist. I would pick up a weapon in self-defense, and I would never condemn an individual or a people for fighting back against oppression. We are under no obligation to let the oppressor's value supercede ours. But when we demonize another group as the Enemy, we cannot clearly judge what danger we are in. When we recognize those who oppose us as human, we open new potential for dialogue and change.

We are continually bombarded with media images and propaganda reinforcing the stereotypes of whichever country, group, party, or people is designated our current enemy. We can name the lies for what they are. The Soviet Union is not "the Evil Empire"; it is a flawed and potentially dangerous system—as is the United States.

We can fraternize with our supposed enemies, can see and know their human faces. An example of a highly successful program countering propaganda is Witness for Peace, which sends groups of North Americans down to the disputed border areas in Nicaragua (See Resources). When witnesses return, they speak to their church groups, schools, community organizations, and personal networks about what they've observed. Reagan's outright lies about the Sandinistas cannot be completely convincing because thousands of North Americans have been to Nicaragua and seen a different reality. Similar witnesses could be organized for other troubled areas.

To challenge the construct of the Enemy, we can embrace the Enemy within: we can stop treating ourselves, our bodies, our desires, our friends and companions as demons to be conquered, resources to be exploited, transgressors to be punished. We can create communities in which we love the Goddess, the immanent life force, in each one of us.

Healing ourselves is an act of community. People often say, "I realized I have to work on myself before I can change the world." But we are not machines to be "worked on," with, say, faulty transmissions to be fixed. We cannot become whole in isolation. What threatens the world is continuously damaging us; to heal the damage we must resist the destruction; to resist the destruction we must create the situations, the community, in which we can be healed.

BUILDING ALLIANCES ACROSS THE BARRIERS OF DIFFERENCE

Our own fears of difference also feed the construct of the Enemy. To stop war, we must challenge all the hierarchical relations that separate us and make some of us "other." The struggle against what Luisah Teish calls "the ism brothers" must be a primary priority, for the ways in which we exploit each other by gender or race, the ways in which our sexuality or religion or color are used to mark us out from the human fold are the very underpinnings of war.

One of the great sources of true wealth and real abundance that we are blessed with in America is the great diversity of our people. I can look out my window as I write and see faces pass by whose ancestors lived on every part of the globe. Their heritages, their cultures, languages, myths, and celebrations embody a lush diversity of perspectives, of different drumbeats to dance to and spices to cook with. Yet instead of savoring this richness, we look at it as a problem. To stop war, we must stop fearing the faces on the street, stop discounting the needs, concerns, and aspirations of those who are unlike us. Our collective challenge is to accept the richness of our wonderful variety. If we are to build a movement that can stop war, it must embrace diversity, allow us to connect across the barriers of difference, and affirm the struggles for freedom of women, people of color, gay and lesbian people, the poor, the disabled. To reconnect across the lines of our common differences of race, gender, class, religion, sexual orientation, physical condition, or appearance is the creative act that founds a new world.[1]

To learn from people of other cultures is to be given great gifts, new insights, new ideas, music, and sensations. Our differences give us binocular vision, quadrophonic sound. Unless we connect with and learn from those who are different from us, our knowledge of the world remains dangerously incomplete.

Crossing barriers can be difficult, however, when we are unsure of our own value. For to learn from others who are different requires that we allow ourselves to enter a new reality and allow our perspectives to be shifted. When we are not grounded in a sense of our own inherent worth, we experience that shift in perspective as invalidation. If I say, "At least we aren't in fear of our lives here in the United States," and my black friend says, "Come on down to Oakland if you believe that, honey," I feel pain. I become aware that my view of the world is limited and insufficient, and my self-hater eagerly holds forth on all my insufficiencies.

Yet if only I could see it, I have just been given a gift, a piece of information I need for my own survival, for my own ability to make choices that can reshape the world.

The dominant culture is known to all. We are continually bombarded with its worldview, with the symbols of its values, and those who are outside it learn its beliefs and nuances in order to survive. But when we are inside the dominant culture, we do not have to learn about the cultures, the values, the realities of others. We are not taught their history in our schools; their writers, poets, artists are not lauded as the arbiters of culture. The dominant culture presents its own style and values as the norm; other cultures are seen as deviant, quaint, backward, less valuable. And so we are all diminished.

We often unconsciously impose a style or an attitude on a group that feels uncomfortable to people of other backgrounds. In white Protestant culture, the way to be spiritual often involves being quiet, still, solemn. In black culture, spirituality is more likely to be expressed through music, rhythm, noise, emotion, and fervor. In Jewish culture, argument, discussion, humor, and concrete action may be seen as acts of spirit. These are, of course, generalizations that never apply to all members of any groups. Some blacks can't carry a tune; some Jews have no sense of humor. However, if you attempt to form a multicultural spiritual group in which people sit around solemnly and silently and pray, don't be surprised if the Jews and the blacks leave. They will be bored.

People of the dominant group also have insights, ideas, and resources to share. At times, solemn quiet has its own special power that nourishes all of us. But it is not the only way to be. If we want to cross barriers of difference, we have to let go of the unconscious assumption that our own way is the only way, or the best way, and see it as one possible way among many, while retaining our love for it and our knowledge of its value. Then we can create a truly multicultural spirituality, in which, for example, we might argue, dance, drum, and silently pray with fervor. The variety and diversity of what we create can enrich us all.

As a woman, a Jew, a white-skinned person, an out-of-the-broom-closet Witch, a bisexual, a highly educated person who has experienced varying economic circumstances, I feel I know something about both prejudice and privilege. Admitting we have privilege is hard when we derive our sense of value from seeing ourselves as King Victim. If our worth derives from our suffering and martyrdom, how can we admit that, compared to others, we don't have it so bad?

In a community based on immanent value, privilege—access to resources or opportunies—can be seen as a gift that neither diminishes nor establishes our inherent worth. A gift, to come alive, to nurture us, must move, must be shared and passed on. But a gift that moves in the right way returns to augment rather than diminish the abundance in our lives.

All our resources are needed for the work of renewal. Nobody benefits by our guilt, or our pretense that we are not fortunate when we are. Our attempts to justify our situation, to somehow prove that we deserve our position only become insulting. If we want to become allies of the oppressed, we can do two things. First, we can admit that we have privilege (and anyone reading this book does compared to millions in the world), that we have, in fact, been damn lucky. Then we can ask, How can I use my resources and opportunities responsibly? Can I share them? Teach them? Reproduce them? How can I use them to help improve conditions for those not so lucky?

We also need to recognize that those who do not have the rights, resources, and opportunities that we enjoy may rightfully be angry. My friend may be angry that she has to tell me that black people are murdered every day by the police, that I am able to remain unconscious of her reality. I may get angry if I hear someone use the term *Christian* as if it were unquestionably associated with goodness. I'm angry because the term excludes me, because my history and the experience of my people with Crusades, pogroms, the Inquisition, and Witch-burnings aren't known or considered important.

People get angry when they are attacked, rendered invisible, symbolically or actually annihilated, relegated to the ranks of those who have no value. That anger furthers our survival, gives us energy to act, to fight, to demand to be heard.

At the same time, anger is easily misdirected. Suffering does not, necessarily make us better, more sensitive people; it is just as likely to make us bitter and destructive, which is one of the many reasons we try to alleviate it. Attacking our allies is safer than attacking our real enemies—for our allies are less likely to destroy us in response. So we destroy ourselves and each other, doing the oppressors' work for them.

When others respond defensively to our anger, we only get angrier, for their defense is a further discounting. What is required is the ability to simply listen, to open to another's perceptions without losing our own. I can understand and acknowledge that *Christian* might, for others, be associated with goodness and community and integrity. I don't want them to deny that reality. I simply want them to acknowledge that it isn't the only reality, and I want them to behave toward me and others so that over time I can come to share those good associations (as in fact has happened in the years I have taught in association with Dominican Matthew Fox, who redeems the creation-centered tradition within Christianity).[2]

When we are asked to shift perspective, when we encounter difference, we often feel fear. The culture of war teaches us to respond with fear to whatever is not familiar. When we act and react out of fear we close ourselves off. We cannot be empathetic or sensitive or aware of another's viewpoint.

Witches say, "Where there's fear, there's power." If we can acknowledge our fear, test our assumptions, ask others for feedback, we may discover an unsuspected power to connect, a power that can free us to become our true selves.

QUESTIONS ABOUT DIFFERENCE

When a group bogs down, when the process is painful and nobody is having any fun, stop and ask the following questions:[3]

1. What is my (our) fear?
2. How can I test it, check it out?
3. Have I manifested it—created the conditions that will prove to me it is justified? How?
4. What could I or we do differently?

To connect across differences, we need to learn to imagine how the world might appear from another position. My frustration at having my car stereo stolen is real to me; but I can imagine that if you don't have food to put on your table, you might not want to hear about my problem. Or maybe you would, because you care about me. If I am aware of you, not oblivious, I can sense whether you really want to offer me sympathy, and if I am in doubt, I can ask you.

At times we need the support that can only be offered by those in the same position as we are. We cannot necessarily become open and vulnerable to those who have oppressed us in the past. Not all men are sexist, but women have no reason to feel automatically safe in their presence. Not all whites are racist, but a black woman who has been used by white groups as a token may have good reason to hesitate before trusting a new group of white women. Real trust is only built over time, when we see what people do, not just what they say.

When we come from a group whose culture has been systematically denied or stolen, we need spaces of separation, safe places in which to nurture each other, to grow, to be ourselves without fear or pressure. Women's circles, support groups for people of color or lesbians or working-class women are vitally important. They provide places in which we can develop our unique strengths and perspectives. Men, white people, those of the dominant culture have also been hurt by sexism and racism, and need support at times from each other. Without such places, we have no base from which to connect with others who are different.

Trust, like bonds of affection and connection, is built by doing things together that feel good. My friend Isis, responding to a draft of this chapter, said: "You're not doing black women any favor by inviting them to come sit around while a bunch of white women beat their breasts and wallow in white guilt. Nobody needs that shit. If it's not fun—why do it?"

If the purpose of the struggle to geld "the ism brothers" is to create a world in which we all feel better, we make no progress by making ourselves and everyone around us miserable. When we think of building alliances, we usually think of inviting people who are different from us to attend political meetings or work on projects. We might build stronger bonds of trust by inviting them to dance parties as well as political parties, or we might go out for dinner, hear good music, do ritual together, share poems, stories, gossip, and laughter. Then we might build the trust that can hold up through meetings, deadlines, and the tension of political work.

Most of the rituals in this book lend themselves to multiracial, multicultural groups. The ritual for crossing barriers of difference (on page 000) was created especially for such situations.

Visualization is another tool we can use to consciously put ourselves in another's place. Once a workshop I was leading nearly dissolved over a conflict between the lesbian women and the heterosexual women. At a certain point in the argument, I suggested, somewhat out of desperation, the following meditation.

MEDITATION ON DIFFERENCE

Close your eyes. Breathe deep, and relax. Imagine yourself walking down a street. People pass you by, and you look into their eyes, and you feel fear, because you know that if they knew how different you really are, they might hate you or kill you. The street is lined with billboards advertising things you have no use for, selling images of what is sexy and beautiful and desirable, and you know that you are different from the images and always will be.

Breathe deep, and walk on down the street. You pass a school, and you know that inside the walls of its classrooms the name for who you are is never even mentioned. None of your heras, your poets, your writers, your artists, your scientists are studied or named: or if they are, their differences are concealed.

Breathe again; keep walking. You pass a church, and you know that from its pulpit your differences are denounced. You walk past shops and workplaces, knowing that if your difference became visible, no one would hire you or sell to you.

You enter your home. See your family; greet them. Do they know who you are? Do they share your difference? Do they strengthen you? Or if they knew who you were, would they hate you? Would they be ashamed?

Breathe deep, and open your eyes. Notice how you feel. Talk about it; write it down. When have you experienced a taste of this reality?

Now close your eyes again. Relax. Imagine yourself back on the street. This time, everything fits. Everything reflects who you are. You walk along, and the eyes of the people you meet reflect pride and appreciation of you. Along the sides of the road are billboards, and the images of beauty and desirability they project look just like you. You know that the schools teach your history and extoll the lives of your great artists and thinkers. You glance inside the church: the God they worship is in your image. Enter your own house; greet your family. Know that they are like you, take pride in you, wouldn't have you be any different from how you are. Open your eyes.

Talk about the meditation. What was it like? How do you feel now? When have you tasted this reality? How was it different?

The real value of this meditation is in the discussion and sharing of feelings that emerge. In the workshop, the meditation only sparked the real healing, which began when a woman stood up and said something like, "My name is Oriethya. I am an Amazon, a lesbian, and a Witch, and I am proud of who I am. Now, I invite other women to stand up and tell us who you are."

One by one, women stood up and named themselves and told us something of how they each felt identified. Some of the statements became stories, small tales of acts of courage, of coming out, of needing and getting support. The afternoon became a ritual as each of the nearly one hundred women there told us who she was. The naming was a deep affirming, a way of saying to the group, "I have value in being who I am."

To further the work of making connections, I suggest establishing the following conditions:

1. Commit yourselves. Ask: Is this really what we want to do right now? Are we moving too quickly away from the support we can

only find in separate space? Are we willing to make this work a firm priority, to let it change our perceptions, our values, our focus, our lives?

2. Affirm that each person has inherent value in being who she or he is. That value cannot be rated or compared, augmented or diminished.
3. Know that the process of connection across differences is an emotional process. It cannot be done with the mind alone; it necessarily involves our feelings, and so becomes rich and fertile ground for our own personal change and growth.
4. Insist on having a good time together. Expect moments of pain, but expect them to be heavily counterbalanced by the joy, the humor, the creative excitement, the added richness of our lives when we can share them. Otherwise, what is the point?

When you decide to commit yourselves to building multicultural community, here are some steps you might take to bridge common differences.

1. Notice who is missing—what groups are not represented.
2. Educate yourselves about other cultures and groups. Read. Learn the history, search out the art, dance to the music.
3. Explore the ways in which you have been conditioned to fear or hate difference. What are your unconscious assumptions? Stereotypes? How did you learn them? What were you taught about differences as a child? How did you feel toward the adults who taught you?
4. Learn to identify "the ism brothers" when they speak through the mouths of your friends, your family, your group members, your co-workers. Name them. Interrupt them; challenge their assumptions. Don't leave it to women to point out sexism, to people of color to point out racism, to lesbians or gay men to name homophobia.
5. What are the issues and priorities of groups from different backgrounds? What issues, what groups, exist in your local area? Can you ally with them? Offer each other support? Begin to broaden your own concerns, to name the interconnections?

    Is your group accessible to people with varied resources and abilities? Can a person in a wheelchair get in the door? Do you provide child care?
6. Do you have resources that other groups might be able to share? Networks that you can expand?
7. Invite people into your group in a meaningful way. Nobody likes to be a token. Meaningful participation means that you should:
    a. Bring people into a project or group early, when they can have real impact on how it develops.
    b. Bring in enough people of another group or culture so that they have strength and support of their own. In forming the WomanEarth Feminist Peace Institute, a network of women of

color and white women, we committed ourselves to parity—
equal representation of white women and women of color. In
practice, this meant limiting the number of white women who
could attend our first conference, and we hated excluding people.
But the energy, the process, the confrontation and learning that
emerged from the group was very different from what could have
come of a conference of hundreds of white women with a few
dark faces sprinkled in between. Because we had parity, the values
of the women of color present were able to shape the group mind.

The commitment to meaningful representation must extend
through every aspect of an organization. If your planning com-
mittee is all white, inviting two black women and a native American to speak at your rally will not change the dynamics of separation. (Although it is better than not inviting them.)

c. Recognize that your organization will change. Be clear yourself
about which goals, focuses, and priorities you are willing to shift.
If you don't want to change certain aspects of your group, communicate clearly what they are. Find those who share those priorities and interests.

Be willing to shift other priorities, to hear criticism and make
changes. Be willing to change your style. Be sure that whatever
face you present publicly reflects your diversity.

d. Let goals, priorities, analyses, and directions emerge from your
diversity.

e. Enjoy the rewards of the work. A circle of faces that reflects the
many shapes and colors and forms of humanness is a beautiful
sight. A party is more lively with a Latin beat. Ritual became
more exciting for me after exposure to Teish's tradition encouraged my own group to learn to drum. When we come together
in diversity, we experience the richness of human possibility. We
should all be enraged that this experience is so rare.

This discussion, of course, is only a bare beginning. All the processes
and qualities discussed earlier for groups that foster freedom are helpful
and important for groups that cross barriers of diversity.

ESTABLISHING REAL PROTECTION

To effectively counter our collective possession by the Defender, we
must also begin to face the challenge of establishing collective safety, true
national and global security. A first step might be to ask ourselves the
question, What would make me feel safe in the world? More powerful
weapons systems are not increasing our real security. What would? How
could we establish mutual security with those we fear?

We cannot stop war unless we can invent some alternative way to defend ourselves. The peace movement has not, in the past, sufficiently considered this question. When it arises debate often stops, as if we ourselves cannot think beyond war.

Yet war is not now our only or even most prevalent way of securing ourselves. We are not on the verge of war with most countries in the world or with our nearest neighbors. In reality, the United States is not faced with the threat of invasion. We have not actually had to defend ourselves since World War II. Our wars have been fought to defend the economic interests of a few, and have all been against smaller and poorer countries.

Let us consider a defense policy concerned only with securing our safety from invasion. Could we not make ourselves an undesirable prize, unconquerable, unrulable, using the same techniques of nonviolent resistance we are developing to challenge war? Imagine trying to govern a nation with a bad attitude, hundreds of millions of people who refuse to comply or cooperate, who force the conquerors at every step to exert the maximum force at their disposal to accomplish the simplest end. Such strategies have, in fact, worked. Scandinavian noncooperation prevented the Nazis from consolidating their conquest of the North in World War II. Czechoslovakian resistance undermined the Soviet invasion in 1967.

Imagine, instead of the military draft, universal preparation for nonviolent resistance. Such training would itself loosen the grip of the King and make people better able to resist domination at home—even if the Soviets never do sail through the Golden Gate. (For this reason, of course, this plan is unlikely to be promoted by the authorities.) It might foster a healthy national pride, based not on the fantasy of ourselves as Rambo strongmen, but on the reality of our readiness to act with integrity and courage in the face of force.

This is, of course, only one scenario. What we need is to begin considering the necessary questions with the belief that we can succeed, and will therefore someday need to know the answers. If we commit ourselves to undoing the systems of power-over that support war, we need to rethink every aspect of culture and society. What type of economy would make war unfeasible? What approach to science, what forms of technology would foster liberation? How might we live? What families, what communities, might we create?

Community is the only real basis of security. While it is unlikely that any of us will face violence at the hands of Soviet invaders on our streets, most of us have faced the threat or reality of rape, robbery, and physical attack on those same streets. Children need the freedom to explore their environment and to engage in unstructured, unsupervised play. Today urban parents are afraid to let their children play in parks or walk to school. If they have resources, they flee to suburbs, which is no guarantee of safety, or arrange endless series of classes, lessons, and after-school programs. If they don't have money, their children are kept confined or are allowed to risk an environment that can be lethal.

In 1961, in her classic work *The Death and Life of Great American Cities,* Jane Jacobs identified the real factors that make city streets safe for children, or anyone else. Safe streets are lively and diversified, with sidewalks where people gather, socialize, and take responsibility for each other. Children can play under the eyes of adults who are conducting their own business but maintain casual surveillance, and so learn "the first fundamental of successful city life: People must take a modicum of public responsibility for each other even if they have no ties to each other."[4]

The economic pressures and planning decisions of the years since 1961 have worked against the diversity Jacobs identified as the prime determinant of a city's health. We cannot replace the organic process by which safe neighborhoods are generated. We can, however, do much to improve the level of real security we feel in our daily lives.

We might organize, block by block and neighborhood by neighborhood, to establish "safe corridors" for children and old people. Many areas have instituted successful Neighborhood Watch programs to discourage burglaries. Similar programs could establish street safety. Parents and other interested adults could volunteer to take shifts as "eyes." Training in nonviolent intervention and conflict resolution could be held. "Safe houses" could be identified and marked with stickers on the door or window. Porch lights could be lit when people are home, so that a woman being followed, or a frightened child, would know where to run for help and shelter. Such projects would also build neighborhood networks and solidarity.

Strong neighborhoods could organize to make physical modifications that would improve street safety. My own street has four lanes of traffic. If it were changed to a two-lane, one-way street, the reclaimed space could be devoted to wide sidewalks, accommodating both play and the variety of adult pursuits that keep the sidewalks lively and interesting. Jacobs recommends sidewalks thirty-five feet wide, to provide for jumping rope and roller skating (today, skateboarding).[5] Parks are no substitute: if they are large, they become unsafe, and if they are small enough to be safe, older children quickly find them boring. Nor do grass or gardens serve the same purpose as sidewalks, for older children want to be mobile, to roam large territories on wheels. In a city laced with a network of safe corridors and wide walkways, a nine year old could ride a bike or skateboard from the local swimming pool to the library, down to the shopping street or over to a friend's house. An older person could walk safely from home to the bank and back. A woman could regain the freedom of the night.

CREATING DIVERSITY OF EXPRESSION

A life-loving culture that escaped the repression of the Censor would be expressive, erotic, alive with art, music, poetry, dance, and ritual; diverse, not monolithic, drawing on many rhythms, many languages; active, not passive. Entertainment would cease to be a spectacle we consume, and become what we do for each other and ourselves; the stories we tell, the rituals we create, our own songs and our own laughter.

ENSURING SUSTAINABILITY

The war culture also treats the earth as enemy. To stop war, we must reembrace the earth, the Mother, the ever-renewing, ever-decaying fertile principle of life. Stopping war means stopping the war on the earth, learning to feed ourselves sustainably, no longer treating her plant and animal life as disposable objects to be exploited, but instead embracing them as the embodiments of the powers that teach us and of our lives' sustenance. Stopping war is an act of the spirit that arises in the body and sings in the flesh, an erotic act, an act of love.

A culture that values the earth must also be sustainable, must preserve its resources for future generations. Its agriculture must improve the soil, not deplete it. Its forestry must extend the groves, not decimate them. Its economy cannot be based on extracting the maximum short-term profit, but must seek its rewards in the harvest that we can count on year after year, generation after generation.

Sustainable culture must take root in place. The society we envision will be diverse, different on the coast than on the prairie. Here in the San Francisco Area, our yearly miracle is the rain's return in autumn, and the slow greening of the dry, straw hills. Where you are, it may be the leaves' blaze of color, or the return of the migrating egret. These are the mysteries we must celebrate. And when we do, when we take root in the land herself, we can begin to heal her and each other.

The healing of our relationship with place begins with the preservation of the natural environment. We cannot go to the wild for renewal if no wilderness is left. The eagle cannot be our power animal when it is extinct, nor can the elements cleanse us when they are polluted. To value ourselves we must protect and heal the greater earth body of which we are a part. Wilderness is necessary for our psychic health even if we never set foot there, for we are not separate from the earth, and the wild places are her places of power, where the life force runs freely and strongly and the vitality of the world is renewed.

Rooting in place also means supporting indigenous peoples in their struggles to retain and regain their lands and determine for themselves how best to preserve their culture. The belief in inherent value is not compatible with genocide or notions of manifest destiny. A society rooted in the earth must acknowledge the value in each culture and tradition. In doing so, we have much to learn and many gifts to receive.

A society based on immanent value is built from the ground up, from the local sense of place out to the global arenas of power. We begin with a community, which might take root in a city, a neighborhood, a rural region. We might begin to think in terms of our bioregions—areas of specific animal and plant communities, watersheds of the great rivers, areas of climate change. To let the biological life of a place determine its political boundaries, interests, and alliances is one way of acknowledging its inherent value, grounding theory in the dirt of reality. For my interests are, in reality, tied to the flow of the Sacramento River and the salinity of San Francisco Bay, as yours may be tied to the purity of Mississippi River water or the forest cover on the slopes of the Rockies. We can begin to learn about the ecology of our own place, for when we know its needs we can fight to preserve and restore its living balance.

The intimate knowledge of place is the only basis for an agriculture and an industry that is sustainable. Sustainable agriculture is small-scale. "With land as with anything else, those who have a lot will tend to think that a little waste is affordable. When land is held in appropriately small parcels, on the other hand, a little waste tends to be noticed, regretted, and corrected, because it is felt that a little loss cannot be afforded. And that is the correct perception; it *cannot* be afforded."[6]

An economy of peace can only be based on a sustainable agriculture and a healthy soil. For however we try to account for unemployment, inflation, stagflation, however much we juggle wages, prices, and interest rates, we ultimately have to feed ourselves. American agriculture is highly productive now because it mines the stored fertility of the soil, banked over thousands of years when it lay unbroken as prairie sod. That soil, another of the great gifts we waste, is rapidly being eroded. Chemical fertilizers and pesticides pollute a third of our stored groundwaters. By the next century, we may be suffering famine instead of exporting surplus grain.

Rooted in place, an economy of peace extends its branches out to nurture the globe. For our interconnectedness stops at no borders. When most of the world goes hungry and children starve, we can know no true comfort or security. The causes of hunger are not, in reality, natural disasters or overpopulation. Hunger results from economic systems that exploit resources for the benefit of the few and political systems that keep people powerless. In *World Hunger: Twelve Myths*, Frances Moore Lappé and Joseph Collins define democracy as accountability to those most affected by decisions. "The root cause of hunger isn't a scarcity of food or land; it's a scarcity of democracy."[7]

Only by transforming our own economy to one of peace can we make possible economic democracy in the Third World or our own country. The present economy generates wars to protect its profits and its short-term interests, while squandering the future. Unless we transform the economy, we cannot end war.

An economy of peace would refuse its resources to war. It would follow no model we have ever seen. Instead of seeking endless expansion, it might take as a model biological homeostasis, a steady state that is not static but ever dynamic, shifting, changing, and moving, yet keeping vital relationships in balance. Certainly, it would not be a capitalist economy, for capital is like a vast confidence trick: a system in which money can apparently breed money removed from any real value or use. But money has no genitalia, no womb and no testes. The profits it "breeds" are leached from the soil, from our labor, from the storehouse of natural resources that have been appropriated by the few.

Nor would an economy of peace be a centralized state economy on the Marxist or socialist model. A centralized economy also concentrates power in the hands of a few, removing too many decisions from those who live with their consequences.

An economy of peace might look more like a mosaic, a crazy quilt of enterprises small enough to be both innovative and sustainable, owned and controlled by those who work in them. Instead of developing huge organizations with multinational exploitative interests, it would encourage the development of regional self-reliance for the necessities of life, both at home and in the Third World. Productive land would be devoted first to feeding a region's own people and only secondarily to export crops. Foreign investors and creditors would not be allowed to shift these priorities.

Knowing our own food, water, housing, and energy needs could be provided from our own nearby region would greatly increase our sense of real security. Cities and suburbs have the potential to produce much of their own food.[8] Self-reliance would necessitate new developments in the technologies of energy conservation and generation from renewable sources, which would be diverse and suited to each specific region.

An economy of peace would also foster interdependence—systems and agreements that encourage mutual cooperation and benefit. Some systems lend themselves to centralization or large-scale coordination; for example, communications and transportation systems. Other enterprises might bring goods from far-off places, knitting many locales together in one fabric of mutual interest. If we begin to think of an economy as an ecosystem to be nurtured and sustained for the long term, we might learn that exploitation is not ultimately beneficial even to the exploiter. If our economic goals were broadened to include the balance sheet of the welfare of succeeding generations, we might understand that exploiting the Third World is not, in the long run, good business.

Our aid to the Third World has only attempted to make countries our helpless dependents. Were we, instead, to offer aid to the Third World that would help these countries develop sustainable, ecologically sound economies, based on technologies appropriate to their local resources and capable of providing self-sufficiency in basic needs, we might find ourselves surrounded by strong allies instead of potential trouble spots. In solving the problems presented by local conditions and developing tools and techniques to meet the challenges presented by each unique place, the

Third World would generate innovations that could improve the quality of our lives and open up new areas of growth for our economy.[9]

The media would have us believe that collective businesses and households declined with the end of the sixties. Many experiments of that era failed but many also succeeded. I know collective households and land groups that have thrived for over a decade. Even the failure of many experiments taught us valuable lessons in what not to do.

If we envision an economy of small pieces, striving for balance rather than eternal growth, we are empowered to begin where we are. We can form our own collectives and engage in creating a livelihood that supports peace. We may find niches in the present economy or generate new products and services. *A Pattern Language,* for example, suggests a model for child care that could easily be adapted to a collective enterprise: a "children's house" that would be the actual home of some adults and would be available to children at any time of the day or night, located close to where they live. The home would not provide a regimented program but would be like a child's second family, a place to hang out, to participate in whatever activities were going on, or to retreat and be alone in a safe environment. Parents would pay a weekly or monthly fee that would entitle them to ever-available child care.[10]

Groups and organizations can pressure for laws and regulations that foster diversity and protect the small. We need farm legislation to protect the small farmer. No democratic country can afford to have a few large corporations controlling the bulk of the world's most productive farmland. The ties of a family to land they have worked for generations cannot be measured against the profits of banks and investors. Bankruptcy laws currently protect families from losing homes, clothing, or automobiles needed for work; similar laws should protect farmers against the loss of their lands and the equipment needed to work the land. The elaborate edifice of subsidies, loans, interest rates, and commodity prices, currently weighted against the small farmer, should be readjusted or done away with. We need land reform in this country as much as it is needed in any underdeveloped dictatorship of the Third World.

Programs could also be instituted, and tax laws and insurance structures adjusted, to aid and encourage small businesses and collective enterprises. Tax incentives could encourage the development of new technologies and the use of renewable resources. When tax credits were available for solar conversions, many small businesses sprang up; when credits were withdrawn, many failed, resulting in a national loss of the potential innovations that they might have produced.

The challenge, of course, is not just to envision a future, but to bring it about. The transformation of the economy will not happen easily. Those who have power and privilege rarely see the benefit of relinquishing it. The need for resistance, vigilance, and sustained troublemaking always remains. The more clearly we identify our goals, the more clearly we can identify the points in the system where sustained pressure will bring the greatest results.

We also need to sustain ourselves through that struggle, to create communities of support. The groups I have discussed in this book can be the nucleus of those communities. They may extend networks throughout the world. But they will be most grounded when they have a base in a physical location: a city neighborhood, a rural county. There, services can be developed, meetings can be conveniently attended, and resources can be shared.

A sustainable culture values diversity, and offers support to a wide variety of life-styles. Alternative community does not necessarily mean moving to the country to live in one large yurt with twenty-five others. Transforming society means transforming the cities; and cities are potentially fertile breeding grounds for diversity. A city neighborhood might include big houses for groups that want to live in collectives or extended families, small apartments for those who prefer to live alone, housing for nuclear families or single parents who might find that city proximity makes shared child care or pooling of resources possible. In smaller towns, or on country land, a similar variety of life-styles could be fostered. City and country groups might link up to exhange resources. City money could help support those who live on the land; in return, the land might provide food, retreat, and recreation space for city dwellers.

In communities of support we can explore new ways of living: collective or cooperative households, shared child care or child rearing, new integrations of work and leisure. In a collective household, the culture of immanent value can become a daily reality. If you choose the right housemates, you are guaranteed perpetual entertainment and stimulation. With luck, you will also find emotional support when you need it, practical help, and growthful confrontation. I admit my bias: I live with eight other people and love it.

Collective living is not, however, for everyone. It demands a willingness to share personal space and give up some control over one's environment, and a willingness to share feelings, stay honest, and spend a lot of time talking about issues and emotions. As my housemate Brook says, "It helps to be gregarious and easygoing." Many fine people are neither. If your most precious time is spent alone, if noise drives you crazy, if you are part of a devoted couple that resents intrusions on your mutual rapture, or if you are a less devoted couple on the verge of a stormy breakup, some other way of living may better preserve your happiness and sanity. To live collectively, you must choose the life-style because you genuinely want it—not because it seems more practical or more politically correct.

Collective households also seem to work best when expectations are reasonable and boundaries clear. To live collectively, we don't necessarily have to share everything. We can retain our own income, lovers, private rooms, and so on. Living with others should enrich our lives, not force us to make sacrifices.

Groups that do live collectively can afford resources that can be shared with a larger community. A network of collective households, such as exists in the Bay Area, provides a base of support for events and projects that knit a community together. For example, a San Francisco group sponsors an anarchist coffeehouse every month. The gathering is held at one of several collective households that have large spaces for people to dance, talk, and listen to the widely varied entertainment provided. Admission is inexpensive and proceeds are devoted each month to a different cause. Most important, the coffeehouse provides a fun, informal place to connect with others, to talk political theory or dance, to show off new clothes, to fall in love, to gossip, to have the spontaneous, unstructured meetings and interactions that give community an organic life.

Organized groups could also pressure for laws, insurance, and lending policies that support alternative experiments in housing and land ownership. The high cost of housing has encouraged many people to consider collective ownership of buildings. Model contracts for group ownership and land trusts exist, and more legal and financial resources could be developed. Groups that want to foster community might also simply consider moving into the same neighborhood. The process of neighborhood-building happens organically in healthy cities; people with similar values and tastes are drawn to the same areas. Today, economic pressures are so intense that they often radically limit our choices, but many city neighborhoods still exist where the variety of buildings can foster diversity. We must take care, however, not to destroy the diversity that exists by displacing people whose resources are even more limited than ours. A sustainable community is not a gentrified, homogeneous collection of people who share the same life-style and income level; it is a mix of those who have both greater and lesser resources, and varied ways of living and types of work. It includes children and old people, new immigrants and long-established residents, owners and renters, and the mixture of races, ethnic groups, and cultures that is our unsung wealth.

OPENING TO MYSTERY

Finally, a free society would open us to mystery: not to any specific religion or dogma but to wonder at the vast, self-praising universe. We would affirm the erotic, the wildness in us; we could rage, or cry, or flirt, be lively, sexy, funny, ecstatic, as the energies moved through us.

Mystery is about compost, worms eating shit, about the way we must continually eat the world, biting off hunks of life, chewing and swallowing, passing life through us and excreting it out again to fertilize other lives until we ourselves are eaten and decay.

We are the mystery, in our diversity, in the splendor of our differences.

The Hopis say that we all began together; that each race went on a journey to learn its own road to power, and changed; that now is the time for us to return, to put the pieces of the puzzle back together, to make the circle whole.[11] Through our differences, we complete each other. Together, we become a new whole. Mystery is vision. When I attempt to envision what the world renewed might look like, I imagine the following.

Fantasy of a Living Future

You are walking the dogs up on the hill they call La Matria, the Mother's Womb. Below is spread a sparkling panorama of the city, a living tapestry of rainbow colors on a warp of green. Toward the west, the Maiden's Breasts thrust their twin peaks up into a clear sky. All during Sunreturn Moon, fireworks lit the sky there, celebrating La Purisima, the festival of the conception of the Virgin. The streets were filled with processions, the Catholics and the Pagans dancing together without arguing about which Virgin they were celebrating, and everyone else in the city, it seemed, joining in just for the fun of it.

Now it is Fruit Blossom Moon, no fog, and the winter rains have turned the hillside green, dotted with the orange of a few early poppies. Three cows graze the hillside; the dogs are used to them and ignore them. You smile a greeting at the young girl who watches them; she is sprawled on her back in the sun, not working too hard. The cows are the project of the kids from your own child's school; the neighborhood market collective buys their milk and cream, and with the money and their own labor, they are constructing what you believe must be the world's most elaborate skateboard run.

Atop the hill stands a circle of stones. You pause for a moment, feeling the energy of the city, the hill, the sky all converge here, remembering the bonfires and the dancing and the rituals. On the Jewish New Year, they blow the shofar, the ancient ram's horn, here. On the Winter Solstice, you climb this hill at dawn to welcome the newborn sun.

To the east stretches the bay. The air is so clear today that you can see all the way to Coyote Mountain in the distant hills. Great flocks of pelicans and seabirds wheel and dive around the fleets of fishing boats, their bright-colored sails plumped out by the breeze. Among them sail the great ocean-going trade ships, their huge sails spread like wings. No need today to switch to the solar batteries; the wind is strong.

You call the dogs and head down the winding, processional way, reveling in the scent of the blossoms from the apple trees that line the walkway. You glance into the gardens of the houses on the hill; it would be a great day to double-dig your tomato bed and plant out the seedlings. The dogs run ahead as you follow the road down, past the park at the bottom of the hill. Sidewalk cafes line the park; you spend pleasant hours there watching the kids play on the slides and swings, taking your turn, as do most of the neighborhood adults, on playground watch.

Now the walkway narrows as you turn down your street. On your left are the front gardens of the old Victorian houses. On your right, a low greenhouse structure lines the roadbed where trolley cars and electric autos run on the one-way street. The greenhouse is the neighborhood waste treatment plant, where banked rows of water hyacinths are aquacultured to purify wastes and generate clean water and compost.[12]

You pass another small park, where a group of older people sit conversing under walnut and almond trees. Like everyone else on the street, they are a mix of races. Africa, Asia, the Americas, Europe, all contribute to their heritage, and you smile with pleasure, for to see a group of elders who embody the Four Quarters is considered extremely good fortune. "Blessed be the elders; blessed be the Four Quarters that complete the circle," you murmer as you pass.

There are several elders' houses on the block: equipped with elevators and intercoms, the older people can live independently in a suite of rooms with someone always on call; some take turns cooking and baking, some pool together and hire local teenagers to cook and clean. In your own house, each of you cook once every two weeks. Once a week, you eat out at friends' or go to restaurants. On another night, you go to the neighborhood dining club, where, for a fixed membership fee, a collective provides a good organic meal. The dining club is a place to meet, talk, socialize, do informal business, and talk local politics.

The fruit trees that line the sidewalks are very old now, planted years ago as an attempt to provide free food for the hungry. Now, of course, no one goes hungry. The very thought is barbaric, amidst all this abundance. No one lacks shelter, or care when sick, or a chance to contribute the work that sustains abundance.

You open the door to your collective house. The dogs run in. Your computer sings to you: someone has left you a message. One of your housemates calls to you to tell you the news.

"The ship's in! The Chocolate Consortium called—they want everyone who can to come down there and help unload."

All thoughts of gardening disappear. You hop on your bicycle and speed down the path that winds past houses, shops, and parks to the docks.

The ship is in from Central America: one of the great winged traders, carrying your long-awaited shipment of cocoa beans and cane sugar. You greet your co-workers from the Truffle Collective and say hello to your friends from the other collectives in the consortium: the Candymakers, the Bakers, the representative from the Ice Cream Consortium, the Chocolate Chip Cooperative.[13] Together, you unload the heavy sacks, count the inventory, and examine their other wares: the finely crafted hammocks, the innovations in intelligent crystal technology in which Central America leads the way. The ship will return laden with fine Sonoma wines, precision tools from the East Bay foundries, artichokes from Santa Cruz, and, of course, a load of state-of-the-art skateboards from the City.

You have arranged this deal yourself and it has been a complicated one. Your work collective is part of an extensive tradeweb, involving the households of your members, your sister collectives in the Delta grain-growing region and the Wine Country, your lover, who works in an East Bay steel mill, where the worker cooperatives pride themselves on pro-ducing the finest alloys in the cleanest, safest plants in the country, your ex-lover, who is a computer genius, and your housemate's brother, who repairs and maintains ships. You can resort to currency if you need to: the City's money is good anywhere, but you prefer to trade when you can. Fortunately, with a few exceptions, everybody loves truffles. The Tofu and Tempeh Consortium won't touch sugar products, but many of the soybean growers have voracious sweet tooths, so it all works out.

The work is hard but you enjoy the physical labor as you all talk and joke together. It's a nice change from the candy kitchen and the computer terminal. The smells and the staccato sound of Spanish remind you of the winter you spent visiting the Cooperativa de Cacao, where the beans come from. You remember the lush fields of corn and vegetables, the sturdy children, the trees you helped plant to hold the slopes of the mountain, the doorways open to the mild nights and the people calling out as you took an evening stroll. The visit cemented the friendships that established your trade contacts.

Finally, the whole shipment is packed away on electrotrucks that will take it back to the factory. The captain invites you and your friends up to her cabin for a cold drink. After you ritually exchange compliments and computer software, you invite her and her compañeros to spend the evening with you. The moon will be full tonight; your ritual circle will meet up on the hill and guests will be welcome. You will dance to the moon and then head downtown, for it is Chinese New Year and the dragon will dance through the streets. There will be fireworks, parades, and celebrations.

You bicycle home. In the last hour of daylight, you have time to pull a few weeds and turn the compost. Your household, like most of the city's living groups, grows much of its own food, providing all its salad greens, most vegetables, many fruits, nuts, and herbs. Your housemate feeds the chickens and milks your goat. You can shower, soak your sore muscles in the hot tub, chat with your child, and relax before dressing for the celebration. It's been a long day—but a good one. Now for some good food, and you'll be ready to dance all night in the friendly streets aglow with moonlight.

BUILDING A MOVEMENT FOR CHANGE

Revolutions have been made by sudden violence, and revolutions have also come from slow, sustained change. But even the latter road is not an easy one. It demands long sustained pressure to undermine the systems of control and ongoing work to create alternative structures.

To build a movement that could transform society without turning to violence, we need to develop long-term strategies. The steps in such a struggle might proceed as follows:

1. Clarify Our Vision.

Begin to imagine the world we want to live in. Then make that vision concrete. What would actually be needed to bring it about? How would work, sustenance, production, education, health care, shelter, art, and ritual function or be provided? What tools and skills would we need? How might they be developed? What changes would be needed in the system that exists? How might they be brought about? Where are the pressure points?

Consider these questions individually and in groups. Explore different answers, analyze, and argue. Ask them in your classrooms and your workplace. Ask, Is what we're learning, is the work we're doing, furthering our vision or feeding war? Be a pain in the ass, a thorn in the foot of the war culture.

2. Withdraw Consent and Support from the Systems of Control.

Don't cooperate with their aims and goals, don't work for them, don't buy their products or lend them your energies. Of course, in the culture of war almost everything we do feeds war. We all need to survive, but we can make choices that withdraw our direct participation from the work of oppression—including the work of oppressing ourselves. Doing this may mean making what seem to be economic sacrifices in the short run. In the long run, refusing to waste your life energies and instead working to create the world you want, brings benefits that cannot be bought or sold.

3. Create Communities of Support.

We need help in this work. In community, we can support each other through lean times and difficult transitions. We can create islands of the culture of immanent value, where we can be nourished and healed. And we can experiment with ways of interacting and organizing on a small scale that can eventually be adapted to larger systems.

4. Mount Ongoing Resistance.

Actively oppose war and all systems of domination. Get in their way. Interfere with their operations. Identify the secret power-holders and make your knowledge public. Call them to account. Speak truth to power. Develop long-term strategies and ongoing campaigns of pressure. Let your community support you in resistance, and let the skills in collective process you develop in the course of actions strengthen your community.

5. Create Alternatives.

We can begin to enact our visions, to try them out and test them in operation, to develop work for ourselves that provides the services or goods needed by a life-serving culture. We can develop new infrastructures that can replace systems of domination. And we can create culture: music, art, drama, writing, and ritual that embodies our values and visions.

6. Build Networks of Common Interest.

Women need organizations that specifically work for women's needs. People of color, gay people, the disabled, any group who must struggle for power needs an organizational base that is primarily devoted to the needs and interests of that group.

7. Build Coalitions.

Organizations based in a specific group still have many interests and aims in common with other groups, although they may also have strong differences. We can learn not to fear our differences, and to build coalitions that allow us to combine our strength. We can enact our vision of a truly multiracial, multicultural, diverse society.

8. Pressure for Positive Changes.

Use the political system that exists to put forth proposals for positive change, to divert resources to programs that further earth-centered values, to hold our representatives accountable and demand responsive leadership.

9. Take the Next Step.

While we work toward a long-term vision, we can identify the small steps we can take immediately, and so begin. The following meditation may be helpful.

NEXT-STEP MEDITATION

Breathe deep, and follow your breath down to your belly, the belly of Spider Woman. Feel the place within you where she spins the thread of your life. Around you stretch all the roads of possibility, like a great web with you at the center. Look around; see which one shines for you. Which one is the future you want to create?

Take a deep breath; draw power from the earth, and jump! Let yourself float out on the breeze, trailing your thread, jumping far, far into the future, until you land in the world you want to create.

Now look down at your feet. Who are you? Where are you?

Turn and look to the East, the South, the West, the North. Breathe deep and notice what you hear and feel and sense and smell and see.

Now look to the center. What is there for you?

How do you live in this world? Who do you live with? How do you get your food?

Who do you love? How do you raise the children? What is your work? What are your rituals and celebrations?

What knowledge do you have in this world that you need at home? What message, what wisdom, do you have for yourself?

Now say good-bye to this world. Say good-bye and thanks to everyone you've met. Thank the East, the South, the West, the North, the Center. Thank yourself.

Now breathe deep, and begin to walk back along the path. Notice what you feel and hear and sense as time rolls by. Feel the ground beneath your feet and the air on your skin, and continue, until you reach a point halfway to the future.

Now look down at your feet. Who are you? Where are you?

Turn and look to the East, the South, the West, the North. Breathe deep and notice what you hear and feel and sense and smell and see.

Now look to the center. What is there for you?

How do you live in this world? Who do you live with? How do you get your food?

Who do you love? How do you raise the children? What is your work? What are your rituals and celebrations?

What knowledge do you have in this world that you need at home? What message, what wisdom, do you have for yourself?

Now say good-bye to this world. Say good-bye and thanks to everyone you've met. Thank the East, the South, the West, the North. Thank yourself.

Now breathe deep, and begin to walk back along the path. Notice what you feel and hear and sense as time rolls by. Feel the ground beneath your feet and the air on your skin, and continue, until you reach a point that is the very first step into the future you want to create.

Breathe deep, and know what that step is for you. How will you take it? What will you do? What will you change?

Breathe deep again, and step back into the center. You are in the center of the web. Look around you. See the roads, as they stretch in so many directions, beckoning and foreboding, shining and dim. Know that the road you have taken is one future, one possibility. You can choose it, or you can make another choice.

Thank the spider, who spins time. Breathe deep, and follow your breath up, up from your belly, up to the place where She spins your cord of life, up into the body that remains here in this room. Breathe deep, and bring back with you your memory of the future, as you come fully back, and become fully awake.

Take time to discuss your visions and your next steps. Share feelings, fears and hopes, excitements and disappointments. Open discussions of planning and strategies.

A similar process can be done as a more intellectual strategy-development exercise.[14]

STRATEGY EXERCISE

In a small group, discuss a vision or a goal to be realized in twenty years. Make it as concrete and realistic as possible. Write it down. Then ask, Where would we need to be in ten years to be halfway to our twenty year goal? Discuss the answer. Again keep discussion concrete. Then ask the same question for five years from now, two years, one year, six months, and tomorrow. As the time frame gets nearer and nearer to the present, tension may rise. Long-term goals or time frames may need to be reevaluated. The exercise is helpful in setting both group and personal priorities.

The vision of a society rooted in the idea of immanent value is a creative, exciting vision. We can convey that excitement in the actions we take on its behalf. When we tell it to people, we can speak in terms of their value. When we take action, we can do so not with self-righteousness but with humor and compassion, never forgetting to care for each other and nurture each other's power.

A life rooted in the mysteries must be a life of action, engaged with the world, not removed from it. The mysteries are the cycles, the patterns, the balance of the world, the arising of great forces that sustain life. When we awaken to them, evoke them, name them as sacred, they flow strongly in us and refuse to be boxed and suppressed. The mysteries have a bad attitude. They make trouble. We want to be out in the storm, not inside under fluorescent lights. We ask inconvenient questions. We awaken from the sleep-fog of compliance and move to a rhythm older and deeper than the laws of the King. We will not keep silent. We care too fiercely. Rage, the sweet fire of survival, is transmuted in us into passion. We desire the abundance, the variety, the blooming life.

We have mourned our dead. Now we will keep open the way of their return, through us, through our children, in the damp earth of spring and the musky pollen. We will not let the pattern of life be broken, nor will we walk the living earth as if we were already dead. For we will be living beacons. The moon, the stars, reflect our light.

of the circling stars
and the ever-renewing flame
As your labor has become her labor

Out of the bone, ash
Out of the ash, pain
Out of the pain, the swelling
Out of the swelling, the opening
Out of the opening, the labor
Out of the labor, the birth
Out of the birth, the turning wheel
  the turning tide
This is the story we like to tell ourselves
In the night
When the labor is too hard, and goes on too long
When the fire seems nothing but dying embers winking
  out
We say we remember
  a time when we were free
We say
  that we are free, still, and always
And the pain we feel
  is that of labor
And the cries we hear
  are those of birth

And so you come to the fire
  where the old ones sit
You are young
  just on the edge of ripening
They are ancient
  their faces lined
  with spiderwebs of wrinkle
Their faces brown, bronze, cream, black
  their eyes are wells of memory
They say
    Listen child
    For this is your night of passage
    And it is time to learn
    Your history
    Tonight you will run free, out into the wild
    Fearing only the spirit of your own power
    And no one in this world would harm you or lay
      a hand on you
  But there was a time
    When children were not safe

The Last Story

And so the time comes when all the people of the earth
   can bring their gifts to the fire
   and look into each other's faces
   unafraid

Breathe deep
Feel the sacred well that is your own breath, and look
   look at that circle
See us come from every direction
   from the four quarters of the earth
See the lines that stretch to the horizon
   the procession, the gifts borne
   see us feed the fire
Feel the earth's life renewed
And the circle is complete again
   and the medicine wheel is formed anew
   and the knowledge within each one of us
   made whole
Feel the great turning, feel the change
   the new life runs through your blood like fire
   and all of nature rises with it
   greening, burgeoning, bursting into flower
At that mighty rising
   do the vines rise up, do the grains rise up
   and the desert turns green
   the wasteland blooms like a garden
Hear the earth sing
   of her own loveliness
   her hillock lands, her valleys
   her furrows well-watered
   her untamed wild places
She arises in you
   as you in her
Your voice becomes her voice
Sing!
Your dance is her dance

And the dark held rape and death and terror
We remember that time

You are growing
Already you know joy in your own body
Soon you will know joy in another
And whoever you choose to love
We will all be glad for your happiness
But there was a time when people were not free to
    love
And suffered pain and shame and loneliness
We remember that time

Go to the stream, kneel down, drink the sweet
    water
As you can anywhere water runs in this world
For it runs clean, and breathe the clear air
And know that there was a time
When the waters and the very air itself
Were poisoned, and the people died
We remember that time

Look around the circle, look at our faces
Each one different, each special
And we so love the hue of our different skins
And the carved planes of our faces
And our beautiful hair, like moss, like water
But there was a time
When people feared each other
And hated what they saw in different eyes
We remember that time

And look up into the sky, see the stars, see the
    moon
Know that there is nothing in the sky
To threaten or harm you
But there was a time
When we were all targets
And we didn't know, from one day to the next
When the bombs might come
Whether we would have a world to leave to you
We remember that time

They are silent
They wait
You look into their eyes, you breathe deep
   and it's as if you knew the world they speak about

You feel its fear seep into your blood
  and you feel also something else
  a memory of strength, of courage
Look at the old ones
See the power in those old eyes and frail, cupped hands
Breathe it in
Know it is your own power, too
You are of them
They live in you as you in them
  and you marvel at them
How did they survive? How did they stand it?
They wait
You realize they are waiting for you
  and you wonder what it is they want you to do
And you think maybe they want you to ask them
  something
So you say
    Tell me, old ones
    How did you do it?
    How did you change it?
And they smile

Listen
Hear what they say to you

    We struggled
    We held out our hands and touched each other
    We remembered to laugh
    We went to endless meetings
    We said no
    We put our bodies on the line
    We said yes
    We invented, we created
    We walked straight through our fears
    We formed the circle
    We danced

    We spoke the truth
    We dared to live it

Notes

Chapter 1: Truth or Dare

1. The Christian devil is a construct of Christian theology. To believe in the devil or worship Satan, one must, therefore, be a Christian. Pagans do not believe in the devil.
2. Actually, this seems to me a perfect example of what Mary Daly calls the "reversals" of patriarchy. By rights, the word *Witch* should ring with associations of noble martyrdom, healing, and goodness, and the word *Christian* should be the one we fear. Not that there aren't good, loving, and noble Christians—but after all, who burned whom?
3. For more information about the basic history, philosophy, and practice of Witchcraft, see Starhawk, *The Spiral Dance: A Rebirth of the Ancient Religion of the Great Goddess* (San Francisco: Harper & Row, 1979). For a discussion of the Witch persecutions, see Starhawk, *Dreaming the Dark: Magic, Sex and Politics* (Boston: Beacon Press, 1982), 183–219.
4. Alice Miller, *Thou Shalt Not Be Aware: Society's Betrayal of the Child,* trans. Hildegarde and Hunter Hannum (New York: Farrar, Straus & Giroux, 1984), 20.
5. Ibid., 19–20.
6. Stanley Milgram, "Behavioral Study of Obedience," in *The Social Animal,* ed. Elliot Aronson (San Francisco: W. H. Freeman, 1981), 33–34. See also Stanley Milgram, *Obedience to Authority* (New York: Harper & Row, 1969).
7. Quoted in Carol Gilligan, *In a Different Voice* (Cambridge, MA: Harvard University Press, 1982), 15.
8. Carolyn Niethammer, *Daughters of the Earth: The Lives and Legends of American Indian Women* (New York: Collier, 1977), 249.
9. Conrad Arensberg, *The Irish Countryman* (Garden City, NY: Natural History Press, 1968), 123–124.
10. The Fall/Redemption model is not the only one in Christianity. In Christian theology, as in Judaism, a current of religious thought has always existed that stresses and celebrates the sacredness of creation. For a full discussion of the creation-centered tradition in Christianity, see Matthew Fox, *Original Blessing: A Primer in Creation Spirituality* (Santa Fe, NM: Bear & Co., 1983). For examples of earth-centered Jewish celebration, see Arthur Waskow, *Seasons of Our Joy: A Celebration of Modern Jewish Renewal* (Toronto: Bantam, 1982).
11. Margery Wolf, "Chinese Women: Old Skills in a New Context," in *Woman, Culture and Society,* ed. Michelle Z. Rosaldo and Louise Lamphere (Stanford, CA: Stanford University Press, 1974).
12. Perhaps no issue is as fraught with pain and contradiction for radical Jews as the question of Israel. We could look at Jewish history as the history of an earth-based religion practiced for thousands of years by people forcibly removed from their land. The strength of the desire for return, the unlikely realization of the dream of a Jewish state, shows the political power of a spiritual idea. Yet, tragically, that dream has become the Palestinian's nightmare, and those who were themselves dispossessed now dispossess others; those who themselves suffered massacres now perpetrate them.

I was raised with Israel as the great shining ideal of hope and freedom—the justification for all the suffering of the Nazi era. To admit that Israel commits injustices is hard. I would prefer to ignore the whole situation: I would much prefer not to write about it, as I'm sure that anything I say will get me in trouble with someone. And I know that the issue is used now by many to foster anti-Semitism, which is again on the rise.

But Jewish tradition teaches that God acts in history—that history must be our teacher. Researching the history for this book has made it clear to me that war breeds war—and in a culture based on war, no one is secure or free. The best hope, the only hope, for Israel's survival has to be a solution based on real justice for Jews and Palestinians, immigrants and refugees alike.

13. Alice Walker, "Choice: A Tribute to Martin Luther King," *In Search of Our Mothers' Gardens* (San Diego, CA: Harcourt Brace Jovanovich, 1983), 144.
14. Naomi Goldenberg, *Changing of the Gods* (Boston: Beacon Press, 1979), 96.
15. Audre Lorde, "The Master's Tools Will Never Dismantle the Master's House," *Sister Outsider* (Trumansburg, NY: Crossing Press, 1984).
16. Gertrude and Rubin Blanck, *Ego Psychology: Theory and Practice* (New York: Columbia University Press, 1974), 101.
17. Personal communication, Sister José Habday, August 1984.
18. Luisah Teish, *Jambalaya: The Natural Woman's Book of Personal Charms and Practical Rituals* (San Francisco: Harper & Row, 1985), 63.
19. Personal communication from Kathleen Adkins, September 1984.
20. Teish, *Jambalaya*, 56.

Chapter 2: The Dismembering of the World

1. Carol Christ, *Laughter of Aphrodite: Reflections on a Journey to the Goddess* (San Francisco: Harper & Row, 1987), 162–165.
2. The assumption made by some Jungians (and others) that we of modern Western culture are more individuated than peoples of the past or of tribal cultures today is perhaps an example of how sheep look different to other sheep. It perpetuates the racist assumption that people of the First World are somehow more sensitive, more differentiated, more "real," and more valued than those of other cultures, and hence entitled to a larger share of the world's resources and rewards.
3. Gerda Lerner, *The Creation of Patriarchy* (New York: Oxford University Press, 1986), 52.
4. Hunting and gathering societies, being nomadic, do not hoard material goods, and stress sharing as an obligation. Most practice a division of labor in which men hunt and women gather. But women retain power and status because their economic contribution is central to survival. "Most hunting-gathering populations could not be maintained without it, whereas they can and do go for long periods without meat," writes Elman R. Service in *The Hunters* (Englewood Cliffs, NJ: Prentice-Hall, 1966), 10.

    For a discussion of the meaning of the prehistoric goddess figures, see Anne Barstow, "The Prehistoric Goddess," in *The Book of the Goddess: Past and Present*, ed. Carl Olson (New York: Crossroad, 1985), 7–16. And see Adrienne Rich, *Of Woman Born: Motherhood as Experience and Institution* (New York: Bantam, 1977), 80–81.
5. Robert J. Braidwood suggests that "around 8000 B.C. the inhabitants of the hills around the fertile crescent had come to know their habitat so well that they were beginning to domesticate the plants and animals they had been collecting and hunting." Robert J. Braidwood, "The Agricultural Revolution," in *Scientific American: Hunters, Farmers and Civilizations: Old World Archaeology* (San Francisco: W. H. Freeman, 1979), 94. His article was written in 1960: since that time, new discoveries and dating techniques have tended to push the origins of agriculture farther back in time, so this is a conservative estimate.
6. See: *Introduction to Anthropology*. ed. Ralph L. Beals, Henry Hoijer, and Alan R. Beals (New York: MacMillan Publishing Co., 1977).
7. The development of animal breeding in this era tells us that people must have known

about the male role in procreation. Clearly, the discovery of fatherhood could not alone have precipitated the transition to patriarchy.

8. I use the designation B.C.E. meaning Before the Common Era, as a substitute for B.C., Before Christ; and I use C.E., meaning Common Era, as a substitute for A.D., Anno Domini.

9. James Mellaart, *Earliest Civilizations of the Near East* (New York: McGraw-Hill, 1965), 84.

10. James Mellaart, "A Neolithic City in Turkey," in *Scientific American: Hunters, Farmers and Civilizations: Old World Archaeology* (San Francisco: W. H. Freeman, 1979), 131.

11. Mellaart, "A Neolithic City," 130.

12. Marija Gimbutas defines Old Europe as the complex of cultures extending from the Aegean and Adriatic seas as far as Czechoslovakia, southern Poland, and the western Ukraine between about 7000 and 3500 B.C.E. See Marija Gimbutas, *The Goddesses and Gods of Old Europe: Myths and Cult Images* (Berkeley, CA: University of California Press, 1982), 17.

13. For the most comprehensive discussion of women's status in Çatal Hüyük, see James Mellaart, *Çatal Hüyük, a Neolithic Town in Anatolia* (New York: MacGraw-Hill, 1967).

14. Mellaart, "A Neolithic City," 132.

15. Ruby Rohrlich, "State Formation in Sumer and the Subjugation of Women," *Feminist Studies* 6 (Spring 1980): 79.

16. Mellaart, *Earliest Civilizations*, 126–31. See also Robert M. Adams, "The Origin of Cities," in *Scientific American: Hunters, Farmers and Civilizations: Old World Archaeology* (San Francisco: W. H. Freeman, 1979), 175.

17. Rohrlich, "State Formation in Sumer," 88.

18. Mellaart, *Earliest Civilizations*, 129.

19. Rohrlich, "State Formation in Sumer," 80.

20. Mellaart, *Earliest Civilizations*, 132.

21. Adams, "The Origin of Cities," 173.

22. Rohrlich, "State Formation in Sumer," 81.

23. Ibid., 87.

24. Merlin Stone, *When God Was a Woman* (New York: Harcourt Brace Jovanovich, 1976), 40. Myths, religious rites and litanies were not written down until a later era, when the transition to patriarchy was already underway, perhaps as an attempt to preserve traditions that might have been lost in times of societal upheaval. Later, writing and codifying texts became a way of "fixing" elements and interpretations that supported the consolidation of power in the hands of upper-class males.

25. Rohrlich, "State Formation in Sumer," 88.

26. Ibid., 85.

27. Thorkild Jacobsen, *The Treasures of Darkness* (New Haven: Yale University Press, 1976), 104.

28. Rohrlich, "State Formation in Sumer," 86.

29. Jacobsen, *Treasures of Darkness*, 36.

30. Judith Ochshorn, *The Female Experience and the Nature of the Divine* (Bloomington: University of Indiana Press, 1981), 89.

31. Rohrlich, "State Formation in Sumer," 34.

32. Adams, "The Origin of Cities," 175.

33. Rohrlich, "State Formation in Sumer," 95.

34. Andrew B. Schmookler, *The Parable of the Tribes* (Boston: Houghton Miflin, 1984), 42.

35. Adams, "The Origin of Cities," 175.

36. See Lerner, *The Creation of Patriarchy*; Rohrlich, "State Formation in Sumer"; and Merlin Stone, *When God Was a Woman* (New York: Harcourt Brace Jovanovich, 1976).

37. This dating comes from Jacobsen, *Treasures of Darkness*.

38. Ibid., 6.

39. Ibid., 26.
40. Ibid., 36.
41. Ibid., 44.
42. Ibid., 47.
43. Ibid., 45, 46.
44. Perhaps missing texts exist that sing the glories of birth control?
45. Jacobsen, *Treasures of Darkness*, 46.
46. Diane Wolkstein and Samuel Noah Kramer, *Inanna, Queen of Heaven and Earth: Her Stories and Hymns from Sumer* (New York: Harper & Row, 1983), 38–39. (Although this work paraphrases some of the ancient texts, I have occasionally referred to it when their variations added poetic qualities without changing the sense of the source material.)
47. Jacobsen, *Treasures of Darkness*, 44.
48. Ibid., 40–41.
49. Wolkstein and Kramer, *Inanna*, 44–45.
50. Jacobsen, *Treasures of Darkness*, 36.
51. Ibid., 48.
52. Ibid., 50.
53. Ibid., 48.
54. Ibid., 62.
55. Personal communication with Marija Gimbutas. In all fairness, she said that she believes from the evidence of folk tales that human sacrifice was practiced in prepatriarchal times, but conceded that no archaeological evidence supports this.
56. C. Leonard Wooley, *The Sumerians* (New York: W. W. Norton, 1965), 39.
57. Lerner, *The Creation of Patriarchy*, 61.
58. Wooley, *The Sumerians*, 40.
59. Jacobsen, *Treasures of Darkness*, 195.
60. Ibid., 208–15.
61. Adams, "The Origin of Cities," 176.
62. N. K. Sandars, ed., *The Epic of Gilgamesh* (Harmondsworth, Middlesex: Penguin, 1960), 62.
63. Merlin Stone suggests that Gilgamesh himself may have been an invading conqueror from a tribe more warlike and patriarchal than the indigenous Sumerians. See Stone, *When God Was a Woman*, 140–41.
64. Sandars, *Gilgamesh*, 63–64.
65. Ibid., 64.
66. Ibid., 65.
67. Ibid., 68.
68. Ibid., 66.
69. Ibid., 76–77.
70. Rohrlich, "State Formation in Sumer," 91.
71. Gwynne Dyer, *War* (New York: Crown, 1985), 6.
72. Ibid., 36.
73. Ibid.
74. Ibid., 36–37.
75. Jacques Boudet, ed., *The Ancient Art of Warfare, Vol. 1: 1300 B.C. to 1650 A.D.* (London: Barrie & Rocklitte, 1969), 30–31.
76. Samuel Kramer, *The Sumerians: Their History, Culture, and Character* (Chicago: University of Chicago Press, 1963), 104.
77. Dyer, *War*, 127.
78. J. Glenn Gray, *The Warriors* (New York: Harper & Row, 1967), 40.
79. Wolkstein and Kramer, *Inanna*, 81.
80. Shepherd Bliss, "The Enemy: A Vet Looks Back," *Awakening in the Nuclear Age Journal* 11 (Fall 1985): 9.
81. Dyer, *War*, 123.
82. Homer, *The Iliad*, trans. E. V. Rieu (Baltimore: Penguin, 1950), 27.
83. Ibid., 28.

84. Rohrlich, "State Formation in Sumer," 95.
85. Kramer, *The Sumerians*, 253.
86. Lerner, *The Creation of Patriarchy*, 89.
87. Sandars, *Gilgamesh*, 85.
88. Ibid., 86–87.
89. Jacobsen, *Treasures of Darkness*, 42.
90. Ibid.
91. Ibid.
92. Ibid., 31.
93. Wolkstein and Kramer, *Inanna*, 45.
94. Rohrlich, "State Formation in Sumer," 86.
95. Ibid., 91.
96. Ibid.
97. Ibid.
98. Ibid., 86.
99. Stone, *When God Was a Woman*, 157.
100. Kramer, *The Sumerians*, 338.
101. Rohrlich, "State Formation in Sumer," 91.
102. Susan Brownmiller, *Against Our Will: Women, Men and Rape* (New York: Bantam, 1975), 28.
103. Edward S. Hyams, *Soil and Civilization* (New York: Harper & Row, 1976), 63.
104. Ibid., 64. See also Marshall Massey, "Carrying Capacity and the Greek Dark Ages," *Coevolution Quarterly*, Winter 1983, 29–35.
105. Sandars, *Gilgamesh*, 86.
106. Ibid., 117.
107. James B. Pritchard, *The Ancient Near East, Vol. 1: An Anthology of Texts and Pictures* (Princeton, NJ: Princeton University Press, 1958), 31.
108. Jacobsen, *Treasures of Darkness*, 167.
109. Ibid., 170.
110. Ibid., 171.
111. Ibid., 174.
112. Gimbutas, *Goddesses and Gods of Old Europe*, 144–45.
113. Gray, *The Warriors*, 133.
114. Lerner, *The Creation of Patriarchy*, 77.
115. Pritchard, *The Ancient Near East*, 34.
116. Jacobsen, *Treasures of Darkness*, 190.
117. Ibid., 180.
118. Pritchard, *The Ancient Near East*, 35.
119. Ibid., 33.
120. Jacobsen, *Treasures of Darkness*, 180.
121. Pritchard, *The Ancient Near East*, 32.
122. Jacobsen, *Treasures of Darkness*, 101.
123. Kramer, *The Sumerians*, 322.
124. Jacobsen, *Treasures of Darkness*, 176. A variant translation is found in Pritchard, *The Ancient Near East*, 32: "Open thy mouth: the cloth will vanish!"
125. Doris Lessing, *The Four-Gated City* (New York: Bantam, 1970), 522–23.

Chapter 3: Fierce Love:
Resisting the Weapons the Culture Has Devised Against the Self

1. Michel Foucault, *Discipline and Punish: The Birth of the Prison*, trans. Alan Sheridan (New York: Vintage, 1979), 183.
2. Craig Haney, Curtis Banks, and Philip Zimbardo, "A Study of Prisoners and Guards in a Simulated Prison," in *The Social Animal*, ed. Elliot Aronson (San Francisco: W. H. Freeman, 1981), 52–68. See also Craig Haney and Philip Zimbardo, "The Socialization into Criminality: On Becoming a Prisoner and a Guard," in *Law, Justice and the*

Individual in Society: Psychological and Legal Issues, ed. June Tapp and Felice J. Levine (New York: Holt, Rinehart & Winston, 1977), 198–223.

3. Solomon E. Asch, "Opinions and Social Pressure," in *The Social Animal,* 13–23.
4. J. Glenn Gray, *The Warriors* (New York: Harper & Row, 1967), 175.
5. Haney and Zimbardo, "The Socialization into Criminality."
6. Terence Des Pres, *The Survivor: An Anatomy of Life in the Death Camps* (Oxford: Oxford University Press, 1976), 59.
7. Stanley, Milgram, *Obedience to Authority* (New York: Harper & Row, 1974), 88.
8. Haney and Zimbardo, "The Socialization into Criminality," 214.
9. Ibid.
10. Ibid., 214–215.
11. Gray, *The Warriors,* 184–85.
12. Haney and Zimbardo, "The Socialization into Criminality," 215.
13. Des Pres, *The Survivor,* 82–83.
14. Ibid., 85.
15. Ibid., 88.
16. Bruno Bettelheim, *The Informed Heart: Autonomy in a Mass Age* (New York: Avon, 1960), 152–53.
17. Des Pres, *The Survivor,* 87.
18. Ibid.
19. Kelly Girl, "Kelly Call Girl," *Processed World* 13:18.
20. Ibid., 19.
21. Sharon Wegscheider, *Another Chance: Hope and Health for the Alcoholic Family* (Palo Alto, CA: Science and Behavior Books, 1981), 104–05. Claudia Black, in *It Will Never Happen to Me* (Denver, CO: M.A.C. Publications, 1981), provides a slightly different set of descriptive terms: the Responsible One, the Placater, the Acting Out child, and get fourth and page reference.
22. Black, *It Will Never Happen to Me,* 31–52.

Chapter 4: Unraveling and Reweaving: Pattern and Ritual

1. Christopher Alexander, *The Timeless Way of Building* (New York: Oxford University Press, 1979), 210.
2. Ibid., 209.
3. Ibid., 14.
4. More detail about ritual structure and forms can be found in Starhawk, *The Spiral Dance: A Rebirth of the Ancient Religion of the Great Goddess* (San Francisco: Harper & Row, 1979).
5. For variations on their meditation, see also: Starhawk, *The Spiral Dance,* 43–44, 49; and Starhawk, *Dreaming the Dark: Magic, Sex, and Politics* (Boston: Beacon Press, 1982), 161–62.
6. Starhawk, *The Spiral Dance,* 149–50.

Chapter 5: The Sacred Spark: Reclaiming Value from the Judge

1. James B. Pritchard, *The Ancient Near East, Vol. 1: An Anthology of Texts and Pictures* (Princeton, NJ: Princeton University Press, 1958), 150.
2. Traditional liturgy, "The Charge of the Goddess," written by Doreen Valiente.
3. Michel Foucault, *Discipline and Punish: The Birth of the Prison,* trans. Alan Sheridan (New York: Vintage, 1979), 200.
4. Ibid., 201.
5. Kim Chernin, *The Obsession: Reflections on the Tyranny of Slenderness* (New York: Harper & Row, 1981), 7.
6. I don't know why we started calling this process "talk—story," but we do.
7. *Twelve Steps and Twelve Traditions* (New York: AA World Services, 1952), 139–40.

8. Ibid., 141.
9. Alice Miller, *For Your Own Good: Hidden Cruelty in Child-rearing and the Roots of Violence*, trans. Hildegarde and Hunter Hannum (New York: Farrar, Straus & Giroux, 1983), 4.
10. J. Sulzer, "Versuch von der Erziehung und Unterweisung der Kinder" [An Essay on the Education and Instruction of Children] (1748), quoted in Miller, *For Your Own Good*, xviii–xvix.
11. Miller, *For Your Own Good*, 8.
12. Perhaps this analogy is unfair to fungi, who, after all, are fulfilling their own useful ecological niche. I'm sorry, fungi. Please don't send me any letters about this.
13. The founders of the New Alchemy Institute credit Saul Mendlovitz of the World Policy Institute with posing this question. Their answer was to institute a project designing wind-powered, easily constructed, low-cost fishing vessels for Third World countries. A description of the project can be found in Nancy Jack Todd and John Todd, *Bio-shelters, Ocean Arks, and City Farming: Ecology as the Basis of Design* (San Francisco: Sierra Club Books, 1984), 32–44.

Chapter 6: Risking the Boundaries: Dethroning the Conqueror

1. Shepherd Bliss, "The Enemy: A Vet Looks Back," *Awakening in the Nuclear Age Journal* 11 (Fall 1985): 8.
2. J. Glenn Gray, *The Warriors* (New York: Harper & Row, 1967), 131–32.
3. Ibid., 146.
4. Ibid., 133.
5. William Broyles, Jr., "Why Men Love War," *Esquire*, November 1984, 61.
6. Angela Davis, *Women, Race and Class* (New York: Vintage, 1983), 185.
7. Susan Griffin, *Pornography and Silence: Culture's Revenge against Nature* (New York: Harper & Row, 1981), 49.
8. See also "Safe Space Spell" and "Spell to Know the Child Within," Starhawk, *The Spiral Dance: A Rebirth of the Ancient Religion of the Great Goddess* (San Francisco: Harper & Row, 1979), 120–21.
9. *Twelve Steps and Twelve Traditions* (New York: AA World Services, 1952), 17.
10. The Abalone Alliance nonviolence guidelines, from which the Livermore Action Group took its guidelines, are:

    1. Our attitude will be one of openness, friendliness, and respect toward all people we encounter.
    2. We will use no violence, physical or verbal, toward any person.
    3. We will not damage any property.
    4. We will not bring or use any drugs or alcohol other than for medicinal purposes.
    5. We will not run.
    6. We will carry no weapons.

    Diablo Canyon Blockade Encampment Handbook (San Luis Obispo, CA: Abalone Alliance, 1981), 6.
11. Griffin, *Pornography and Silence*, 47.
12. Broyles, "Why Men Love War," 61–62.
13. *Twelve Steps*, 21.
14. Ibid.
15. Ibid., 6–8.
16. Anne Cameron, *Daughters of Copper Woman* (Vancouver: Press Gang, 1981), 133–35.

Chapter 7: Finding a Voice: Breaking the Censor's Silence

1. Claudia Black, *It Will Never Happen to Me* (Denver, CO: M.A.C. Publications, 1981), 34.

2. Alice Miller, *Thou Shalt Not Be Aware: Society's Betrayal of the Child,* trans. Hildegarde and Hunter Hannum (New York: Farrar, Straus & Giroux, 1984), 119.

3. Sandy Butler, *Conspiracy of Silence: The Trauma of Incest* (San Francisco: Volcano Press, 1978), 147–48.

4. Ibid., 39.

5. *Twelve Steps and Twelve Traditions* (New York: AA World Services, 1952), 55.

6. Ibid., 56–57.

7. Carol Christ, *Diving Deep and Surfacing: Women Writers on Spiritual Quest* (Boston: Beacon Press, 1980), 1.

8. William Hinton, *Fanshen* (New York: Vintage, 1966), 132–33.

9. An excellent resource on consensus and feminist process is: Virginia Coover, Charles Esser, Ellen Deacon, and Christopher Moore, *Resource Manual for a Living Revolution* (Philadelphia: New Society Publishers, 1978), available from New Society Publishers, 4722 Baltimore Ave., Philadelphia, PA 19143.

10. I learned this from Cerridwen Fallingstar, who learned it from her mother.

11. Paulo Freire, *Pedagogy of the Oppressed,* trans. Myra Bergman Ramos (New York: Continuum, 1981).

12. Alice Walker, "On Writing *The Color Purple,*" In *Search of Our Mothers' Gardens* (San Diego, CA: Harcourt Brace Jovanovich, 1983), 359.

Chapter 8: Creating Sustainable Culture:
Serving No Masters

1. Thorkild Jacobsen, *The Treasures of Darkness* (New Haven: Yale University Press, 1976), 181.

2. Quoted in Gwynne Dyer, *War* (New York: Crown, 1985), 141.

3. In World War II, officer casualties were approximately twice as high as those of lower ranks. See Dyer, *War,* 141.

4. Lisa Leghorn and Katherine Parker, *Woman's Worth: Sexual Economics and the World of Women* (Boston: Routledge & Kegan Paul, 1981), 179.

5. Ibid., 28.

6. Louisa May Alcott, *Work* (New York: Schocken Books, 1977), 19.

7. Leghorn and Parker, *Woman's Worth,* 184.

8. Gerda Lerner, *The Creation of Patriarchy* (New York: Oxford University Press, 1986), 89.

9. Sigmund Freud, "The Transformations of Puberty," *The Basic Writings of Sigmund Freud,* trans. A. A. Brill (New York: Modern Library, 1938), 612.

10. Quoted in Sandy Butler, *Conspiracy of Silence: The Trauma of Incest* (San Francisco: Volcano Press, 1978), 83.

11. Ibid., 73.

12. Butler cites statistics showing that half to three-quarters of men serving time in prison for sex offenses were themselves victims of abuse. See Butler, *Conspiracy of Silence,* 67. This still raises questions: since most abuse is male to female, what happens to all the abused female children who presumably do not grow up to be abusers? It seems that childhood abuse may instill the Master/Servant pattern, but whether one then is more likely to act out the role of abuser or continues as victim may be a function of gender roles.

13. Susan Brownmiller, *Against Our Will: Women, Men and Rape* (New York: Bantam, 1975), 23.

14. Butler, *Conspiracy of Silence,* 54.

15. Susan Griffin, *Pornography and Silence: Culture's Revenge against Nature* (New York: Harper & Row, 1981), 204–5.

16. Ibid., 215.

17. Ibid., 216.

18. *Twelve Steps and Twelve Traditions* (New York: AA World Services, 1952), 106.

19. Ibid., 106–17.

20. Lewis Hyde, *The Gift: Imagination and the Erotic Life of Property* (New York: Vintage, 1983), 4.
21. Ibid., 47.
22. Marshall Massey, "Carrying Capacity and the Greek Dark Ages," *Co-Evolution Quarterly*, Winter 1983, 35.
23. Bryce and Margaret Muir, "Where've You Been, Stranger? Disintermediation in the Maritimes," *Co-Evolution Quarterly*, Summer 1981, 77.
24. Ibid., 76.
25. Edward S. Hyams, *Soil and Civilization* (New York: Harper & Row, 1976) 24–32.
26. *Twelve Steps*, 17.
27. My understanding of permaculture has been influenced by discussions with Sago of the Permaculture Institute, Seattle, Washington, and Susan Davidson of Community Alternatives, Alder Grove, British Columbia. See also John Quinney, "Designing Sustainable Small Farms and Homesteads," *Mother Earth News* 88 (July-August 1984), 54–65.
28. This project was described to me by organizer Dennis Livingstone, whose ideas influenced this section.
29. Quinney, "Designing Sustainable Small Farms and Homesteads," 57.
30. Discussions with Bill Moyer helped me formulate ideas about succession and group development. See Bill Moyer, "The Movement Action Plan," *The Dandelion: Newsletter of Movement for a New Society* (Fall 1986).

Chapter 9: Evoking Mystery:
Restoring Organic Order

1. Gwynne Dyer, *War* (New York: Crown, 1985), 136.
2. David Kubrin, "The War Against the Earth," *The Ley Hunter* 100, (Winter/Spring 1986), 8.
3. Gelsey Kirkland (with Gene Lawrence), *Dancing on My Grave* (Garden City, NY: Doubleday, 1986), 55–56.
4. Ibid., 33.
5. Ibid., 45.
6. See also "The Mirror," in Starhawk, *Dreaming the Dark: Magic, Sex and Politics* (Boston: Beacon Press, 1982), 147; and "Spell to Be Friends with your Womb," in Starhawk, *The Spiral Dance: A Rebirth of the Ancient Religion of the Great Goddess* (San Francisco: Harper & Row, 1979), 121.
7. For a discussion of the physical component of alcoholism, see James Milam, Robert Ketcham and Katherine Ketcham, *Under the Influence* (Seattle: Madrona Publications, 1981).
8. *Alcoholics Anonymous* (New York: AA World Services, 1976), 433.
9. Ibid., 443.
10. Ibid., 375.
11. Ibid., 435.
12. Quoted in Claudia Black, *It Will Never Happen to Me* (Denver, CO: M.A.C. Publications, 1981), 9.
13. Ibid., 17.
14. John Keegan, *The Face of Battle* (New York: Viking, 1976), 326.
15. *Twelve Steps and Twelve Traditions* (New York: AA World Services, 1952), 5, 21.
16. Ibid., 5.
17. Alice Walker, "On Writing *The Color Purple*," *In Search of Our Mothers' Gardens* (San Diego, CA: Harcourt Brace Jovanovich, 1983), 356.
18. Ibid., 358–59.

Chapter 10: Toward Community:
Structure and Leadership in Groups

1. This chant was created in a workshop I led with the Institute for Culture and Creation Spirituality at Omega Center, New York, in 1985.

2. Bill Moyer proposes eight stages for social movements in "The Movement Action Plan." *The Dandelion: Newsletter of Movement for a New Society* (Fall 1986).
3. See Starhawk, *Dreaming the Dark: Magic, Sex and Politics* (Boston: Beacon, 1982), 128–30.

Chapter 11: Ritual to Build Community

1. A beautiful description of a womanhood ritual for a young girl is found in Carol Christ, *Laughter of Aphrodite: Reflections on a Journey to the Goddess* (San Francisco: Harper & Row, 1987) 192–199.

Chapter 12: Toward Renewal

1. This material draws on the work of the WomanEarth Feminist Peace Institute, especially the learning and struggles I experienced as part of the core collective in 1985. Discussions with Rachel Bagby and Isis Coble also helped shape this section.
2. The program I refer to, sponsored by the Institute for Culture and Creation Spirituality, offers both a one-year master's degree program in religious studies and a series of summer workshops. It is based at Holy Names College in Oakland, California. See Resources.
3. To develop these questions, I drew on experiences with two excellent facilitators: Mary Arnold, to whom I will forever be grateful for teaching me to say, "That's not my problem—that's *your* problem!" and Lily Alan of the National Black Women's Health Network.
4. Jane Jacobs, *Death and Life of Great American Cities* (New York: Vintage, 1961), 81.
5. Ibid., 87.
6. Wendell Berry, *The Gift of Good Land* (San Francisco: North Point Press, 1981), xii.
7. Frances Moore Lappé and Joseph Collins, *World Hunger: Twelve Myths* (New York: Grove Press, 1986) 4.
8. Nancy Jack Todd and John Todd, *Bioshelters, Ocean Arks, City Farming: Ecology as the Basis for Design* (San Francisco: Sierra Club Books, 1984).
9. For considerations about economic relations between developed and underdeveloped countries, see Jacobs's discussion of "Why Backward Cities Need Each Other," in Jacobs, *Cities and the Wealth of Nations* (New York: Random House, 1984), 134–56.
10. Christopher Alexander, Sara Ishikawa, and Murray Silverstein, *A Pattern Language* (New York: Oxford University Press, 1977), 426–30.
11. Buck Ghosthorse of the Institute for Culture and Creation. Spirituality taught me about the Hopi prophecies.
12. Similar systems are described in Todd and Todd, *Bioshelters, Ocean Arks and City Farming*, 98–105.
13. This is my vision—if you want a sugarless, dairyless, carob-ridden future, go make one of your own. And don't send me any letters.
14. An excellent resource for stategy exercises is Virginia Coover, Charles Esser, Ellen Deacon, and Christopher Moore, *Resource Manual for a Living Revolution* (Philadelphia: New Society Publishers, 1978).

Bibliography

Adair, Margo. *Working Inside Out: Tools for Change.* Berkeley, CA: Wingbow Press, 1984.

Adams, Robert M. "The Origin of Cities." In *Scientific American: Hunters, Farmers and Civilizations: Old World Archaeology.* San Francisco: W. H. Freeman, 1979.

Adelman, Penina. *Miriams Well: Rituals for Jewish Women Around the Year.* Fresh Meadows, NY: Biblio Press, 1986.

Adler, Margot. *Drawing Down the Moon.* Boston: Beacon Press, 1986.

Adorno, T. W., Elsa Frenkel-Brunswik, Daniel J. Levinson, and R. Nevitt Sanford. *The Authoritarian Personality.* New York: Science Editions, 1964.

Alcoholics Anonymous. New York: AA World Services, 1976.

Alcott, Louisa May. *Work.* New York: Schocken Books, 1977.

Alexander, Christopher. *The Timeless Way of Building.* New York: Oxford University Press, 1979.

Alexander, Christopher, Sara Ishikawa, and Murray Silverstein. *A Pattern Language.* New York: Oxford University Press, 1977.

Arendt, Hannah. *The Origins of Totalitarianism.* San Diego, CA: Harcourt Brace Jovanovich, 1973.

Arensberg, Conrad. *The Irish Countryman.* Garden City, NY: Natural History Press, 1968.

Asch, Solomon E. "Opinions and Social Pressure." In *The Social Animal,* ed. Elliot Aronson. San Francisco: W. H. Freeman, 1981.

Barstow, Anne. "The Prehistoric Goddess." In *The Book of the Goddess: Past and Present,* ed. Carl Olson. New York: Crossroad, 1985.

Beals, Ralph L., Henry Hoijer and Alan R. Beals, eds. *Introduction to Anthropology.* New York: MacMillan Publishing Co., 1977.

Berry, Wendell. *A Continuous Harmony: Essays Cultural and Agricultural.* San Diego, CA: Harcourt Brace Jovanovich, 1970.

———. *The Gift of Good Land.* San Francisco: North Point Press, 1981.

Bettelheim, Bruno. *The Informed Heart: Autonomy in a Mass Age.* New York: Avon, 1960.

Black, Claudia. *It Will Never Happen to Me.* Denver, CO: M.A.C. Publications, 1981.

———. *Repeat after Me.* Denver, CO: M.A.C. Publications, 1985.

Blanck, Gertrude and Rubin. *Ego Psychology: Theory and Practice.* New York: Columbia University Press, 1974.

Bliss, Shepherd. "The Enemy: A Vet Looks Back." *Awakening in the Nuclear Age Journal* 11 (Fall 1985): 8–12.

Bookchin, Murray. *Post-Scarcity Anarchism*. Montreal: Black Rose Books, 1971.

_____. *The Ecology of Freedom*. Palo Alto, CA: Cheshire Books, 1982.

Boudet, Jacques, ed. *The Ancient Art of Warfare, Vol 1: 1300 B.C. to 1650 A.D.* London: Barrie & Rockcliffe, 1969.

Braidwood, Linda. *Digging Beyond the Tigris*. New York: Henry Schuman, 1953.

Braidwood, Robert J. "The Agricultural Revolution." In *Scientific American: Hunters, Farmers and Civilizations: Old World Archaeology*. San Francisco: W. H. Freeman, 1979.

Brownmiller, Susan. *Against Our Will: Women, Men and Rape*. New York: Bantam, 1975.

Broyles, William, Jr. "Why Men Love War." *Esquire,* November 1984, 55–66.

Butler, Sandy. *Conspiracy of Silence: The Trauma of Incest*. San Francisco: Volcano Press, 1978.

Caldecott, Leonie & Stephanie Leacock. *Reclaim the Earth: Women Speak Out for Life on Earth*. London: The Women's Press, 1983.

Califia, Pat. "Jessie." In *Coming to Power*, ed. Samois Collective. San Francisco: Samois, 1981.

_____. "Feminism and Sado-Masochism." *Co-Evolution Quarterly,* Spring 1982, 37.

Cameron, Anne. *Daughters of Copper Woman*. Vancouver: Press Gang, 1981.

Capra, Fritjof, and Charlene Spretnak, in collaboration with Rudiger Lutz. *Green Politics*. New York: E. P. Dutton, 1984.

Center for Conflict Resolution. *Manual for Group Facilitators*. Madison, WI: New Society Publishers, 1977.

Chagnon, Napoleon A. *Yanomamo: The Fierce People*. New York: Holt, Rinehart & Winston, 1983.

Chaliand, Gerard, ed. *Guerrilla Strategies: An Historical Anthology from the Long March to Afghanistan*. Berkeley: University of California Press, 1982.

Chernin, Kim. *The Obsession: Reflections on the Tyranny of Slenderness*. New York: Harper & Row, 1981.

_____. *In My Mother's House*. New York: Harper & Row, 1984.

Chesler, Phyllis. *Women and Madness*. New York: Avon, 1972.

Christ, Carol. *Diving Deep and Surfacing: Women Writers on Spiritual Quest*. Boston: Beacon Press, 1980.

_____. *Laughter of Aphrodite: Reflections on a Journey to the Goddess*. San Francisco: Harper & Row, 1987.

Coogan, Tim Pat. *On the Blanket: The H Block Story*. Dublin: Ward River Press, 1980.

Coover, Virginia, Charles Esser, Ellen Deacon, and Christopher Moore. *Resource Manual for a Living Revolution*. Philadelphia: New Society Publishers, 1981.

Daly, Mary. *Gyn/Ecology: The Metaethics of Radical Feminism*. Boston: Beacon Press, 1978.

_____. *Pure Lust: Elemental Feminist Philosophy*. Boston: Beacon Press, 1984.

Davis, Angela. *Women, Race and Class*. New York: Vintage, 1983.

Day, Dorothy. *The Long Loneliness*. San Francisco: Harper & Row, 1981.

Deming, Barbara. *Prison Notes*. Boston: Beacon Press, 1970.

Des Pres, Terrence. *The Survivor: An Anatomy of Life in the Death Camps*. New York: Oxford University Press, 1976.

Diablo Canyon Blockade Encampment Handbook. San Luis Obispo, CA: Abalone Alliance, 1981.

Dupuy, R. Ernest, and Trevor N. Dupuy. *The Encyclopedia of Military History from 3500 B.C. to the Present*. New York: Harper & Row, 1970.

Dworkin, Andrea. *Right-Wing Women*. New York: Perigee Books, 1983.

Dyer, Gwynne. *War*. New York: Crown, 1985.

Ehrlich, Howard J., Carol Ehrlich, David DeLeon, and Glenda Morris. *Reinventing Anarchy: What Are Anarchists Thinking These Days?* London: Routledge & Kegan Paul, 1979.

Engels, Frederick. *The Origin of the Family, Private Property, and the State*. New York: International Publishers, 1942.

Evans, Sara. *Personal Politics: The Roots of Women's Liberation in the Civil Rights Movement and the New Left*. New York: Alfred A. Knopf, 1979.

Falk, Nancy Auer, and Rita M. Gross. *Unspoken Worlds: Women's Religious Lives in Non-Western Cultures*. San Francisco: Harper & Row, 1980.

Fanon, Frantz. *The Wretched of the Earth*. Trans. Constance Farrington. New York: Grove Press, 1963.

Farr, Susan. "The Art of Discipline: Creating Erotic Dramas of Play and Power." In *Coming to Power*, ed. Samois Collective. San Francisco: Samois, 1981.

Festinger, Leon. "Cognitive Dissonance." In *The Social Animal*, ed. Elliot Aronson. San Francisco: W. H. Freeman, 1981.

Fischer, Louis. *Gandhi*. New York: Mentor, 1962.

Flexner, Eleanor. *Century of Struggle: The Woman's Rights Movement in the United States*. New York: Atheneum, 1973.

Flynn, Elizabeth Gurley. *The Alderson Story: My Life as a Political Prisoner*. New York: International Publishers, 1963.

Fortune, Dion. *The Secrets of Dr. Taverner*. St. Paul, MN: Llewellyn, 1962.

———. *The Winged Bull*. London: Aquarian Press, 1971.

———. *Moon Magic*. New York: Samuel Weiser, 1972.

Foucault, Michel. *Discipline and Punish: The Birth of the Prison*. New York: Vintage, 1979.

Fox, Matthew. *Original Blessing: A Primer in Creation Spirituality*. Santa Fe, NM: Bear & Co., 1983.

Freire, Paulo. *Pedagogy of the Oppressed*. Trans. Myra Bergman Ramos. New York: Continuum, 1981.

Freud, Sigmund. *The Basic Writings of Sigmund Freud*. Trans. A. A. Brill. New York: Modern Library, 1938.

Gandhi, Mohandas K. *An Autobiography*. Boston: Beacon Press, 1957.

———. *All Men Are Brothers*. New York: UNESCO, 1958.

Gilligan, Carol. *In a Different Voice*. Cambridge: Harvard University Press, 1982.

Gimbutas, Marija. *The Goddesses and Gods of Old Europe: Myths and Cult Images*. Berkeley, CA: University of California Press, 1982.

Goldenberg, Naomi. *Changing of the Gods*. Boston: Beacon Press, 1979.

Gowan, Susanne, George Lakey, William Moyer, and Richard Taylor. *Moving toward a New Society*. Philadelphia: New Society Publishers, 1976.

Grahn, Judy. *The Work of a Common Woman*. Trumansburg, NY: Crossing Press, 1978.

———. *Another Mother Tongue: Gay Words, Gay Worlds*. Boston: Beacon Press, 1984.

Gray, J. Glenn. *The Warriors*. New York: Harper & Row, 1967.

Green, Hannah. *I Never Promised You a Rose Garden*. New York: Signet, 1964.

Griffin, Susan. *Woman and Nature: The Roaring Inside Her*. New York: Harper & Row, 1978.

———. *Rape: The Power of Consciousness*. New York: Harper & Row, 1979.

———. *Pornography and Silence: Culture's Revenge against Nature*. New York: Harper & Row, 1981.

———. *Made from This Earth*. New York: Harper & Row, 1982.

Grossinger, Richard, and Linda Hough. *Nuclear Strategy and the Code of the Warrior: Faces of Mars and Shiva in the Crisis of Human Survival*. Berkeley, CA: North Atlantic Books, 1984.

Halifax, Joan. *Shamanic Voices*. New York: E. P. Dutton, 1979.

Haney, Craig, and Philip Zimbardo. "The Socialization into Criminality: On Becoming a Prisoner and a Guard." *Law, Justice and the Individual in Society: Psychological and Legal Issues*, ed. J. Tapp and F. Levine. 1977.

Haney, Craig, Curtis Banks, and Philip Zimbardo. "A Study of Prisoners and Guards in a Simulated Prison." In *The Social Animal*, ed. Elliot Aronson. San Francisco: W. H. Freeman, 1981.

Harner, Michael. *The Way of the Shaman: A Guide to Power and Healing*. New York: Bantam, 1980.

Harp, Carl. *Love and Rage: Entries in a Prison Diary*. Vancouver: Pulp Press, 1981.

Harragan, Betty L. *Games Mother Never Taught You: Corporate Gamesmanship for Women*. New York: Warner, 1977.

Hawken, Paul. *The Next Economy*. New York: Ballantine, 1983.

Heidel, Alexander. *The Babylonian Genesis: The Story of Creation*. Chicago: University of Chicago Press, 1963.

Hennig, Margaret, and Anne Jardim. *The Managerial Woman*. New York: Pocket Books, 1977.

Hertz, J. H., ed. *The Soncino Edition of the Pentateuch and Haftorahs*. London: Soncino Press, 1964.

Hinton, William. *Fanshen*. New York: Vintage, 1966.

Holy Bible: King James Version. Nashville, TN: Thomas Nelson, 1977.

Homer. *The Iliad*. Trans. E. V. Rieu. Baltimore: Penguin, 1950.

Howard, Michael, ed. *The Theory and Practice of War*. Bloomington: Indiana University Press, 1965.

Hurley, Judith. "From Argentina to Iowa: The Global Farm Debt Crisis." Excerpted from *Who Owes Whom Newsletter* in *Utne Reader*, Oct./Nov. 1986, 98–106.

Hurston, Zora Neale. *Dust Tracks on a Road: An Autobiography*. Urbana: University of Illinois Press, 1984.

Hyams, Edward. *Soil and Civilization*, New York: Harper & Row, 1976.

Hyde, Lewis. *The Gift: Imagination and the Erotic Life of Property*. New York: Vintage, 1983.

Iglehart, Hallie Austen. *Womanspirit: A Guide to Women's Wisdom.* San Francisco: Harper & Row, 1983.

Jacobs, Jane. *The Death and Life of Great American Cities.* New York: Vintage, 1961.

————. *The Economy of Cities.* New York: Vintage, 1970.

————. *Cities and the Wealth of Nations: Principles of Economic Life.* New York: Random House, 1984.

Jacobsen, Thorkild. *The Treasures of Darkness.* New Haven: Yale University Press, 1976.

Jaggar, Alison M., and Paula Rothenberg Struhl, eds. *Feminist Frameworks: Alternative Theoretical Accounts of the Relations between Women and Men.* New York: McGraw-Hill, 1978.

Jones, Mary Harris. *The Autobiography of Mother Jones.* Chicago: Charles H. Kerr, 1980.

Kagan, Paul. *New World Utopias: A Photographic History of the Search for Community.* New York: Penguin Books, 1975.

Kanter, Rosabeth Moss. *Men and Women of the Corporation.* New York: Basic Books, 1977.

Keegan, John. *The Face of Battle.* New York: Viking, 1976.

Kelly Girl. "Kelly Call Girl." *Processed World* 13:18.

Kirkland, Gelsey (with Gene Lawrence). *Dancing on My Grave.* Garden City, NY: Doubleday, 1986.

Kogon, Eugen. *The Theory and Practice of Hell.* Trans. Henry Norden. New York: Farrar, Straus & Giroux, 1949.

Konopka, Gisela. *The Adolescent Girl in Conflict.* Englewood Cliffs, NJ: Prentice-Hall, 1966.

Kramer, Samuel Noah. *History Begins at Sumer.* New York: Doubleday, 1959.

————. *The Sumerians: Their History, Culture, and Character.* Chicago: University of Chicago Press, 1963.

————. "The Sumerians." In *Scientific American: Hunters, Farmers and Civilizations: Old World Archaeology.* San Francisco: W. H. Freeman, 1979.

Kropotkin, Peter. *Kropotkin's Revolutionary Pamphlets.* New York: Benjamin Blom, 1968.

Lappé, Frances Moore; Joseph Collins. *World Hunger: Twelve Myths.* New York: Grove Press, 1986.

Leacock, Eleanor. "Women in Egalitarian Societies." In *Becoming Visible: Women in European History,* ed. K. Bridenthal and C. Koonz. Boston Houghton Mifflin, 1977.

Lederer, Laura, ed. *Take Back the Night: Women on Pornography.* New York: Bantam, 1980.

Leghorn, Lisa, and Katherine Parker. *Woman's Worth: Sexual Economics and the World of Women.* Boston: Routledge & Kegan Paul, 1981.

Lerner, Gerda. *The Creation of Patriarchy.* New York: Oxford University Press, 1986.

Lessing, Doris. *The Four-Gated City.* New York: Bantam, 1970.

————. *Canopus in Argos: Archives: Re: Colonised Planet 5: Shikasta.* London: Panther, 1979.

————. *Canopus in Argos: Archives: The Marriages between Zones Three, Four, and Five.* New York: Vintage Books, 1980.

————. *Canopus in Argos: Archives: The Making of the Representative for Planet 8*. London: Granada, 1982.

————. *Canopus in Argos: Archives: The Sirian Experiments*. New York: Vintage, 1982.

————. *Canopus in Argos: Archives: The Sentimental Agents in the Volven Empire*. London: Panther, 1985.

Livermore Weapons Lab Blockade/Demonstration Handbook. Berkeley, CA: Livermore Action Group, 1982.

Lloyd, Seton. *The Archaeology of Mesopotamia: From the Old Stone Age to the Persian Conquest*. New York: Thames & Hudson, 1984.

Lorde, Audre. *Sister Outsider*. Trumansburg, New York: Crossing Press, 1984.

Lorde, Audre, and Susan Leigh Starr. "Interview with Audre Lorde." In *Against Sadomasochism: A Radical Feminist Analysis,* eds. Robin Ruth Linden, Darlene R. Pagano, Diana E. H. Russell, and Susan Leigh Starr. East Palo Alto, CA: Frog in the Well, 1982.

Lovins, Amory B. *Soft Energy Paths: Toward a Durable Peace.* New York: Harper & Row, 1977.

Margolin, Malcolm, ed. *The Way We Lived: California Indian Reminiscences, Stories and Songs*. Berkeley, CA: Heyday Books, 1981.

Massey, Marshall. "Carrying Capacity and the Greek Dark Ages." *Coevolution Quarterly,* Winter 1983, 29–35.

Masters, Anthony. *Bakunin, the Father of Anarchism*. New York: E. P. Dutton, 1974.

McAllister, Pam, ed. *Reweaving the Web of Life: Feminism and Nonviolence*. Philadelphia: New Society Publishers, 1982.

Mellaart, James. *Earliest Civilizations of the Near East*. New York: McGraw-Hill, 1965.

————. *Çatal Hüyük, a Neolithic Town in Anatolia*. New York: McGraw-Hill, 1967.

————. "A Neolithic City in Turkey." In *Scientific American: Hunters, Farmers and Civilizations: Old World Archaeology*. San Francisco: W. H. Freeman, 1979.

Menninger, Karl. *The Crime of Punishment*. New York: Viking, 1968.

Milam, James, Robert Ketcham, and Katherine Ketcham. *Under The Influence*. Seattle: Madrona Publications, 1981.

Milgram, Stanley. *Obedience to Authority*. New York: Harper & Row, 1969.

————. "Behavioral Study of Obedience." In *The Social Animal,* ed. Elliot Aronson. San Francisco: W. H. Freeman, 1981.

Miller, Alice. *For Your Own Good: Hidden Cruelty in Child-rearing and the Roots of Violence*. Trans. Hildegarde and Hunter Hannum. New York: Farrar, Straus & Giroux, 1983.

————. *Thou Shalt Not Be Aware: Society's Betrayal of the Child*. Trans. Hildegarde and Hunter Hannum. New York: Farrar, Straus & Giroux, 1984.

Mills, Stephanie. "Feminism and Pornography." *Co-Evolution Quarterly,* Spring 1982, 32.

Mitford, Jessica. *Kind and Usual Punishment: The Prison Business*. New York: Alfred A. Knopf, 1974.

Morgan, Robin. *Going Too Far*. New York: Random House, 1977.

Muir, Bryce, and Margaret Muir. "Where've You Been, Stranger? Disintermediation in the Maritimes." *Co-Evolution Quarterly,* Summer 1981, 77.

Niethammer, Carolyn. *Daughters of the Earth: The Lives and Legends of American Indian Women.* New York: Collier, 1977.

Ochshorn, Judith. *The Female Experience and the Nature of the Divine.* Bloomington: University of Indiana Press, 1981.

Olson, Carl, ed. *The Book of the Goddess Past and Present.* New York: Crossroad, 1985.

Osherow, Neal. "Making Sense of the Nonsensical: An Analysis of Jonestown." In *The Social Animal,* ed. Elliott Aronson. San Francisco: W. H. Freeman, 1981.

Perera, Sylvia. *Descent to the Goddess.* Toronto: Inner City Books, 1981.

Piercy, Marge. *The Moon Is Always Female.* New York: Alfred A. Knopf, 1985.

Pilgrim, Peace. *Peace Pilgrim: Her Life and Work in Her Own Words.* Santa Fe, NM: Ocean Tree, 1983.

Pritchard, James B. *The Ancient Near East, Vol. 1: An Anthology of Texts and Pictures.* Princeton, NJ: Princeton University Press, 1958.

Radical Therapist Collective. *The Radical Therapist.* Produced by Jerome Agel. New York: Ballantine Books, 1971.

Randall, Margaret. *Sandino's Daughters: Testimonies of Nicaraguan Women in Struggle.* Vancouver: New Starr Books, 1981.

Renfrew, Colin. *Before Civilization: The Radiocarbon Revolution and Prehistoric Europe.* New York: Cambridge University Press, 1979.

Reich, Wilhelm. *The Mass Psychology of Fascism.* Trans. Vincent R. Carfagno. New York: Farrar, Straus & Giroux, 1970.

Rich, Adrienne. *Of Woman Born: Motherhood as Experience and Institution.* New York: Bantam, 1977.

Rohrlich, Ruby. "State Formation in Sumer and the Subjugation of Women." *Feminist Studies* 6 (Spring 1980): 77–102.

Rohrlich, Ruby, and June Nash. "Patriarchal Puzzle: State Formation in Mesopotamia and Mesoamerica." *Heresies* 4, no. 1 (1981): 60–63.

Rohrlich, Ruby, and Elaine Hoffman Baruch, eds. *Women in Search of Utopia: Mavericks and Mythmakers.* New York: Schocken Books, 1984.

Ruby Rohrlich. "Women in Transition—Crete and Sumer." *Becoming Visible: Women in European History,* ed. K. Bridenthal and C. Koonz. Boston: Houghton, Mifflin, 1977.

Rosset, Peter, and John Vandermeer, eds. *The Nicaraguan Reader: Documents of a Revolution under Fire.* New York: Grove, 1983.

Rossman, Michael. *On Learning and Social Change.* New York: Vintage, 1972.

———. *New Age Blues: On the Politics of Consciousness.* New York: E. P. Dutton, 1979.

Roth, Geneen. *Feeding the Hungry Heart: The Experience of Compulsive Eating.* New York: Signet, 1983.

Rothenberg, Jerome, ed. *Technicians of the Sacred: A Range of Poetries from Africa, America, Asia, and Oceania.* Garden City, NY: Anchor, 1968.

Ruether, Rosemary Radford. *New Woman/New Earth: Sexist Ideologies and Human Liberation.* New York: Seabury Press, 1975.

Sandars, N. K., ed. *The Epic of Gilgamesh.* Harmondsworth, Middlesex: Penguin, 1960.

Schaef, Anne Wilson. *When Society Becomes An Addict*. San Francisco: Harper & Row, 1987.

Schmookler, Andrew B. *The Parable of the Tribes*. Berkeley, CA: University of California Press, 1984.

Service, Elman R. *The Hunters*. Englewood Cliffs, NJ: Prentice-Hall, 1966.

Sharp, Gene. *The Politics of Nonviolent Action: Part One: Power and Struggle*. Boston: Porter Sargent Publishers, 1973.

Shulman, Alix Kates, ed. *Red Emma Speaks: An Emma Goldman Reader*. New York: Schocken Books, 1983.

Sjöö Monica, and Barbara Mor. The Great Cosmic Mother: Rediscovering the Religion of the Earth. San Francisco: Harper & Row, 1987.

Snortum, John R., and Ilana Hader, eds. *Criminal Justice: Allies and Adversaries*. Pacific Palisades, CA: Palisades Publishers, 1978.

Spretnak, Charlene, ed. *The Politics of Women's Spirituality*. Garden City, NY: Anchor, 1982.

Starhawk. *The Spiral Dance: A Rebirth of the Ancient Religion of the Great Goddess*. San Francisco: Harper & Row, 1979.

———. *Dreaming the Dark: Magic, Sex and Politics*. Boston: Beacon Press, 1982.

Stein, Diane. *The Women's Spirituality Book*. St. Paul, MN: Llewellyn, 1987.

Stevens, Doris. *Jailed for Freedom*. New York: Schocken Books, 1976.

Stone, Merlin. *When God Was a Woman*. New York: Harcourt Brace Jovanovich, 1976.

———. *Ancient Mirrors of Womanhood*. Boston: Beacon Press, 1979.

———. *Three Thousand Years of Racism: Recurring Patterns in Racism*. New York: New Sibylline Books, 1981.

Sun Tzu. *The Art of War*. Ed. James Clavell. New York: Delacorte, 1983.

Szasz, Thomas. *Ideology and Insanity: Essays on the Psychiatric Dehumanization of Man*. Garden City, NY: Anchor Books, 1970.

———. *The Myth of Psychotherapy*. Garden City, NY: Anchor Books, 1979.

Teish, Luisah. *Jambalaya: The Natural Woman's Book of Personal Charms and Practical Rituals*. San Francisco: Harper & Row, 1985.

Toch, Hans. *Living in Prison: The Ecology of Survival*. New York: Macmillan, 1977.

Todd, Nancy Jack, and John Todd. *Bioshelters, Ocean Arks, City Farming: Ecology as the Basis of Design*. San Francisco: Sierra Club Books, 1984.

Tokar, Brian. *A Green Primer*. San Pedro, CA: R. & E. Miles, 1987.

Training/Action Affinity Group of Movement for a New Society. *Building Social Change Communities*. Philadelphia: Movement for a New Society, 1979.

Tucker, Robert C., ed. *The Marx-Engels Reader*. New York: W. W. Norton, 1978.

Turnbull, Colin M. *The Mountain People*. New York: Touchstone, 1972.

Turner, William W. *The Police Establishment*. New York: G. P. Putnam's Sons, 1968.

Twelve Steps and Twelve Traditions. New York: AA World Services, 1952.

Valiente, Doreen. *Witchcraft for Tomorrow*. Custer, WA: Phoenix Publishing, 1978.

Walker, Alice. "A Letter of the Times, or Should This Sado-Masochism Be Saved?" In *Against Sadomasochism: A Radical Feminist Analysis,* ed.

Robin Ruth Linden, Darlene R. Pagano, Diana E. H. Russell, and Susan Leigh Starr. East Palo Alto, CA: Frog in the Well, 1982.

————. *In Search of Our Mothers' Gardens*. San Diego, CA: Harcourt Brace Jovanovich, 1983.

Walker, Barbara. *The Skeptical Feminist*. San Francisco: Harper & Row, 1987.

Walker, Barbara. *The Woman's Encyclopedia of Myths and Secrets*. San Francisco: Harper & Row, 1983.

Waskow, Arthur. *Seasons of Our Joy: A Celebration of Modern Jewish Renewal*. Toronto: Bantam, 1982.

Wegscheider, Sharon. *Another Chance: Hope and Health for the Alcoholic Family*. Palo Alto, CA: Science and Behavior Books, 1981.

Wilson, Edmund. *To the Finland Station: A Study in the Writing and Acting of History*. Garden City, NY: Doubleday, 1953.

Wolf, Margery. "Chinese Women: Old Skills in a New Context." In *Woman, Culture and Society*, ed. Michelle Z. Rosaldo and Louise Lamphere. Stanford, CA: Stanford University Press, 1974.

Wolkstein, Diane and Samuel Noah Kramer. *Inanna, Queen of Heaven and Earth: Her Stories and Hymns from Sumer*. New York: Harper & Row, 1983.

Woman of Power, Winter/Spring 1986.

Woodman, Marion. *Addiction to Perfection: The Still Unravished Bride*. Toronto: Inner City Books, 1982.

Woolley, C. Leonard. *Digging Up the Past*. Westport, CT: Greenwood Press, 1954.

————. *The Sumerians*. New York: W. W. Norton, 1965.

Zaroulis, Nancy, and Gerald Sullivan. *Who Spoke Up? American Protest against the War in Vietnam 1963–1975*. Garden City, NY: Doubleday, 1984.

RESOURCES

Circle
Box 219
Mt. Horeb, WI 53572

Pagan networking and newsletter. Write them for contacts.

Covenant of The Goddess
P.O. Box 1226
Berkeley, CA 94704

National legally recognized Wiccan church.

Institute for Culture and Creation Spirituality
P.O. Box 19216
Oakland, CA 94602

Reclaiming
P.O. Box 14404
S.F. CA 94114

My own collective that provides classes and summer programs in ritual, as well as a newsletter. Tape of chants available.

Witness for Peace
515 Broadway
Santa Cruz, CA 95060

Nonviolent peace witness in Nicaragua—most groups are Christian in orientation.

Index